GLOBAL FINANCIAL CONTAGION

This book is an authoritative and engaging account of the economic and political origins of the 2008 financial crisis examining why it was triggered in the United States; why it morphed into the Great Recession; why and how the advanced economies (the U.S., the Eurozone, and Japan) were hit particularly hard; how and why the contagion spread with such ferocity to Eastern Europe, Russia, China, India, South Korea, the Middle East, and the world's poorest countries; the nature and effectiveness of the official policy responses – with focus on how the Obama administration and the EU have dealt with the unprecedented challenges in their realm, and why some economies have rebounded faster than others; and why the G-20's efforts to create a "Bretton Woods II" or a new international financial architecture is most likely to fall short. *Global Financial Contagion* will long be regarded as the standard account of the global financial crisis, the Great Recession, and their aftermath.

Shalendra D. Sharma is a professor in the Department of Politics at the University of San Francisco. He also teaches International political economy for the MA program in the Department of Economics and at the Center for the Asia Pacific Rim. He is the author of several books, including the 2010 Alpha Sigma Nu Book Award winner *China and India in the Age of Globalization* (Cambridge University Press, 2009); *Achieving Economic Development in the Era of Globalization* (2007); *The Asian Financial Crisis: Crisis, Reform and Recovery* (2003); and *Democracy and Development in India* (1999), which won the 1999 Choice Outstanding Academic Title. He is also the editor of *The Asia-Pacific in the New Millennium: Geopolitics, Security, and Foreign Policy* (2000).

D0059722

Global Financial Contagion

Building a Resilient World Economy after the Subprime Crisis

SHALENDRA D. SHARMA

University of San Francisco

CAMBRIDGE
UNIVERSITY PRESS

CAMBRIDGE
UNIVERSITY PRESS

32 Avenue of the Americas, New York, NY 10013-2473, USA

Cambridge University Press is part of the University of Cambridge.

It furthers the University's mission by disseminating knowledge in the pursuit of education, learning, and research at the highest international levels of excellence.

www.cambridge.org
Information on this title: www.cambridge.org/9781107609617

© Shalendra D. Sharma 2014

First published 2014

Printed in the United States of America

A catalog record for this publication is available from the British Library.

Library of Congress Cataloging in Publication data
Sharma, Shalendra D.
Global financial contagion : building a resilient world economy after the subprime crisis / by Shalendra D. Sharma.
pages   cm
Includes bibliographical references and index.
ISBN 978-1-107-02720-6 (hardback) –
ISBN 978-1-107-60961-7 (pbk.)
1. Global Financial Crisis, 2008–2009.   2. International finance.
3. International trade.   4. International economic relations.
5. International relations.   6. Economic policy.   I. Title.
HB37172008.S53   2014
332′.042–dc23   2013015857

ISBN 978-1-107-02720-6 Hardback
ISBN 978-1-107-60961-7 Paperback

Contents

Figures

Tables

Acknowledgments

This book is a product of my attempt to make some sense of the economic and political roots of the subprime-mortgage crisis and the resultant Great Recession of 2008 as well as their implications for the United States and the global economy. Little did I realize that it would quickly become an all-consuming project spanning many months in the making. In the process I have incurred enormous debts, both professional and personal, to colleagues and friends from around the world who are simply too numerous to adequately acknowledge. The extensive bibliography confirms my intellectual debt to many individuals and organizations – though all should be absolved of responsibility for remaining errors.

It is with great pleasure that I extend my appreciation to some of them, with apologies to those I have inadvertently left out. I would like to thank the University of San Francisco's Elliot Neaman, Hartmut Fischer, Vamsee Juluri, Michael Lehmann, Max Neiman (emeritus professor, UC Riverside), Tony Fels, John Nelson, Steve Roddy, Rob Toia, Sunny Wong, Horacio Camblong, Nicholas Imparato, Xiaohua Yang, Patrick Hatcher, Phil Carleton, Pawel Lutomski, Kouslaa Kessler-Mata, Laleh Shahideh, Cecilia Santos, John Pinelli, James Taylor, Julio Moreno, Tanu Sankalia, Pedro Lange-Churion, Bryan Whaley, James Wiser, Jay Gonzales, Bruce Wydick, Roberta Johnson, and Stanley Nel. Over the years they have been wonderful colleagues whose support and counsel I greatly value. Special thanks to my outstanding research assistants, Cass Gordon Krughoff and Christina Hunter O'Leary. Cass has my abiding thanks for his tireless efforts to gather and analyze all pertinent material on the topic with great skill and proficiency. I am also grateful for the assistance provided by a number of my talented students, including Chris Mclachlan, Li Li, Aidi Ma, and Nicholas Stafford. For proficient administrative assistance and unwavering support for all things big and small, I extend my many thanks to Spencer Rangitsch, whose always incisive comments and deep, critical insights were of great help to me.

A number of friends and colleagues from around the world have my deepest gratitude for their unwavering support. These include colleagues at the International Monetary Fund (who kindly made available some of the data used in this study), especially Professor Jacques Artus (formerly at the IMF); Professor Barry Eichengreen at UC Berkeley; Dr. Bal Gopal Shrestha at Oxford University; Professors Emeritus Jon Quah and Stella Quah from the National University of Singapore; Dr. Andrew Marble, formerly at the National Bureau of Asian Research in Seattle; Dr. Francis Schortgen at the University of Mount Union; my former students, Kittiyaratch Thanakornmonkkonchai, now a Ph.D. candidate at the Claremont Graduate School, and Alexandra Ghosh, now a Ph.D. candidate at the Leibniz Center for Tropical Marine Ecology; Dr. Salim Lakha and Dr. Nadeem Malik at the University of Melbourne; Sally Tam, analyst at NERA Economic Consulting at San Francisco; David Jihhsiu Tai at the Taipei Economic and Cultural Office in San Francisco; and Rattan Dodeja at Merrill Lynch/Bank of America. Rattan's deep knowledge of global financial markets and his remarkable ability to explain complex financial concepts and instruments with clarity and humor proved invaluable to me.

I have nothing but the highest praise for Cambridge University Press. I can say without even the slightest risk of exaggeration that this study would not have been possible if not for the support and encouragement of Scott Parris at Cambridge University Press. One could not ask for a more thoughtful and meticulous editor. I am deeply indebted to Scott for his interest in this project and for his always sound advice and professional guidance. I only hope I have met Scott's high expectations. I would also like to extend my appreciation to Scott's assistant, Kristin Purdy, who, after Scott's departure to Oxford University Press, handled all my questions with professionalism and grace and helped transform a massive manuscript into a readable book. It has been a great pleasure working with both of them. I am deeply indebted to the reviewers at Cambridge University Press, who provided thoughtful, detailed, and trenchant criticisms and suggestions that have significantly improved this book. I have tried my best to incorporate their critique, suggestions, and recommendations in the following pages. However, I take full responsibility for remaining flaws and omissions.

My greatest debt, however, is to my wife Vivian and our son Krishan and our very large families. They have been a pillar of support from the beginning to the end. For their unconditional love and support, I humbly dedicate this book to all of them with gratitude and affection – with special dedication to my mother, the late, Krishna K. Sharma, and the newest addition to the Sharma clan, Rohan D. Sharma.

Introduction

The Great Recession of 2007–2009

The months of August–September 2008 will forever be remembered as the time when the economic tsunami hit Wall Street. On September 7 the venerable "models" of mortgage finance (the government-sponsored enterprises Fannie Mae and Freddie Mac), which together had more than $5 trillion in mortgage-backed securities and debt outstanding, collapsed.[1] The authorities placed both into conservatorship in the hopes of stabilizing the housing and mortgage-finance markets. This clearly did not happen. On September 15, the world witnessed the fire sale of the investment bank and stock-market "bull" Merrill Lynch to Bank of America and, more ominously, the bankruptcy of the 154-year-old investment bank, Lehman Brothers, the largest company ever to fail in the United States.[2] The collapse of Lehman

---

[1] The Federal National Mortgage Association (Fannie Mae) and the Federal Home Loan Mortgage Corporation (Freddie Mac) are government-sponsored enterprises (GSEs). They were established by Congress to achieve specific goals set by Congress. Both are privately owned, but as GSEs they enjoy tax and regulatory breaks such as being exempted from state and local income taxes.

[2] Lehman Brothers survived the U.S. Civil War, two World Wars, and the Great Depression. After the Fed and the Treasury failed to find a buyer for the firm, Lehman filed for bankruptcy. Its collapse was the largest corporate bankruptcy in U.S. history. On the other hand, Merrill Lynch was acquired by Bank of America for $50 billion. Allan Meltzer (2009) has argued that allowing Lehman to fail was a "major error" that "deepened and lengthened the current deep recession". A lingering question remains: why was Lehman allowed to fail while AIG and Citigroup were spared? To some, Citigroup had a prominent asset that Lehman did not: Robert Rubin, who was the Treasury secretary under the Clinton administration and executive at Citi. However, a more plausible explanation is that both the U.S. Treasury and the Federal Reserve were concerned about the moral hazard of placing Lehman into a government conservatorship. It should be kept in mind that Lehman was the most leveraged of the major investment banks, and bailing it out would have been costly. Bernanke has noted many times that the Federal Reserve lacked legal authority to bail out Lehman because Lehman did not have good collateral.

(which had more than $600 billion in assets and some 25,000 employees), proved to be a fork in the road – an inauspicious event – that transformed the subprime crisis into a catastrophic global financial crisis and ushered in the "Great Recession."[3]

As Lehman was a counterparty in many financial transactions across several key markets, its failure predictably triggered defaults on contracts all over the world. Lehman's collapse rapidly reverberated throughout the financial system, destroying confidence in money market funds, which in turn, exacerbated problems in the commercial-paper market. Deeply concerned that a massive run on the money markets could destroy the commercial-paper market and thereby bring the entire economy to its knees, the Federal Reserve Board intervened by providing liquidity to money market investors and insured all money market deposits (Allen and Moessner 2011; Mehrling 2011; Wessel 2009). Yet the collateral damage continued unabated. The very next day (September 16), it became public that the nation's largest insurer, American International Group (AIG), could no longer honor the credit-default swaps (CDS) it had sold to banks.[4] Fearful that AIG's collapse

For a range of views, see FDIC (2011); McDonald and Robinson (2009); Paulson (2010); Sorkin (2009); and Zuckerman (2009).

[3] The term Great Recession is used to describe the eighteen-month-long global economic downturn officially dated from December 2007 to June 2009.

[4] In essence, credit-default swaps (CDSs) are contracts between buyers and sellers of protection against default. It is a form of debt insurance, or more precisely, derivatives contracts that investors buy to either insure against or profit from a default. In this way CDS contracts act as a form of debt insurance in that they provide a means of protection against credit risk. "Buyers" pay premiums to "sellers" for insurance, and if an insured bond or loan fails or goes into default, the seller is obligated to pay off the value of the debt. More specifically, the buyer of the CDS contract receives compensation by the seller if a "credit event" (which could include default of some underlying assets such as a government bond, bankruptcy, restructuring, and a credit-rating downgrade) occurs to a third party or the "reference entity" within a specified period of time. For credit protection, the CDS buyer pays a fee or "premium," and since CDS contracts are between two parties rather than on an exchange, the CDS contracts are mainly traded over the counter. Reference entities are usually corporations, governments, and asset-backed securities. The CDS concept was first introduced by J.P. Morgan in 1997. Jarrow (2011) points out that the CDS was primarily designed to limit the firm's exposure to billions of dollars in loans it had made to governments and corporations. In 1998, the estimated total size of the CDS market was around $180 billion. However, by June 2008, it had skyrocketed to around $57 trillion (Stulz 2010, 78). The exponential growth of CDSs took place because they proved to be highly profitable; insurers (banks, insurance companies, and other financial institutions) earned hefty fees for insuring "events" they assumed would never occur or that constituted an extremely low risk. For example, banks purchased CDSs from AIG (mainly from its Financial Products division, a noninsurance operation based in London) to hedge the mortgage-backed securities they held, in the case of mortgage defaults. Of course, AIG did not anticipate the total collapse of the market for mortgage-backed securities. When

would have a domino effect and bring down banks and investment firms, the Federal Reserve Board gave AIG an emergency credit line totaling $85 billion to facilitate an "orderly" downsizing of the company.[5]

Yet again, the financial hemorrhaging continued unabated. By the second week of September, funding markets had come to a virtual standstill in the United States (and many other countries), with bank funding markets essentially ceasing to function at terms longer than overnight. As the startled former Federal Reserve chair Alan Greenspan (2010, 18) noted, "Evaporation of the global supply of short-term credits within hours or days of the Lehman failure is.... without historical precedent." The credit panic became self-fulfilling – that is, as the uncertainty among banks and other financial institutions about the creditworthiness of their counterparts grew, it further exacerbated counterparty risk. This was vividly reflected in the soaring rates banks were charging each other for short-term loans. As money market fund managers tightened lending, credit lines to businesses (including healthy ones) dried up, triggering fears of a general liquidity crisis (Paulson 2010). Predictably, the corporate bond spreads widened to all-time highs, equity markets experienced sharp declines, and foreign-exchange volatility increased sharply. On September 19, the Bush administration, led by U.S. Treasury Secretary Hank Paulson, finally abandoned their "hands-off" policy and confronted the spiraling financial conflagration by hastily cobbling together an unprecedented "rescue" plan (to critics, a "bailout" plan) under the aegis of TARP (Troubled Assets Relief Program), a government agency with the authority to purchase some $700 billion of distressed assets from failing and failed private financial companies.[6]

Even as this massive plan was being announced, the economic landscape in the United States was already undergoing irrevocable transformation. Just a few months earlier, in the tightly cloistered world of U.S. banking, there were five major investment banks. By the end of September 2008, there were none (Lowenstein 2010). Bear Stearns, the canary in the coal

---

these hard-to-price securities (unlike traditional types of insurance, CDSs were unregulated before the crisis, and the market for them so opaque it was difficult to know the extent of the risks) did collapse, AIG (like Bear Stearns) stood exposed. When asset prices fell sharply, and the banks made collateral calls, AIG could not meet them. Burdened with huge liabilities and without sufficient capital to cover its obligations, AIG was forced to seek taxpayer support.

[5] The government loan was in exchange for a 79.9 percent equity stake in AIG.

[6] The Emergency Economic Stabilization Act of 2008 authorized the Treasury Secretary to purchase troubled assets from financial institutions through December 31, 2009. The law also placed limits on compensation and prohibited "golden parachutes" for senior executive officers whose company assets were purchased under the plan.

mine, and which had put its eggs in the mortgage-backed securities basket was pushed into the arms of J.P. Morgan Chase on March 16, 2008 as
house prices further tumbled.[7] Lehman simply went bust, Merrill Lynch
sold itself to Bank of America, and Morgan Stanley and Goldman Sachs
announced on September 22 that they were becoming commercial banks.[8]
On September 26, Washington Mutual (a $300 billion thrift), announced
that most of its assets would be acquired by J.P. Morgan. On September
29, Citigroup announced that it would acquire the banking operations of
Wachovia Corporation in a deal facilitated by the Federal Deposit Insurance
Corporation (FDIC). Citigroup agreed to absorb up to $42 billion of losses
from Wachovia's $312 billion loan portfolio, with the FDIC covering the
remaining losses. With so many of the mighty falling and the era of the
independent investment banking coming to an ignominious end, the country that had long prided itself on its unabashedly free-market system and
individual enterprise began contemplating what just days earlier had been
unthinkable: socialist-style state intervention – wherein the state would
pump in huge amounts of monetary and fiscal stimuli and financial institutions would be outright nationalized in order to stabilize the collapsing
economy.[9]

On September 29 the markets reacted negatively to Congress's rejection
of TARP. The stock market sell-off was dramatic: the Dow fell nearly 7 percent – a one-day drop that has been matched only seventeen times since
the index's creation in 1896. With apocalyptic predictions of another Great
Depression, growing populist anger, and unrelenting admonition and political arm-twisting by Congressional leaders, the White House, and the two

---

[7] The investment bank Bear Stearns had not only heavily invested in residential
     mortgage-backed securities, it was also highly leveraged and depended heavily on
     overnight loans to fund its investments. In early March 2008, when the firm's creditors
     refused to provide funding, Bear Stearns found itself on the verge of bankruptcy (it was
     unable to roll over its short-term financing). The Federal Reserve and the Treasury were
     forced to arrange the sale of Bear Stearns to J.P. Morgan Chase – but not without first
     providing government guarantees on some of Bear Stearns' assets. Given Bear Stearns'
     complex inter-linkages with other financial institutions through derivative trading and
     loans, the Fed determined that letting Bear Stearns fail would exacerbate the stress in the
     financial markets.
[8] Both Morgan Stanley and Goldman Sachs have two years to conform to federal supervi-
     sion and meet capital requirements and other rules that govern such commercial banks as
     Wells Fargo, Bank of America, and Citigroup.
[9] Cassidy (2009, 4) has captured this well, noting "The Bush administration, after eight
     years of preaching the virtues of free markets, tax cuts, and small government, had turned
     the U.S. Treasury into part owner and the effective guarantor of every big bank in the
     country... it had stumbled into the most sweeping extension of state intervention in the
     economy since the 1930s."

Table I.1. *Trends in world stock markets*

Index	May 2008	Nov 2008	% Decrease (May to Oct 2008)
DJIA (NY)	12,800	8,693	−68
FTSE (London)	6,200	4,268	−69
Nikkei (Tokyo)	13,750	8,696	−63
Sensex (Mumbai)	17,000	9,956	−56
SSE180 (Shanghai)	8,500	4,076	−48

Source: Bloomberg and Shanghai Stock Exchange, 2008.

presidential candidates (Barak Obama and John McCain), Congress finally passed the $700 billion rescue package on October 3. It was the biggest bail-out in U.S. history.[10] However, even this unprecedented fiscal indulgence underwritten by U.S. taxpayers failed to stop the financial bleeding. In fact, efforts by governments around the world to stem the panic via sovereign guarantees on bank deposits and loans, recapitalizing banks, passing legislation to use public funds to purchase troubled assets from banks, injection by several central banks of massive amounts of liquidity into the banking system, and widespread use of the Federal Reserve's swap networks or "reciprocal currency arrangements" (which at its peak on December 4, 2008 provided US$586.1 billion to other central banks) failed to calm the markets. To the contrary, the credit markets around the world froze. The commercial-paper market shut down, three-month Treasuries yields dipped below zero, and the money market mutual fund "broke the buck" for only the second time in history, precipitating a $200 billion net outflow of funds from that market (Table I.1). In this environment of fast-evaporating investor confidence and the seizing-up of interbank credit markets, fear and panic gripped the world's capitals and financial markets (Brunnermeier 2009).

Indeed, the world found itself facing the specter of the worst financial shock since the Great Depression. As 2009 rolled in, some hundreds of billions (if not trillions) of dollars in capital value had already been lost in the stock and equity markets. Still, the crisis showed no signs of abating.[11] In

[10] Milton Friedman and Anna Schwartz (1963) argued in their seminal *A Monetary History of the United States* that the root cause of the Great Depression was not the stock-market crash but a "great contraction" of credit due to large-scale bank failures.

[11] Drawing on data from the IMF and U.S. Federal Reserve, Altman (2009, 5) notes that

Americans have lost one-quarter of their net worth in just a year and a half, since June 30, 2007, and the trend continues. Americans' largest single asset is the equity in their homes.

the United States, the economy remained in the grips of a sharp contraction with almost two million jobs lost, and the number of home foreclosures and bankruptcies on the rise. With the U.S. budget deficit for 2008 trebling and the ratio of public-plus-private-debt to GDP at more than 300 percent, there was recognition (and palpable anxiety) that the world's economic hegemon was profoundly constrained in what it could do to boost growth. Not surprisingly, observers were generally unanimous in projecting that world economic growth would further contract in 2009 to its lowest rate in sixty years – a projection that came to pass as world economic growth fell at an annual rate of −6.4 percent in the fourth quarter of 2008 and −7.4 percent in the first quarter of 2009 (IMF 2009a; 2009b).

The Focus of this Study

Although there are no recent precedents of an economic crisis of such a catastrophic magnitude, in retrospect, the writing of a financial meltdown was on the wall. In the United States, the signs of speculation and risk had been evident for some time: ubiquitous growth of global economic imbalances, worsening macroeconomic fundamentals, mounting debt levels, low household savings, skyrocketing asset prices, and the proclivity of Americans (presumably blinded by rising wealth effects[12]) to live beyond their means and rely on consumer borrowing to finance hedonistic spending and consumption. Thus, the crisis was hardly a discordant black swan event.[13] Nevertheless, in spite of the growing preponderance of evidence,

> Total home equity in the United States, which was valued at $13 trillion at its peak in 2006, had dropped to $8.8 trillion by mid-2008.... Total retirement assets, American's second-largest household asset, dropped by 22 percent, from $10.3 trillion in 2006 to $8 trillion in mid-2008. During the same period, savings and investment assets (apart from retirement savings) lost $1.2 trillion and pension assets lost $1.3 trillion. Taken together, these losses total a staggering $8.3 trillion.

Drawing on more recent dataset, Emmons and Noeth (2012, 11) point out that

> Household wealth declined almost $17 trillion in inflation-adjusted terms, or 26 percent, from its peak in mid-2007 to the trough in early 2009. Only about two-fifths of that loss had been recovered by early 2012. Looking at individual asset categories between June 30, 2007, and March 31, 2009, the inflation-adjusted value of households' real-estate holdings declined 26 percent ($5.4 trillion), while stock-market equity holdings declined in value by 51.5 percent ($10.8 trillion) after adjusting for inflation.

[12] "Wealth effects" means individuals and households feeling wealthier than they actually were because of rapidly rising asset values.

[13] Nassim Nicholas Taleb (2007), in the second edition of his best seller, *The Black Swan*, notes that the crash of 2008 was not a "black swan" event. Chapter 1 elaborates.

policy makers and the economists remained blissfully oblivious, if not in denial.[14] The only professional economist prescient enough to warn about the impending danger, the indefatigable Nouriel Roubini, was dismissed as an iconoclast, sarcastically dubbed "Dr. Doom," and ignored.

In hindsight, the reasons behind the existential economic calamity of our times and what must be done to prevent future ones have become more obvious. We now have a more nuanced understanding of the roots of the financial meltdown. The introspection and soul-searching in both the policymaking and academic circles regarding the causes and consequences of the crisis and how best to reduce the financial systems' vulnerabilities in the future have the potential to provide essential lessons (and solutions) regarding how best to mitigate the incalculable economic toll and dislocation the crisis has left (and continues to leave) in its wake. As Milton Friedman (1962, 9) reminded us years ago, "Only a crisis – actual or perceived – produces real change... [when] the politically impossible becomes the politically inevitable." Similarly, Gourevitch (1986, 9) has noted that economic crises can act as potential "critical junctures" where "old relationships crumble and new ones have to be constructed." Whether this rethinking and reevaluation of the prevailing orthodoxies galvanizes action at both the national and global levels and open paths to new possibilities and "new equilibriums," or as Friedman warned, the moment is imperceptibly overtaken by the "tyranny of the status quo" remains an open question.

The following narrative contributes to this discussion by adjudicating and reassessing a number of interrelated questions, namely: Why was the crisis triggered in the United States – a country renowned for its deep, resilient, and innovative financial system that is undergirded by extensive and modern regulatory and supervisory oversight? Why did the crisis, which began with the implosion of a relatively small and ubiquitous part of the U.S. housing market (the so-called subprime residential mortgages), quickly morph into a credit crunch and then a full-blown global financial crisis? How were the problems in the U.S. financial system amplified both domestically and globally? Why did the contagion spread so quickly to all corners of the globe? What were the specific "transmission channels" via which the crisis reverberated and impacted such diverse economies – from the EU (European Union), the eurozone, Russia and Eastern Europe, Asia (including Asia's four largest economies – China, India, Japan, and South Korea), the

---

[14] Cassidy (2009) compellingly implicates the economics profession for the crisis. He argues that the professions' infatuation with "rational expectations" and "perfect financial markets," led them to downplay the need for government regulation and support of deregulation of financial markets. Krugman (2009b) makes similar charges.

Middle East, and the world's poorest and globally least integrated nations? What explains the rather significant variations across countries in terms of the contagion's reach and impact? What explains why advanced economies (the United States, the EU, and Japan) have been hit particularly hard, and why some countries (notably China, South Korea, and India) seemed better insulated and have rebounded quickly – with China notching an impressive 8.7 percent growth in 2009? How precisely have political leaders and national governments (with focus on the United States and the EU), indeed, public authorities around the world, as well as international organizations, namely the Group of 20 (G-20), and the International Monetary Fund (IMF), dealt with the crisis and resultant economic downturn? How effective have their policies and programs been in responding to the crisis, including their stated goal of creating a "Bretton Woods II" or a new international financial architecture capable of preventing such crises in the future?

As Table I.2 shows, governments of the world's major economies have agreed to implement a wide variety of measures to mitigate the financial crisis.

Although there is broad unanimity that the unprecedented public interventions around the world (including the United States) helped avoid a prolonged worldwide economic depression (Blinder and Zandi 2010), there are also valid concerns regarding why such huge public largess failed to produce the predicted "bang for the buck." Certainly, the compendium of prodigious fiscal stimulus packages, the nationalization of private-sector debt, bailouts, and reduced tax revenues have sharply contracted economic activity, thus worsening debt-to-GDP levels and leaving governments with huge bills. In the advanced economies, especially in the United States, colossal spending has produced only meager results, failing to jump-start economic growth and especially job growth. In fact, in the United States and other advanced economies, budget deficits have already reached a staggering 10 percent of GDP – a figure that will only worsen with the inevitable continued government borrowing and further accumulation of debt. By the end of 2012, U.S. debt passed an astronomical $16 trillion with $1.5 trillion in annual government deficits.[15] According to the

---

[15] This grim picture does not include the state and local government debt, which at the end of the first quarter of 2010 stood at $2.8 trillion (CRS 2011). Nor does it count the ballooning "unfunded" public-sector pension or retiree health benefit liabilities (an outstanding liability is not covered by an asset of greater or equal value). Recent defaults by a number of cities underscore growing fiscal woes. For example, in June 2012, the city of Stockton, California, filed for chapter 9 bankruptcy as it could not meet its $700 million financial liabilities. This was followed in August 2012 by San Bernardino, California, filing for bankruptcy protection largely because its employee retirement costs in 2012 were double the 2006–07 values.

Table I.2. *Classification of events*

Central Bank – Monetary Policy and Liquidity Support

Interest Rate Change
• Reduction of interest rates

Liquidity Support
• Reserve requirements, longer funding terms, more auctions and/or higher credit lines
• Domestic system lender of last resort: broader set of eligible institutions, wider collateral rules, and/or eligible collateral
• Other liquidity support (e.g., support of money market funds)
• Foreign exchange lender of last resort: forex swap lines (with other central banks) and forex repos

Government – Financial Sector Stabilization Measures

Recapitalization
• Capital injection (common stock/preferred equity)
• Capital injection (subordinated debt)

Liability Guarantees[a]
• Enhancement of depositor protection
• Debt guarantee (all liabilities)
• Debt guarantee (new liabilities)
• Government lending to an individual institution

Asset Purchases[b]
• Asset purchases (individual assets, bank by bank)
• Asset purchases (individual "bad bank")
• Provisions of liquidity in context of bad asset purchases/removal
• On-balance-sheet "ring-fencing" with toxic assets kept in the bank
• Off-balance-sheet "ring-fencing" with toxic assets moved to a "bad bank" Asset guarantees

[a] Includes the Federal Reserve's liquidity support to AIG for toxic-asset removal to a special-purpose vehicle, coupled with government's loss sharing.
[b] Includes business-loan guarantees as part of financial sector stabilization measures (e.g., the United Kingdom, Germany); for some countries, asset purchases were not conducted by the government, but (also) by the central bank (or a central bank-sponsored) agent, such as in the case of the United States and Switzerland.
Source: *Global Financial Stability Report*, October (IMF 2009a, 120).

Congressional Budget Office (CBO 2012), if the current trajectory is not reversed, by 2020, annual interest owed on U.S. debt will approach $1 trillion or roughly 21 percent of the projected federal revenue for that year. Analysis of how governments around the world have attempted to get their fiscal houses in order and the challenges they face will help shed light on the

efficacy of various government policies and programs. Finally, at the 2009 G-20 Summit, President Obama deftly announced that "from now on the Group of 20 will be the primary organization responsible for coordinating global economic policy." Indeed, the G-20 has placed the creation of a bold and forward-looking "new global financial architecture" at the core of its agenda. The concluding chapter will assess the G-20's efforts in creating the so-called new Bretton Woods.

These questions are examined through the prism of a broad political-economic approach that illustrates how mutable human decisions made in response to political calculations and changes in the global and domestic financial systems created perverse incentives to engage in risky economic behavior. Such an inclusive and encompassing approach better captures the subtle nuances and complexities of a prodigiously multifaceted event with a large cast of players and provides an important corrective to the formulaic "economistic" or "market-failure" analysis of the crash of 2008. More specifically, this study goes beyond conventional economic narratives that see the crisis as inadvertently rooted, inter alia in the permeability of and disequilibrium caused by globalized capital, the adoption of flawed fiscal and monetary policies, excessive reliance on technocratic expertise, the procyclicality of the financial system; Wall Street hubris, avarice, financial chicanery, incompetence, excessive risk-taking by market participants due to avowedly perverse incentives (namely, distorted compensation schemes at major financial institutions), inaccurate measures of financial risk exposures due to narrow cost-benefit analysis of complex securities, and the alleged lack of moral guidance in the promiscuously free-wheeling globalized capitalism (Ahmed 2009; Cohan 2009; Farrell 2010; Madrick 2010; Tett 2009; Yavlinsky 2011).

A Political Economy of the Subprime Crisis

To Ben Bernanke (2005), the taciturn (and endlessly introspective) chair of the U.S. Federal Reserve, the real culprit behind the financial meltdown was the pervasive and ubiquitous buildup of the "global savings glut" and the resultant surge in capital inflows from emerging market economies to the United States.[16] These massive inflows contributed to significant declines in

---

[16] In his important speech "The Global Saving Glut and the U.S. Current Account Deficit," Bernanke (2005) offered a novel explanation for the rapid rise of the U.S. trade deficit in recent years. To Bernanke, the source of the problem was not the United States but China and the other booming economies of East and Southeast Asia. He argued that in the

long-term interest rates in the United States and other industrial economies and imbalances and distortions in the U.S. real-estate sector. To others, including the perpetually prickly Nobel Laureate Joseph Stiglitz (2010), the roots of the problem lay in the Federal Reserve's flagrantly misguided policy of low interest rates (also Dowd and Hutchinson 2010; Sachs 2009). Although concern about deflation in wake of the dot-com-bust-induced recession forced the Federal Reserve to drastically reduce the federal fund rate, Taylor (2009) judiciously shows that the unusually long period of negative real U.S. interest rate from 2001 to 2005 fueled the housing bubble.[17] More specifically, by lowering short-term interest rates, the Federal Reserve pushed down the longer-maturity mortgage interest rates. This, in turn, pushed up demand for housing, leading to a sharp spike in house prices. Inevitably, the upward pressure on housing prices led to even more investment in real estate and construction in the residential-housing sector, but this monetary-policy-induced housing boom resulted in an oversupply and eventually a housing bust.

Still others, while acknowledging the role of misguided monetary policy, focus the blame on unduly loose lending standards typified by the subprime-mortgage loans. They argue that the easy extension of credit to risky borrowers created the housing boom and set the stage for the later massive defaults (Cassidy 2009; Posner 2010). Also, a number of studies have highlighted the macro-picture, namely, the problems in the wider economy, such as the unsustainable U.S. current account deficit, growing global imbalances, and excessive credit growth and leverage in the financial system (Munchau 2010; Reinhart and Rogoff 2009). The claim is that a combination of extremely low interest rates with unlimited liquidity and low market volatility prompted investors to search for higher yields without adequate appreciation of the inherent risks. In order to meet investor demand, financial institutions created new, "exotic" instruments and products (Lewis 2010). Investors snapped these up without due consideration of

---

mid-1990s, these economies had become significant importers of capital by borrowing abroad to finance their ambitious development, but that in the aftermath of the Asian financial crisis of 1997–98, they made a sharp volte-face. Cognizant of the fact that absence of foreign hard currency reserves had made them vulnerable, they began to protect themselves (on the IMF's advice) against future crisis by amassing huge war chests of foreign assets.

[17] In the United States, the Federal Reserve slashed interest rates from 6.5 percent at the beginning of 2001 to 1 percent by mid-2003 and maintained this rate until mid-2004. However, concerns about inflation forced the Fed to gradually increase the rates. In May 2006, the rates had increased to about 5 percent.

risk. Since many investors relied on the assessments of credit-rating agencies, namely Standard & Poor's, Fitch, and Moody's, only to learn too late that these very agencies were also in the business of advising how to develop and market the very products they were receiving hefty fees to assess the credit of.[18] Inevitably, such an incestuous relationship, coupled with a lack of market discipline, resulted in a calamitous economic buildup and financial denouement.

Several commentators, including Gary Gorton (2010), Robert Shiller (2008), George Soros (2008), and the influential former chair of the Federal Reserve, Alan Greenspan (2011; 2010a; 2010b; 2008) have argued that the Great Recession is rooted in hubris and cognitive dissonance reflected in the failure of borrowers, lenders, and investors to prudently assess the risks of complex assets. To Greenspan, the Wall Street meltdown happened because "risk-modelers" tended to limit their data analysis to periods when the market was performing well and carried out what in hindsight was clearly only perfunctory risk analysis (also Thibodeau 2008). Shiller (2008, 4) identifies the problem as stemming from "an epidemic of irrational public enthusiasm" – the end result of professional economists and policy makers, enamored of their seemingly elegant "rational-decision making" models, confusing desired outcomes with actual outcomes. Nobel laureate Paul Krugman (2009, 2) is more biting: "As I see it, the economics profession went astray because economists, as a group, mistook beauty, clad in impressive-looking mathematics, for truth." This oversight prevented economists from paying attention to swings in market sentiments. Undoubtedly, these are valid points, but the question remains: why? The authors provide two explanations – although one has greater resonance than the other. First, there is no dispute regarding the claim that a benign economic environment often leads to credit booms and to the creation of marginal assets. Certainly, homebuyers, investors, and lenders had every reason to be bullish as U.S. housing prices had increased every year since 1991, even during the dot-com bust and recession of 2001. The high distributions of returns on housing made it look like a sure bet, and securitization only made the new financial instruments more complex and opaque, limiting investors' ability to carefully assess their portfolios and financial institutions and accurately value assets on their balance sheets. Although many homebuyers knew that the housing bubble could not last forever, they had no way of knowing when the bubble would burst, much less how severe the fallout would be. However, the authors' second claim, that if

---

[18] Sinclair (2005) provides a good overview on the global politics of "creditworthiness."

these market actors (especially investors and financial institutions) had access to better information, they would not have made such grave errors of judgment, is not entirely plausible. After all, a vast body of research has shown that markets are inherently fragile and may not always work efficiently due to externalities, coordination failures, and information asymmetries, including well-placed firms and individuals using their power and privileged access for private gain. Thus, more or better information by itself is no panacea.

The reality is that these market failure explanations are only a part of a much larger and complex story. They tend to mostly highlight the proximate causes and capture the most glaring manifestations and symptoms of the crisis and not necessarily the underlying causes. Indeed, anyone familiar with monetary and fiscal policy knows that governments explicitly or implicitly create the environment for economic behavior. Therefore, purely economic explanations do not adequately reveal the fundamental determinants that created the environment where such narcissistic and recklessly speculative behavior was allowed to flourish. For example, if credit expansion occurred because of the adverse incentives inherent in the originate-to-distribute system of mortgage lending, why did the authorities not limit, if not end, such practice? Similarly, the argument by Gorton (2010) and others that the progressively deregulated and fragmented system of prudential oversight was simply not up to the task brings up another question. What explains the lack of oversight on the part of the United States' veritable army of regulators with overlapping mandates and powers ostensibly meant to supervise the financial sector?[19] Also, if the problem was merely flawed monetary policy, how does one account for the discrepancy that the U.S. monetary policy was quite similar to that of most of the advanced economies, why did not all these countries experienced the massive mortgage delinquencies and a housing bust? A key reason why the Canadian and the Australian financial sectors remained mostly unscathed by the crisis is that their systems of home financing prevented the buildup of risky home loans such as subprime mortgages. In both Canada and Australia, mortgage insurance is not only mandatory, but banks are required to hold these mortgages rather than unload them via securitization. Moreover, mortgage interest is not tax deductible, and a market for

---

[19] National-level regulatory agencies include the Federal Reserve, the Office of the Comptroller of the Currency, the Office of Thrift Supervision, the National Credit Union Administration, and the Federal Deposit Insurance Corporation. Financial markets regulators include the Securities and Exchange Commission and the Commodities Futures Trading Commission. In addition, there is the Department of the Treasury, and each state also has banking and insurance regulators.

adjustable-rate, interest-only – subprime – mortgages does not exist (Booth 2009; Northcott et al., 2009).

Addressing this puzzle means dispassionately scrutinizing the broader political economy at the root of the crisis in the U.S. housing sector. Fundamentally this means asking what explains the relative absence of effective supervision, surveillance, and prudential regulation in this vital sector? Why did the usually risk-averse, seasoned, and prudent market participants behave with such cavalier disregard of the risks, or display such irrational exuberance about markets, particularly the housing sector with its long and checkered history of booms and busts? More explicitly, why did millions of homeowners and financial institutions that held their mortgage loans underestimate the true risks associated with subprime loans?

Johnson and Kwak (2010), in their provocative *Thirteen Bankers: The Wall Street Takeover and the Next Financial Meltdown*, blame the perverse monopoly of power in the United States enjoyed by Wall Street elites or "oligarchs" as the root of the problem (see Ferguson, 2012, for a similar argument). These oligarchs exert significant influence over the political system as their lobbying, campaign contributions, and influence peddling has created a veritable revolving-door relationship between Washington and Wall Street. This usurpation has given these oligarchs and their legions of lobbyists undue access and influence in the corridors of power, including the ability to weaken and undermine regulatory policies, including the unprecedented ability to keep their profits private in good times and socialize their losses during the bad. Predictably, the end result has been a financial system that has delivered unparalleled wealth to the few, while at the same time becoming highly prone to recurrent crises.

Indeed, the following pages will illustrate that the Great Recession was the result of a confluence of political and economic factors coming together like a perfect storm. That is, the crisis of 2008 was just as much a case of government failure as of market failure. However, government failure is more than outrageously egregious control and manipulation by unscrupulous oligarchs or an unwillingness or inability by sanctimonious politicians/legislators and obsequious supervisory authorities to enforce legal-prudential regulations. Government failure is fundamentally about the role mutable human decisions and prerogatives played in creating the crisis. It means examining the nature and extent of the culpability of both the executive and legislative branches of the U.S. government, particularly the blatantly self-serving and duplicitous actions of influential law makers and legislators in promoting an array of government policies and programs that led to the housing bubble and other macroeconomic distortions. These actions include political elites' supplication and passive acquiescence to Wall Street interests, their solicitousness, complicity, connivance, ingeniousness, flawed policies, lax regulations, and tendency to dismiss glaring incongruities as minor anomalies.

An appraisal of the experience of the United States confirms that although both market actors and regulators failed to adequately assess the risks of the complex assets, law makers in both the executive and legislative branches of the U.S. government, including regulators who were responsible for exercising due diligence and scrutiny against the buildup of distortions and risks across the financial system and providing warnings about potentially destructive behaviors and fatally risky financial instruments failed in their most fundamental fiduciary responsibilities. Arguably, this incongruity was because prominent regulators, in particular Alan Greenspan (a disciple of the enigmatic free-market philosopher Ayn Rand and an enthusiastic "market fundamentalist") not only had limited faith in the ability of regulators and governments to correct market distortions, they also believed that unfettered markets are intrinsically efficient and self-correcting and best left unregulated. Indeed, the prevailing efficient market hypothesis claimed that market participants are their own best information-gatherers and judges of an asset's "true" value. To stalwarts like Greenspan (and others), for whom such thinking was sacrosanct, financial institutions would act unabashedly in their own self-interest to protect their investments.[20] Indeed, the failure of markets to act in utilitarian rationality led Greenspan (2008) to grudgingly admit that "those of us who have looked to the self-interest of lending institutions to protect stockholders' equity, myself included, are in a state of disbelief."

Although, only a handful of strategically-placed and influential legislators (both Democrats and Republicans), were perhaps true-believers in "market fundamentalism," they were, nonetheless, cynically "prudent" in the sense they understood the exigencies of electoral politics and deft at shifting their allegiances as circumstances dictated. They could count on campaign contributions from an array of deep-pocketed interests and lobbies from Wall Street to Main Street by indulgently championing deregulation in the real-estate sector – indeed, pushing for overall financial deregulation and reduction in the role of government in the economic sphere at large (Wallison 2009). To satisfy their goal of creating a "homeownership society," the Clinton

---

[20] To Greenspan (2007; 2010; 2011), even the most prescient regulator cannot anticipate or prevent financial crises. Rather, as crises are inherent to capitalism, the most effective regulator is the market itself. For a good overview of the workings of the Fed, see Axilrod (2009), Reichley (1981), and Wessel (2009).

administration and Republican senator Phil Gramm deregulated the banking sector with the repeal of Glass-Steagall and the Community Reinvestment Act (CRA), cajoling and coercing banks to provide loans to borrowers with poor credit histories. And Democrats in Congress, particularly Connecticut Senator Chris Dodd and the notoriously pugnacious Massachusetts congressman Barney Frank, via the government-sponsored Fannie Mae and Freddie Mac, funneled trillions of dollars of home subprime and Alt-A mortgages to risky borrowers. Not surprisingly, Freddie and Fannie, along with Wall Street, were major campaign contributors to Dodd and Frank – and Dodd, the chairman of the Senate Banking Committee, apparently received discounted "VIP loans" by Countrywide Financial, a large subprime mortgage company.[21]

Cumulatively, the actions (or more appropriately, inactions) of regulators, coupled with the obscurantist machinations and prevarications of powerful legislators and key decision makers, resulted in systematic deregulation (and evisceration) that gravely undermined financial risk management in the United States at a time of unprecedented change and rapid innovation in the global financial markets. The absence of effective oversight and regulation over trillions of dollars in complex and seemingly free-wheeling financial instruments such as derivatives (financial instruments whose value derives from something else, such as a mortgage-backed security or a commodity like oil), not only encouraged financial institutions and intrepid investors to take on too much risk, they also used these instruments to evade regulation and exploit regulatory loopholes to minimize taxes and maximize gains.[22] Exacerbating this, the complexity (and opaqueness) of these new financial instruments overwhelmed the checks and balances of risk management and supervision. Unambiguous and well-defined rules and regulatory oversight, especially more intrusive supervision, would have placed some degree of constraint on imprudent behavior and prevented the buildup of speculative bubbles in the economy. To the contrary, egregiously weak regulation, lack of diligent oversight, and seeming abdication on the part of policy makers and regulators exacerbated the problem by making the U.S. financial system unduly vulnerable to shifts in market sentiments. The U.S. experience demonstrates that although the crisis was triggered by economic factors that were independent of political institutions and party

---

[21] In the aftermath of the crisis, Dodd was also criticized for his role in writing a bill that protected bonuses for executives at bailed-out insurer AIG.

[22] Over-the-counter derivatives grew explosively in the past decade with the face value of outstanding transactions rising sixfold to an estimated $700 trillion in 2008.

affiliations, they were not independent of powerful law makers in both branches of the U.S. government.

The Contagion

Why did the contagion spread with such choreographed rapidity and virulence around the globe? In short, via three channels – finance, trade, and the expectations or confidence of investors and consumers. Certainly, global capital markets allocate resources more efficiently than domestic ones, helping spread wealth and affluence more widely than ever before (and in the process enabling millions to better their lives). However, alongside this, intimacy and unwavering interconnections between economies, in particular the unprecedented level of integration between financial institutions, both within and across borders, causes problems in one area to rapidly amplify across the entire gamut. With financial integration blurring distinctions, business cycles becoming increasingly permeable and synchronized across countries, and the financial sector rapidly growing as a larger percentage of economic activity, there has been a simultaneous increase in the incidence of financial crises, including banking crises, currency crises, debt crises, and "sudden stops" in lending – referred by some as the "crisis of financialization" (Freeman 2010; Galbraith 2012). For example, increased trade between banks, especially the need to refinance in foreign currencies, has sharply increased the banking sector's balance sheet exposure to foreign currencies. Compounding this, the integration of inherently fragile and unstable financial markets has made the financial system more prone to excess and more vulnerable to cycles of booms and busts. Mishkin (2011; 2006) points out that financial globalization not only makes it easier for capital (especially inflows) to fuel excessive risk taking by market participants, it also facilitates a simultaneous and rapid buildup of systemic risks across national boundaries, enabling financial shocks to spread more rapidly within and across countries.

Krugman (2008) succinctly describes the contagion spreading like a chain reaction via what he calls an international version of the "financial multiplier process" where a fall in asset values in one country depresses the balance sheets of highly leveraged institutions. This in turn not only depresses the demand for financial assets in other countries, but also reduces asset prices and wreaks havoc with bank balance sheets, and so on. In other words, the deepening integration of global financial markets has meant more rapid and powerful spillover across economies through both traditional and newer types of transmission channels. Although spillovers through the traditional trade channel remains a central transmission mechanism (even though global trade patterns have become more diversified), financial spillovers have become more pronounced as the rising correlation of global equity prices and the potential for sudden capital flow reversals mean that shocks in the core can be transmitted with great speed and force through the financial system. For example, as U.S. financial institutions began to sell their assets to raise cash, stock prices in Europe, Japan, and emerging economies dropped sharply, and the value of the U.S. dollar increased against other currencies. There was also a sharp reversal in capital flows and a shortage of liquid foreign reserves.

Bordo and Eichengreen (2002; 1999) have identified some 139 financial crises between 1973 and 1997 (of which 44 occurred in high-income countries), compared with a total of 38 between 1945 and 1971. They point out that global economic crises are twice as common as they were before 1914, in part because the early period of financial stability creates confidence and cautious risk taking that eventually leads to recklessness and instability. Of course, Hyman Minsky (1986; 1982) first proposed that long periods of stability lead to excessive debt and eventually collapse. Minsky's "credit cycle model" proposes five stages: displacement, boom, euphoria, profit taking, and panic. Displacement occurs when investors are wooed by new developments – in the current phase, the securitization of exotic financial products. This leads to speculative booms and overvaluation of assets, which, in turn, gives way to euphoria. As Minsky noted, the major manifestation of this euphoria is that banks and other lenders drop their guard and extend credit to all sorts of borrowers. Junk bonds played that role in the 1980s; in the current crisis, it was the securitization of mortgages, especially subprime mortgages. Indeed, this new development prompted even more bank lending as it enabled banks to provide home loans without concern as to whether they would be repaid because defaults would be the problem of investors who bought these new securities. Panic is triggered by a dramatic and unanticipated collapse – in the current crisis, it was the collapse of two Bear Stearns hedge funds and Lehman Brothers, who had invested heavily in mortgage securities.

Bordo and Eichengreen (2002) also point out that financial markets operate on the basis of trust as financial transactions are fundamentally a series of promises (people deposit money in banks based on the promise that they can withdraw it at any time). However, when this trust is brought into question or broken by recklessness, callous deception, and deliberate wrongdoing, the gentile and fragile edifice of trust and confidence can quickly unravel, with potentially disastrous consequences. The realization that the advancements in financial innovations – the so-called sophisticated and exotic financial products – were not as benign, safe, or profitable as they were advertised to be came as a shock to market participants, shattering their confidence. Rather, the democratization of credit – the easy availability of credit made possible by dramatic advances in information technology and financial product innovations, particularly the securitization of debt and use of financial derivatives – came with many hidden and little understood risks. Subprime mortgages turned out to be both attractive and toxic at the same time because "securitization" made these highly risky products seem more secure and safe than they really were. Securitization allowed subprime mortgages to be traded directly as securities, and they were repackaged to create even more complex financial instruments (derivatives[23]), such as collateralized debt obligations (CDOs). The derivatives were again split into and repackaged in various tranches several times over. Each stage of the securitization process sharply increased the leverage or debt accumulated by financial institutions as they were often purchasing these securities and derivatives with borrowed money. This greatly limited their ability to adequately value their holdings, raising uncertainty about the solvency of borrowers.

Nevertheless, banks and financial institutions obliged borrowers, including those with poor credit history, by making credit easily available in the form of these new and innovative types of mortgages and mortgage-related securities. Despite the risks, these securitized mortgage products also offered bigger returns and profits. As a result, they not only attracted first-time home buyers and investors in the United States, they also attracted foreign investors who poured billions of dollars into the U.S. economy. In fact, the incongruity, fragmentation, and lack of harmonization of financial supervision and regulation at the international level gave rise to the problem of regulatory arbitrage (the practice of taking advantage of a regulatory difference between two or more markets) by both U.S. and foreign financial institutions. However, when these risky mortgage-backed securities eventually plummeted in value, financial institutions in the United States and around the world were affected (and in some cases, brought down). As markets reassessed credit risk, a global flight to quality ensued. Funds were rapidly repatriated from emerging markets to shore up balance sheets of financial institutions in the advanced economies. This explains

---

[23] Derivatives are used by financial institutions and corporations to adjust their exposure to particular financial risks, such as the default of a borrower or wild swings in interest rates.

why the contagion spread with such speed and ferocity, and why unlike previous crises, which had been restricted to sovereign entities and private financial institutions (where key participants could resolve matters behind closed boardroom doors), this crisis was not amenable to such resolution as numerous actors from the high-powered world of capital and finance, small-time investors, and legions of "six-pack Joes" representing all manner of residential real estate were involved.

Similarly, profound changes in the global economy, in particular, the widening global imbalances (again, dismissed as benign), turned out to carry hidden, and in hindsight, fatal flaws. Global imbalance refers to the huge current account deficits and surpluses that had built up in the global economy starting in the late 1990s and was widely viewed as a benign response to the global primacy of the U.S. dollar (Cooper 2007, 2008; Caballero, Farhi, and Gourinchas 2008; Dooley, Folkerts-Landau, and Garber 2005). The United States, along with a number of other advanced economies, including the United Kingdom and Italy, built up large deficits, while China, Japan, Germany, Russia, Brazil, and the oil-exporting economies built up huge dollar surpluses. These surpluses were massive; global central bank reserves skyrocketed from a paltry $200 billion in 1990 to some $8 trillion by 2009, with sovereign wealth funds accounting for an additional $4 trillion (Taylor 2011, 95).

Economic theory states that wealthier countries tend to have higher savings, lower investment, and large or healthy current account surpluses, whereas emerging and developing economies tend to have low savings and high investment rates, there were several interrelated factors that contributed to this counterintuitive pattern of capital flows.[24] Specifically, many emerging market economies adopted an export-based strategy, necessitating the maintenance of highly competitive exchange rates. Or, put another way, many emerging economies adopted exchange rate policies that effectively prevented real exchange rate adjustment. This in turn led to the accumulation of substantial foreign-exchange reserves. By maintaining undervalued exchange rates (such as China's currency policy) and stoically compressing domestic demand to promote export-led growth, the emerging Asian markets were able to accumulate massive international reserves, mostly in U.S. dollars. These huge surpluses, what Bernanke called a "global savings glut," became even larger as Asian economies cut back on investment and increased savings to self-insure against liquidity shocks following their bitter experience with the IMF during the Asian financial crisis in 1997. Moreover, the underdeveloped

---

[24] This pattern tends to contradict Milton Friedman's (1957) "permanent income hypothesis."

financial systems in many emerging economies (most notably China) forced these countries to divert their savings to the advanced economies by investing in typically safe sovereign financial assets.

The United States accommodated (indeed, welcomed) these savings-cum-largess. However, these massive (and invasive) capital inflows also drove down the real interest rates in the United States and elsewhere, further fueling consumption and speculation. Warnock and Warnock (2009) estimate that if there had been no foreign official purchases of U.S. government bonds between May 2004 and May 2005, the ten-year Treasury yield would have been around 80 points higher. These developments, combined with the already low household savings rates in the United States, led to a rapid rise in the U.S. current account deficit. As noted, these were seen as generally benign developments for two reasons – first, the inherent "safety" of U.S. financial assets created sustained demand for those assets, and second, the assumption that because the dollar functions as a de facto global currency, the buildup of dollar reserves by foreign countries was not only inevitable but also a positive development for the United States because it brought in a disproportionately large share of world capital flows for investment.

However, widening global imbalance also created deep and pernicious distortions that made the global economy extremely vulnerable to a downturn in the U.S. economy. Although a handful of analysts, namely Roubini and, to a lesser extent, Raghuram Rajan (2005), expressed apprehension that these growing imbalances could lead to an unsustainable buildup in external claims on deficit countries like the United States and potentially substantial dollar depreciation, the overall consensus was that these imbalances could be sustained as long as the structural factors noted above remained in place. Seduced by immediate gains, overzealous market participants and policy makers failed to adequately appreciate how persistent imbalances were also spawning a serious buildup of leverage, the creation of risky assets, and a real-estate bubble in the United States and other advanced economies by contributing to a long period of low interest rates (especially in the advanced economies) and large capital inflows into U.S. and European banks. Post-crisis research confirms that the obstinate patterns of global imbalances played a significant role in contributing to the subprime mess and the financial crisis because foreign investors, in their search for safe investments, forced the U.S. financial sector to create products that were increasingly risky (Caballero 2009; Wolf 2008). Specifically, as China and other countries with significant foreign reserves began to accumulate large volumes of U.S. Treasury bonds, they not only pushed down yields (making

Table I.3. *Percentage of daily average FX turnover divided by currency*

	2001	2004	2007	2010
U.S. dollar	89.9	88.0	85.6	84.9
Japanese yen	23.5	20.8	17.2	19.0
Euro	37.9	37.4	37.0	39.1
Pound sterling	13.0	16.5	14.9	12.9

Source: Bank of International Settlements Triennial FX Turnover Survey.

Treasuries less attractive), but the growing demand for higher-yielding U.S. debt provided incentives to the investment banking industry to create new types of higher-yielding securities – in particular, the collateralized debt obligations.

The sheer size of the U.S. financial market, the United States' disproportionate share of the world economy (27 percent in 2010), the fact that the U.S. dollar is the world's reserve currency because it is a good "store of value" and the currency most used in international transactions all guaranteed that any shock to the U.S. financial markets and economy would have immediate and far-reaching global repercussions.[25] Given the world's seemingly insatiable appetite for dollar-denominated assets, a very large portion of international payments are made in dollars, and a substantial portion of international trade (even trade not directly involving the United States) is denominated in U.S. dollars. Roughly 85 percent of foreign-exchange transactions are trades of other currencies for dollars (Table I.3). In addition, globally traded commodities (such as oil and foodgrains) are priced in dollars, making it necessary for foreign banks to hold portfolios of dollar assets and liabilities. Overall, some two-thirds of the world's official foreign-exchange reserves of $6.7 trillion are held in dollars (Table I.4). This means that central banks around the world not only hold more U.S. dollars and dollar securities than they do assets in any other foreign currency, they also know that these dollar reserves are essential to stabilize the value of their own national currencies.

The U.S. dollar's status as the world's reserve currency means that financial shocks can be rapidly transmitted across borders. Although that status allows the United States to finance its huge trade and fiscal deficits without transaction costs, it also encouraged emerging economies (most

---

[25] For the classic statement, see Krugman (1984).

Table I.4. *U.S. dollar's share of official global foreign-exchange reserves (%)*

2001	2004	2007	2010
71.5	65.9	64.1	61.3

Source: Bank of International Settlements Triennial FX Turnover Survey.

notably, China) to peg their currencies to the dollar, creating an artificially low exchange rate, in order to gain a trade advantage and amass vast amounts of foreign-exchange reserves (much of which is denominated in dollars) in the process. As U.S. and other investors (both private and sovereign) began to move their investments to the safety of U.S. government bonds, the value of the dollar was lifted.[26] For the rest of the world, this meant a dollar crunch and an exacerbation of economic woes, especially in countries attempting to refinance debt, and those for whom foreign investment and aid was rolled back. In addition, because the massive accumulation of U.S. dollar assets around the world saddled banks with significant funding requirements, the acute shortages of dollar liquidity (particularly in the weeks following Lehman's collapse), both within and outside the United States, created serious problems for financial institutions as many could not access dollars when they needed them most.[27] This undermined the interbank money markets and resulted in a sharp rise in the cost of exchanging foreign currency for dollars in the FX swap markets. If not for the far-reaching policy measures adopted by central banks around the world, including international swap arrangements with the U.S. Federal

---

[26] According to the Federal Reserve, since mid-2008, the dollar has risen by 13 percent against major foreign currencies after adjusting for inflation. Foreign holdings of Treasury bills rose by $456 billion in 2008.

[27] International financial institutions and businesses need U.S. dollars to fund their dollar-denominated investments such as retail and corporate loans, holdings of structured finance products based on U.S. mortgages, and other underlying assets. Although the shocks to the U.S. subprime and mortgage-based securities markets further weakened the dollar (by about 8.5 percent in real effective terms between June 2007 and July 2008), the dire predictions of a massive flight from U.S. assets and a sudden drop in the value of the dollar failed to materialize. Indeed, the assumption that if the U.S. economy went into a sharp downturn, foreign central banks would be reluctant to invest their national savings in the U.S. dollar proved to be incorrect. Rather, the dollar was once again affirmed as the global reserve currency. The massive "flight to safety" by panicked investors following the collapse of Lehman Brothers into U.S. Treasuries only confirmed that the U.S. government is still the safest investment in the world.

Reserve, banks would not have been able to provide dollars to financial institutions in their respective jurisdictions. Finally, the massive deleveraging contributed to large and wild swings in the currencies of many emerging economies, including South Korea, Brazil, and Mexico.[28]

Contagion via Global Trade

Reinhart and Rogoff (2009) persuasively illustrate that crises originating in advanced economies or in global financial centers tend to be highly contagious because they lead to a sudden stop in lending and a massive liquidity squeeze.[29] Although the origins of the Great Recession and its rapid transmission lay in the financial sector, world trade was not immune for very long. Economies, especially emerging economies, experienced twin shocks – first, a sudden stop of capital inflows driven by global deleveraging (and the resultant unwinding of positions), and second, a collapse in export demand.

World trade began to decline at the end of 2008, and by the first quarter of 2009, the pace of decline had picked up dramatically. All 104 nations for which the WTO collects data experienced a drop in trade starting the second half of 2008 and the first half of 2009 (Baldwin 2009), leading some to compare the contraction to the collapse of trade during the Great Depression (Eichengreen and O'Rourke 2009). As Table I.5 shows, global trade not only experienced a precipitous decline, the collapse was fairly broad-based across trading partners. As the fall in external demand began to have impact, exports and cross-border trade contracted – although, given the centrifugal nature of global integration, the size of the shock varied between countries, depending on the country's exports – high-value manufactured goods, labor-intensive manufactured goods, or basic commodities and raw materials (Hausmann et al. 2007). Countries with poor or limited global financial linkages (the least-developed countries or LDCs) were mainly impacted through the trade channel, whereas countries with deeper financial linkages were impacted via the financial channel. However, countries with particular vulnerabilities, including high current account deficits, high levels of indebtedness, low foreign-exchange reserves, and imprudent credit growth were most adversely impacted. Conversely, countries with

---

[28] Of course, large currency depreciation (usually the result of countries having few foreign assets, but extensive liabilities denominated in a foreign currency like the U.S. dollar, can severely undermine the real economy.

[29] Banking crises that originate in global financial centers (like the subprime crisis) result in sudden stops in lending to other economies.

Table I.5. *Financial crisis and impact on world exports*

	Peak month	Trough month	Peak to trough (change in %)
Advanced Economies	April 2008	January 2009	−23.3
United States	July 2008	April 2009	−24.7
Euro area	April 2008	February 2009	−23.1
Japan	January 2008	March 2009	−41.4
Emerging Economies	April 2008	January 2009	−21.5
Asia	July 2008	January 2009	−24.7
Latin America	January 2008	August 2009	−21.1
Central & Eastern Europe	January 2008	May 2009	−30.8
Africa & Middle East	April 2008	April 2009	−12.8

Source: Wynne (2009, 6).

more flexible exchange rates and a robust stock of international foreign reserves experienced more modest impact (Berkmen et al. 2009).

Research also tends to underscore two key factors behind the sharp contraction in global trade (see Alessandria et al. 2010; Baldwin 2009; Baldwin and Evenett 2009; Levchenko et al. 2010; Wynne 2009). The first is expanding vertical specialization, where countries specialize in a particular stage of a good's manufacture or assembly, causing increased dependency on global supply chains.[30] This is because intermediate goods typically cross borders several times before being assembled into a final product, and any disruption of product inputs negatively impacts all, especially countries "downstream" or at the later phases of production as they have higher imported content in their exports (Yi 2009). Second, since international trade requires various types of financing (such as letters of guarantee provided by banks, loans from public sector export-import banks and intra or inter-business financing, among others), the extremely tight credit conditions and the resultant shortage of liquidity (especially U.S. dollars), coupled with skyrocketing cost of trade finance, contributed to a sharp fall in economic activity (Chauffour

---

[30] The example of the iPhone is illustrative. Contessi and El-Ghazaly (2010, 10) describe the manufacturing and assembly process:

The iPhone's CPU and video processing are made in Singapore. Its digital camera, circuit boards and metal casings are made in Taiwan. Its touch screen controllers are made in the U.S. From these countries, all components are then shipped and assembled in Shenzhen, China, before being delivered to final consumers in various countries. Complete iPhones arrive to American consumers after the phones' components have crossed at least four borders, including the U.S. border twice.

and Malouche 2011). To fill this gap, in April 2009, the G-20 agreed on a $250 billion support facility to expand trade finance via export credit agencies and multilateral development banks. Not surprisingly, the average utilization rate of the facility was initially 70 percent, but dropped to around 40 percent in the fourth quarter of 2009 as the supply of credit from private sources began to pick up.[31]

With illustrations from the EU and countries as diverse as the United Kingdom, Iceland, Ireland, Russia, Japan, South Korea, China, India, the oil-producing Gulf States, and the world's poorest countries in Africa and elsewhere, this book elaborates the multifarious ways in which the crisis spread globally from its epicenter. The United States and Western Europe had both become dependent on the financial sector (their growth engines were at the very heart of the crisis), and Eastern Europe had become highly dependent on large-scale capital imports from Western European banks and was saddled with growing current account deficits and inadequate reserves. Both were hit hard by the reversal of capital flows. The high-performing Asian economies were affected because of sharp declines in export growth and tightening of credit due to sudden capital flow reversals as part of global deleveraging, but their healthy reserves enabled them to use aggressive countercyclical fiscal policies to better withstand the shocks (Kose and Prasad 2010). However, most developing economies were negatively impacted because of large-scale drops in commodity prices, deterioration in their terms of trade, and the tightening of global credit.

Free Markets and Keynesian State Capitalism

To some, the U.S.-induced subprime crisis and the global economic meltdown only further underscore the inherent (and deadly) flaws of Anglo-American free-wheeling market capitalism – often interchangeably and disparagingly caricatured as the "Anglo-American model," "market fundamentalism," "neoliberalism," "the Washington Consensus," and so forth (see Crotty 2009). This apparent disillusionment with technocratic neoliberal economic orthodoxy also provides prima facie evidence (and vindication) of the relevance of greater governmental action via planning and intervention – often dubbed neo-Keynesianism or the "new structuralism."

---

[31] Although there is broad consensus that the tight credit conditions exacerbated global trade, there is no agreement regarding the role of trade finance, in particular, if lack of it was the primary reason for global trade contraction. For example, Levchenko et al. (2010, 214) found "no support for the hypothesis that trade credit played a role in the recent trade collapse." See Asmundson (2011) for a similar conclusion.

As is well known, the celebrated British economist John Maynard Keynes, in his magnum-opus, *General Theory of Employment, Interest and Money*, published in 1936, rejected the classical nineteenth-century laissez-faire notion of a benevolent self-equilibrating economy, claiming that targeted government intervention ("heterodox" policies), by boosting aggregate demand, was necessary to correct market failure and prevent recessions. In the midst of the crisis, Krugman (2009) and others triumphantly (and nostalgically) concluded that we are all "Keynesians now" – not only because the policy ideas of Keynes such as the use of expansionary fiscal policy to stem the massive deflationary pressures were successfully adopted on a global scale to restore ailing economies to health, but also because the "twentieth century's most influential economist" provides a coherent set of epistemological guidelines as to how to construct a more viable "path to global economic prosperity" (Clarke 2009; Davidson 2009; Eatwell and Milgate 2011; Kotz 2009; Madrick 2008; Posner 2009; Reich 2010; Skidelsky 2009).

Undoubtedly, the crash of 2008 has profoundly shaken what was once an article of faith in the United States and other Western capitals: the innate superiority of the free-market system, combined with a deep and abiding mistrust of "statism" or big government. In the aftermath of the crisis, the view that markets are inherently volatile, unpredictable, and prone to booms and busts, and thus require the guiding hand of a benevolent state to repair wrecked economies and protect average citizens from the corrosive impact of crises and crashes they had no role in creating, seems to be again ascendant. Bremmer (2009, 41), in an aptly titled article, "State Capitalism Comes of Age," argues that "state capitalism, a system in which the state functions as the leading economic actor and uses markets primarily for political gain," and which takes eclectic forms, ranging from the hybrid Chinese-style statist-authoritarian capitalism to the more traditional Keynesian-inspired welfare and social-democratic state capitalism, is emerging as a viable alternative, not only in the United States (the quintessential citadel of unbridled laissez-faire capitalism), but around the world. Bremmer (2009, 49) notes that "until very recently, New York City was the world's financial capital. It no longer is even the financial capital of the United States. That distinction now falls on Washington, where members of Congress and the executive branch make decisions with long-term market impact on a scale not seen since the 1930s."

Of course, it remains to be seen if the shift toward state capitalism and activist governments reflects a fleeting and ephemeral pendulum swing (the debate regarding markets and government is old) or signals a "paradigm shift" and a more durable and enduring realignments in national and global political economy. In the United States at least, contrary impulses – from the Tea Party's vitriolic rejection of "big government," to the Occupy Wall Street's equally shrill demand for state-mandated "wealth redistribution" illustrate that the issue is far from resolved. This book argues that although Keynesian-inspired policies and programs to boost aggregate demand in the initial phase of the crisis were entirely justified, that is hardly a long-term economic solution. Rather, the seemingly wholesale adoption of neo-Keynesian policies epitomized in massive government spending and a deepening of the state's presence in the economy in the United States and other advanced economies carries huge and unmitigated risks.

Undoubtedly, the current infatuation with Keynesianism is in part based on a wistfully naïve optimism about what states can do as well as on a deep misdiagnoses of the crisis, namely, that since the crisis and the Great Recession was fundamentally the result of systemic failure of markets (namely, neoliberal capitalism), a complete restructuring of the economic order along more Keynesian-cum-statist lines is in order. In the advanced economies, both the free-wheeling Anglo-American "Liberal Market Economies" (LMEs) and the more cooperative and welfare-Keynesian type "Coordinated Market Economies" (CMEs), succumbed to the crisis – although, some liberal market economies such as Canada and Australia remained relatively immune (Konzelmann et al. 2012), The fact that the outcome was similar for these economies with very different political institutional arrangements should give pause to those claiming that Keynesian and statist systems are inherently superior in both managing and overcoming the cycles of boom and bust inherent to globalized capitalism.[32] Needless to say, such simplification and eagerness toward more state intervention in political and economic life is also attractive to law makers and politicians who face constant pressure to find quick (and simple) solutions to complex economic problems, and are only too eager to operate under the pretense that if markets don't work, there are no alternatives to governments.

Perhaps more troubling, the latest incarnation of state capitalism epitomized by the highly centralized and interventionist Chinese *guanxi*,

---

[32] Hall and Soskice (2001), in their influential *Varieties of Capitalism*, pointed out that a country's overall economic performance is much better if it fits into one of two basic types of capitalism: the Liberal Market Economies (LME), a variant characteristic of Anglo-Saxon economies (in particular, the United States and the United Kingdom), and Coordinated Market Economies (CME), a variant typical of continental Europe, notably Germany. As the following chapters show, the fact that both systems suffered from similar structural flaws and were hit equally hard by the crisis of 2008 indicates that the forces of financial globalization have created far deeper convergence than earlier assumed.

or network, capitalism, which is rooted in top-down Leninist management and control of the "commanding heights" of the economy, informal and opaque relationships between the party-state and private networks, and party-state sponsorship of compliant and "strategic" private business interests is, as Bremmer (2010) has argued, intrinsically incompatible with the competitive and rules-based liberal global economic order.[33] In fact, the expansion and adoption of such radical variants of neo-Keynesianism can severely emasculate the free-market system so conspicuously responsible for generating worldwide prosperity during the post-war era. If history is any guide, top-down state planning has produced disastrous outcomes, and once entrenched can become intransigent and difficult to reverse (Scott 1998). Indeed, burdened by the weight of its many pathologies, statism carries the potential to do more long-term economic harm than the financial crises associated with the open liberal market system.

A New National and Global Financial Architecture

Although markets are inherently unpredictable and prone to cycles of booms and busts, in the long-run, they are also essential to correcting market failure – captured in this pithy observation: "Markets fail. That's why we need markets" (Kling and Schulz 2009). Yet, as Karl Polanyi (1944) reminded us decades ago, although market economies provide numerous incentives for businesses and firms to advance their interest, extreme selfish behavior, if unchecked, can also undermine and destroy the foundations of market economies. Hence, political institutions are necessary as they can help temper and regulate such narrow self-interested behavior. To more effectively balance regulation and risk, a creative synergy of markets and government, or what the "varieties of capitalism" school has described as "institutional complementarities," is needed (Amable 2003; Crouch 2005; Hall and Soskice 2001). That is, institutions are integrated in such a manner that each enhances the other. However, the crisis of 2007 also shows that institutions that reinforce incentives for financial innovation and risk taking must also have countervailing institutions to compensate for or provide checks against reckless market behavior. Thus, "compensatory" institutions are just as important as the "reinforcing" sets of institutions (Kenworthy 2006). These are much easier to put in place at the domestic level than globally (Campbell 2004).

---

[33] The term "*guanxi*," or network, capitalism is used by McNally (2011).

It is important to reiterate that the subprime-induced global crisis was hardly a case of total market failure, but a specific case of failure in the financial sector. In other words, the crisis was fundamentally a financial crisis, the result of poorly regulated banks and financial institutions taking reckless gambles in search of quick profits. This is what explains that even during the midst of the crisis, market activities in the so-called "real economy," such as the exchange of goods and services, continued to function relatively smoothly. The meltdown occurred in the financial sector with its speculative and increasingly high-risk activities, especially in regard to securitized assets (the result of imprudent deregulation and failure of regulatory oversight). Instead of the total economic restructuring and overhaul the Keynesians are blithely propagating, more dispassionate financial regulation and oversight can greatly help to mitigate the types of colossal financial meltdown the global economy has just experienced. In other words, national authorities must use a surgeon's scalpel instead of a sledge hammer. Besides overhauling financial regulation to build a more stable and transparent financial system with the ability to withstand abrupt swings and sharp shocks, regulators must also impose stronger capital requirements to limit the banking and financial sector from making risky investment bets with borrowed money, and they must have the authority to oversee consumer protection.

Like previous economic crises, this crisis has also renewed calls for the creation of a new international financial architecture – indeed, an ostensible "Bretton Woods II" – that is resilient to financial shocks and more equitable sustainable. Already, a wide range of prescriptions have been enunciated as how best to deal with both the immediate and long-term ramifications of the financial crisis and to set the global economy on a sustainable growth path. However, if past experience is any guide, one may be forgiven for seeing this exercise as akin to Hegel's Owl of Minerva – the collective wisdom taking flight after dusk when the damage is already done, and the proclivity is to react to the previous crisis, rather than to anticipate the next one. Will the lessons of the Great Recession be learned and acted upon, or will the ponderously slow and exasperating etiquette that defines multilateral negotiations on how to fix the global economy again prove too little and come too late?

Charles Kindelberger (1973), in his magnificent *The World in Depression: 1929–1939*, compellingly argued that "the 1929 depression was so wide, so deep, and so long because the international economic system was rendered unstable by British inability and U.S. unwillingness to assume responsibility for stabilizing it" (p. 291). The conspicuous absence today of a global leader is again making the painstaking work of stabilizing the international order exceedingly difficult. With the United States weary and lacking both the political will and economic wherewithal, the EU preoccupied with its own existential challenges, and China torn between engagement and quiescence and not yet willing or ready to fill the vacuum, the global system today lacks a pivotal hegemon or even a concert of powers that can assume leadership to provide a stable, rule-based international order for open trade and commerce to thrive. This explains why governments around the world seem to have already abdicated in favor of organizations such as the IMF and multilateral bodies such as the G-20 to pick up the pieces. The hope is that with deeper institutionalization, the world's premier multilateral body, the G-20, along with the IMF will be able to produce broadly coordinated and coherent policy responses to both domestic and global economic problems. Certainly, in the absence of a hegemon, or even a concert of powers, multilateral economic cooperation is essential to building a stable and durable global economic order. Nevertheless, Chapter 10 will argue that the current reality appears to validate Kindleberger's pessimistic observation – because, among other things, this second-best strategy is proving incapable of resolving pressing problems such as the buildup of imbalances in the global economy – without which there cannot be sustained and balanced recovery. However, the gloomy predictions are hardly certainties. The verdict is still out if meaningful multilateral cooperation to create a more balanced and sustainable international economic order can be achieved.

ONE

The United States

Why the Trigger?

In their authoritative study, *This Time Is Different: Eight Centuries of Financial Folly*, Reinhart and Rogoff (2009) points out that the past can be the prologue as they show that financial panics and crises are not episodic, but have occurred with remarkable frequency throughout recorded history. In the United States, major crises occurred with debilitating frequency: in 1792, 1797, 1819, 1837, 1857, 1873, 1893, 1907, and 1929–33. Then, for the next several decades, although there were bumps, there were no major financial crises. Since the 1980s the "Great Moderation" further underscored the notion that macroeconomic volatility was a thing of the past. As Figure 1.1 illustrates, beginning in the mid-1980s, the volatility of the U.S. economy was markedly lower than it was in the earlier part of the postwar period, and certainly much less than during the interwar period.

Overall, during the period from 1980 to mid-2000 growth rate volatility underwent a dramatic moderation from the 1950s to the 1970s. The largest recession of the postWorld War II era was in 1982 when real per capita GDP fell by 3 percent and the unemployment rate peaked at nearly 11 percent. After 1984, the growth rates were only about half as volatile than they were during the earlier postwar period. By 2000, the U.S. fiscal situation looked robust. The federal budget recorded a surplus of 2.4 percent of GDP, and the Congressional Budget Office (CBO 2001) boldly projected a surplus of some $5.6 trillion by 2011. In fact, even as late as September 2008 – in the midst of a gigantic financial meltdown – the CBO (2008) was confidently predicting only a "mild recession" with GDP growing by only 0.9 percent in 2008 but rebounding back to 1.8 percent in 2009.

Arguably, such an exceptionally uninterrupted period of relative calm and sustained prosperity made policy makers, market participants, and analysts, among others, unduly complacent. The somber and cautionary experiences of history were forgotten and hubristically replaced with a combustible mix

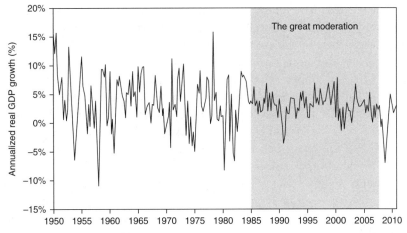

Figure 1.1. U.S. real GDP growth, 1950–2010.
Source: http://www.wikipedia.org.

of arrogance and overconfidence. The Great Moderation, now increasingly seen as the "new normal," meant that policy makers no longer had to concern themselves with such mundane tasks as risk management, and market actors could devote their energies and talents to the pursuit of profit. After all, the prevailing view reinforced the belief that sharp economic downturn, if it did occur at all, would be far less severe than in the past, and in the worst-case scenario, the new, sophisticated (and foolproof) risk management tools and complex mathematical models that produced superior understanding of the secrets of "counter-cyclical monetary policy" would eventually allow regulators and market actors to cure the economy's pathology and nudge it back on track (Patterson 2010). Put bluntly, the abiding faith in the market ("market fundamentalism") and technocratic expertise, coupled with equal measure of cognitive dissonance and arrogance (i.e., the mood of the market could always be read and necessary corrections made when needed), not only made legislators, regulators, and market actors consistently underestimate risk and push the limits of an inherently fragile financial system; it also prevented more rigorous oversight and the creation of the necessary regulatory and supervisory institutions capable of keeping up with the inexorably fast changes in the domestic and global economic landscape.

On top of this, successive administrations in Washington expediently convinced themselves (and their constituencies) that they could simultaneously increase expenditure, cut taxes, and balance the budget without any permanent corrosive repercussions for either the domestic or international economy.[1] The obvious corollary of such tendentious claims was that it led lawmakers in both the executive and legislative branches of government to explicitly and indirectly "encourage" reckless behavior. For example, the "moral hazard" inherent in the bailout of the Continental Illinois Bank in 1984, the massive Savings and Loan bailout in the late 1980s, and the equally massive bailout of Long Term Capital Management, orchestrated by the Federal Reserve of New York a decade earlier, set the precedent and established the strong belief among private financial institutions that the Feds would always "send in the cavalry" to rescue the financial sector in a liquidity squeeze. The unqualified optimism or the "irrational exuberance" that such a promiscuous culture spawned took the underestimation of both risk and risk taking to new heights by inducing banks, non-bank financial institutions, and institutional and individual investors to increase their leverage and take increasingly aggressive (and risky) gambles. In an environment such as this, seemingly devoid of clear regulations (and ineffective regulators), rules, guidelines, and constraints (laws), the ability to devise new and unrestrained ways to get rich fast was limited only by one's imagination and creativity. Perhaps nowhere were these symptoms more pronounced than in the U.S. housing sector.

The U.S. Housing Market

For decades the residential mortgage market in the United States worked quite well, enabling millions of individuals and families to achieve the dream of owning a home. The road to home ownership was simple: most homebuyers had only one option for borrowing money to purchase a home: pay a fair down payment and meet the requirements of a rather strict mortgage-lending standard to receive a thirty-year fixed-rate amortized loan. In return, these mortgages offered homebuyers both affordability and stability in the form of equal monthly payments – a far cry from the volatile and predatory five-year "balloon loans" common before the Great Depression.[2] For their part, the lenders (usually the local depository institutions such as banks and the Savings and Loans), which used deposits to fund the home loans, functioned not only as the "originators" of the loans, but also kept or

---

[1] The misguided tenet of Reaganism – that tax cuts are always self-financing – still has a strong sway over the Republican Party.

[2] Under amortized mortgages, borrowers pay off part of the capital owed as well as the interest accrued for each period. This means that by the end of the loan period the original sum has been prepaid in full.

"held" (hence the "originate-and-hold model") them in their portfolios, and in so doing also held the credit risk, including the market risk of interest-rate fluctuations. However, in their effort to provide greater liquidity to the mortgage market, the federal government in 1938 created Fannie Mae, or the Federal National Mortgage Association. In purchasing only mortgages that conformed to clear underwriting standards (that is, prime mortgages) Fannie Mae successfully created a vibrant secondary market for mortgages, allowing millions of Americans to purchase their first homes.

The home-ownership rate was close to a record 70 percent by the 1990s, and politicians from both parties valorized home ownership, boasting that an ecumenical American "ownership society" was the cornerstone of the country's economic stability. They championed the need to extend this inalienable right to the pursuit of the American Dream to the excluded 30 percent, many of whom, politicians claimed, through no fault of their own, had been shut out of the housing market (McLean and Nocera 2010). For example, President George W. Bush, in October 2002, boldly proclaimed: "You see, we want everybody in America to own their own home. That's what we want. That is – an ownership society is a compassion-ate society."[3] But, as Andrews (2009) wryly notes, the "ownership society" mantra, always a politically unassailable theme, was carefully orchestrated by Bush's political strategist, Karl Rove, to expand the Republican support among the white middle and working class and especially racial and eth-nic minorities, a disproportionate percentage of whom were potential first-time homebuyers.[4]

Fortuitously, a number of developments beginning in the 1990s made it possible to translate the political rhetoric of "affordable housing" and "own-ership society" into reality. First, rising housing prices (between 1997 and 2006, the median housing price increased by some 125 percent) led many to assume that they would continue to increase for the foreseeable future. Coupled with low interest rates (between 2000 and 2003, the federal fund rate target declined from 6.5 percent to 1 percent), this meant that individu-als could buy a house with no money down as they could borrow by taking out either home-equity loans or second mortgages on their existing homes.

[3] http://www.whitehouse.gov/news/releases/2002

[4] Cannato (2010, 77) notes:

Before the compassionate conservatism of George W. Bush, there was the empowerment conservatism of Jack Kemp. As a member of Congress in the 1970s and '80s, and as secre-tary of HUD under President George H. W. Bush, Kemp made it his mission to broaden the reach of the Republican Party beyond the white middle class, reaching out to minori-ties and the poor.

Second, with housing prices trending upward, a quick (and easy) way for banks and other financial institutions to increase yield and profits was to expand their mortgage lending. The excluded 30 percent of households were seen as a particularly lucrative market because the higher interest rates could be levied against those with poor credit scores and inadequate down payment and incomes.

Second, technological innovations in financial products, particularly loan securitization, enabled banks to create mortgage loans by packaging and reselling a whole array of assets under intricately entwined and often poorly understood "bundles," "pools," and "tranches." In other words, securitization allowed banks to use large pools of mortgages as collateral to issue securities, namely mortgage-backed securities. These included the new hybrid ARMs (adjustable-rate mortgages), which began with a low, fixed interest rate for several years followed by a much higher market rate. Some of these securities were made up of the so-called nontraditional mortgages, including interest-only mortgages (where amortization of principal was not required during the first few years of the loan); negative-amortization mortgages (that offered initial payments well below the amount required to cover interest and amortize principal); mortgages with "teaser" rates; and "balloon payment loans," which required a large lump-sum payment at the end of the loan. Unlike the subprime mortgage products (to be discussed), these nontraditional mortgages were often used by first-time homebuyers and investors who either could not afford or did not wish to make a large down payment.

The more "creative" (and riskier) were the credit-market instruments such as derivatives on asset-backed securities and the structured investment vehicles SIVs (Gorton 2009). These were quite difficult to price as they were based not simply on mortgage loans, but rather on home mortgage loans collateralized with an assortment of commercial paper of varying quality, including credit card loans and student loans, among others. Perhaps most corrosive and pernicious of the securitized credit were the mortgage-backed securities (MBS), particularly the residential mortgage-backed securities (RMBS), in which thousands of mortgages were collected into mortgage pools. Moreover, the tranches from one mortgage pool were often combined with tranches from other mortgage pools, creating collateralized mortgage obligations (CMOs), while collateralized loan obligations (CLOs) were created by combining tranches from different pools made of commercial mortgages, auto loans, student loans, small business loans, and even credit card receivables. The returns on these pools were then divided or "sliced" into several tranches and sold to investors as securities. Some of these tranches, namely the most "senior" ones, received the highest AAA rating but carried a lower interest rate. The middle or "mezzanine" tranches carried greater risk but a higher rate of return, and the lowest or the unrated "equity" tranches, with below-investment-grade credit ratings, were at the very bottom. Some of these asset-backed securities, made up of "subprime mortgages" for the marginal and risky borrowers, including those with inadequate income relative to their debts, were packaged and sold to banks, investors, pension funds, and equities worldwide. These assets attracted a wide range of investors: from those with large pools of available funds (notably pension funds, insurance companies, and sovereign governments around the world) to those who could use leverage and borrow money more cheaply[5] (such as commercial and investment banks, hedge funds, insurance companies, and private investors). After all, not only did these securities pay more interest; their predominantly AAA ratings also gave them the appearance of low-risk and high-yield investments.

The third development was the overreliance of the finance and banking industries on inaccurate mathematical models to assess investment risk. As Nassim Nicholas Taleb (2010) points out in his best-selling book, *The Black Swan*, the crash of 2008 was not a "black swan" event. A black swan is a highly improbable and unpredictable event, such as the 9/11 terrorist attacks. In contrast, the crash of 2008 – a totally predictable event – was made improbable by flawed mathematical models of risk assessment in the banking and financial sectors. Even as these models artificially suppressed all signs of risk and volatility, a dangerous buildup of risk was silently accumulating, with the eventual and predictable explosion its inevitable denouement. Indeed, Scott Patterson (2010), in his aptly titled book, *The Quants: How a New Breed of Math Whizzes Conquered Wall Street and Nearly Destroyed It*, lucidly chronicles how math and physics "geeks" creatively used advances in information technology to enable both the traditional (and relatively transparent) commercial banking sector and the less regulated "shadow banking" system to create a whole array of seemingly robust and flamboyant asset-backed securities or financial derivatives and off-balance-sheet investment vehicles (all of which looked statistically robust) as a way to provide easy access to credit.[6] Securitization and other new and "creative"

---

[5] That is, one could make money by borrowing at a low interest rate and then turning around and buying the MBS.

[6] As Gorton (2009; 2010) and Gorton and Metrick (2010) point out, although the shadow-banking system performs a role similar to that of traditional banks, the lenders and borrowers using the shadow-banking system are large businesses, broker-dealers, and institutional investors who invest and lend millions and billions of dollars at any given time.

financial products allowed banks and financial institutions to engage in "disintermediation" or to shift assets off their balance sheets. Large mortgage finance companies and banks including Countywide, Washington Mutual, First Franklin, Lehman Brothers, and Ameriquest made huge profits by developing and selling mortgage loans to Wall Street investment firms such as Morgan Stanley, Barclays, Merrill Lynch, Bear Stearns, Goldman Sachs, Deutsche Bank, Credit Suisse, JP Morgan, and Citigroup. For its part, the insurance giant AIG became heavily involved in guaranteeing these mortgage-backed securities – in hindsight – without much oversight. Last but by far not least (as discussed later in the book), policy makers and regulators share much responsibility because they had failed to thwart this high-risk financial engineering by systematically relaxing the underwriting standards and failing to enforce existing rules to mitigate some of the worst excesses.

Loan Securitization

Securitization began in the United States in the 1970s, when home mortgages were pooled or "bundled" together into securities by government-backed agencies. These mortgage-backed securities were backed by mortgage loans, both commercial and residential. Later, asset-backed securities based on any asset with a stable cash flow were created.

Hence, securitization is a process under which various types of assets are pooled and then bundled and repackaged into interest-bearing securities. These securities are then sold to investors who benefit from the interest and principal payments from the assets. For financial institutions, securitization served as a useful tool to transfer the credit risk of the assets they originated from their balance sheets to other financial institutions, including insurance companies, banks, Freddie Mac and Fannie Mae, and to hedge funds, which now carried both the credit and market risks. Securitization also allowed banks to greatly reduce the amount of capital reserves required (roughly 8–10 percent) against their existing loans, and thereby allowed them to lend more. Schwartz (2009, 21) lucidly notes that

Furthermore, much of the credit intermediation in the shadow-banking system takes the form of maturity transformation with short-term, liquid liabilities issued against longer-term, less-liquid assets. Gorton (2009) notes that the shadow-banking system emerged gradually over the past three to four decades as traditional banking became less profitable. Specifically, restricted from paying interest on demand deposits, including insurance and securities underwriting services, and facing increasing competition from interest-bearing services offered by nonbanks such as money market mutual funds, banks began to shift their activities toward more profitable activities that shadow banking offered.

"securitization substituted the 'originate to distribute securities' model of mortgage lending in lieu of the traditional 'originate to hold mortgages'" model. That is, under this new model, dubbed the "origination, securitization and servicing model," an investment bank like Bear Stearns, Lehman Brothers, Merrill Lynch, or Goldman Sachs would request mortgage banks to make home loans – often by providing them with capital. In return, these investment banks would purchase these loans and package them into large securities, particularly the "residential mortgage backed securities" designed to get 100 percent financing or cash-out financing as homeowners borrowed against the equity in their homes. Through this process, securitization allowed mortgages to be assembled or bundled together into thousands of types of loans and bonds that were then sold to investors.

As noted, in the past, mortgage lenders usually held onto the entire mortgage until it was fully repaid. If the borrowers defaulted, the banks would have to bear the losses. This gave banks every incentive to diligently assess the borrowers' creditworthiness before extending loans. Securitization allowed lenders to put many such mortgages into a single pool, dividing the interests into different asset groups or tranches, and thus allowed financial risk to be more widely dispersed rather than concentrated in the loan originator. Each tranche not only offered differing yields, but also carried a different level of payout risk. That is, both the investment returns (principal and interest payments) as well as losses were spread among the various tranches (Barth et al. 2009; Gorton 2010). A "senior" tranche was the least risky and a "junior" one the most risky because each tranche could be sold to several investors, and in the process the risks of any one mortgage would be spread among many lenders. The more creative lenders took securitization a step further by converting mortgage-backed securities (CDSs) into even more complicated structured products such as the collateralized debt obligations (CDOs).

Indeed, securitization was widely seen as win-win as it spread both the gains and risks associated with credit, interest rate, and currency broadly (Patterson 2010). Not surprisingly, by "mid-2008, more than 60 percent of all U.S. mortgages were securitized" (Blanchard 2009, 37). In addition to providing a more diverse source of funding for residential home mortgages, this also provided a wider range of mortgage products for borrowers and eased accessibility to credit for hundreds of thousands of first-time homebuyers searching for a starter house. Investors, including speculators (both domestic and foreign), had every incentive to invest and expand their portfolios in real estate as mortgage-backed securities carried higher yields than those offered by safe investments such as the U.S. Treasury bonds.[7] Not surprisingly, according to the IMF (2007; 2008), the issuance of selected structured credit products in the United States and Europe grew from $500 billion in 2000 to $2.6 trillion in 2007.[8]

However, securitization also carried a number of fatal, if hidden, risks. Specifically, securitized assets were not only more risky than originally assumed, but the risks were hardly spread broadly or evenly. To the contrary, banks simply earned fees for originating loans without the burden of holding them on their balance sheets. In fact, mortgage originators held virtually none of the debt they created as they quickly sold it for a fee after the mortgage was signed, and the purchaser (usually Wall Street) quickly bundled these mortgages into securitized instruments and, like the originators, sold it off to investors. Suffice it to say that with total fees from home sales and mortgage securitization from 2003 to 2007 totaling some $2 trillion, neither party had any interest in the quality of the credit they were extending. For their part, investors desperately searching for yield in a low-interest-rate environment got assets that yielded more than government bonds and represented claims on a diversified group of borrowers. Unlike the originators and packagers, they had every interest in the quality of credit. Yet they failed grievously to exercise due diligence, part because these assets were difficult to value, but also because they naively assumed the assets they purchased were safe (Barth et al. 2009). Those minority of investors who did see some potential risk in the instruments they were purchasing took out credit default swaps to insure against default – but the institutions selling the swaps, namely AIG, failed to provision sufficiently against possible losses as they felt there was no risk of default (Gorton 2010). With hindsight, we now know that AIG based its decisions on seemingly implausible projections – even selling insurance to investors who did not own the underlying instrument they were betting against.

Predictably, loan originators and packagers (the major beneficiaries) developed a voracious appetite for these mortgages (Andrews 2009; Bitner 2008). The packagers not only encouraged the originators to deliver more and more mortgages; they also developed new innovative ways to further slice and dice the mortgages into even more "exotic" (risky) instruments to supply the demand. Again, this was greatly facilitated by the new

---

[7]   While the securitization of home mortgages began in the early 1980s, it was the technological innovations of the 1990s that made its reach worldwide.

[8]   Acharya and Richardson (2009, 200) note that "in the aggregate, securitization worldwide went from $767 billion at the end of 2001 to $1.4 trillion in 2004 to $2.7 trillion at the peak of the 'bubble' in December 2006."

technologies. The real-time securitization of debt lowered transaction costs by allowing lenders and an array of financial brokers to quickly price a loan with instantaneous credit-scoring technology and then extend credit to an even wider spectrum of possible borrowers.

Here, the credit-rating agencies, principally Standard & Poor's, Fitch, and Moody's (whose task was to assess the quality of the credit), failed miserably in their responsibilities. This was not simply because they conducted only perfunctory assessments, or because the assortment of mortgages haphazardly bundled together were difficult to price, or even because the agencies were not up to the task and made an honest mistake.[9] Rather, these agencies not only displayed deep arrogance, but also deliberately misled investors by legitimizing suspect and risky securities by invasively inflating their value by giving them AAA ratings. Undoubtedly, as willing partners in this enterprise, rating agencies were grossly derelict in their activities. As Schwartz (2009, 21) notes, "The rating agencies had no formula for this task. They assigned ratings to complex securities as if they were ordinary corporate bonds and without examining the individual categories in the pool. Ratings tended to overstate the value of the securities and were fundamentally arbitrary." Moreover, there was a conflict of interest: as credit-rating agencies received hefty fees for making the mortgage instruments look credible, they hardly ever noticed the many anomalies and compliantly provided the ratings the mortgage packagers and issuers wanted. Otherwise they would lose this lucrative business to a more willing and pliant competitor (Gorton 2010). Yet this still begs the question of why the rating agencies enjoyed such a free reign and what gave their ratings such an essential seal of approval. The answer: with regulators largely sidelined (if not made irrelevant) by excessive political and bureaucratic rules and interference (to be discussed), credit-rating agencies literally became the sole providers of supposedly "objective" and "transparent" information to markets about risks. As noted, the rating agencies grossly failed in their task, and their underestimation of risk had catastrophic consequences.

The Subprime Mortgage Market

Beginning in the second half of the 1990s, a new type of mortgage loan, the so-called subprime residential mortgage loan, gained widespread

---

[9] To be fair, there is some truth in this claim. Credit-rating agencies did emphasize that they rated only the risk of actual default (i.e., credit risk), but not the liquidity and market risks.

popularity among borrowers and lenders alike. Demyanyk and Hermet (2008) note that between 2001 and 2005, the number of subprime mortgages issued increased from 624,000 to 3.44 million while the average value rose from $151,000 in 2001 to $259,000 in 2006. In other words, if in 2000, subprime originations accounted for about 6 percent of total residential mortgage originations, by 2006, their share had risen to about 25 percent. By the end of 2007, the number of outstanding subprime mortgage loans totaled about 7.7 million, or 14 percent of the overall mortgage market.[10] In addition, from 2001 to 2004, the spread between prime and subprime mortgages declined from 2.8 percent to only slightly more than 0.6 percent, rising to slightly more than 1 percent in 2007. With house prices notching double-digit gains in 2004 and 2005, the subprime loans were seen as a quick ticket to get a piece of the housing market (indeed, a piece of the American dream) before it was too late. Between 2005 and 2006, of the $6.1 trillion in home mortgages originated in the United States, some $1.25 trillion were subprime mortgages (Gorton 2010).

The subprime mortgage loan, unlike the "prime" one, is deemed a lower-quality mortgage. In the United States there are broadly four types of mortgages:

1. Prime mortgages made to creditworthy borrowers who meet requirements that enable originators to sell them to the two quasi-private organizations, known as government-sponsored enterprises (GSEs): the Federal National Mortgage Association (Fannie Mae) and the Federal Home Loan Mortgage Corporation (Freddie Mac).[11]

---

[10] See Randall S. Kroszner, "The Challenges Facing Subprime Mortgage Borrowers," Federal Reserve Governor at the Consumer Bankers Association 2007 Fair Lending Conference, Washington, DC, November 5, 2007, http://www.federalreserve.gov/newsevents/speech/kroszner20071105a.htm#f2

[11] The Federal National Mortgage Association (Fannie Mae) and the Federal Home Loan Mortgage Corporation (Freddie Mac) are government-sponsored enterprises (GSEs). They were established by Congress to achieve a specific goal. Although, both are privately owned, as GSEs they enjoy tax and regulatory breaks such as exemption from state and local income taxes. As GSEs, Fannie and Freddie are able to borrow money at below-market interest rates, which they use to buy existing mortgages that generate a higher interest revenue stream. The difference in rates not only generates income for the GSEs, but also allows them to purchase more mortgages. These GSEs also purchase loans from mortgage originators to provide funds to the mortgage market. These loans are then packaged into mortgage-backed securities and sold to investors – the GSEs guarantee the principal and interest payments on these mortgage-backed securities. The Johnson Administration reorganized Fannie Mae to both lend money and hold mortgages, while the newly created Freddie Mac was to provide completion for Fannie Mae. To insure these mortgages against risk of default, the government also created the National Mortgage Association – Ginnie Mae.

2. Jumbo mortgages that exceed the limits set by Fannie Mae and Freddie Mac. The 2008 limit set by Congress was $729,750.
3. Alt-A mortgages, which carry a potentially higher default risk because they have a higher loan-to-income ratio and a higher loan-to-value ratio.
4. Subprime mortgages, which fall below Alt-A mortgages as the Alt-A loans are viewed as having a lower risk (and carrying lower interest rates) than the subprime loans.

Although the subprime mainly covered mortgages to individuals with poor or spotty credit histories, including a previous record of delinquency, foreclosure, bankruptcy, and/or a credit score of 580 or lower,[12] not all subprime borrowers were credit-impaired by poor credit record or low income. Some were individuals who could have qualified for the traditional prime mortgages but were steered to the subprime by disreputable brokers seeking the more generous commissions these loans usually offered, as well as homeowners with equity in their properties because the property could be sold for enough in foreclosure to cover the borrower's debt.[13] Some borrowers with good credit took subprime loans because of the low "teaser rates," often using them to buy second homes or investment properties. Regardless, all subprime mortgages shared common traits: there was greater penalty for borrowing in the subprime market, including much higher up-front fees (such as application and appraisal fees), much higher insurance costs, punitive fines for late payment or delinquency, and much higher interest rates (Gorton 2009). Although the subprime mortgages came with both fixed and adjustable interest rates, and borrowers were granted some "protection" under the subprime mortgages, such as allowance to spread loan payments over time, overall the terms decidedly protected the lender. Such terms included greater discretion allotted to the lender in underwriting standards and, most importantly, in setting the interest rate depending on a "loan grade" assigned in light of the borrower's credit history.

For example, the interest rates on the hybrid adjustable-rate mortgages (ARMs) could be pegged to a benchmark rate such as the six-month Libor rate or the one-year Treasury bill rate.[14] However, the most common ARM

---

[12] Though standards vary, in general a credit score of 660 or higher qualifies one for a prime loan. For the near-prime Alt-A category of loans, borrowers need credit scores between 580 and 660. Subprime borrowers usually are those with credit scores lower than 580.

[13] This explains why so many loans involve refinancing or home equity loans. Such "predatory loans" are issued to homeowners on the guise they will use the money for home improvements. In most cases, these homeowners got into way more debt than they could handle.

[14] ARMs typically offer a lower interest rate for a fixed number of years. After that the rates rise or decline each year depending on the prevailing interest rates. ARMs were not

was the so-called 2/28 or 3/27. A 2/28 hybrid ARM carried a fixed rate for two years, after which the loan would "reset" and become an adjustable-rate mortgage for the remaining twenty-eight years. As noted, the interest premiums on the subprime mortgages were quite high (averaging about 4 percentage points) to cover the apparently higher risk of default these loans posed. As Campbell (2007) points out, this meant that a thirty-year, $250,000 loan at the subprime rate of just 2 percentage point higher than the prime would require monthly payments of $1,904 compared with $1,563 for a prime loan, or a difference of more than $4,000 a year. Subprime lenders justified this on the grounds that their loans were not intended as long-term financing for houses, but were designed to help borrowers who lacked the necessary down payment or adequate credit history qualify for the prime (or even Alt-A) financing. In fact, subprime ARMs came to be described as "bridge loans" – a short-term fix allowing borrowers to redeem themselves by rebuilding their credit record, accumulating equity in their house, and eventually refinancing into a lower-priced mortgage.

However, in reality, the "variable rate" was a misnomer. Like anything too good to be true, subprime mortgages also came with "hidden" risks. The most notable of these was the fact that subprime mortgages originated with high loan-to-value (LTV) and debt-to-income (DTI) ratios, which made them extremely sensitive to declines in housing prices. Gorton (2010, 18) aptly notes that no "other consumer loan has the design feature in which the borrower's ability to repay is so sensitively linked to appreciation of an underlying asset." Specifically, the subprime mortgages' artificially low initial interest rates (which kept initial payments small and made it easier for applicants to qualify), was preprogrammed to include a significant interest-rate hike after just a few (usually two to three) years. Moreover, while the rates would "adjust" to the new higher market rates, they would not fall when market rates declined. That is why the initial rate was dubbed a "teaser" – the low rates and the interest-only or negative-amortization payment options were designed to make them seem more affordable to borrowers than they really were. Although this allowed borrowers to take out larger mortgages, it also meant larger payments down the road when the teaser rate expired or principal repayments began. Indeed, it can be argued that the teaser rate was deliberately devised to suck in as many borrowers as possible with no regard for the longer-term consequences: namely, the borrowers' inability to meet their payment obligations on time. This

---

deemed attractive in the run-up to the financial crisis because ARM rates were competitive with the fixed-rate mortgages.

was evident not only from the fact that subprime resets involved a sharp increase in the size of the monthly payments (doubling, in some cases) but also the prepayment penalties that many subprime loans carried made it prohibitively expensive for borrowers to refinance during the first two or three years.

If for decades the securitization of residential mortgages was dominated by Fannie Mae and Freddie Mac (whose primary task was to extend securitized loans to creditworthy borrowers), all this changed with the proliferation of the so-called "private-label" residential mortgage-backed securities (RMBSs) issued by banks, brokerage firms, and even large private investors. These loans were purchased from banks and mortgage companies and then repackaged into complex bundles. These RMBSs, representing claims on the principal and interest payments made by borrowers on the bundle of loans, were then sold to investors. For example, the RMBSs were often sliced into five to fifteen different tranches with the senior-level tranche, typically rated AAA, being the first to be paid back in the event there was a problem with some of the underlying loans. The next tranche would be rated AA, followed by the rest, down to the junk level. The lowest level, the so-called junior level, would take the first losses and were paid higher yields for this risk. Because it was hard to sell some of the lower-level tranches, investment banks created another security called the collateralized debt obligation (CDO). Through fancy bookkeeping by the rating agencies, the CDOs themselves were sliced into tranches and transformed into respectable AAA bonds – akin to making sow's ears into silk.[15]

Mortgage-Backed Securities Structure
Investment Grade
Super Senior AAA
AAA Mezzanine
AA
A
BBB
Non-Investment/Junk Grade
BB
B
Equity/Unrated

[15] In fact, to cover the risk of default on subprime mortgages, CDO holders purchased CDSs or credit-default swaps. As noted, CDSs are basically an insurance contract that lenders purchased in case of a "credit event" such as bankruptcy, credit-rating downgrades, or default.

Even if investors could review their portfolios, the bundling of assets into complex packages made it exceedingly difficult to accurately value the opaque structured credits. As a result, lending institutions and investors in securities tended to underestimate the riskiness of subprime loans and thus looked to credit-rating agencies for assessments of risk. And because a very large share of the value of structured investments originally was in highly rated tranches (AAA or AA), most concluded that their investments were safe. As noted, rating agencies not only failed to conduct objective and independent credit assessments, they also made overly optimistic assumptions on new and untested types of mortgages. The high ratings were hardly surprising as these agencies were paid generously to structure the same financial instruments that they would later grade. The conflict of interest inherent in this practice made these ratings mostly unreliable, but few saw this contradiction at that time.

Although subprime mortgages initially contributed to an increase in U.S. home ownership, these gains proved short-lived. Because one in five subprime mortgage borrowers was burdened with a combination of low credit scores, high levels of debt compared to income, high mortgages compared to their home's value, and most ominously, minimal or no down payments on their homes, most of these high-risk borrowers could not hold on to their homes. Demyanyk (2009) points out that many of the estimated one million borrowers who took out subprime mortgage loans between 2000 and 2006 to finance the purchase of their first home defaulted within a couple of years of origination. More specifically, approximately 10 percent of the mortgages originated between 2001 and 2005 were delinquent or in default within the first year of loan origination, as were approximately 20 percent of the mortgages originated in 2006 and 2007. On the other hand, those attracted by subprime mortgages for speculative purposes also preferred mortgages with the smallest down payment and the lowest interest rate. Suffice it to note, they usually chose the adjustable-rate mortgage option. Having little "skin in the game," they could and did simply walk away (Calomiris 2008; Jaffe and Perlow 2008). Finally, although securitization and derivatives trading were designed to distribute the risks underlying subprime mortgages throughout the financial system, this reallocation clearly failed to dissipate systemic risks. On the contrary, as each stage of the securitization process increased not only the number of financial institutions involved in the process but also the leverage these financial institutions took on (after all, they were purchasing the securities and derivatives with borrowed money), securitization greatly amplified the problems and negatively affected balance sheets across the financial sector.

Administrative and Regulatory Failure

Why did legislators and regulators fail to oversee the proliferation of new financial products and halt risky financing engineering, in particular, the blatant conflict of interest between credit-rating agencies and loan securitizers and packagers? The short answer: because influential legislators through government policies and programs were complicit in creating a friendly environment for such practices to emerge and thrive. Knott (2012, 82) aptly refers to this as "*political moral hazard* – a condition in which public officials and private interests had strong incentives to take actions mutually beneficial to them but adverse to the overall economy and the interests of the general public – that led to a decline in institutional checks and balances in economic regulation." Indeed, "over the past few decades presidents and congressional leaders of both parties have pushed for deregulation... political moral hazard by Congress to collude with private industry to mutual benefit has reduced efforts by regulatory agencies to provide sound regulation of the banking, housing, and investment industries" (Knott 2012, 87, 93). The following sections as well as Chapter 2 show, government actions (and inaction) due to the "political moral hazard" and "regulatory capture" directly and indirectly contributed to the depth and severity of the crisis.

Democrat and Republican lawmakers in both the executive and legislative branches of government provided strong (if not unqualified) support for the subprime mortgage credit expansion – right up to the meltdown in the housing market in 2007. They had invested interest in doing so. Over two decades of bipartisan push by Congress to create universal homeownership led to the implementation of a series of perverse laws, incentives, and regulations, including the rapid expansion of the role of two government-sponsored enterprises: Fannie Mae and Freddie Mac.[16] Beginning in the early 1990s, Congress pushed both Freddie and Fannie to increase their purchases of mortgages targeting low- and moderate-income borrowers, a disproportionate percentage of whom were non-whites. Although it is usually assumed that Congress's intention was well-meaning and admirable (real-estate ownership serving as the "great leveler"), the manner in which the policy was formulated and carried out jeopardized the entire mortgage system by fundamentally weakening traditional precautionary mortgage-lending standards, especially loan-underwriting standards.

---

[16] Of course, the idea to create mortgage-backed securities goes back to the Johnson administration when the president and the Democratic Congress – to fulfill the administration's "Great Society" goals – decided to assist the baby-boom generation and low-income Americans in purchasing a home.

Mian, Sufi, and Trebbi's (2010) examination of the relationship between the rapid expansion of the subprime market and Congressional politics and policy between 2002 and 2007 find a dramatic increase in campaign contributions and lobbying by the mortgage industry. Specifically, they find that between 1998 and 2002, the contributions were modest but increased by some 80 percent between 2002 and 2006. In fact, Knott (2012, 94) notes that "the Fannie Mae Foundation spent $650 million opening offices in Congressional districts, and the two mortgage companies also spent $170 million in lobbying activities from 1998 to 2008 ... in 2006, Freddie Mac agreed to pay a $3.8 million fine to settle allegations that it made illegal campaign contributions." Mian, Sufi, and Trebbi (2010) show that "beginning in 2002, mortgage industry campaign contributions increasingly targeted U.S. representatives from districts with a large fraction of subprime borrowers," and that not only "mortgage industry campaign contributions... predicted congressional voting behavior on housing related legislation" but also "both subprime mortgage lenders and subprime mortgage borrowers influenced government policy toward housing finance during the subprime mortgage credit expansion" (pp. 1–2).

The authors conclude that members of Congress had every incentive not to place regulation on subprime lenders and to increase mortgage support for subprime borrowers.

In 1993, Henry Cisneros, secretary of HUD (the Department of Housing and Urban Development) under President Clinton, launched the "National Homeownership Strategy" under which proof of income was reduced from five to three years, borrowers could use their own appraisers, and lenders such as Countrywide were encouraged to provide borrowers with poor credit with subprime loans.[17] In 1994, HUD required that 30 percent of Fannie and Freddie's mortgage purchases consist of "affordable-housing" mortgages. However, "apparently doubting that Fannie and Freddie were doing all they could for affordable housing" (Wallison 2009, 369), in 1996, HUD ordered Fannie and Freddie to meet an explicit target: 42 percent of their mortgage financing had to go to borrowers with income below the median in their area (Friedman 2009). The target increased to 50 percent in 2000 and to 56 percent in 2004.[18] In similar fashion, HUD required that

---

[17] After leaving HUD, Cisneros set up a housing development company that was later fined for approving poorly documented loans.

[18] As Cannato (2010, 78) notes, "Clinton's first HUD secretary, Henry Cisneros, pushed the two 'government-sponsored enterprises' toward requiring that 40% of all the mortgages they traded originate from low- and moderate-income borrowers. Cisneros's successor, Andrew Cuomo, pushed the benchmark to 50%."

12 percent of all mortgages purchased by Fannie and Freddie be "special affordable loans" designed for borrowers with incomes less than 60 percent of their area's median income. The percentage was increased to 20 in 2000 and 22 in 2005 (Roberts 2008). Not surprisingly, "Freddie Mac and Fannie Mae purchased almost no subprime mortgage backed securities in 2000. Between 2004 and 2006, the two agencies purchased $434 billion in securities backed by subprime loans" (Mian, Sufi, and Trebbi 2010, 6). Overall, "from 2005 to 2007, Fannie and Freddie bought approximately $1 trillion in subprime and Alt-A loans, amounting to about 40 percent of their mortgage purchases" (Wallison 2009, 370). Fannie and Freddie met these huge targets by pumping billions of dollars of loans – the bulk of which were subprime and adjustable-rate loans – to borrowers with poor credit histories who bought houses with down payments of, in most cases, less than 5 percent. As a result, rather cynically, some of the subprime mortgages came to be called "ninja" loans – from "no income, no job, and no assets."

Indeed, these developments created incentives for mortgage lenders such as Countrywide, Indymac, and WAMU to make even more risky loans because they could easily sell them to Fannie and Freddie. Not surprisingly, Freddie and Fannie soon became the primary securitizers of home mortgages as they used their state guarantees to purchase more risky loans and expand the subprime market. In 2003, efforts to bring Freddie and Fannie under tighter regulatory control were defeated in Congress by the Democrats, who were concerned that tighter regulation would hamper these agencies' ability to meet affordable housing goals. Indeed, Morgenson and Rosner (2011) allege that Fannie Mae, in league with the rapacious mortgage industry and community groups such as ACORN (Association of Community Groups for Reform Now – who could directly file complaints with the FDIC if any bank refused to provide subsidized loans) and blessed by an opportunistic Congress, were fundamentally responsible for the real-estate bubble and eventual financial crisis. Although the administration of George W. Bush eventually put a cap on the amount of mortgage lending that Fannie and Freddie themselves could engage in, placing limits on these government-sponsored entities also had the unintended effect of bringing more private lenders into the marketplace to peddle even more risky subprime mortgages (Gramlich 2007). Undoubtedly, without Freddie and Fannie's implicit guarantee of government support, the mortgage-backed securities market, especially the subprime portion of it, would not have expanded so rapidly. Rather, the actions of Freddie and Fannie not only led to over-investment in residential real estate, the implicit government guarantee also created the problem of widespread systemic risk.[19]

Compounding this were two other "incentives" which in time would cause a housing bubble. First, the 1977 passage into law of the Community Reinvestment Act (CRA) by Congress, which required banks to conduct business across the entirety of the geographic areas in which they operated. After Congress amended the CRA in 1989, it gave regulators even greater power over the banks, including the power to deny banks with low CRA ratings the right to merge with other banks or open and acquire new branches. In effect, via the CRA, the U.S. Congress forced banks to serve a politically motivated "common good" by requiring them to increase the percentage of their "affordable loans" to low and moderate-income households, including individuals with poor credit histories. Under new rules adopted in May 1995, the government threatened banks and thrifts with more regulations and punitive legal challenges if they did not extend more loans to poor neighborhoods, especially minority communities. The Fed explicitly warned that "failure to comply with the Equal Credit Opportunity Act or Regulation B can subject a financial institution to civil liability for actual and punitive damages in individual or class actions" (Liebowitz 2008). As Wallison (2009, 366) bluntly notes, "amendments to the CRA ... pressured banks into making loans they would not otherwise have made."

Second was the tax incentive proposed by President Clinton at the 1996 Democratic National Convention.[20] Clinton's tax break, approved by Congress in 1997 under the Taxpayer Relief Act of 1997, exempted most home sales from capital-gains taxes in one bold stroke. The first $500,000 in realized capital gains from any home sale was exempt from taxes for a married couple provided they had lived in the home for at least two of the previous five years. For singles, the first $250,000 was exempt. Moreover, homeowners could deduct from their taxes mortgage interest payments and subtract the cost of renovations to their homes done over many years from their taxable gain. Even renovations on previous homes qualified as

---

[19] While we now know that many politicians from both parties were recipients of campaign contributions from the Fannie and Freddie slush funds, the Democrats were major beneficiaries, especially Barney Frank in the House and Chris Dodd in the Senate. For an excellent overview of Fannie and Freddie and why they were "guaranteed to fail" see Acharya, et al. (2011).

[20] Apparently, Clinton's tax proposal was designed to preempt Senator Bob Dole's (Clinton's Republican opponent in the 1996 presidential election) call for a wide-ranging tax cut, including an across-the-board reduction in the capital-gains tax. Clinton's political advisers not only charged that the Dole tax cut would cause the deficit to skyrocket, but quickly came up with their own generous tax proposal.

long as owners had deferred the tax in the past by buying a new house at least as valuable as their old one. This meant that for the first time in history, Americans did not have to pay tax on profits made on a property sale. In effect, allowing home sales to become tax-free windfalls not only gave individuals a new incentive to plow money into real estate but also to engage in "flipping" or buying and selling real estate for a quick profit. For private lenders the real-estate market provided a huge opportunity. Hedge fund investors often engaged in highly speculative activities while banks controlling trillions of dollars engaged in "disintermediation" to shift assets off their balance sheets. Unintentionally, by unduly favoring real estate, tax rules pushed many Americans to view their houses more as ATM cash cows rather than as homes.[21] Indeed, Shiller (2008, 41) describes the housing boom as a form of "social contagion" where rising prices fed the expectation of a perpetual boom. Not surprisingly, it seemed to make sense to invest in real estate – the highest-yielding investment with the highest tax benefit.

Although the weakening of mortgage-lending standards did succeed in increasing the rate of home ownership, it also created other unintended outcomes: a sharp rise in homes prices (inevitably creating a housing "bubble"), and a significant buildup of equity in the homes. The ability to refinance a mortgage without penalty and the "cash-out-refinancing" provision allowed property owners to cash out a significant portion of the equity (estimated at some \$330 billion in 2006) and use the funds for consumption – or as Wallison (2009, 372) notes, "buy cars, boats, or second homes, or to pay for other family expenditures." Moreover, because interest on home-equity loans is a tax deduction, but consumer loans such as credit cards and auto loans are not, individuals were encouraged to take out home-equity loans to pay off consumer loans – in the process leaving them with little equity or the incentive to continue making payments on their mortgage when housing prices eventually fell.

Similarly, regulation of banks and mortgage companies was weakened as Democrats and Republicans in both the executive and legislative branches, claimed that no regulation or self-regulation would be more effective than

---

[21] I thank my colleague Hartmut Fischer for his pithy quote: "housing has increasingly become a way for the average American to make money and to save for the future. In particular, an expansion of interest rate deductibility for mortgages up to \$1 million, a change in rollover provisions and right to unlock equity by selling your first or second home without payment of capital gains taxes – albeit there are limits to this." On top of this, "you also have the development of the reverse mortgage market and changes which made it easier to get tax deductible home equity lines of credit. All of this meant that the average American has way overinvested in housing as compared to other assets."

government regulation. With the full blessing of Federal Reserve Chair Alan Greenspan, the Republican-controlled Congress and the Clinton administration passed two laws that, via deregulation, fundamentally transformed the U.S. financial industry. First, in 1999, Congress abolished the Glass-Steagall Act of 1933 with the passage of the "Financial Services Modernization Act of 1999" led by Republican Senator Phil Gramm (henceforth known as the Gramm-Leach-Bliley Act of 1999). For decades, Glass-Steagall maintained clear separation between the relatively transparent commercial banks and less-regulated investment-banking sector by prohibiting investment-banking activities such as underwriting and securities trading, and commercial bank's loan-making business from being conducted in the same institution. This act also prohibited banks from serving as insurance companies.[22] This separation helped mitigate potential conflict of interest and prevent bank concentration and thereby "too big-too-fail" institutions within the banking sector. Just as important, by introducing the federal deposit insurance through the Federal Deposit Insurance Corporation (FDIC) and expanding federal bank supervision, Glass Steagall helped to end the perennial banking crises. In particular, prudential regulation and oversight enhanced public confidence in the financial system, while deposit insurance gave consumers protection and, thereby, insulated banks from destructive "deposit" or "bank runs." As a result, systemic banking crises in the United States essentially became a rare occurrence after 1933.

The end of Glass-Steagall meant the end of the stability and security that both insurance and regulation had long provided the banking and financial sectors. Specifically, the blurring of the lines between commercial and investment banks not only resulted in greater bank concentration,[23] but also the rapid expansion of the activities of what Gorton (2010) has succinctly described as the "shadow banking system," made up of investment banks, insurance companies, money market funds, hedge funds and other financial entities that engage in large-scale credit intermediation – outside the regular banking system.[24] In other words, even as "shadow banks" function

---

[22] Although distinctions within the financial sector are hardly clear-cut, a *commercial bank* generally takes deposits and lends out the funds (deposits) to generate higher returns than it pays on the interest for the deposits. On the other hand, *an investment bank's* central goal is to raise money for firms and businesses, usually through initial public offerings.

[23] Zingales (2009, 30) notes that "in 1980, there were 14,434 banks in the United States, about the same number as in 1934. By 2000, [this number had dropped] to 8,315. In 2009, the number stands below 7,100."

[24] Bord and Santos (2012, 12) note "that banks have been an important contributor to the so-called shadow banking system. For example, in 1993, of the $22.7 billion in term loans originated, banks sold $2.2 billion to the shadow banking system. By comparison, in 2007,

as traditional financial intermediaries conducting the full gamut of credit intermediation, they serve large businesses and billion-dollar institutional investors by issuing short-term, liquid liabilities against longer-term, less liquid assets, including creating asset-backed securities, financial derivatives (which Warren Buffett famously called "financial weapons of mass destruction"), and off-balance-sheet investment vehicles. Also, because shadow banks operate without access to central-bank liquidity or public-sector credit guarantees, the prudential regulatory standards governing them are either loose or nonexistent.

The repeal of Glass-Steagall had profound implications. In the political sphere, Zingales (2009, 31) points out: "under the old regime, commercial banks, investment banks and insurance companies had different agendas, and so their lobbying efforts tended to offset one another. But, after the restrictions were lifted, the interests of all the major players in the financial industry became aligned, giving the industry disproportionate power in shaping the political agenda. The concentration of the banking industry only added to this power." The impact on the economic sphere was even more negative. Since Gramm-Leach-Bliley allowed banks to offer both commercial and investment banking, plus insurance services to boot, under a Financial Services Holding Company, it spawned intricate interconnectedness and concentration within the banking and financial sectors. Securitization further facilitated integration by bringing together the activities of the commercial banks (that is, making loans), with investment banking such as underwriting mortgage-backed securities and "originating" derivatives and other opaque (and even riskier) financial instruments.

Second, Robert Rubin and Lawrence Summers, the Treasury secretaries under Clinton, both aggressively pushed for the passage of the Commodity Futures Modernization Act of 2000. This act, which Clinton signed into law in 2000, allowed single-stock futures contracts and deregulated numerous over-the-counter (OTC) derivatives, including swaps. Moreover, it exempted the notorious credit-default swaps from federal regulation, besides enabling for a more wide-ranging deregulation of Wall Street.[25] It is fair to say that without the credit-default swaps, buyers would have been more cautious (and hesitant) in purchasing asset-backed securities.

---

of the $315 billion in term loans originated, they sold $125 billion to the shadow-banking system. In about two decades, the annual volume of term loans that banks supplied to nonaffiliated shadow-banking institutions increased by $123 billion."

[25] Lest we forget, Larry Summers and Gary Gensler (treasury undersecretary in the Clinton administration) joined Phil Gramm to eliminate regulation of the derivative markets that have since brought the banking system to collapse.

In addition, lawmakers in both political parties made certain that the watchdog Securities and Exchange Commission (SEC) saw and heard no evil. The systematic watering down of the securities regulation, in particular, the government's decision not to regulate the asset-backed securities market, resulted in risky unregulated trading of asset-backed securities. As Wade (2008) points out, while the financial innovation was producing robust economic growth, legislators and regulators thwarted all regulatory attempts because they believed that the market was more than capable of controlling its own risks.[26] In early 2004, following much lobbying from investment banks, the SEC created the Consolidated Supervised Entities (CSE) program, which effectively removed the regulatory capital requirements of the five largest investment banks and their holding companies, including securities firms.

By enrolling in the CSE program, investment banks could gain access to reduced capital requirements. This allowed these firms to move capital from safer to more profitable, if not riskier, investments. It also meant that securities firms no longer had to set aside a fixed percentage of capital to ensure solvency in event of a crisis. The new SEC rules violated all prudence by allowing these firms to use non-cash assets, in particular, asset-backed securities, as a hedge to offset risk (Blinder 2009). On March 28, 2004, the SEC became irrelevant when it removed the ceiling on the risk that U.S. investment banks could take on securitized loans – in effect, announcing its abdication and allowing investment banks to regulate themselves. The final nail in the SEC's coffin was in 2007 when the new SEC chair, Christopher Cox (a longtime proponent of deregulation appointed by President George W. Bush) made it a requirement that SEC officials obtain approval from SEC commissioners before they sanctioned violators. As Knott (2012, 93) notes, "this rule created delays, demoralized officials, and caused many officials to leave, reducing sanctions by 51%."

Ultimately, the net results of all this proved disastrous. With such free reign, these firms in turn developed complex and risky financial instruments, including varieties of subprime mortgages, securitization, derivatives, credit-default swaps, and an array of hedge funds, and bundled them into mortgage-backed securities. The investment banks were motivated purely by the transaction fees and had little or no stake in the ultimate performance of the loans they helped to arrange. For a hefty fee they sold them

---

[26] Wade (2008) notes that Alan Greenspan, Robert Rubin, and Arthur Levitt (chair of the SEC), were instrumental in championing this cause because they felt that regulation would undermine the efficiency of the securities market.

to Freddie and Fannie and to investors in the United States and around the world, who in turn sold them, sometimes deliberately, but usually recklessly, to individuals with limited resources or capacity to pay.

This seemingly "lawless" environment fostered a vicarious casino mentality where all caution was thrown to the wind. While providing credit, lenders, and mortgage brokers in particular (who could earn fees while passing along any credit risk) casually winked at underwriting standards on mortgage debt, deliberately ignored critical data such as debt-to-income requirements, and most egregious, did not demand proper documentation of borrowers' credit history, employment status, income, and assets in their zeal to extend credit (Wilcox 2009). In fact, not subject to government regulation and legal action, and seduced by irresistible fees, brokers and related intermediaries bent all rules to lure people into mortgages that they could not afford. On their part, investors holding RMBSs remained complacent because the green light from rating agencies, rising home prices and securitization by spreading risk created an aura of invulnerability. As a result, housing market mortgage originators were happy to accept no security at all, lending 100 percent of the value of the house, because they thought house prices would continue to rise (in fact, the conventional view was that home prices would not fall, but, in the worst-case scenario would "moderate" in a "soft landing"), and that the market would be liquid enough for them to sell off the mortgages to other investors.

In their impassioned book, *Winner-Take-All Politics*, Hacker and Pierson (2010) forcefully attribute the growing income inequality in the United States to policies adopted by politicians in Washington (both Republicans and Democrats) since the late 1970s. They argue that both the executive and legislative branches, in tandem with big businesses and their lobbyists, have worked to undermine regulations and the progressive tax policies that had helped promote a more fair distribution of income and opportunities to the middle class. The authors provide a corrective to the view that sees the growing income inequality in the United States as a result of economic globalization, namely the hollowing-out of America's manufacturing base, the technological changes in the workplace, or the "education gap" that have made U.S. workers less competitive. In similar fashion, Krippner (2011) claims that the progressive deregulation of the U.S. banking and financial sector was the direct result of policymakers' inability to respond to competing and incompatible socioeconomic demands as postwar economic prosperity stalled beginning in the late 1960s and 1970s. To generate growth, policymakers enacted a series of measures that both deliberately and inadvertently privileged "financialization" – via the deregulation of domestic credit markets, more flexible monetary policy, and openness to international capital flows and global market integration. The growing volatility of financial markets is largely the end product of the state's actions.

More provocatively, Prasad (2012) argues that the United States has long promoted consumption-driven economic growth as an alternative to a welfare state. Hence, easy credit serves as a substitute to the country's poorly developed social-welfare system. In his thought-provoking book, *Fault Lines*, Rajan (2010) argues that the growth of subprime lending was fueled by policymakers' failure to address the root causes of rising income inequality in the United States. This failure forced them to make access to credit easier, especially for middle- and low-income households, in order to support their spending. The astronomical expansion of household debt as a share of household income is the sad result of this failure (also see Bivens 2011). Rajan notes

The political response to rising inequality – whether carefully planned or an unpremeditated reaction to constituent demands – was to expand lending to households, especially low incomes ones. The benefits – growing consumption and more jobs – were immediate, whereas paying the inevitable bill could be postponed into the future. Cynical as it may seem, easy credit has been used as a palliative throughout history by governments that are unable to address the deeper anxieties of the middle class directly. (p. 9)

While one can quibble with Rajan's view as to why politicians, who are usually sensitive to high-income voters, should care about low-income ones, he persuasively argues that powerful politicians and policymakers were only too happy to leave the mortgage markets alone as the expanding U.S. housing market played a key role in stimulating the U.S. economy after the 2001 dot-com crash. The easy lending practices brought in first-time buyers who had previously been shut out of the housing market and allowed existing owners to move up to bigger houses (with bigger mortgages), creating hundreds of thousands of construction and related jobs in the residential and commercial real-estate sectors. Furthermore, equity from the rapidly appreciating real estate yielded billions of dollars in cash for households to spend.

The surge in "wealth effects" prompted households to withdraw equity from their properties, resulting in a significant boost in consumption as homeowners went into a spending spree on all manner of goods and services. The ill effects of increased household debt relative to income and a decline in the personal savings rate to near zero were assumed to be offset by the sharp increase in real-estate value. Mian and Sufi (2009), in their analysis of a dataset of roughly 70,000 anonymous individual homeowner credit files covering end-1997 to 2008, find that between 2002 and 2007, the debt-to-income ratio for U.S. households doubled, and home equity-based borrowing averaged 2.8 percent of GDP between 2002 and 2006, or $1.45 trillion. They estimate that the average homeowner increased spending by 25 to 30 cents for every dollar of home-equity borrowing, much of it directed toward consumer goods and services.[27] In their more recent study, Mian and Sufi (2012) show that between 2001 and 2007, household debt doubled from $7 trillion to $14 trillion, and homeowners' debt-to-GDP ratio jumped from 0.7 to 1.0 during the same period. Therefore, it is hardly surprising that as house-price appreciation jumped to dizzying heights, the resultant growth in housing demand was accompanied by increased availability of mortgage loans, especially subprime loans, and expanding limits on credit cards.[28]

The government's low interest rates also indirectly added fuel to mortgage lending. John Taylor (2009), in his aptly titled, *Getting off Track: How Government Actions and Interventions Caused, Prolonged and Worsened the Financial Crisis*, has argued that the monetary excesses were the main cause of the boom. That is, in response to the crash of the dot-com bubble in 2000 and the resultant recession that began in 2001, the Federal Reserve Board began expanding the money supply by cutting short-term interest rates from about 6.5 percent to 1 percent between 2001 and 2003, with real interest rates negative – the lowest they had been since 1958. In addition, the ten-year Treasury note rate fell from 6 percent in 2000 to 4 percent in 2003 before rising to 4.8 percent in 2006. The Fed made ARMs cheap by lowering short-term rates relative to the thirty-year fixed-rate mortgages.[29] Hardly surprising, new mortgage borrowers pushed away from mortgages with thirty-year rates into ARMs, and lenders and investors seeking higher yields turned to the subprime mortgage market.[30] Taylor compellingly illustrates that the Fed, in violating the famous "Taylor rule" (where a short-term nominal interest rate or the federal funds rate is adjusted in response to inflation and some measure of real economic activity), seriously undermined economic performance.

---

[27] This large dataset was provided by the National Consumer Credit Bureau and included samples from every major U.S. metropolitan area

[28] Home prices increased nationally at an average annual rate of nearly 9 percent from 2000 to 2006.

[29] In 2001, non-teaser ARM rates on average were 1.13 percent cheaper than thirty-year fixed-rate mortgages (5.84 percent versus 6.97 percent). By 2004, the gap had widened to 1.94 percent (3.90 percent versus 5.84) percent.

[30] The nominal federal funds rate was below 3 percent continuously from September 2001 through June 2005.

Undeniably, under Alan Greenspan, the Federal Reserve's less-than-prudent "easy-money policy" helped expand the money supply well beyond the growth in the nation's gross domestic product by keeping interest rates too low for too long. In turn, this served to create too much liquidity and drove interest rates to artificially low levels. Eventually, the Fed's easy money policy created an excess of cash that inflated equity and asset prices. The skyrocketing house prices and a booming stock market fostered a sort of cognitive dissonance leading investors and homeowners to conclude (wrongly) that their real net worth was not only higher than perceived, but that their wealth would continue to increase in perpetuity. This not only made individuals feel richer than they actually were, but the abundant money supply, coupled with low interest rates, spurred buying. Prudence and caution were thrown to the wind as saving for retirement was deemed unnecessary, and people borrowed more and more against their ever-rising home equity to pay for all kinds of goods, services, and more real estate. Such credit-fueled spending further reinforced rising asset prices. Since the supply of housing is relatively limited, it is a much sought-after asset. As a result, real-estate prices tend to rise faster as everyone tries to get a share of the "dream" before it becomes out of reach. Hence, excessive money growth fueled the technology bubble of the late 1990s and the real estate bubble in 2007.

The Housing Problem Amplifies

As the economic historian Anna Schwartz (2007, 158) warned: "among the consequences of the policy of maintaining interest rates at an inappropriate low level were credit and mortgage market distortions, discouragement of personal savings, incipient inflation, and depreciation of the dollar foreign exchange rate. 'Wealth' built on sand has a way of quickly collapsing." In the summer of 2004, when short-term interest rates rose dramatically, subprime loans began to reset with much larger payments. However, it was believed that the problem was temporary and still manageable. But as the housing bubble began to lose steam and home prices began to fall, subprime borrowers had a harder time refinancing to better loans or selling their properties. By the middle of 2005, mortgage-loan delinquencies and foreclosure rates began to increase. The fact that there were fundamental flaws in the subprime market became hard to ignore by early 2006 as housing prices not only stopped their upward trajectory, but began to decline in many parts of the United States, including traditionally strong markets such as California, Nevada, and Florida (Reyes 2010). Arguably, like a giant Ponzi scheme, the subprime mortgages could remain viable only in an environment of continued easy credit and rising home prices. As these began to sputter, borrowers of subprime mortgages, including many with the Alt-A mortgages, realized that they had unduly overextended themselves, especially those who had bought homes at the peak of the market or had drained equity by borrowing against the price appreciation of their house.[31]

Exacerbating this was the bitter realization that many borrowers, lenders, brokers, and appraisers had grossly inflated house prices and borrowers' incomes on loan applications. Now, more realistic (that is, lower) appraisals made it difficult for borrowers to refinance and possibly avoid foreclosure. Without the continuing house-price appreciation, many of these mortgages simply became unaffordable. Since most borrowers' ability (and willingness) to remain current on payments was largely based on the rate of appreciation of their house's market value, the declining home prices took away both this incentive and ability. If in the past a robust housing sector with rising prices allowed even the most lax borrower the ability to avoid defaulting by selling the property or refinancing the mortgage, declining house prices and fast evaporating equity closed this window. The only remaining options were mortgage delinquency or outright default. Not surprisingly, many borrowers who fell behind on payments or found themselves "underwater" (industry parlance for borrowers who owe more on their mortgage than their houses are worth) responded by simply walking away from their homes.[32] According to McKinsey Global Institute (2010), up to 35 percent of the defaults resulted from households simply walking away from their homes. In the process, thousands of households lost their homes through foreclosure.[33]

It seems that by the second half of 2006 it finally dawned on market participants that the problem in the housing sector was not localized or even regional, but systemic and nationwide and that things were going to get much worse. As this reality sunk in, the deterioration in the performance of subprime loans became sudden and painful. This was in part because the supposed structured nature of the investments (with each tranche representing

---

[31] This also explains the difficulties in refinancing faced by homeowners who have good credit and make their monthly payments on time but who bought during the boom years. As the value of their home plummeted, banks became reluctant to refinance.

[32] Since in 11 of the 50 states, including hard-hit California and Arizona, mortgages are "without recourse," it is legal for homeowners to default on their mortgages without penalty. More specifically, as mortgages are nonrecourse loans in these states, lenders cannot pursue the other assets or income of borrowers who default.

[33] On the other hand, as my colleague Jacques Artus mentioned to me, "People that purchased a house with a subprime mortgage with negative amortization did not lose a house they did not have one to begin with. They enjoyed a nice house for free for a few years."

a different level of risk) proved to be a selling gimmick. The assumption that the "senior" rated tranche had little correlation with the riskier, lower-rated tranches, proved to be false despite the AAA ratings. As the poor quality of the subprime loans became apparent and the securities were downgraded, the various tranches began to fall like dominos in value together. In fact, by August 2007, the AAA-rated U.S. residential MBSs were priced at about the same level as the BBB-rated corporate bonds. Consequently, throughout the second half of 2006 to the early months of 2007, subprime mortgage delinquencies continued their steady rise. A quick sampling of headline economic news underscores this: on April 2, 2007, New Century Financial Corporation, a leading subprime mortgage lender, filed for Chapter 11 bankruptcy protection. On June 2007 Standard and Poor's and Moody's Investor Services downgraded more than 100 bonds backed by second-lien subprime mortgages. On June 7, 2007 Bear Stearns informed its investors that it was suspending redemptions from its High-Grade Structured Credit Strategies Enhanced Leverage Fund. On July 11, 2007 Standard & Poor's placed 612 securities backed by subprime residential mortgages on a credit watch. The unabated continuation of delinquencies in subprime mortgages resulted in further drops in the prices of triple-A-rated mortgage-backed securities and raised suspicions about the value of their underlying assets. The fact that banks held these securities (either directly or through SIVs) raised legitimate concerns regarding the health of the banks' balance sheets. By mid-August 2007, interbank lending rates had spiked to levels well above those in the federal funds market. Hardly surprising, on August 16, 2007 Fitch Ratings downgraded Countrywide Financial Corporation to BBB+, its third-lowest investment-grade rating, and Countrywide borrowed the entire $11.5 billion available in its credit lines with other banks.

When the subprime mortgage originations ceased after several subprime mortgage lenders filed for bankruptcy in mid-2007, the housing bubble finally burst. As "negative equity" or mortgage debt greater than the market value of the house skyrocketed, delinquencies and foreclosures rose sharply, the value of mortgage backed securities and derivatives fell, and defaults were widespread.[34] By October 2007, nearly 1.3 million U.S. housing properties were subject to foreclosure activity. Suffice it to note that for lenders, reselling foreclosed properties in a declining housing market proved to be a major challenge.

---

[34] Negative amortization occurs when monthly payments do not cover all the interest owed. The interest that is not paid in the monthly payment is added to the loan balance. This means that even after making many payments, a borrower could owe more than at the start of the loan.

Furthermore, the housing bubble's burst exposed deep-rooted problems in the real-estate sector and financial intermediation that were not limited to the original subprime loans. Indeed, there was genuine fear that if the housing market failed to improve quickly, the problem would get worse, especially as there was a large volume of adjustable-rate mortgages scheduled to reset over the next two years. In October 2007 the worst seemed to happen: for the first time, the number of prime mortgages in delinquency exceeded the subprime loans in danger of default, especially in the "epicenters" or high-growth regions such as Arizona, Nevada, Florida, California, but also in other states. In part, the recession made it tougher for homeowners to pay their mortgages, but more importantly, crashing home prices left growing numbers of borrowers "underwater" and unable to sell or refinance their way out of trouble.

The problem was further exacerbated by "deleveraging" as firms and consumers attempted to reduce their debt exposure at a time when economies around the world were slowing due to sharply rising oil and other commodity prices. The liquidity shock and the bursting of the housing bubble only heightened concerns about all leveraged positions, effectively ending the credit boom. The residential mortgage market in the United States is an $11 trillion market. The banks' highly leveraged balance sheets and minimal down payments on home loans meant that even a minor drop in home prices and rise in defaults would result in a large hit to banks' capital and threaten the very solvency of financial institutions. The loss of confidence in credit ratings and revaluation of risks led investors to pull back from a wide range of securities, especially structured credit products. The spillover effects were fast and furious: a sharp credit crunch and chaos in the stock markets, the banking industry, and the global money markets. Specifically, as the markets for subprime mortgage backed securities literally evaporated, the high leveraged investors such as hedge funds could no longer trade – that is, liquidate their large positions in the troubled securities. This, in turn, meant that the CDO and derivatives markets simply ceased to function (Gorton and Metrick 2010; Stulz 2009). International banks, especially those in Europe, were particularly impacted as many had purchased the high-yielding mortgage securities.

The Gloves Come off

Financier George Soros (2009) argues that the decision to let Lehman fail was "the game changer" because it transformed a potentially localized crisis related to problems with structured financial products in the United

States into a full-fledged global liquidity crisis. Soros argues that Lehman's bankruptcy "had the same shock effect on the behavior of consumers and businesses as the bank failures of the 1930s." Taylor (2009) offers a slightly different view, arguing that it was not so much the Lehman collapse as the haphazard way Lehman was dealt with and the uncertainty it created about when and under what circumstances the government would support financial institutions that made the bad situation truly worse.

Certainly, the collapse of Lehman was a seminal moment. Overnight, there was a virtual halt of interbank lending. The spillover effect was particular painful because the balance sheets of many banks and financial institutions burdened by illiquid, impaired assets simply could not cope. Although financial institutions worldwide tried (often aggressively) to deleverage (or offload at acceptable prices some of their stock of impaired assets and bring down their leverage ratios), this proved futile, in part because illiquid assets made up of mortgage-backed securities are difficult to value during times of crisis. Not surprisingly, credit markets became tight as banks and other financial institutions tried to reduce their exposure to each other.[35] Banks became reluctant to lend because of deep concerns over counter-party risk: that is, who owns the impaired mortgage backed and other assets, and what are the odds of repayment in the interbank market for funds. The tightening of credit was reflected not only in the interbank lending in the United States and abroad, but also in the sharp contraction in availability and cost of credit to even good, creditworthy borrowers. Rather, maturities shortened, the cost of hedging against default risk sharply rose, and the range of assets accepted as collateral narrowed. It was now a just a matter of time before the liquidity crisis and stresses in the financial system would spread to the real economy. This realization finally prompted the "hand-offs" by the Bush administration to acknowledge the escalating problems and respond to the economic maelstrom with an unprecedented intervention in the U.S. private capital markets.

---

[35] The dollar interbank credit contraction is a worldwide occurrence because the loan portfolios of U.S. banks and financial institutions are mostly dollar-denominated. Most foreign banks are in the same boat because they also have sizeable portfolios in dollars.

TWO

The Bush and Obama Administrations' Response

In September 2008, the U.S. economy (indeed, the global economy) teetered on a precipice of a depression that would rival the scale of the Great Depression. In a matter of weeks, several of the world's premier financial institutions had collapsed, credit markets had ceased to function, trillions of dollars in household savings had evaporated as stocks, pensions, and home values plummeted, and hundreds of thousands of people had lost their jobs. As widespread feelings of loss, insecurity, and panic gripped the land, authorities jumped into action to avert a large-scale economic depression. Leading the charge for bold and vigorous action was the Federal Reserve's Ben Bernanke. An economic historian, Bernanke understood the cost of inaction and of inappropriate action. After all, Milton Friedman and Anna Schwartz's classic *A Monetary History of the United States* – which has long provided the standard history of U.S. monetary and financial experience – warned about the dangers of both. Friedman and Schwartz had compellingly argued that the crash of 1929 rapidly morphed into the Great Depression because of the Federal Reserve Board's inept response, which resulted in a large contraction of the U.S. money supply. This view has long been conventional wisdom, to the point that scholars of the Great Depression uniformly blame that era's policymakers for making a bad situation worse by failing to decisively respond to the unfolding economic crisis. Clearly, Bernanke was determined not to repeat these errors. Seen in this context, Bernanke's strong support of the Bush, and later the Obama, administrations' massive stimulus program, including the decision to drive interest rates rapidly down to essentially zero was hardly surprising.

The White House (both the Bush and Obama administrations) and Congress, via the Federal Reserve, the U.S. Treasury, the Federal Deposit Insurance Corporation (FDIC), and other federal agencies, used their considerable prerogatives to quickly put in place a number of emergency measures to stabilize the financial system. In effect, the U.S. government, acting as provider of liquidity and last-resort lender, pumped billions of dollars to bail out failing and failed financial institutions and to jump-start the spluttering economy – both directly through capital infusions and indirectly by providing a wide array of liquidity facilities and guarantees. According to the CBO (Congressional Budget Office 2010), the treasury, the Federal Reserve, and the FDIC set aside nearly $3 trillion in assistance. The Federal Reserve's short-term collateralized lending to financial institutions (both depository and non-depository institutions) constituted about half, with the treasury funding some thirteen programs from the $700 billion in TARP or the "Troubled Asset Relief Program" authorized by Congress in late September 2008.

If the cornerstone of the Bush administration's plan was the unprecedented $700 billion in TARP funds, the Obama administration, which took over the reins of government a few weeks later, not only extended TARP but also added its own even more ambitious and costly programs dubbed the "Financial Stability Plan" and the "American Recovery and Reinvestment Act," (ARRA) among others.[1] Although these programs, introduced during

---

[1]   Sources consulted for the U.S. government programs and policies include the following:
CBO (Congressional Budget Office). 2010. *The Budgetary Impact and Subsidy Costs of the Federal Reserve's Actions during the Financial Crisis*. May.
   2009a. *The Budget and Economic Outlook: Fiscal Years 2009 to 2019*. January. http://www.cbo.gov/ftpdocs/99xx/doc9957/01–07-Outlook.pdf
   2009b. *The Budget and Economic Outlook: An Update* http://www.cbo.gov/ftpdocs/105xx/doc10521/2009BudgetUpdate_Summary.pdf
   2009c. *A Preliminary Analysis of the President's Budget and an Update of CBO's Budget and Economic Outlook*. March. http://www.cbo.gov/ftpdocs/100xx/doc10014/03–20-PresidentBudget.pdf.
   2009d. *An Analysis of the President's Budgetary Proposals for Fiscal Year 2010*. June. http://www.cbo.gov/ftpdocs/102xx/doc10296/06–16-AnalysisPresBudget_forWeb.pdf.
   2009e. *Measuring the Effects of the Business Cycle on the Federal Budget*. June. http://www.cbo.gov/ftpdocs/102xx/doc10299/06–23-BusinessCycle.pdf.
   2001. *The Budget and Economic Outlook: Fiscal Years 2002–2011*. January. http://www.cbo.gov/ftpdocs/27xx/doc2727/entire-report.pdf.
CRS (Congressional Research Service). 2009a. *The Global Financial Crisis: Analysis and Policy Implications*. 25 November. CRS Report RL34742 by Dick K. Nanto.
   2009b. *Economic Stimulus: Issues and Policies*. 10 November. CRS Report R40104 by Jane G. Gravelle, Thomas L. Hungerford, and Marc Labonte.
   2009c. *The Global Financial Crisis: Analysis and Policy Implications*. 2 October. CRS Report RL34742 by Dick K. Nanto.
   2009d. *Financial Turmoil: Federal Reserve Policy Responses*. 10 July. CRS Report RL34427 by Marc Labonte.
   2009e. *American Recovery and Reinvestment Act of 2009 (P.L. 111–5): Summary and Legislative History*. 20 April. CRS Report R40537 by Clinton T. Brass, Carol Hardy Vincent, Pamela J. Jackson, Jennifer E. Lake, Karen Spar, and Robert Keith.

the peak of the crisis, helped arrest a devastating financial meltdown, they failed to live up to their architects' bold claims of quickly kick-starting a stalled economy and creating hundreds of thousands of jobs.[2] Rather, these

2009f. *Troubled Asset Relief Program: Legislation and Treasury Implementation.* 24 March. CRS Report RL34730 by Baird Webel and Edward V. Murphy.

2009g. *Financial Market Intervention.* 29 January. CRS Report RS22963 by Baird Webel and Edward V. Murphy.

2008. *The Emergency Economic Stabilization Act and Current Financial Turmoil: Issues and Analysis.* 25 November. CRS Report RL34730 by Baird Webel and Edward V. Murphy.

United States, Government Accountability Office. 2008. *Housing Government-Sponsored Enterprises: A Single Regulator Will Better Ensure Safety and Soundness and Mission Achievement,* Statement of William B. Shear, Director, Financial Markets and Community Investment. March 6.

http://www.gao.gov/new.items/d08563t.pdf

United States, Government Printing Office. 2008a. *The Economic Stimulus Act of 2008* (Pub.L. 110–185, 122 Stat. 613, enacted February 13). United States: National Archives and Records Administration.

United States, Government Printing Office. 2008b. *The Housing and Economic Recovery Act of 2008* (Pub.L. 110–289, enacted July 30). United States: National Archives and Records Administration.

U.S. Government: Office of Management and Budget. 2009. *A New Era of Responsibility: Renewing America's Promise.* Washington, D.C.: US Government Printing Office.

2008. *Mid-Session Review, Budget of the U.S. Government, Fiscal Year 2009.* July 2008. www.whitehouse.gov/omb/budget/fy2009/pdf/09msr.pdf.

United States. President Barak Obama. 2009. *Remarks of President Barack Obama: Address to Joint Session of Congress.* 24 February.

http://www.whitehouse.gov/the_press_office/remarks-of-president-barack-obamaaddress-to-joint-session-of-congress

United States Department of the Treasury. 2009a. *Financial Stability Plan Fact Sheet.* 10 February. http://financialstability.gov/docs/fact-sheet.pdf

United States Department of the Treasury. 2009b. *Secretary Geithner Introduces Financial Stability Plan* press release. 10 February.

http://www.treas.gov/press/releases/tg18.htm

United States Department of the Treasury. 2009c. *Homeowner Affordability and Stability Plan Fact Sheet,* February 18.

http://www.treasury.gov/initiatives/eesa/homeowner-affordability-plan/FactSheet.pdf

United States Department of the Treasury. 2008a. *Statement by Secretary Henry M. Paulson, Jr. on Treasury and Federal Housing Finance Agency Action to Protect Financial Markets and Taxpayers.* September 7.

http://www.ustreas.gov/press/releases/hp1129.htm

United States Department of the Treasury, Office of Public Affairs. 2008b. *Government Sponsored Enterprise Credit Facility Fact Sheet.* September 7.

http://www.ustreas.gov/press/releases/reports/gsecf_factsheet_090708.pdf

United States Department of the Treasury, Office of Public Affairs. 2008c. *Treasury Senior Preferred Stock Purchase Agreement Fact Sheet.* September 7.

http://www.treas.gov/press/releases/reports/pspa_factsheet_090708%20hp1128.pdf

[2] However, in fairness, Blinder and Zandi (2010) note that without fiscal stimulus, the unemployment rate in 2010 would have been around 11 percent instead of the actual 9.6 percent and that the economy would be experiencing deflation, instead of low inflation.

programs have saddled the U.S. taxpayer with unprecedented levels of debt. No doubt, making and enacting policy and programs during emergency conditions is fraught with dangers. Yet, it is conceivable that these programs would have produced better outcomes if they were better thought through, administered, or executed, and especially if the banks and financial institutions were held more accountable to the generous public funds they received. Perhaps meaningful bipartisan cooperation could have resulted in greater public support and more targeted programs.

Yet, as this chapter shows, TARP and its successor programs failed to live up to their billing because the policies and programs were unusually unimaginative and based on deeply flawed assumptions about the problems facing the U.S. economy. In particular, the prevailing view that the crisis was a result of a catastrophic "market failure" and that an unprecedented Keynesian state intervention was in order to put the economy back on track was a gross misdiagnosis of the problem and unduly raised expectations about a quick recovery. The failure of the massive stimulus coupled with poorly conceived and half-hearted reform measures to jump-start the economy, especially job growth, underscores how incommensurate the various government policies and programs were to the problem at hand. If the recent past is any guide, excessive state intervention may end up further entrenching a vicious cycle by monetizing the national debt and encouraging even more deficit spending.

The Bush Administration's Response

The U.S. Congress passed the Emergency Economic Stabilization Act of 2008 (EESA) on October 3, 2008, giving the treasury the authority to establish the $700 billion Troubled Asset Relief Program. Initially, the TARP funds were to allow the U.S. Treasury to buy troubled assets from financial institutions. The treasury hoped that removing these non-performing assets from the banks' balance sheets would encourage eligible U.S. financial institutions to build capital and provide credit to both businesses and consumers. Under this voluntary program, the treasury agreed to purchase up to $250 billion (of the $700 billion) of senior preferred shares from qualifying financial institutions, while as part of the EESA, Congress temporarily raised deposit insurance limits to $250,000 through December 31, 2009 to prevent a possible bank run and calm a nervous public.

As the bankruptcy of Lehman Brothers and the near-collapse of AIG triggered severe disruptions (and panic) in short-term money markets and as investors in prime money market funds sought shelter in treasury securities, the Federal Reserve had little choice but to use its balance sheet to support the credit markets. On October 7, the Federal Reserve announced a "radical plan" to buy massive amounts of short-term debts to break through the credit crisis. Normally, about $100 billion of these short-term IOUs are outstanding at any given time, waiting to be sold to money market mutual funds, pension funds, and other investors. However, this market had virtually dried up as investors became too nervous to purchase paper longer than overnight or a couple days. To alleviate these difficulties, the Fed invoked a Depression-era power under the so-called "unusual and exigent circumstances" to buy commercial paper that companies rely on to finance their day-to-day operations such as purchasing supplies or making payrolls.[3] As the demand for liquidity grew, the Federal Reserve introduced two new liquidity facilities called the Asset-Backed Commercial Paper Money Market Mutual Fund Liquidity Facility (AMLF), and the Money Market Investor Funding Facility (MMIFF). Both these facilities were introduced to provide funds to markets by extending loans to banking organizations to finance their purchases of high-quality asset-backed commercial paper (ABCP) from money market mutual funds. The AMLF was designed to provide nonrecourse discount window loans to banks to enable them to purchase asset-backed commercial paper from money market mutual funds, and the MMIFF was designed to provide loans to a private-sector vehicle established to purchase a broad range of assets from these funds.

On October 8, the Federal Reserve, in a coordinated effort with other central banks, cut a key U.S. interest rate from 2 percent to 1.5 percent to calm investors increasingly worried about the stagnant credit markets. For millions of Americans, the cut meant that borrowing would become cheaper. As home equity loans, credit cards, and other floating-rate loans all fluctuate depending on what the Federal Reserve does, the Bank of America, Wells Fargo, and other banks cut their prime rate by half a point to 4.5 percent – the lowest in more than four years. Similarly, the Bank of England cut its rate by half a point to 4.5 percent, and the European Central Bank reduced its rate to 3.75 percent. Similar actions were also adopted by the central banks of China, Canada, Sweden, and Switzerland. Yet, despite this coordinated effort, credit markets failed to show signs of stability – making it apparent that a rate reduction alone was not enough to make credit availability easier for businesses and consumers. Desperate to unlock the

---

[3] The $99.4 billion daily market for this crucial financing virtually dried up as investors became too jittery to buy paper. This made it difficult and expensive for companies to raise money to fund their day-to-day operations.

seemingly frozen credit markets, on October 10, the treasury announced the government's intention to take stakes in major financial institutions instead of simply buying these institutions' illiquid assets (United States Department of Treasury 2009a; 2008c).

From the very early stages of the crisis, the Fed also provided commensurate volumes of liquidity to financial institutions to ease capital and liquidity pressures. For example, in December 2007, the Fed introduced a new auction system named the "Term Auction Facility" (TAF) to distribute discount window loans. Auctions of longer-term (up to 84-day) loans were added to address the shortage of term funding in the money markets as underscored by the exceptionally high spreads of term versus overnight Libor (London Interbank Offered Rate) loans. On March 14, 2008, the Fed created a limited-liability company called Maiden Lane I (ML I) to purchase approximately $30 billion in assets from the mortgage desk at Bear Stearns thereby facilitating J.P. Morgan Chase's acquisition of Bear Stearns. In September 2008, Maiden Lane II (ML II) and Maiden Lane III (ML III) were created to reduce liquidity pressures on AIG. Specifically, this was accomplished by ML II's purchase of $20.5 billion in residential mortgage-backed securities (RMBSs) from several of AIG's U.S. insurance subsidiaries. ML III purchased some $29.3 billion in collateralized debt obligations from certain AIG counterparties to ease capital and liquidity pressures emanating from the credit-default swap contracts backed by AIG. On October 14, the federal government took additional steps to "shore-up market stability" by announcing the Capital Purchase Program (a program within TARP), which would provide funds to eligible institutions. On the same day, the FDIC announced the Temporary Liquidity Guarantee Program (TLG) to preserve confidence and encourage liquidity in the banking system. The program consisted of two basic components. First, a temporary guarantee of newly issued senior unsecured debt (the Debt Guarantee Program), and second, a temporary unlimited guarantee of funds in noninterest-bearing transaction accounts (the Transaction Account Guarantee Program), at "eligible entities." These eligible institutions had until December 5, 2008 to opt out of the TLG Program. Institutions could elect to opt out of either the Debt Guarantee Program or the Transaction Account Guarantee Program, or both. The primary purpose of the Debt Guarantee Program was to provide liquidity to the interbank lending market and promote stability in the unsecured funding market for banks. The Debt Guarantee Program was designed to temporarily guarantee certain newly issued senior unsecured debt, including purchases of federal funds with a maturity greater than thirty days. On October 21, the Federal Reserve announced that it would buy commercial paper from money market mutual funds to break the credit clog. In addition, the Fed supported the provision of offshore dollar liquidity through expansion of swap lines with foreign central banks.[4] In total, the treasury advanced some $205 billion to more than 700 financial institutions in 48 states at interest rates of between 5 and 7.7 percent between October 2008 and December 2009. And, finally, by December 2008, the Federal Reserve had established swap lines with fourteen central banks.

On November 12, the treasury announced that TARP was insufficient to overcome to the difficulties posted by the fragile credit markets and thus would no longer be used to purchase troubled assets. It seems that the plan to purchase the non-performing or "toxic" assets was abandoned when the authorities realized that there was no clear mechanism to determine the value of the assets. Rather, it was deemed that TARP would continue to inject capital into financial institutions via the purchase of senior preferred shares and equity stakes in banks and other nonbank financial institutions as had been done through the existing Capital Purchase Program. It was hoped that such an approach would improve the capital position of banks, remove uncertainty from lenders' balance sheets, and restore liquidity to and confidence in the financial system. Moreover, treasury officials indicated that future uses of the TARP could include improving the capital positions of bank and nonbank financial institutions, securitizing consumer credit such as credit-card receivables, auto loans, and student loans, and increasing foreclosure-mitigation efforts. Initially, investors and governments around the world remained cautious – apparently waiting for details as to how exactly the treasury was going to buy $700 billion of U.S. banks' mortgage assets. This partly explains why the treasury bill yields remained extremely low, suggesting that investors such as money market mutual funds were still sticking to the safety of short-term government debt rather than the short-term corporate debt known as "commercial paper."

As the preceding illustrates, contrary to widespread perception, the Bush administration's response to the crisis was extensive, aggressive, and expensive. As liquidity pressures on financial markets increased, the Fed responded decisively to mitigate the difficulties, and the various measures they put in place no doubt helped prevent a complete systemic financial collapse. Yet, despite these efforts, the economic toll in terms of lost output, lost jobs, and lost wealth continued to mount. As *The Economist* (2009b) noted,

[4] Swap lines make dollars available to other central banks when these banks post their own currency as collateral. In turn, these central banks provide financing to "sound" commercial banks that need dollar funding.

"lenders balked at the requirement that they first write down the principal,"[5] rendering both President Bush's plan and the Democrats' plan to ease the crisis ineffective. The Bush plan to help some 240,000 delinquent subprime borrowers refinance their debts into government-backed fixed-rate mortgages resulted in only 4,000 such refinances, and the Democrats' much-touted $300 billion plan to guarantee up to 400,000 mortgages received only 517 applications. By mid-January 2009, a week before President Bush's term expired, more than 2.3 million American homeowners faced foreclosure proceedings, an 81 percent increase from 2007. Nationwide, more than 860,000 properties were actually repossessed by lenders – more than double the 2007 level.[6]

What explains this disconnect between such ambitious public policy and outcomes? In retrospect, a large part of the problem was that the TARP funds simply failed to trickle down. In particular, not enough of the TARP money that banks received was pumped back into the economy in the form of loans, despite that fact that by mid-January 2009 some $350 billion of the TARP funds had been utilized. Clearly TARP failed to deliver – despite the fact the treasury bought equity stakes in failing banks assuming that with more capital on hand these banks would begin to lend. It seems what John Maynard Keynes called a "liquidity trap" was already at work. That is, banks were reluctant to lend not because they lacked sufficient capital, but because they were deeply concerned, indeed fearful, about the solvency of all borrowers, even creditworthy ones. Arguably, if TARP had explicitly required these recipients of tax dollars to demonstrate that they were using the funds to extend credit, this problem could have been somewhat mitigated.

Taylor (2009) provides additional insight. Although he blames the Federal Reserve (and Fannie and Freddie) for causing the crisis, he holds the Bush administration responsible for misdiagnosing and exacerbating the problem. Specifically, to Taylor, since the Fed assumed that the problem was one of liquidity, all its efforts were designed to inject more liquidity into the financial system. Yet, Taylor argues, liquidity was not the fundamental problem. Rather, the root problem was "counterparty risk." To illustrate this, he compares finance to the classic card game of "hearts." Of course, in hearts, you do not want to get stuck with the queen of spades. The queens of spades in finance, he notes, "were the securities with bad mortgages in them," and, moreover, "people didn't know where they were" (p. 13). Thus,

5   *The Economist*. 2009. "The Foreclosure Plan: Can't Pay or Won't Pay?," February 19 http://www.economist.com/world/unitedstates/displaystory.cfm?story_id=13145396.
6   http://news.yahoo.com/s/ap/20090115/ap_on_bi_ge/foreclosure_rates

increasing liquidity by increasing the money supply failed to address the problem. Taylor's claim that the problem was "risk" is based on his comparison of two interest-rate spreads, the Libor-OIS spread (i.e., the three-month London Interbank Offered Rate minus the three-month overnight index swap). As the OIS measures market expectations of the federal-funds rate over a three-month period, the size of the Libor-OIS spread gives an idea about both risk and liquidity. Taylor's second spread, which measures the difference between the Libor and the interest rate on secured loans, shows that the size of the spread was due to risk. Taylor's findings compellingly show that the Libor-OIS spread did not widen much after the Lehman bankruptcy. Rather, it widened after Bernanke's and Paulson's September 23, 2008 testimony, when both warned of dire consequences if the bailout program was not passed. According to Taylor, this only exacerbated market panic and made the crisis far worse.

Obama's Plans: More Ambitious and Costlier

Even before the Obama administration formally took over the reins of power on January 21, 2009, there was talk that the crisis may be so fundamentally different from previous ones that the traditional policy measures may not work. This was in part because the Federal Reserve's typical line of defense against sharp downturns and recessions, cutting interest rates, was not working as expected (the Fed had already cut the rates it controlled basically to zero). Instead, the view that was gaining momentum with the incoming Obama administration was that only a massive fiscal stimulus involving broad-based government spending (a view similar to what the then president-elect was proposing) would work. This was because a number of analysts felt that the crisis was already so severe that the U.S. economy was caught in a "deflationary trap" and heading inexorably toward a deep, prolonged slump with double-digit unemployment rates.

Given this, the Obama administration made it clear that it planned to use the remaining $350 billion of the TARP funds to help "Main Street" by reducing the number of home foreclosures, in addition to funneling capital directly to banks who were willing to lend. At the request of incoming President Obama, President Bush asked Congress to make the remaining $350 billion available to the incoming administration without delay. On January 15, 2009, just a few days before Obama's inauguration, the Senate voted 52 to 42 to permit the incoming administration to spend the remaining $350 billion to stabilize the financial system. Through its vote the Senate defeated a resolution that would have blocked the funds from flowing to the treasury department. On January 16, again at the incoming administration's request, the treasury asked the banks in which it had injected capital to provide monthly reports on their lending – implicitly to check the number of loans made to consumers.

However, President Obama made no secret of the fact that the $350 billion was just his first down payment of a much larger public expenditure to fight the crisis on behalf of Main Street. Underscoring the urgency of the problems, even before his swearing-in on January 21, Obama worked closely with the House Democrats to release a preliminary proposal-cum-legislation that called for $825 billion in federal spending and tax cuts to revive the economy. Specifically, the proposed legislation called for $550 billion in federal spending and $275 billion in tax cuts over two years. Despite the President's appeal to lawmakers in both parties to move quickly in approving the legislation (and predicting economic disaster if they failed to act), on January 29 the House Democrats passed the $819 billion bill to cut taxes and increase public spending. Not a single Republican member of the House voted for the Economic Stimulus Bill.

The passage of the bill generated much debate about the merits of the stimulus package and an outpouring of "advice" to the Senate, where the bill was headed. In early February 2009, as if to assure both the lawmakers and the markets, the new treasury secretary, Timothy Geithner, publicly rejected any suggestion of nationalizing financial institutions by taking large ownership stakes. Rather, he claimed that the federal government was interested only in getting the banks to increase lending. He outlined in broad terms how the administration aimed to provide incentives to investors in the form of commitments to absorb some of the losses from any assets they purchased should their values continue to decline. Geithner reiterated that it was his fervent hope that this combination of private involvement and government guarantees would not only reduce the government's exposure to losses and avoid the problem of valuing assets that financial institutions were unable to sell, but in relieving banks of their worst assets, get them to lend again.

After much heated debate, the Senate passed the Economic Stimulus Bill on February 10, 2009 – a bill the president and Congressional Democrats called crucial to pull the U.S. economy away from the brink of an economic precipice. The Senators voted 61 to 37 (only three Republicans voted in favor) to approve the bill, which, according to the Congressional Budget Office (CBO), would cost $838 billion over ten years. The Republicans, who favored a smaller stimulus package with more tax cuts, labeled the bill as wasteful – tantamount to what John McCain called a "generational theft" of

Table 2.1. *Financial stability plan (core proposals)*

- Financial Stability Trust
    - A Comprehensive Stress Test for Major Banks
    - Increased Balance Sheet Transparency and Disclosure
    - Capital Assistance Program
- Public-Private Investment Fund ($500 billion–$1 trillion)
- Consumer and Business Lending Initiative (up to $1 trillion)
- Transparency and Accountability Agenda – Including Dividend Limitation
- Affordable Housing Support and Foreclosure Prevention Plan
- Small Business and Community Lending Initiative

---

borrowing from one's children to pay for current mismanagement and greed. The Republicans' charge that the bill contained too much "pork" (programs for "social engineering"), was not without merit. Instead of authoring the bill himself, Obama had allowed some of the longest-serving Democrats in the House of Representatives to write the bill. By ceding control of the stimulus to the liberal Congressional Democrats, Obama perhaps missed the opportunity to have broad support from both parties. Instead, the stimulus bill became a divisive partisan battle. Nevertheless, with this phase over, the bill headed to a House-Senate conference to resolve differences between the two versions. The Senate vote came as Geithner (joined by Ben Bernanke, FDIC Chair Sheila Bair, Office of Thrift Supervision Director John Reich, and Comptroller of the Currency John Dugan) announced a massive new rescue plan dubbed the Financial Stability Plan (Table 2.1) for the financial sector.

The program recognized that until the hundreds of billions of dollars of impaired assets weighing down bank balance sheets were removed, credit flows would continue to be restricted. To alleviate this problem, the program planned to put together some $2 trillion from the treasury, private investors, and the Federal Reserve. It was hoped that by pumping such a large dose of capital into banks and financial institutions to unfreeze credit markets, more accurately determine the prices of toxic assets, and stem the growing foreclosures would stabilize the financial system. Specifically, Geithner's program proposed (1) the creation of a Public Private Investment Fund, run jointly by the treasury and the Fed and with financing from private investors, to buy the troubled assets burdening banks and financial institutions. The new fund, often described as a "bad bank," would start with $500 billion with a goal of eventually buying up to $1 trillion in assets; (2) capital injections into banks using the remaining $350 billion in the treasury's rescue program; and (3) an expansion of lending program that the treasury and Federal Reserve had already announced, aimed at financing consumer loans. The two agencies had originally announced their intention to finance as much as $200 billion in loans for student and car loans and credit-card debt. Now the program was expanded to about $1 trillion.

Despite raising expectations that the "policy response will be comprehensive and forceful," Geithner's plan provided surprisingly few details on the crucial "how" questions. Despite weeks of preparation, the plan did not delineate how precisely the Obama administration planned to deal with the root cause of the crisis: namely how to stem the foreclosure problem remained inexplicably unanswered. Although Geithner promised to provide details "in the coming weeks" regarding specific programs to reduce mortgage-foreclosure rates, he left tantalizing suggestions that banks that received government funds would be expected to cooperate with these programs. However, on specifics, the $50 billion program to curb foreclosures was not only deemed too small, it also lacked details. For example, it was not clear if the program would include incentives for mortgage lenders and brokers to write down borrowers' principal – seen as critical to stop the spreading bankruptcies. After all, there was no dispute that unless the foreclosure surge eased, no amount of federal spending would spur an economic recovery. That is, with more than one million residences already in foreclosure since 2006 and an additional 5.9 million expected over the next four years, no amount of stimulus could possibly solve this problem by itself. Rather, at a minimum, lenders and investors would not only have to acknowledge huge losses but also work out how to keep borrowers (especially those whose equity had evaporated) to make at least some monthly payments. Of course, the subprime mortgage mess was just a part of the problem. An estimated $5 to $7 trillion, including commercial real-estate loans, consumer credit-card debt, and high-yield bonds and leveraged loans were also at risk of losing much of their value. This did not include trillions of additional dollars in high-grade corporate bonds and loans and jumbo prime mortgages whose worth would surely move south if the recession deepened and more firms and households defaulted on their loans and mortgages.

Although Geithner promised to "stress-test" banks with assets of more than $100 billion to see if they were sufficiently capitalized to withstand a severe and lengthy recession and provide them "contingent" capital if they were not, he again offered few details about the terms, especially as to whether this plan could eventually mean a backdoor route to temporary bank nationalization. According to "tier-one capital," the usual measure of assessing banks' capital adequacy, the United States' ten biggest banks by assets appeared to be in reasonably good shape as their ratios of tier-one capital to risk-weighted assets exceeded 10 percent. Yet, as Walter Bagehot's famous dictum confirmed, if you have to prove you are worthy of credit, your credit is already gone. Indeed, the markets were cognizant of the fact that the quality of the banks' tier-one capital had become progressively poor. Not surprisingly, the markets preferred tangible common equity, which is undiluted by hybrid capital such as preferred stock. Making matters worse, the United States' five largest banks (Citibank, Bank of America, HSBC Bank USA, Wells Fargo Bank, and J.P. Morgan Chase), which already had received $145 billion in bailout funds, still faced potentially catastrophic losses from exotic investments if economic conditions were to substantially worsen. The big concern was about these banks' "current" net loss risks from derivatives (insurance-like bets tied to a loan or other underlying asset). This meant that corporate bankruptcies could lead to a domino-like chain reaction that could deprive the banks of hundreds of billions of dollars in insurance they bought on risky debt or force them to pay out massive sums to cover debt they guaranteed. Even more troubling were the banks' holdings of trillions of dollars of credit-default swaps, which provided insurance against defaults on loans such as subprime mortgages and guarantees of payments on loans of borrowers who walked away from their debts.

The widespread perception that for many banks passing the stress test would be difficult given their large volumes of toxic assets and their inability to build reserves was not without merit. In fact, there was genuine fear that many banks were either close to being or already were insolvent. After all, the value of write-downs by U.S. banks had already surpassed $1 trillion, and the IMF and Goldman Sachs were predicting further losses of more than $2 trillion. Given this, Geithner's plan for "stress testing" banks and separating the "viable" institutions from bankrupt ones and establishing an investment fund with private and public money to purchase bad assets was already moot, if not dead on arrival, because it assumed that the system was still largely solvent. Although officials from the treasury and the Federal Reserve, including Bernanke during his Congressional testimony on February 23, 2009, noted that nationalization "is when the government seizes the bank and zeroes out the shareholders ... we don't plan anything like that," concerns that nationalization may become unavoidable remained palpable. Indeed, a number of prominent Republicans and "fiscal conservatives," most notably former Federal Reserve Chair Alan Greenspan and Senator Lindsey Graham, publicly stated that the government should consider nationalizing the most troubled institutions, including Citigroup, Bank of America, and Wells Fargo. Others argued that quasi-nationalization or "conservatorship" had already occurred via debt guarantees, loss-sharing agreements, central-bank facilities, and massive capital infusions. Clearly, as Krugman indignantly noted, throwing yet more public capital at weak banks risked perpetuating "lemon socialism" – where banks reap the gains but taxpayers bear the losses. Nevertheless, even as the idea of cleaning the Augean banking stables was gaining popularity, critics of bank nation-alization pointed out the dangers: done haphazardly, the seizure of one bank could easily start a run on the liabilities of others, including healthy banks. Second, there was concern that finding a viable exit strategy to unload nationalized banks may not be easy, and a further cost to taxpayers. After all, it took the FDIC seven years in the early 1990s to sell the failed Continental Illinois. In other words, government takeovers are highly risky amid a systemic crisis because of the scale and distribution of creditors' potential losses.

On February 26, 2009, the Obama administration finally provided details of the "bank stress test" designed to identify, in advance, the bad assets on bank balance sheets by using financial models to project future loan values and loss rates under different economic conditions. According to the new treasury department guidelines, the banks would have to assume that the economy would contract by 3.3 percent in 2009 and remain flat in 2010, that housing prices would fall by another 22 percent in 2009, and that unemploy-ment would jump to 8.9 percent in 2009 and 10.3 percent in 2010. Nineteen of the nation's biggest banks were ordered to undergo stress tests to see if whether they could hold up to the new guidelines. In addition, the "big banks" (those with more than $100 billion in assets), were ordered to carry out supervised tests by the end of April 2009 to see how much their capital would be depleted under the treasury's assumptions. If federal regulators concluded that a bank would not have enough capital, the bank would have to raise the extra money within six months or get it from the government in exchange for a potentially big ownership stake. Specifically, the treasury made it clear that it would provide new capital in exchange for shares of pre-ferred stock. These would be converted to shares of common stock at a price slightly below the level at which the shares traded on February 9, 2009.

For many of the big banks this would mean extremely low prices com-pared with what they would have received a year prior. The case of Citigroup is illustrative. On March 5, 2009, shares of Citigroup (once the world's most valuable bank), tumbled below $1, taking their year-to-date drop to 85 per-cent. Citigroup, a Dow component, fell more than 13 percent to an intra-day low of $0.98, spurred by continued fears over the bank's health and ability to avert nationalization. Two years prior, Citigroup's market value was more than $270 billion. In March 2009, its market cap barely exceeded $5.4 billion. The Obama administration hoped that its strategy would allay fears about bank nationalizations as it would reaffirm that the nation's big banks remained adequately capitalized to withstand further downturns in the economy. Of course, this remained to be seen as there was no guarantee that many of these banks could absorb the full brunt of losses and still remain solvent. In any case, the real challenge was how best to value bank assets. Geithner had long tried to make a distinction between the "basic inherent economic value" of troubled assets and their "artificially depressed value," and although he may have been right, the fact remained that no one really knew the true value of these assets. What was known, however, was that if prices were set too low, banks would lose value and may even collapse. If prices were too high, the remaining shareholders would be unjustly enriched. After all, it was this dilemma that undermined Paulson's plan to remove toxic assets, and no amount of Geithner's stress testing could address this conundrum. This explains why some (most notably, Paul Krugman) argued that it was more prudent to temporarily nationalize undercapitalized banks, and thereby remove the fear surrounding the financial system. On the other hand, since the government already owned big shares in many banks and enjoyed immense powers over them without direct ownership, nationalization was not deemed necessary.

The big question in early 2009 was what would it take for banks receiving public funds to lend? Although many Democrats (and many Republicans) had harshly criticized the Bush administration for mismanaging the TARP funds by not requiring banks receiving assistance to increase their lending, Geithner's plan also failed to come up with a set of clear rules for banks to provide more loans. Similarly, Geithner provided few details of the crucial asset-purchase plan. In particular, how the public and private sector partnership would work, and whether the public-private partnerships would end up being a pretext for a bank bailout at taxpayers' expense. At best, Geithner's plan for a public-private investment fund to buy toxic assets implied the government's willingness to guarantee the floor value of the assets and to provide cheap financing – hardly an incentive given the lack of clarity regarding how the troubled assets would be valued. These two issues were at the heart of the financial crisis: how to value the potentially trillions of dollars of unsellable assets, many of them directly tied to the collapse of the mortgage market, that were weighing down financial institutions, and how to provide assistance to homeowners to stem the rising foreclosures.

Thus, Geithner's plan failed to live up to the Obama administration's boast that it would mark a sharp departure from the earlier "haphazard" plan under the Bush administration. Geithner's inexplicable failure to deliver a plan that provided more clarity than Paulson's only served to further fuel uncertainty and concern. Not surprisingly, the market greeted Geithner's plan with a mix of anxiety and disappointment. If Geithner's aim was to instill confidence, he clearly failed. The reality was that the market simply did not know enough (yet) to make a judgment on the plan's prospects. Even as Geithner was concluding his remarks, stocks plunged, with the Dow Jones Industrial Average shedding 300 points and the tech-heavy Nasdaq and the Standard & Poor's 500-stock index each falling more than 4 percent. Finally, one of the criticisms of Paulson's bailout plan was that it was difficult for the public to discern how taxpayer dollars were being spent. Geithner pledged to make his plan more transparent – even establishing a Web-site to keep track of bank lending. Yet, this "transparency" did not necessarily put pressure on the banks to lend. After all, markets knew that since money is fungible it is always difficult to effectively keep track of its flow.

On February 11, 2009, the House and Senate leaders finally came to an agreement on a massive 1,100-page, $789 billion economic stimulus bill (smaller than either the House or Senate had earlier proposed) after little more than 24 hours of negotiations with the Obama administration. On February 13, 2009, both chambers of Congress approved the $787 billion stimulus bill called the American Recovery and Reinvestment Act (ARRA). Although President Obama personally courted Republicans to support the bill, it passed the House by 246–183 without a single Republican vote, and the Senate by 60–38 with the help of just three Republicans. The majority Republican lawmakers lost no time in denouncing the bill as too laden with big spending and too short on tax relief. Perhaps the bill deserved more bipartisan support. After all, the original bill was reduced by more than $100 billion, and many of the offending earmarks had been removed. Moreover, it not only spared some 24 million middle-class taxpayers from increases they were due from the Alternative Minimum Tax, it also allowed small business to cut tax obligations by using losses to offset profits in the previous five years and encouraged capital improvements by allowing accelerated depreciation – all programs Republicans support. President Obama signed the bill into law on February 17.

The final stimulus bill was divided as follows: $505 billion in spending programs and $282 billion (about 35 percent) in tax relief, including a much scaled-back "Making Work Pay" and middle-class tax cut designed to give credits of up to $400 for individuals and $800 for families within certain income limits in 2009 and 2010. Businesses also received tax breaks, including accelerated depreciation (by 50 percent) of capital assets like new machinery brought in service in 2009. However, a provision that would have allowed businesses to claim tax credits by applying current-year losses to profits earned in the past five years was scaled back to only businesses with $15 million or less in gross receipts. The bill also provided a one-time payment of $250 to recipients of Social Security and government disability support and funding for the president's pet initiatives – $19 billion for the expansion of computerized information technology in the health-care industry and more than $45 billion in new spending and tax breaks for programs to promote energy efficiency and renewable energy. In addition, the bill provided tax credits of up to $7,500 to buyers of new hybrid vehicles and $18 billion for environmental projects, like clean water systems, flood control, and "pollution cleanup work." Education, another top priority for Obama, received $100 billion in emergency funds over two years for public schools, universities, and child-care centers, and health care, in particular Medicaid (the health-insurance program for low-income people) received $87 billion. Without these funds many of these programs would have disappeared as state governments were already slashing funding to such programs.

The bill also offered financial help to the unemployed by enabling them to temporarily keep group health benefits under the 1986 Cobra law. As the cost is often prohibitive because workers must pay the entire premium, including the employer's share, under the bill the federal government agreed to provide subsidies – paying 65 percent of the cost for up to nine months. In addition, this aid was to be made available to workers who lost their jobs between September 1, 2008 and December 31, 2009. To qualify, workers had to certify that their income did not exceed $125,000 for individuals or $250,000 for families.

The public-works or infrastructure spending in the stimulus package totaled $120 billion. However, the bill failed to create the "national infrastructure bank" that Obama had called for to set national priorities, especially for big projects. Highways and bridges were slated to get the largest share, $29 billion, because the bill claimed those projects would create 835,000 jobs. The bulk of the funds for roads were to be distributed under existing formulas that gave a percentage to each state regardless of its needs or the merits of its projects. Finally, although the administration claimed that the offending "Buy American" provisions in the stimulus bill that favored U.S. steel, iron, and manufactured goods for government projects conformed to WTO (World Trade Organization) rules, the action created friction with U.S. trading partners (Hufbauer and Schott 2009). The last worry an already jittery global market needed was fears of "creeping protectionism" and the emboldening of protectionist and nationalist impulses in the United States and elsewhere.

Between December 2007 and February 2009, the United States had already shed 4.4 million jobs, including more than 600,000 each of the three months December 2008–February 2009. The unemployment rate jumped to 8.1 percent in February 2009, the highest in a quarter-century. Sadly, President Obama's prediction that his bill would create four million jobs had not been realized. Moreover, during this period the U.S. national debt also increased sharply. The Obama administration's own assessments expected that the 2009 deficit (for the budget year that began October 1, 2008), would jump to $1.6 trillion or about three times the previous fiscal year's shortfall. Overall, the national debt (the sum of all annual budget deficits) stood at $10.7 trillion, roughly equivalent to about $36,000 for every American man, woman, and child. Interest payment alone on the national debt was estimated at nearly $500 billion, making it the fourth-largest federal expenditure after Medicare-Medicaid, Social Security, and defense.

Assessment of the Bush and Obama Plans: Sept. 2007–Feb. 2009

The Bush, and Obama administrations' massive stimulus package adopted a textbook Keynesian strategy to fight the unprecedented economic crisis. According to Keynesian theory the effect of a change in fiscal policy on real GDP is more than one for one. That is, the "multiplier effect" of government spending on GDP is greater than one – or that a dollar spent by the government begets more than a dollar's worth of additional economic output. On the other hand, the multiplier effect of tax cuts on GDP is less than that for government spending because savings from tax cuts may not be spent. Therefore, when economic uncertainty forces firms and consumers to cut back, government spending is a prudent way to boost demand – the optimal outcome being getting the multiplier effect from spending to kick in immediately. Here, it is worth reiterating that the idea to use fiscal policy to boost the economy during a severe downturn championed by Keynes during the Great Depression remains shrouded in controversy. As is well known, Keynes argued that when market economies suffer downturns, only large infusions of government stimulus can revive growth. However, Milton Friedman (1963) challenged this assumption by showing that the Great Depression was caused by a failure of government monetary policy, not a failure of markets as Keynes had claimed.

However, because to the Obama administration, the economic contraction that followed the subprime meltdown was due to a decline in aggregate demand, direct government spending was seen as the appropriate remedy. In fact, the Obama administration released a document titled "The Job Impact of the American Recovery and Reinvestment Plan," in which it boldly claimed that the "government-purchases multiplier" (or the multiplier for direct spending) would be 1.57 while the tax-cut multiplier would be 0.99. That is, every dollar of government spending would yield $1.57 in aggregate demand, while every dollar in tax cuts would yield only 99 cents in increased demand.

However, the $505 billion spending boost did not result in actual spending because the states tended to use the funds to meet their own budget shortfalls rather than stimulate economic activity. Taylor (2011, 701) points out that the ARRA and the earlier stimulus initiatives "did not have a positive effect on consumption and government purchases, and thus did not counter the decline in investment during the recessions as the basic Keynesian textbook model would suggest" because "state and local governments used the stimulus grants to reduce their net borrowing (largely by acquiring more financial assets) rather than to increase expenditures, and they shifted expenditures away from purchases toward transfers." Similarly, the $282 billion in tax cuts failed to generate the assumed increases in consumer or business spending. With unemployment at record highs, both businesses and individuals were more concerned with paying down debt and saving what they could. Indeed, Barro (2009) compellingly argues that the "Ricardian equivalence" was already at work. That is, households and businesses that viewed the skyrocketing government deficit as creating increased future tax liabilities were responding by reducing their present levels of spending. Perhaps most fundamentally, the bill failed to adequately address the core problem without which there could be no meaningful recovery: the plummeting value of home prices. With more and more homes technically underwater and foreclosures a growing problem, the real-estate sector remained unstable. To the markets, even if the supposedly $100 billion in mortgage relief waiting in the next installment of the stimulus package materialized, they feared (quite correctly) that it would most probably help just a small number of homeowners keep their homes, and not the vast majority who had already lost their homes or were in the process of losing them.[7]

---

[7] By February 2009, about 2.3 million U.S. households faced foreclosure. This number was certain to rise as more adjustable-rate mortgages reset, driving more millions into foreclosure and causing home prices to drop further.

Similarly, the impact of the massive stimulus in job creation has been modest, if not insignificant – hence, the term "jobless recovery."[8] This is mainly because unemployment problem in the United States has become increasingly structural, rather than cyclical. Therefore, boosting aggregate demand failed to meaningfully alleviate the problem. Specifically, employment growth in the United States over the past two decades has been in the non-tradable sectors, namely, government, health care, and until recently, construction. It seems unlikely that these non-tradable sectors can sustain employment growth. With the tradable sector increasingly uncompetitive and the non-tradable sector reaching its limits, the U.S. economy lacks the ability to create jobs. Yet, even as the Keynesian multiplier involving government spending was not working, the Keynesians, or more aptly, the many born-again Keynesians, seemed unfazed. To the contrary, Larry Summers (Obama's chief economic advisor), put a new spin by boldly claiming that the multiplier was working as theory informed – at a rate of 1.5 (Mitchell 2009).

Despite the growing evidence to the contrary, it seems that the Reagan-era belief in "supply-side" economics which held that across-the-board cuts in income-tax rates would raise overall tax revenues was replaced by the other extreme: the demand-side view that the multiplier effect of government spending on output is greater than one. Conveniently overlooked was the fact that the world today is quite different than during Keynes's time. First, economies during the Great Depression were largely closed with little international trade. In contrast, in today's globalized world massive, uncoordinated spending by national governments has more potential to produce currency and bond market volatility than a return to growth. Second, and again unlike the 1930s, the United States and other major OECD economies are burdened with unprecedented levels of indebtedness. Governments, corporations, and individual households have accumulated huge debts, with average household debt some 141 percent of disposable income in the United States and 177 percent in Britain. The U.S. Federal Reserve's (2009) "Survey of Consumer Finances" (a triennial report on the assets and liabilities of U.S. households), confirmed that the United States is a nation of borrowers and spenders, not savers. The personal-savings rate dropped from 9 percent in the 1980s to 5 percent in the 1990s, to just 0.6 percent from 2005 to 2007, and household debt grew much faster than personal income. Similarly, the many blue-chip American and European banks now had

---

[8]   A "jobless recovery" occurs when output growth during an economic recovery remains steady but employment lags behind.

liabilities ranging anywhere from 40, 60, or even 100 times the amount of their capital. The markets plausibly concluded that the skyrocketing costs of the stimulus package could force the United States to run a deficit of more than 10 percent of GDP. Given this, how piling on more debt was going to solve a crisis that was already made worse by building more debt was never addressed by the Obama administration.

The Obama administration's mounting stimulus spending was also a tacit acknowledgement that monetary policy had failed to stimulate the economy. It seems there was growing consensus within the administration that the United States faced what Japan did during the 1990s – when even interest rates of zero could not revive the economy. Arguably, this is what pushed the policy makers to adopt a Keynesian fiscal policy or a program that lowers taxes or increases government spending or both. However, the experience of Japan shows that Keynesian strategy is hardly a magic bullet. Japan spent trillions of dollars to lift its economy from a severe downturn caused by the bursting of a real-estate bubble in the late 1980s. Over the course of some two decades, Japan accumulated the largest public debt in the developed world, totaling an estimated 180 percent of its $5.5 trillion economy. Yet all this failed to jump-start its economy. Eventually, Japan was able to escape from its stagnation because the global boom in the United States and China boosted its exports, not because of its colossal spending, especially spending on infrastructure. Thus, Japan's expensive stimulus did not deliver the desired results, and even when the economy eventually expanded, consumers refused to spend – underscoring Keynes's famous "paradox of thrift." Between 2001 and 2007, per-capita consumer spending rose only 0.2 percent. Public spending only sunk Japan deeper into debt, thereby leaving an enormous tax burden for future generations. Also, Japan which already had good infrastructure, investments in infrastructure turned out to be akin to digging and refilling potholes and building roads and bridges to nowhere. On the other hand, infrastructure in the United States, suffering from decades of neglect, could have used investments for improvements and job creation. But, this potential was wasted because the investment funds earmarked for infrastructure became a source of political pork. Equally troubling, the Obama administration's boast about its many "shovel-ready" projects turned out to be mostly nonexistent.

Both the Bush and Obama administrations plans also lacked a clear strategy as how to remove the bad assets from the troubled banking system. Of course, the least problem was posed by banks that had already gone bust and under government control. However, excising toxic assets from banks that were still, at least officially, private and viable, proved tricky.

Although there was broad agreement for a solution through the creation of a "bad bank" to assume the bad assets, leaving "good banks" to resume the daily business of lending, the details as to how this would work in practice remained elusive. Nevertheless, this did not stop some from suggesting (both seriously and in jest) that the Federal Reserve could serve as a "bad bank" as it already had purchased large volumes of undisclosed assets from banks, and that it was already a "bad bank" as its balance sheet had grown from just over $900 billion to more than $2 trillion in a matter of weeks. As noted earlier, another possible solution (and most unpalatable) was bank nationalization. To most Americans "nationalization" was blasphemous, but that did not prevent a number of distinguished analysts, including Paul Krugman (2009) from advocating it. Yet, nationalization was never in the cards – not only because of domestic political considerations, but also because Bernanke and other senior officials recognized that nationalization came with huge costs and risks. These included the difficulty in getting rid of large volumes of unwanted bank assets, not to mention that it could take years for the government to privatize "their" banks. Moreover, few needed to be remained of the pervasive problems inherent in state-owned banks, namely, that it could fuel politically motivated lending as politicians would be tempted to turn these banks into instruments of state policy, including using funds for their pet projects and rent-seeking activities.

However, an idea that did gain some traction was the creation of an "aggregator bank" – meaning one large bad bank (instead of splitting every sick bank into a good bank and a bad bank) which then took bad assets off the balance sheets of many banks. This idea was hardly new. The good bank/bad bank solution was first tried in the early 1990s when the government created the Resolution Trust Corporation to sell off the loans and underlying collateral of hundreds of failed savings banks, or thrifts. In fact, some elements of the good bank/bad bank were put in place with the Federal Reserve creating a facility for asset-backed securities designed to relieve banks of bad loans. Yet, even this idea failed to alleviate investors' concern. It seems that neither the banks nor the investors were convinced that the so-called aggregator banks would remove problem assets from the banking system. Clearly, the markets were cognizant of the fact that, unlike with Resolution Trust, a bad bank during the depth of the 2008 crisis faced additional problems, in particular, how to set prices for assets that both the bank and the seller could agree on. This was less of an issue in the early 1990s because the assets largely came from banks that had already failed or were under government control. However, in 2008, if the bad bank paid above the fair market value, it would raise taxpayer costs, and if it paid fair value or less, banks might be reluctant to participate. The Obama administration had no convincing answers to these essential questions.

The Obama Plans: Feb. 2009–October 2009

The Foreclosure Fix

On February 18, 2009, President Obama pledged $75 billion (funded from the second half of the $700 billion bailout) to reduce the mortgage payments of some four million homeowners at risk of default and to halt the free-falling home prices. The plan had several components with ample amounts of carrots and sticks. First, it was reasoned that after the treasury invested an additional $200 billion in Fannie and Freddie preferred shares, it would allow both these organizations (which were considered to be insolvent) to refinance conforming loans (up to $729,750) without the requirement that the refinanced loan be no larger than 80 percent of the value of the house. The assumption was that such a change would allow even borrowers who were underwater access to lower mortgage rates. This in turn would reduce payments and fewer defaults. Second, the plan provided more clear rules regarding mortgage modification, which was already obligatory for banks that had accepted TARP funds. Under the plan, lenders, mortgage investors, and other loan servicers would have to agree on a lower interest rate (rather than principal write-downs) that would be designed to reduce the borrower's mortgage payments to 38 percent of their pretax income. The government would then provide financing (totaling $75 billion in taxpayer subsidies) to bring that ratio down to 31 percent of pretax income. Lenders who helped homeowners refinance their mortgages would receive matching subsidies from the federal government, including fees for successful loan modifications. Specifically, the plan agreed to provide (a) fees to mortgage servicers and borrowers for every assisted borrower who did not default again, and (b) the Treasury Department, via an insurance fund agreed to give protection to participating lenders if house prices fell further. Also, borrowers with little or no equity in their homes, but who were meeting their payment obligations would be eligible to refinance in order to take advantage of the lower interest rates of around 5 percent. In effect, this plan lifted the guideline that borrowers have at least 20 percent equity to refinance, allowing those with loans as large as 105 percent of their home's value to qualify. Third, as a stick, the administration proposed a "cramdown" designed to allow judicial modification of home mortgages for borrowers who had run out of options – albeit, it was duly noted that since this would require changes to the bankruptcy code, it would entail federal legislation.

On March 4, 2009, the Obama administration released more details about its $75 billion "Homeowner Affordability and Stability Plan" to stabilize the housing market "by helping as many as 9 million homeowners" (up from the original 4 million) refinance or modify their mortgages. The administration's "Making Home Affordable" plan consisted of two main parts: one aimed at "prudent" homeowners interested in refinancing into a lower rate, and the other aimed at "struggling" homeowners hoping to lower their heavy monthly mortgage payments. The first program, called "Home Affordable Refinance," was designed to help homeowners whose homes had lost value as housing prices plummeted. It would now allow them to refinance their current mortgage even if there was little or no equity left in their homes. Borrowers with "conforming" loans backed by Fannie Mae and Freddie Mac would be able to refinance even if they no longer had 20 percent equity in their homes. In other words, the plan was open only to homeowners with loans owned or guaranteed by Fannie and Freddie. To qualify, homeowners had to be current on their loan, the property had to be owner-occupied, and the principal balance could not exceed $729,750 – albeit, there was no ceiling as to how high their income was provided they were in danger of losing their homes. The plan also required borrowers to document their income and sign an affidavit of financial hardship. The plan was set to expire on June 2010.

On the other hand, under the "Home Affordable Modification" plan, the government agreed to provide incentives for lenders to lower mortgage payments for struggling homeowners to 31 percent of their monthly gross income. This could come from lowering the interest rate to as little as 2 percent or extending the terms of the loan. In addition, lenders were to be given incentives to lower the principal owed by the borrower and stop charging interest on a portion of the loan (i.e. "principal forbearance"). Specifically, under the new loan modification guidelines, the treasury agreed to offer mortgage-servicing companies upfront incentive payments of $1,000 for every loan they modified and additional payments of $1,000 a year for the first three years if the borrower remained current. Moreover, the treasury agreed to contribute $1,000 a year to directly reduce the borrower's loan amount if the borrower stayed up-to-date on payments. To finance the plan, the treasury agreed to provide Freddie and Fannie with up to $200 billion in additional capital on top of $200 billion that it had already pledged. This plan was open to individuals who obtained a mortgage before January 1, 2009, and borrowers could apply for loan modifications until the end of 2012.

Despite the extensive scope of the plans, it is important to note that the plan was not designed to help every homeowner in financial trouble. The plan also did not have any provision for a large percentage of homeowners: those whose income had evaporated because of unemployment and those swamped by debts beyond their mortgages. Similarly, there was no fix for the growing numbers of homeowners who were falling behind in their payments because they were either underemployed or because one income earner was unemployed. More importantly, the plan never did reconcile the fundamental problem of what was driving the wave of foreclosures. Was it that homeowners could not afford to pay, or was it that they were refusing to do so because of "negative equity" as their homes were now worth less than their mortgages? Not surprisingly, the waves of foreclosures continued unabated. In its review of residential mortgages in forty-three U.S. states and Washington, D.C, First American CoreLogic, the United States' largest provider of property and ownership information and residential mortgage risk management, reported that one in five U.S. homeowners with mortgages owed more than their properties were worth. About 8.31 million properties had negative equity at the end of 2008 – up 9 percent from 7.63 million at the end of September. The percentage of underwater borrowers rose to 20 percent from 18 percent, and the value of residential properties fell to $19.1 trillion at year-end from $21.5 trillion a year earlier, with half the decline in California. More ominous, the report noted that another 2.16 million properties could go underwater if home prices fell another 5 percent, and that the housing crisis would get worse as housing values dropped in states that had so far avoided the worst of the crisis.[9] Given the oversupply in housing inventory caused by overbuilding and foreclosures, a problem further compounded by stubbornly high unemployment and uncertainty in the labor market, the problem of delinquency could not be wished away (Immergluck 2009; Kiff and Klyuev 2009).

On March 5, 2009, the House passed a bill 234–191 (mostly along party lines), to give bankruptcy judges (who until then had the authority to modify car and student loans but not for primary residences) new powers of "cramdown" to reduce the interest rate and principal on a home mortgage. Bankruptcy would be the last option as homeowners could approach a bankruptcy court only after they failed to work out a fair arrangement with their lenders. It would be up to the court to decide whether the home loan company had made a reasonable offer to change the terms to allow the

---

[9] First American CoreLogic. 2009. *Negative Equity Report: December, 2008.* http://www. loanperformance.com/loanperformance_hpi.aspx. Similarly, according to the Mortgage Bankers Association, about one in every eight U.S. households ended 2008 behind on their mortgage payments or were in the foreclosure process.

homeowner to reduce monthly payments to one-third of household income, including protecting loan-servicing companies from lawsuits by investors. Backers of the bill argued that the "carrot and stick" approach would prod banks to negotiate with homeowners for more affordable terms. The "stick," or the threat of a mortgage modification in bankruptcy court, and the "carrot" of financial incentives to the mortgage-servicing companies overseeing two-thirds of all home loans in the country, including Citigroup, J.P. Morgan Chase, Bank of America, and Wells Fargo would make them eager to participate. On the other hand, critics pointed out, the measure would only create a flood of new bankruptcy filings which ultimately would drive up mortgage rates for everyone and further destabilize an already-battered housing market as lenders raised interest rates in anticipation of losses they could suffer in bankruptcy court. Moreover, markets knew that any plan that forces mortgage holders to reduce the amount of money they are owed could potentially also reduce the value of mortgage-backed securities held by banks, Fannie and Freddie, the Fed, and other financial institutions. Over the long term, a judicial cramdown could also negatively impact potential borrowers as it would weaken the balance sheets of potential lenders forcing banks to limit their overall mortgage lending – which has the potential to hurt homebuyers over the long term.

The President's Budget in Perspective

In February 2009 the commerce department released figures that showed that the United States' GDP (the nation's output of goods and services), had plunged at an annual rate of 6.2 percent in the final quarter of 2008. This was the sharpest drop in GDP since the first quarter of 1982. On February 25, 2009, President Obama, in his first address to a joint session of Congress, pledged to cut the federal budget deficit in half by 2013 to boost the sagging economy. Most viewed this to be overly optimistic, especially since the president's budget for the 2010 fiscal year (that begins in October 2009) totaled an unprecedented $3.6 trillion. The CBO projected that the deficit for 2009 would be a record $1.75 trillion when the fiscal year ended September 30, or 12.3 percent of the overall economy – the highest since 1945. The fiscal deficit in 2010 was projected to be around $1.2 trillion, and this forecast did not include the president's massive stimulus package or potential spending increases in further bailouts for troubled financial institutions. Although at the time few disputed the need for deficit spending to stimulate a stagnant economy, there was nevertheless palpable concern that such large deficits may become the norm. In retrospect they have.

The president's projected budget improvement by 2013 was premised on economic recovery beginning in 2010. Specifically, the administration predicted that the overall economy (as measured by GDP) would shrink by 1.2 percent in 2009 but grow by 3.2 percent in 2010, 4 percent in 2011, 4.6 percent in 2012, and 4.2 percent in 2013. The administration claimed that such sustained growth would mean more tax revenues and lower deficits in coming years. As a result, the administration forecasted that the deficit would decline to $1.17 trillion in 2010, $912 billion in 2011, $581 billion in 2012, and $533 billion in 2013. Yet again, the administration's was unduly optimistic in its assessments. It conveniently overlooked the lesson of history which shows that, given the depth of the 2007–09 recession, the rebound may be more U-shaped than V-shaped – meaning that the downturn could last much longer than expected and the recovery more slow and modest.[10]

To its credit, the Obama administration recognized that reducing the deficit was imperative. Without a reduction in deficit, foreign lenders (China and oil-rich Arab states) who had long financed U.S. deficits and were paying for the bulk of the stimulus and bailouts, might choose to stop, especially if repayment came in the form of depreciating dollars. Indeed, without constraining the United States' debt-fueled spending, economic recovery would be exceedingly difficult. However, in order to meet the president's ambitious deficit-reduction goals, at a minimum, the administration would have to do some deep spending cuts or raise taxes by at least $800 billion a year. Much of the deficit reduction was set to come from reduced spending on the wars in Iraq and Afghanistan and higher taxes on "wealthy individuals." That is, because the president promised that 98 percent of families (couples earning less than $250,000 per year and individuals earning less than $200,000 per year), would not be taxed, meant that the remaining 2 percent of "richest Americans" would see their marginal rates go up to 39.6 percent with and their tax deductions capped at 28 percent. On the other hand, the new and expanded refundable tax credits would increase

[10] On one hand, the Obama administration needs to be congratulated for getting rid of the tricks past administrations have used to hide the real costs of government programs and proposed tax cuts (for example, by bringing spending into the budget that was previously in supplemental appropriations, including the funding for the wars in Iraq and Afghanistan). On the other, the administration has also resorted to one of the oldest gimmicks governments use in "cooking budgets" – relying on overly optimistic economic assumptions in order to artificially shrink predictions of future budget deficits. This tactic was used most ostensibly during the Reagan years (hence the joke during the Reagan years that the highest-ranking woman in the administration was Rosy Scenario) and is full of grave risks.

the percentage of taxpayers who paid no income taxes to almost 50 percent from 38 percent.[11] To the markets this was a nonstarter. The problem with the plan was that if the burden of taxation fell on only 2 percent of the "rich," it would not produce enough funds to cover government spending, and it would set a bad precedent as it would create a "free-rider" class with no stake in controlling the cost of government. It would be business as usual as 98 percent of the population would enjoy no taxes or tax cuts, including health care, access to twenty-first-century education, and the green light to continue shopping until they dropped. Not surprisingly, the markets correctly concluded that it would be impossible for the administration to actually make any real dent in the deficit, let alone reduce it from $1.75 trillion to less than a third by 2013 as projected. It seemed that, without a sense of common purpose and shared sacrifice – which fundamentally meant exploding the myth that the American people can have everything they want, but do not first have to pay for it – the president's budget turned out to be simply more of the same.

However, in all fairness, it is important to recognize that the president adopted the budget he did because of his firm belief that his budget with its emphasis on tax cuts and generous spending on education, health care, and related social programs would directly benefit middle-class and low-income Americans who had been excluded from the nation's rising prosperity prior to the financial crisis.[12] The Obama administration explicitly pointed out that its goal was to reverse the trend that began during the Reagan years, which saw lower- and middle-class incomes stagnate, while the incomes of the wealthiest skyrocketed due to the tax-cutting mantra of that era. The tax cuts enacted under George W. Bush only accelerated the trend as they disproportionately benefited the wealthy. In 1980, the richest 1 percent of Americans claimed 10 percent of all national income. In 2004, they claimed 22 percent, even as the incomes at lower and medium levels stagnated.

Despite the Obama administration's noble intentions, few were convinced that social engineering was the most prudent way to correct these

---

[11] The fear is that increasing the top tax rates on earnings to 39.6 percent and on capital gains and dividends to 20 percent will reduce incentives for the most productive citizens and small businesses.

[12] To help defray the rising cost of higher education the budget proposed to expand and stabilize funding for two signature programs for lower-income students: Pell grants and Perkins loans. The president hoped to expand the Perkins loans to include 2.7 million more students. Moreover, more of the loans will be targeted toward colleges that offer more need-based financial aid – which serves low-income students. The budget would also make permanent the $2,500 American Opportunity Tax Credit passed earlier in the economic stimulus bill to help families pay for college.

inequalities. Even if the Republican claim that Obama's budget was tantamount to "class warfare" and that higher taxes on the affluent would only dampen their entrepreneurial energy seemed like a good political soundbite, there are more fundamental structural forces at work that explain the growing income divide – forces that may not be amenable to a government-led fix. Specifically, during the post-war economic boom (1945–80) income inequalities in the United States eased and standards of living sharply improved for the average person because of the availability of secure, well-paying jobs in heavy industry, manufacturing, and related sectors of the economy. Powerful unions were able to negotiate relatively good contracts for their members, including the relatively unskilled workers, who earned much more than their counterparts in earlier times. However, in the 1980s, as manufacturing and heavy industry gave way to an increasingly globalized economy based on services and technology, workers found few opportunities in these new sectors as they required better educated and skilled workers. The loss of traditional manufacturing jobs has translated into lower and more unequal incomes. Unless these structural problems are addressed, government action will have limited lasting impact and can even make the situation much worse.

More Fixes for an Unresponsive Economy

The week of March 16, 2009 was marked with righteous indignation on Capitol Hill as politicians channeled their calibrated outrage over the $165 million in bonuses handed out by AIG. During his congressional testimony, Edward Liddy, the embattled CEO of AIG, stated that he had asked employees to give half of their bonuses back and that some had already voluntarily given all back. However, it soon became public that Senator Chris Dodd and Treasury Secretary Geithner had both signed off on the contractually promised bonuses after concluding that the government had no legal recourse to prevent them from being paid. Even as House Republican leader John Boehner noted that it was "nothing more than an attempt for everybody to cover their butt up here on Capitol Hill," the House overwhelmingly passed a measure to tax, at a rate of 90 percent, not just the AIG bonuses in dispute, but the bulk of bonuses paid since the start of the year to all employees making more than $250,000 a year at firms receiving more than $5 billion of the TARP funds. The Senate also announced its own "clawback bill," designed to tax at a rate of 70 percent performance bonuses starting at $50,000 and on all retention bonuses given by companies that received $100 million or more in TARP funds. However, the scandal only underscored the administration's own growing credibility crisis. As the anti-bonus bills would apply to virtually every major bank – including Citigroup, Bank of America, Wells Fargo, Goldman Sachs, Morgan Stanley, and J.P. Morgan Chase, as well as AIG, Fannie Mae and Freddie Mac, it only spooked the already nervous markets.

Preoccupation, if not obsession, with the bonuses overshadowed an important policy issue. On March 19, 2009, the Federal Reserve, in its efforts to bolster the faltering economy, announced its plan to purchase $1 trillion in long-term treasury bonds and mortgage securities. This marked a sharp departure from its normal policy of buying only short-term debt and blurred the line between fiscal and monetary policy. Arguably, having already reduced the key interest rate it controlled to almost zero, the central bank felt that it had little choice but to buy securities to pump more dollars into the economy. Although investors responded favorably (the Dow Jones industrial average, which had been down about 50 points just before the announcement, jumped immediately and ended the day up almost 91 points at 7,486.58), the policy was not without risks. Specifically, the concern was that the Fed's action could weaken the value of the dollar and set the stage for future inflation. Indeed, gold prices rose by another $26.60 an ounce (to $942) – a sign of declining confidence in the dollar. Predictably, the dollar, which had been losing value in recent weeks to the euro and the yen, dropped sharply against other major currencies almost immediately (the dollar fell about 5 percent against the euro). More broadly, not everyone shared the view that the central bank could solve the economy's problems by simply pumping in cheap money. For example, even if the Fed made interest rates negative, there was no guarantee that it would help because the private sector, especially in recessionary times, tends to save more. In such situations, piling more money on top of money that is already available usually tends to exacerbate problems. On the other hand, as the Fed had failed to get lenders to lend and borrowers to borrow, its seemingly desperate action was seen as an attempt to bypass the private banking system and act as a lender in its own right.

As noted, a perennial problem regarding the government's plan to buy bank assets through an asset auction was that the taxpayer could end up overpaying for the assets because no one really knew the true value of the assets. On March 23, 2009, the Obama administration (via the treasury secretary) unveiled yet another plan to end the paralysis surrounding bank assets and lack of lending. At its core, the new Public-Private Investment Program envisioned the government teaming with private investors to initially buy up to half a trillion dollars of bad bank assets (what the government termed "legacy assets") and ease credit for consumers and businesses.

Less charitably, at the core of Geithner's plan was the use of taxpayer dollars to encourage private investors such as hedge funds, pension plans, and financial institutions to buy bank assets in order to use private competition to determine the worth of these assets. Altogether, Geithner's expectation was that the cost of these purchases could grow to more than $1 trillion.

To get the plan up and running the administration announced that the government planned to use $75 billion to $100 billion (from the existing $700 billion TARP funds), including funds supported by loans from the FDIC and a loan facility (the Term Asset-Backed Securities Loan Facility, or TALF), a joint treasury and Federal Reserve program. While the treasury would help finance a series of public-private investment funds to buy up unwanted mortgage-backed securities, the FDIC would set up an auction for each bank portfolio, thereby allowing a bank to sell the mortgages to the investor who offered the highest bid. For the investor the real incentive was that the government would lend as much as 85 percent of the purchase price for each portfolio of mortgages. In addition, the treasury would invest one dollar of taxpayer money for every dollar of private equity capital to cover the remaining 15 percent of the portfolio's purchase price. Thus, under a typical transaction, for every $100 in soured mortgages being purchased from banks, the private sector (including pension funds, insurance companies, and hedge funds) would put up $7, and that would be matched by $7 from the government. The remaining $86 would be covered by a government loan provided mostly by the FDIC.[13] No doubt, the treasury secretary was offering private investors very generous terms. For example, on the one hand, if the asset rose in value over time, both the treasury and the private investors would share the profits equally. On the other, if the assets lost value, their losses would be modest: if the price dropped below $100, their losses would be limited to the $7 they put in. In other words, the downside loss to private investors was greatly limited by the equity they put in, while the upside gain could far exceed their initial equity. Another significant incentive for private investors was the government's willingness to provide "nonrecourse" loans to institutions that purchased the unwanted assets. A nonrecourse loan is secured only by the underlying property

---

[13] The Treasury Department offered the following example to illustrate how the program would work. A pool of bad residential mortgage loans with a face value of, say, $100 is auctioned by the FDIC. Private investors submit their bids. In the example, the top bidder, a private investor offering $84, wins and purchases the pool. The FDIC guarantees loans for $72 of that purchase price. The Treasury then invests in half the $12 equity, with funds coming from the $700 billion bailout program; the private investor contributes the remaining $6.

such as a home or building. Thus, if the borrower defaults, the government would only be able to seize the real estate. If the mortgages or the securities generated bigger losses than expected, the government and not the private investors would have to absorb the brunt of those losses.[14]

Although Geithner acknowledged that "the government is taking a big risk," he also noted that the alternative was to do nothing and risk a more prolonged recession or have the government burdened with all of the risk. Of course, Geithner's plan was hardly novel. Former treasury secretary Paulson had come up with a similar "solution." Like Paulson's, Geithner's plan failed to provide clear rules regarding how to price assets or confirm if there were sufficient government resources. In light of the all-out Wall Street-bashing that went on in the White House and the Congress, many private investors expressed reluctance to participate in the program for fear that Congress would subject them to more punitive restrictions. Others correctly pointed out that Geithner's "cash for trash" plan was deeply flawed because it assumed that the banks were fundamentally sound and that the toxic assets on banks' books were worth much more than the jittery markets were willing to pay for them.

On March 26, 2009, Geithner finally unveiled the long-awaited details of the administration's proposals to strengthen the financial system. For starters, since the plan would give the administration a broad "resolution authority" to allow orderly dissolution of insolvent firms whose failure would threaten the stability of the financial system, including vast new powers over "systemically important" banks and other financial institutions, it would require Congressional approval. Geithner's plan centered on mitigating "systemic risk" (the potential for one or a few large and closely intertwined institutions to seriously undermine the U.S. economy as they failed), and it also

---

[14] Stiglitz (2009) notes that although the Obama administration's plan "has been described by some in the financial markets as a win-win-win proposal, actually, it is a win-win-lose proposal: the banks win, investors win – and taxpayers lose." (p. A31) This is because

In theory, the administration's plan is based on letting the market determine the prices of the banks' "toxic assets" – including outstanding house loans and securities based on those loans. The reality, though, is that the market will not be pricing the toxic assets themselves, but options on those assets. The two have little to do with each other. The government plan in effect involves insuring almost all losses. Since the private investors are spared most losses, then they primarily "value" their potential gains. This is exactly the same as being given an option.... What the Obama administration is doing is far worse than nationalization: it is ersatz capitalism, the privatizing of gains and the socializing of losses. It is a "partnership" in which one partner robs the other. And such partnerships – with the private sector in control – have perverse incentives, worse even than the ones that got us into the mess. (p. A31)

offered strict new government supervision of hedge funds and traders of exotic financial instruments, in particular, credit-default swaps and other types of derivatives. Specifically, hedge funds, private equity funds, and venture capital funds (which operate largely outside the regulation of either the Securities and Exchange Commission or the Federal Reserve), would have to register with the SEC and provide information (on a confidential basis), on how much they borrowed to leverage their investments, including information about their investors and trading partners. The plan would also give the government the power to take over major nonbank financial firms such as insurers and hedge funds if their failure threatened the entire system.

In April 2009 the U.S. economy sent mixed messages: the stock market seemed to be rebounding and the banks announced (surprisingly) high earnings. For example, Wells Fargo announced its best quarterly earnings ever, and Goldman Sachs announced a healthy increase in profits from fourth-quarter 2008 to first-quarter 2009. Ben Bernanke suggested that "green shoots" were finally appearing, while Obama saw "glimmers of hope" that the economy was finally recovering. On the other hand, U.S. industrial production hit a ten-year low, housing starts remained extremely weak, losses in commercial real estate continued to surge, and unemployment kept rising. Given the contradictory picture, most analysts concluded that the lull was misleading – in large part because foreclosures (which dropped as mortgage companies waited for details of the administration's housing plans), began to surge again. Similarly, the glowing bank profits were seen to be problematic because, among other things, Goldman had changed its definition of "quarter" by removing the month of December, which happened to be a bad one for the bank, and Wells Fargo had engaged in dubious accounting practices to boost its reported earnings. Therefore, as April 2009 came to an end, it was far from certain that the worst was over.

On May 7, 2009, the treasury (with the FDIC, the Office of the Comptroller of the Currency, and the Federal Reserve) announced the results of their long-awaited "stress test" or review of the capital position of the country's nineteen largest banks. The tests were conducted to allay concerns about the financial health of the banks and the damage this was causing to confidence and economic activity, and to provide markets with greater transparency and accountability. These somewhat punitive tests were designed to assess the strength of the banks, in particular, to estimate their potential future losses as well as their ability to lend even if the recession worsened. Through careful review of the banks' loan data, potential earnings with existing reserves and capital which were then evaluated against strict minimum capital standards in terms of both overall capital and tangible common equity, the authorities concluded that ten of the nineteen banks would need a total of about $75 billion in new capital to withstand losses if the recession worsened. These banks and the amounts they would need included: Bank of America Corp., $33.9 billion; Wells Fargo, $13.7 billion; GMAC LLC, $11.5 billion; Citigroup Inc., $5.5 billion; and Morgan Stanley, $1.8 billion. The other five requiring capital were regional banks: Regions Financial Corporation of Birmingham, Ala., would need to raise $2.5 billion; SunTrust Banks Inc. of Atlanta, $2.2 billion; KeyCorp of Cleveland, $1.8 billion; Fifth Third Bancorp of Cincinnati, $1.1 billion; and PNC Financial Services Group Inc. of Pittsburgh, $600 million. These banks were given until June 8, 2009 to develop a plan to raise capital and have it approved by regulators.

Again, this failed to generate confidence as there was gnawing suspicion that the resulting smaller capital deficits were a result of the Federal Reserve using a much looser measurement of bank-capital levels than the market was expecting. It seems that in its attempt to maintain a balance between trying to restore confidence and maintaining credibility, the former won. As Krugman (2009a) noted:

I won't weigh in on the debate over the quality of the stress tests themselves, except to repeat what many observers have noted: the regulators didn't have the resources to make a really careful assessment of the banks' assets, and in any case they allowed the banks to bargain over what the results would say. A rigorous audit it wasn't.... What we're really seeing here is a decision on the part of President Obama and his officials to muddle through the financial crisis, hoping that the banks can earn their way back to health.

Similarly, not everyone was convinced that the banks had the where-withal to cover anticipated losses because the revenue-growth projections were simply too optimistic. Finally, there was genuine concern that if unemployment continued to rise and house prices continued to drop, it would make it harder for consumers and businesses to repay loans. This in turn, would cause banks' assets to lose more value. Beyond this, there was justified cynicism that Washington had no stomach to take on Wall Street as many politicians (both Democrats and Republicans) have strong ties to Wall Street, in particular, big banks, who are their biggest campaign contributors.

On June 17, 2009 President Obama unveiled what he described as "a sweeping overhaul of the financial regulatory system, a transformation on a scale not seen since the reforms that followed the Great Depression" (CRS 2009h). The eighty-eight-page white paper proposed major regulatory reforms of the financial sector by giving new powers to the Federal Reserve to protect consumers of financial products via the creation of the Consumer Financial Protection Agency (CFPA), and to make derivatives trading more transparent. In addition, it proposed giving government the power to take over large bank holding companies or troubled investment banks, including requiring large banks to hold more capital and liquidity than smaller firms, such as some of the mortgage-backed securities they create and sell to investors. By giving the Federal Reserve the power to regulate any large financial institution it deemed "systemically important," including the authority to seize such institutions if they appeared insolvent (the FDIC already has this authority with traditional banks), marked an important step toward regulating free-wheeling institutions such as AIG and Lehman. However, surprisingly, the Obama plan again failed to establish clear rules regarding the "too big to fail" or "Tier 1 Financial Holding Companies." The proposal to regulate these companies more "robustly" remained so vague that it led the *Economist* to dub it "less audacity and more timidity."[15] Similarly, few were convinced how the proposed CFPA would deter predatory lending if the lenders were required to hold just 5 percent of their loans, instead of selling everything off. After all, the profit margin by selling everything off would be so great that holding such a nominal amount would hardly prevent irresponsible lending. Equally troubling, the proposal did little to rein in the incestuous rating agencies that so blatantly approved dubious securities because they were on the take. In any case, the plan did not terribly upset the markets as it required approval in Congress. This meant that the final product would be more watered down than Obama's "ambitious" document.

On August 25, 2009, the White House budget office and the CBO (a non-partisan arm of Congress), released its economic forecasts and deficit estimates. Although the deficit estimate for the 2009 fiscal year (which ends September 30), declined to $1.58 trillion from $1.84 trillion (as the billions of dollars originally set aside for bank rescues were not used), the ten-year budget-deficit projection jumped by about $2 trillion from $7.1 trillion, as forecasted by the Obama administration. In other words, the budget projections showed a cumulative deficit of some $9 trillion over the next decade. Yet, despite the gloomy news, end-August also suggested that finally the worst may be over. This optimism stemmed from the hope that the world economy had finally stopped shrinking, and led by China and India, the Asian economies were rebounding with several notching positive growth.

---

[15] *The Economist*. 2009. "Financial Reform in America: New Foundation, Walls Intact," June 18. http://www.economist.com/businessfinance/displaystory.cfm?story_id=13856191

The biggest surprise was Japan, which saw its output rise at an annualized rate of 3.7 percent. In Europe, both Germany and France saw 1 percent growth rates, while in the United States, the economy showed signs of recovery with a steady rise in home sales and decline in job losses. Not surprisingly, this resulted in much discussion about what shape the recovery (if it was real) would take – "V," "U," or "W." A V-shaped recovery would be the fastest as it unleashes pent-up demand. A U-shaped one would mean a slower, more gradual recovery, and a W-shape would mean a short period of growth (say over one or two quarters) that would quickly fall back to the negative. Suffice it to note that analysts remained divided over the prospects. If the optimists felt that the massive scale of the economic downturn augured for a strong and sustained rebound, the pessimists feared the double dip of a W. This, they argued quite correctly, was because unlike earlier post-war recessions rooted in high interest rates, high levels of indebtedness, and weak balance sheets, the current collapse was due to the implosion of the financial sector with broad negative ramifications – similar to how Japan's banking crisis in the 1990s left that economy stagnant for over a decade. To the pessimists, the current rebound was temporary, the result of massive stimulus spending and all manner of government subsidies such as the "cash for clunkers" scheme.

Toward Dodd-Frank

By mid-2010, although the U.S. economy seemed to have stabilized, it still faced significant hurdles. The housing market remained extremely fragile with foreclosure rates still very high and palpable fears that it would get worse once the temporary homebuyers' tax credit ended and unemployment rates remained high or rose. Reflecting the general pessimism, consumer spending remained depressed with households desperately trying to pay down debt and save for an uncertain future. Nevertheless, on July 21, 2010, President Obama could finally say with some justification that his administration had passed the most comprehensive set of financial reform measures since Glass-Steagall by signing into law the 2,300-page Dodd-Frank Wall Street Reform and Consumer Protection Act of 2010.[16] The Dodd-Frank Act (DFA) attempts to reverse the deregulatory trend of the previous

---

[16] The law, better known as the "Dodd-Frank Act," was named after the two legislators (Senator Chris Dodd and Congressman Barney Frank) who were instrumental in creating it. It was first introduced by Dodd on March 15, 2010 and passed by the Senate on May 20. The bill was revised by Frank and approved by the House on June 30.

decades via wide-ranging measures that include: (1) better regulation of credit cards, loans, and mortgages via an empowered Consumer Financial Protection Agency (CFPA) – with the responsibility to regulate credit, debit, mortgage underwriting, and bank fees; (2) the Financial Stability Oversight Council to monitor the entire financial industry with an eye on preventing the problem of too-big-too-fail; (3) the "Volcker Rule" designed to bar commercial banks from engaging in proprietary trading (or investments that banks make on their own behalf, rather than their clients); (4) regulation of derivatives, like credit-default swaps and hedge funds by the SEC or the Commodity Futures Trading Commission (CFTC); (5) the creation of the Office of Credit Rating at the SEC to regulate credit-ratings agencies like Moody's and Standard & Poor's; (6) the creation of a new Federal Insurance Office under the Treasury Department to supervise insurance companies like AIG; (7) reform of the Federal Reserve by allowing the Government Accountability Office (GAO) to audit the Fed's emergency loans during the financial crisis and prohibiting the Fed from making emergency loan to a single entity such as AIG without the approval of the Treasury Department; and (8) giving the Federal Reserve authority over all systemic institutions and the responsibility to safeguard financial stability.

No doubt, on paper at least, the DFA is comprehensive, and if effectively implemented can go a long way in correcting some of the most egregious abuses, including the dangerous risk-trading and moral hazard problems in the financial sector.[17] There is broad agreement that Dodd-Frank's s new emphasis on macroprudential regulation (away from purely microprudential regulation) is an important step. This is because the crisis of 2008 vividly showed that a micro focus ignores the interconnections and externalities (namely, spillover effects) that can generate system-wide risk within the financial sector. Nevertheless, the DFA suffers from a number of fatal flaws. Specifically, the idea of breaking up large banks has become highly unlikely as the Volcker Rule, intended to restore Glass-Steagall, has been considerably watered down. This is a huge missed opportunity as one of the key lessons of the crisis was the dangers inherent in allowing very large banks to operate in highly leveraged form with huge debts and very little equity. As Johnson and Kwak (2010) have compellingly pointed out, the status-quo is fundamentally unfair, not only because the implicit subsidies given to "too-big-to-fail" companies allow them to increase their CEO's compensation, it

---

[17] Because the implementation of Dodd-Frank requires the development of about 250 new regulatory rules and various mandated studies and the responsibility to research and evaluate best measures, implementation will take some time.

also imposes potentially huge costs on taxpayers (see also Wilmarth 2011). By preventing banks with government-guaranteed deposits from speculating with depositors' hard-earned money, the Volcker Rule arguably could have prevented J.P. Morgan Chase from its $2 billion loss in May 2012. The fact that J.P. Morgan Chase was using derivatives (among the most complex and opaque of financial instruments) to make bets on the safety of corporate debt (knowing full well that such bets on housing had brought AIG to its knees just a few years before), underscores the notion that Wall Street has not fully learned the lessons of the great crash of 2008.

Furthermore, although Dodd-Frank fails to address the government's role in fostering the crisis and how to mitigate this problem, it greatly overextends the reach of government in the financial sector. As Acharya and his co-authors (2010, 8) note, with "over 225 new financial rules across 11 federal agencies... the attempt at regulatory consolidation has been minimal and the very regulators who dropped the ball in the current crisis have garnered more, not less, authority." Furthermore, "the Act does not deal with the mispricing of pervasive government guarantees throughout the financial sector." Arguably, this omission was not an oversight. The findings of the Financial Crisis Inquiry Commission (FCIC), the only body authorized by Congress to investigate "the causes, domestic and global, of the current financial and economic crisis in the USA" were ignored. On January 27, 2011, the FCIC's ten-member bipartisan panel (six appointed by the Democrats and four by the Republicans), delivered a 662-page report based on some one year and a half of investigation during which more than 700 witnesses were interviewed in public hearings (FCIC 2011). Although the final report was not unanimous, with the Republican members adding a "minority report," it provided a mostly balanced review of both the role of the market and government in creating the financial crisis. However, as one of the dissenting members of the FCIC, Peter Wallison, notes:

The question I have been most frequently asked about the Financial Crisis Inquiry Commission ... is why Congress bothered to authorize it at all. Without waiting for the Commission's insights into the causes of the financial crisis, Congress passed and the President signed the Dodd-Frank Act (DFA), far reaching and highly consequential regulatory legislation. Congress and the President acted without seeking to understand the true causes of the wrenching events of 2008. (FCIC 2011, 443)

Not surprisingly, the part of the report written by the Democratic majority makes some astonishing claims – that Fannie Mae and Freddie Mac's portfolio of subprime loans "performed significantly better" than those packaged into mortgage-backed securities by private issuers. This goes against the overwhelming evidence that holds these two government-sponsored enterprises as the driving force behind the growth in subprime home lending and the eventual financial crisis. Similarly, rather than holding the 1977 Community Reinvestment Act as mainly responsible for forcing banks into making risky loans, the majority report inexplicably faults banks for failing to lend to lower-income households as the problem. The failure by the majority to take into account the government's role in the crisis and its regulatory mistakes may come back and haunt the DFA. Indeed, financial interests have already brought court cases against key provisions of Dodd-Frank, and it is not clear how effectively the DFA will be implemented (Sorkin 2011).

By mid-2012, the combination of massive fiscal stimulus packages, bailouts, and reduced tax revenues due to the sharp contraction in economic activity had severely worsened debt-to-GDP levels. The budget deficit reached a staggering 10 percent of GDP, and the unprecedented levels of government borrowing and accumulation of debt (the U.S. debt is already more than $16 trillion with $1.5 trillion in annual government deficits) raised fears about the United States' bondholders demanding a serious deficit-reduction plan and a potential sovereign debt default. Most disappointing, despite massive spending, the economy continued to experience a fragile and slow recovery, with home values still depressed and unemployment stubbornly high. For the more than 20 million unemployed Americans (only 15 million of whom are labeled "officially unemployed," government policies and programs have failed to end what must seem like a perpetual depression.

THREE

From the U.S. to the European Crisis

In early September 2008, as the subprime-induced financial contagion began to rapidly spread throughout the U.S. financial system, Europeans were confident that their economy would remain immune. German finance minister Peer Steinbruck scornfully dismissed the financial crisis as an "American problem" – the result of Anglo-American greed and inept regulation that may very well cost the United States its "superpower status." Similar sentiments were echoed in other European capitals (Nicoll 2008). Italy's prime minister, Silvio Berlusconi, blamed the spreading crisis on the "speculative capitalism" of the United States, Gordon Brown, the British prime minister, noted that the crisis "has come from America," French leaders flatly blamed the "*le capitalisme sauvage*" of the Anglo-Americans – excoriating their worship of the markets and lack of business ethics and moral discipline – and the Kremlin saw the crisis as a Western problem that would leave Russia unscathed (Evans-Pritchard 2008). Indeed, in June 2008, Russian president Dimitri Medvedev unabashedly predicted that the Russian ruble would be the future reserve currency of Eurasia (Trenin 2009).

It is hardly surprising, then, that on September 19, 2008, when the Bush administration finally cobbled together an unprecedented $700 billion "rescue plan" to help distressed financial companies, the Europeans condescendingly rebuffed Treasury Secretary Hank Paulson's pleas for a collaborative U.S.-European rescue effort. However, Europe's immunity was short-lived. The Europeans' sense of hubris and complacency was abruptly shattered as the Continent began to scramble to prevent a fast-moving contagion from bringing down major banks, wrecking financial markets, and negatively impacting national economies (Table 3.1).

Although the problems associated with housing bubbles had become noticeable in the United Kingdom and in a number of eurozone countries almost immediately with the outbreak of the subprime-mortgage

Table 3.1. *Advanced economies: current account positions*
(% of GDP)

	2007	2008	2009	2010
Advanced Economies	−1.0	−1.1	−1.0	−1.0
Euro Area*	0.2	−0.7	−1.1	−1.2
Germany	7.5	6.4	2.3	2.4
France	−1.0	−1.6	−0.4	−0.9
Italy	−2.4	−3.2	−3.0	−3.1
Spain	−10.1	−9.6	−5.4	−4.4
Netherlands	6.1	4.4	2.4	2.1
Belgium	1.7	−2.5	−2.4	−3.0
Greece	−14.1	−14.4	−13.5	−12.6
Austria	3.2	2.9	1.3	1.3
Portugal	−9.5	−12.0	−9.1	−8.8
Finland	4.1	2.5	1.0	0.6
Ireland	−5.4	−4.5	−2.7	−1.8
Slovak Republic	−5.4	−6.3	−5.7	−5.0
Slovenia	−4.2	−5.9	−4.0	−5.0
Luxembourg	9.8	9.1	7.6	7.0
Cyprus	−11.6	−18.3	−10.3	−10.1
Malta	−6.1	−6.3	−5.1	−5.2
United Kingdom	−2.9	−1.7	−2.0	−1.5
Sweden	8.6	8.3	6.9	7.4
Switzerland	10.1	9.1	7.6	8.1
Czech Republic	−3.2	−3.1	−2.7	−3.0
Norway	15.9	18.4	11.0	12.6
Denmark	0.7	0.5	−1.2	−1.1
Iceland	−15.4	−34.7	0.6	−2.1
United States	−5.3	−4.7	−2.8	−2.8

*Calculated as the sum of the balances of individual euro area countries.
Source: IMF. 2009. *World Economic Outlook: Crisis and Recovery April*, World Economic and Financial Surveys, Washington, D.C.: IMF. p. 74.

crisis in the United States in September 2007, the full onslaught didn't begin until September 29, 2008, when Icelandic authorities were forced to partly nationalize Glitnir, one of the country's biggest banks. On October 3, 2008, Steinbruck was forced to orchestrate Germany's largest bank bailout with a massive €35 billion ($62 billion) loan package to save commercial-property lender Hypo Real Estate. Visibly shaken, German Chancellor Angela Merkel and her finance minister, in their efforts to reassure depositors and calm a nervous public, appeared before news cameras to promise that all bank deposits would be protected. The following day, Belgium was forced to nationalize Fortis, a large banking and insurance company based in Brussels with businesses across much of the Continent, with help from the Netherlands and Luxembourg, followed a day later by a bailout for another company, Dexia, with help from the French government. A few days later, the Irish government issued a blanket guarantee of the deposits and debts, including all liabilities of its six largest lenders – reminiscent of the Scandinavian bank rescues in the early 1990s. This was followed by the Greek government publicly announcing that it too would guarantee bank deposits. On October 6, the Danish government announced its decision to guarantee bank deposits. Similarly, the United Kingdom, which thought that the worst was over with the nationalization of Northern Rock, one of the country's largest mortgage lenders in terms of gross lending, in February 2008, the hastily announced merger of Halifax Bank of Scotland (HBOS) with U.K. bank Lloyds TSB on September 17, 2008 came as a rude shock. However, it was the September 29 nationalization of Bradford and Bingley, including the fire sale of the bank's deposits and branch network to the Spanish bank Grupo Santander, as well as the government's bailout of the Royal Bank of Scotland (RBS), HBOS, and Lloyds TSB at a cost of £37 billion ($64 billion/€47 billion) that unambiguously demonstrated that Europe was not only not immune, but caught in the vortex of an unprecedented financial maelstrom.

Like in the United States, neither the individual European governments' bailouts nor the European Central Bank's (ECB) efforts to support the EU's banking sector via the purchase of sovereign debt and provision of dollar funding by using a swap line with the U.S. Federal Reserve helped to calm the markets (Fleming and Klagge 2010). Despite receiving €11.2 billion in bailout, Fortis was unable to continue operations. Just a week after the initial bailout, it folded, forcing the Dutch government to seize its operations in the Netherlands. A few days later, the Belgian authorities pushed the French bank BNP-Paribas to take over what was left of Fortis. In early October, during the hastily arranged European Summit meeting, French President Nicolas Sarkozy and his counterparts from Germany, Britain, and Italy vowed to prevent a Lehman-like bankruptcy in Europe. To show resolve, they adopted a concerted "action plan" with the stated aim of restoring confidence in the markets and the quick resumption of the financial system. On October 13, 2008, leaders of the seventeen eurozone countries pledged to end their much criticized "country-by-country" strategies by announcing a common strategy to revive the crippled credit markets and calm jittery investors. Taking to heart Sarkozy's claim that "none of our countries acting alone can end this crisis," the European leaders pledged to guarantee, until the end of 2009, bank debt issues with maturities up to five years and to keep distressed lenders afloat. Furthermore, eurozone governments agreed to buy stock in cash-strapped companies, issue qualifying capital to financial institutions through preferred shares and other instruments, provide resources to stabilize long-term maturities, and instruct the ECB to create a facility for accepting commercial paper from financial institutions and other companies as collateral for funding. Yet, like earlier efforts, these too failed to placate the markets. Despite the massive bailout packages for Greece, Ireland, and Portugal, and the EU's unprecedented €750 billion war chest, the eurozone's sovereign-debt crisis continued to spiral out of control.

What explains why Europe proved so vulnerable to the contagion? What explains why and how so many advanced European economies have become burdened with such manifestly unsustainable debts? How and why did the crisis morph into a wider eurozone crisis? Why have the so-called peripheral eurozone countries (also referred to uncharitably as the PIIGS – Portugal, Ireland, Italy, Greece, and Spain), in particular, Greece, Ireland, Portugal, and non-eurozone countries like Iceland been so severely impacted? Why have the various policy responses (by both the EU and national governments) acting as provider of liquidity and lender of last resort not proven to be very effective? And, is there a way out of this seemingly unending crisis? This chapter addresses these related questions.

Globalization and Europe's Vulnerabilities

The ferociously fast-moving contagion vividly underscores the notion that in this age of globalization no country is an island. Rather, in an inseparably intertwined and interdependent world, the more closely an economy is interlinked to and dependent on the global economic system, the more virulently it will feel the ripple effects, especially if the waves are emanating from the Titanic in the system – the U.S. economy. Europe is particularly vulnerable as its economies are very open in terms of trade, and its financial sector is closely integrated with the U.S. and, indeed, the world economy.

Furthermore, the European economy is profoundly different today than it was a few decades ago. Specifically, since the end of the Cold War, Europe has not only become very open in terms of trade but also unprecedented levels of economic and political convergence have taken place within Europe via deep and complex financial and trade linkages. For example, in the 1990s, few banks in Europe had cross-border operations on a significant scale. However, the use of the single currency and waves of mergers over the past few years have created giants like HSBC and Deutsche Bank, whose vast and complex web of operations and networks are closely linked throughout Europe and to the global financial markets. This means that a shock in one part of the European economy, in particular, within the euro-zone, send ripples throughout the European and the global economy.

Although most European banks were burdened with only a modest amount of U.S. subprime assets, they nevertheless owned a lot of bad assets and were more highly leveraged than U.S. banks.[1] According to the World Economic Forum, with the exception of the Canadian banking system (which is ranked number one or the soundest in the world), European banks were even less "sound" than U.S. banks, which are ranked 40; Germany and Britain are ranked 39 and 44 respectively.[2] The financial crisis bluntly exposed that like their U.S. counterparts, EU banks were burdened with prohibitively high levels of debt because they too had been issuing easy credit, including mortgage loans. As a result, several countries on the Continent were burdened with expanding household debt and a significant housing "bubble" problem due to real-estate speculation. For example, Great Britain's (and as will be discussed) Ireland's housing bubble was twice as large as the United States'.

When the contagion finally made its impact felt, and the banking sector became besieged (literally pushing many near insolvency), European governments (like their counterparts elsewhere) intervened and extended guarantees to their banking sector to prevent panic, bank runs, and a potential collapse of their financial sector. However, such large explicit and implicit bank guarantees and bailouts only "transferred" the problem to the governments' balance sheets, further exacerbating the problem of sovereign debt (see Table 3.2 and 3.3; Figure 3.1), and raising doubts about the solvency of governments. This explains why the combined debt of Greece, Ireland, and Portugal, although small relative to the size of the eurozone economy,

---

[1]	Gros and Micossi (2009, p. 30) point out that "the dozen largest European banks have now on average an overall leverage ratio (shareholder equity to total assets) of 35 compared to less than 20 for the largest US banks."

[2]	The average capital reserves for Canada's big six banks – defined as Tier 1 capital (common shares, retained earnings, and noncumulative preferred shares) to risk-adjusted assets – is 9.8 percent or several percentage points above the 7 percent required by Canada's federal bank regulator. The average capital ratio is about 4 percent for U.S. investment banks and 3.3 percent for European commercial banks. Moreover, Canada's investment banks are subject to the same strict rules as commercial banks, while in the U.S., investment banks were subject to light supervision from the Securities and Exchange Commission. Bordo et al. (2011), point out that that the Canadian banking system came out of the crisis relatively unscathed because it is subject to effective regulation. Nevertheless, the authors point out, "Greater stability may have come at a cost. A more concentrated and regulated financial system may have been slower to innovate, may have been slower to invest in emerging sectors, and may have provided services at monopoly prices" (p. 4)

Table 3.2. *Gross national debt in selected EU countries (2010 in U.S.$)*

Country	Debt	% of GDP
Germany	3 trillion	83.2
Italy	2.6 trillion	119.0
France	2.3 trillion	81.7
United Kingdom	1.9 trillion	80.0
Spain	908.4 billion	60.1
Greece	467.3 billion	142.8
Portugal	228.2 billion	93.0
Ireland	210.6 billion	96.2
Belgium	485.0 billion	96.8
Austria	291.8 billion	72.3
Netherlands	527.7 billion	62.7
Finland	124.0 billion	48.4
Poland	228.2 billion	93.0
Sweden	208.2 billion	39.8
Denmark	145.2 billion	43.6
Hungary	111.3 billion	80.2
Latvia	11.4 billion	44.7
Estonia	1.4 billion	6.6

Source: Compiled from Eurostat.com.

Table 3.3. *Government debt as a percentage of GDP*

	Spain	Ireland	Portugal	Greece
2005	34.71	15.92	57.95	84.07
2006	30.53	12.16	58.77	81.66
2007	26.52	12.18	58.1	80.35
2008	30.36	23.04	61.13	83.4
2009	43.73	36.41	72.08	96.83

Source: IMF *World Economic Outlook* (various years).

raised concerns about the overall health of Europe's banking sector, in particular, fears that the mounting private and sovereign debt could result in a systemic crisis, including sovereign default.

The Euro's Janus Face

Is the debt problem in the eurozone the result of the adoption of the euro? More specifically, would the peripheral countries been better off if

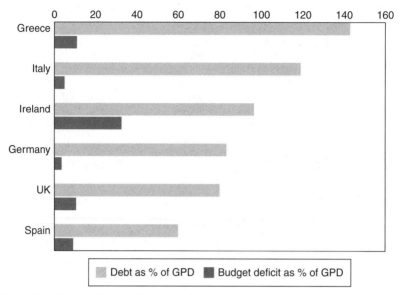

Figure 3.1. Country debts and budget deficits.
Source: Eurostat.

they did not use the euro? At best, the answer is ambiguous as the euro seems to be both a felicitous blessing and a hidden curse. On the positive, the monetary union ended the exchange-rate volatility that plagued the Continent since the collapse of the Bretton Woods system of fixed rates in the 1970s. Furthermore, the common currency eliminated cross-border transaction costs, facilitating European economic and political integration and increasing intra-continental trade. To the inflation-prone countries of Southern Europe, the euro provided much-needed price stability, a buffer against frequent currency crises, and a significant reduction in transaction costs for individuals and businesses, allowing them to finance their investments more cheaply (Pisani-Ferry and Posen 2009). These attributes explain why *euroization* is widespread – like the dollar, the euro is now used alongside or in place of national currencies in several countries outside the eurozone. Arguably, the fact that the United Kingdom and Iceland (both outside the eurozone) experienced credit booms and debt problems, similar to those that plague the PIIGS, show that the euro per se is not the problem. Rather, the problem is due to ineffective regulation and supervision of the financial sector. Eurozone banks, like British banks, engaged in extensive borrowing on the interbank market, fueling a housing bubble, and Icelandic banks imprudently borrowed billions of dollars and euros to finance a massive domestic consumption binge and purchase questionable foreign assets.

Nevertheless, the hope and belief that the euro would instill all-round fiscal discipline, fix long-standing structural weaknesses in the economies of weaker eurozone members, provide a sanctuary for the peripheral economies as they integrated, and heal the bitter estrangement that has long divided the Continent turned out to be no more than a illusion. In fact, the euro has unequivocally proved that it is no panacea for fiscal indiscipline as many eurozone countries have been plagued with similar ills such as running large current account and fiscal deficits, including high debt ratios and anemic growth. For example, before Greece, Ireland, or Portugal joined the eurozone they faced much higher interest rates than countries like Germany or the Netherlands, not to mention that Greece's public debt was more than 100 percent of GDP (EC 2008; 2009). Yet, in order to qualify for membership in the European Monetary Union (EMU), Greece and the other peripherals put in place the necessary measures to meet the strict requirements. Once in, the euro, magic-wand-like, made Greece's and the other peripherals' chronic budgetary and debt problems seemingly disappear. Moreover, with the ECB now in charge of setting monetary policy for the entire eurozone, markets concluded that the ECB would continue the determined anti-inflation policies of the union's key member – Germany's central bank, the Deutsche Bundesbank. To investors, this meant that their investments in peripheral countries' debt instruments could not be eroded through currency depreciation and inflation. Clearly, markets felt that the remaining credit or default risk was not real.

Eurozone membership also gave the PIIGS access to much lower interest rates which allowed them to refinance their debt to more manageable terms and enabled them to borrow funds at lower rates (borrowing in the euro carried lower exchange-rate risk). The interest rates on these countries' debts dropped sharply because investors concluded that the value of their investments would no longer be subjected to losses via currency depreciation. That is, the "security" offered by the euro led markets to assume that an implicit guarantee protected the debt of all eurozone members. This also resulted in a callous underpricing of risk because as debts became "cheaper," reliance on foreign funding, especially funding raised in the markets (that is, wholesale funding) sharply increased. European banks, and German and French banks in particular, were awash with liquidity and only too eager to lend.[3]

---

[3] The German banks' exposure to banks in Portugal, Greece, Ireland, and Spain was estimated at just over €392 billion in February 2010 (*Europe's World* 2011, 56).

Indeed, easy access to credit, in particular, cheap credit that came with low interest rates spurred unrestrained spending and investments in equal measure – with the bulk of the funds used to fuel massive credit-led public and private consumption and real-estate bubbles, rather than productive investment essential to generate an income stream to service the borrowing. The case of Greece is illustrative: even as the Greek economy grew by an average of 4 percent a year during 2001–08, the budget deficits also grew rapidly, and by the middle of 2008, Greece's current-account deficit had widened to more than 12 percent of GDP.[4]

The experience of Greece and the PIIGS paradoxically underscore that eurozone membership could actually shield countries from making fiscal policies with prudence and due diligence and allow them to hide their profligacy, in some cases, like Greece, through deliberate "creative" bookkeeping. The belated realization that the euro did not necessarily enforce discipline and protections served to further spook the already jittery markets and resulted in a sharp reassessment of credit risk. When the hammer finally fell with the collapse of Lehmann Brothers in October 2008, the wholesale funding markets came to an abrupt halt making it impossible for the banks in the periphery to finance their credit-driven growth or meet their external obligations. Having the euro became a liability. Krugman (2011, 2) notes the gravest flaw:

> By going on the euro, Spain and Italy in effect reduced themselves to the status of third-world countries that have to borrow in someone else's currency, with all the loss of flexibility that implies. In particular, since euro-area countries can't print money even in an emergency, they're subject to funding disruptions in a way that nations that kept their own currencies aren't – and the result is what you see right now. America, which borrows in dollars, doesn't have that problem.

The Contradictions of the EMU

The problem lies not so much with the euro, but in the idiosyncratic design of the EMU, which everyone now agrees is anachronistically at odds with

---

[4] Carmen and Vincent Reinhart (2010, BO3) note

> Before it [Greece] joined the Eurozone, Greece's household debt was only 6 percent of the nation's GDP. By 2009, it was nearly 50 percent of GDP. And by the end of 2009, government debt had marched upward to about 115 percent of GDP. In that sense, the euro did pave the way to this crisis. However, Greece was not the only country on a borrowing bender. Iceland and the United Kingdom, not to mention the United States, dramatically increased domestic and international borrowing, even as they retained their national currencies. Rather, why did lenders facilitate such overborrowing? Across continents good economic times bred complacency among investors, who believed that past performance promised a bright future.

the dictates of economic logic. Namely, even as the EMU united Europe's disparate currencies under the banner of the euro (with the premise that the benefits of a common currency would outweigh each having their own currency), it left the union's fiscal policies completely uncoordinated (Feldstein 2012; 2010; Issing 2008; Moravcsik 2012). This has meant that even as the European economies have become closely integrated, including sharing a common currency, the European Union (unlike the United States) does not have in place continent-wide institutional mechanisms to deal with continent-wide economic problems. Put more bluntly, the eurozone is a monetary union without a fiscal union. This means that it has a sort of a central bank, but not a treasury. The central bank can (and has) provided liquidity, but only a treasury can address solvency issues. Unlike the U.S. Federal Reserve, the ECB has limited powers (mostly over interest rates and broader monetary policy) and lacks parallel oversight over private banks. Also, unlike the Federal Reserve, the ECB cannot act as a lender of last resort as its charter precludes it from providing direct financing to governments. Therefore, on one hand, national debts are the responsibility of member states, but on the other, no one is charge of the common currency – this crucial task is left to dozens of regulators across the Continent. This patchwork system of national central banks in each of the eurozone countries (where each still retain broad powers within their own borders), ultimately served to limit effective official supervision of the banking sector, especially warnings about the risks associated with their growing U.S. and Eastern European financial exposure.

Contrary to expectations, the eurozone never did become the "optimum currency area" its architects had hoped it would.[5] In other words, the expected economic homogenization of the member states' economies, in particular, the convergence of the inflation rates within the eurozone, failed to materialize. Rather, as "euro-skeptics" had long warned, the economic divergence within the eurozone became even more pervasive and pronounced. The PIIGS's problems only confirmed the dangers of binding a group of starkly divergent economies (from high-savings, asset-rich, and productive countries in the "north" and an uncompetitive, profligate, and debt-ridden "south") in a currency zone with no effective mechanism such as a central fiscal authority to oversee country budgets and manage domestic

---

[5] The economic theory of optimal currency area pioneered by Mundell (1961) argues that in order to make a monetary union sustainable, monetary policy autonomy (which countries forego when adopting a common currency, should also be composed of countries with similar fiscal policies, overlapping business cycles, and free mobility of goods, services, capital, and labor.

distortions.[6] This meant that in practice, the EU's much-hyped so-called "Maastricht criteria" (also called the "convergence criteria"), which specified that a country could become a member only if its deficit was less than 3 percent of GDP and its public debt less than 60 percent, could not be enforced.[7] Similarly, the EU's much-vaunted Stability and Growth Pact (SGP), tasked to monitor each nation's budgets via annual evaluations, failed in its responsibilities. The EU and national financial regulators (like the SEC in the United States) succumbed to complacency and remained asleep at the wheel, failing to flag the rising credit risk that the growing inter-connectedness of national financial systems posed to the entire EU until it was too late.

The extent to which economic integration outpaced the coordination of even basic macroeconomic and financial policies in the eurozone is vividly reflected in the fact that no eurozone member country has ever been fined during the euro's twelve-year history for not having its budget in compliance. Indeed, there was nothing the EMU could do about it. This partly explains why several eurozone countries could run deficits beyond permissible levels (the average deficit of the eurozone countries on the eve of the Greek crisis exceeded 7 percent of GDP), or that European banks could take such big risks when they fueled a massive credit boom. While the eurozone's defenders argued that if countries got themselves into debt and deficit problems it was their individual problem because the ECB was explicitly prohibited from bailing out profligate members, they did not always appreciate that there was no mechanism for the debtor country to expeditiously exit from the monetary union. Also, even while the ECB is prohibited from guaranteeing all the sovereign debt of individual member countries, the fact that the debt is denominated in the same currency meant that all would suffer from the repercussions. After all, to the markets, the price of any euro asset incorporated some compensation for currency risk.

Implications of the Eurozone's Architecture

In the current hard times, the eurozone's flawed economic and political architecture has not only served to widen the gulf between the so-called

---

[6] Milton Friedman famously said that a common currency area (or a monetary union) could not be sustained without enduring economic and political union. This is because a smooth functioning market economy requires both a strong central fiscal authority and a strong central bank.

[7] To join the Eurozone, countries had to meet the "convergence criteria" before adopting the euro. The criteria set out the economic and legal preconditions for each member's participation.

conscientious and successful "northern" economies (like Germany, the Netherlands, and Finland) and what they see as their undisciplined and spendthrift southern "Club-Med" partners, it has made it exceedingly difficult for the eurozone to speak with a unified voice.[8] As the following pages will show, this has further exacerbated divisions, making policy differences over economic management and reform more intractable.[9] For example, even as the peripheral underdogs call for fiscal federalism, and, by extension, greater "collective responsibility" and "burden sharing" in the form of eurobonds, the northern economies, led by Germany and aware that bailouts for the peripherals are unpopular with their publics, staunchly oppose these measures, insisting that domestic structural and policy reforms in the peripheral economies must take top priority. In fact, some northern policymakers and politicians have gone on record to say that the austerity measures countries like Greece, Ireland, and Portugal have agreed too are not tough enough. They argue that these "irresponsible" debtors should be required to adopt the Latvian and Estonian strategy of "internal devaluation" under which wages and benefits were immediately reduced by 20 to 30 percent, with equally sharp corresponding cuts in government spending (Aslund and Dombrovskis 2010; Berglof and Annenkov 2011). By stoically following the IMF-backed program and prudently downsizing its economy, Latvia's economy not only became more consonant with market realities but was also put on the path to recovery. In 2011, Latvia's real GDP grew by 5.5 percent, and by mid-2011 the country could once again borrow on the international capital markets (it has actually issued two euro-bonds rated "investment grade" since mid-2011). In December 2011, Latvia successfully completed its IMF-supported program. Similarly, Estonia, which saw its GDP drop by 5.1 percent in 2008 and another 13.8 percent in 2009, adopted "a number of austerity packages combining expenditure reductions and tax

---

[8]   Finland's insistence on collateral from Greece in exchange for its share of funding for the July 2011 bailout is an example of this growing gulf. In fact, Finland and the other AAA-rated Eurozone nations have become increasingly critical of the expansion of the rescue packages.

[9]   Eichengreen (2012) argues

> The deficit that prevents Europe from drawing a line under its crisis is a deficit of trust.... there is a lack of trust among European Union member states. The real reason why the northern Europeans have been unwilling to provide a "big bazooka" – that is, extend more financial assistance to Southern Europe – is that they don't trust the beneficiaries to use it wisely. They fear, for example, that additional securities purchases by the European Central Bank, aimed at bringing down Spain's borrowing costs, would only lead the Spanish government to relax its reform effort. As a result, Germany and its allies are prepared to provide just enough assistance to keep the ship from capsizing, but not enough to set it on an even keel.

increases in order to constrain the deficit" and saw its economy rebound in 2010 (Raudla and Kattel 2011, 164).

On the other hand, peripherals, notably Greece, strongly reject such claims, noting that the draconian austerity programs they have been forced to adopt are already quite exacting and more punitive measures could very well strangle their economies. Athens has stated that its implementation of biting fiscal austerity measures has already meant sharp reductions in public-sector wages, higher unemployment, higher taxes, and reduced pensions and social security payments – all of which have led to an overall economic decline of 7 percent of GDP in 2011. To Athens, the reason these measures have failed to generate growth and restore investor confidence is not because the austerity measures are too lax but because these arbitrary and punitive "growth-killing" measures have produced a prolonged "austerity-induced recession." Indeed, to many Greeks, the northern countries are simply playing politics by pandering to the prejudices of their voters who hold the profligate Greeks and other PIIGS responsible for their problems and feel that some sort of collective humiliation and retribution is a much-needed lesson in prudence.

Sadly, forgotten in the acrimony is the fact that the eurozone crisis is hardly a morality play between virtuous northerners and irresponsible southerners. Rather, both sides bear responsibility for the present crisis. If the less creditworthy peripherals (both governments and their banks) used the security of the monetary union to borrow imprudently and spend profligately on consumption (rather than on productive investments), the northern governments and their banks facilitated the problem by imprudently issuing euro-denominated loans to governments and private borrowers in the south. German and French banks, including such heavyweights as Société Générale and BNP-Paribas, face massive losses because they not only chose to treat bonds issued by peripherals as risk-free (or as if they were equal to the triple-A German bunds), they also ignored country-risk because the fees earned for underwriting sovereign debt sold to other investors were simply too profitable to pass. Rather, in their obsessive search for yield, northern banks readily bought the higher-yield bonds of peripheral countries, ignoring the mounting evidence of fiscal problems in these countries, most notably Greece and Spain, and to a lesser extent in Ireland and Portugal. Of course, neither northern governments nor their banks complained when the easy credit was adding to their balance sheets and boosting exports, especially exports from Germany – including such high-ticket items as BMWs and Mercedes-Benzes. Not surprisingly, some have cynically likened the north's response as gratuitous "blaming the credit addicts, but not their pushers" (*Europe's World* 2011, 56). The next chapter examines the eurozone's attempt to respond to the challenges, including what it has to do to alleviate these problems before it is too late.

The United Kingdom and Iceland: The Harbingers

As noted, the problem of bubbles and debts is hardly restricted only to countries using the euro. The case of British banks is illustrative. In 2008, London had little choice but to quickly come up with $87 billion to bail out the banking system and establish a separate liquidity fund of some $348 billion to offer short-term loans to financial institutions to help them cover their day-to-day operations. Despite the fact that some of the country's biggest banks, including Barclays, Lloyds TSB, and the RBS were partially nationalized (in return for the capital infusion, the government received "preference shares"), the efforts failed to calm investors or encourage banks to lend – for similar reasons such an approach failed in the United States (Dimsdale 2009). The gravity of Britain's bubble problem and resultant banking meltdown explains why, on January 19, 2009, the authorities unveiled measures to further stimulate lending, including a guarantee scheme designed to protect banks against losses on bad assets and an increase in its stake in the RBS to 70 percent. This gave it a controlling interest. On January 23, 2009, the British economy was officially declared in recession. The country's Office for National Statistics unveiled that the economy contracted by a sharp 1.5 percent in the fourth quarter of 2008 and the unemployment rate jumped to 6.1 percent – up almost a full percent from the previous year – and the value of the beleaguered pound sunk to a twenty-three-year low (Bank of England 2008). This, despite massive government-funded packages to stimulate the economy, including lending by banks and guarantees to protect them against losses on bad assets. However, the United Kingdom problems were just a pin-prick compared to Iceland's travails.

Throughout much of its history Iceland was little more than a port of call for the North Atlantic fishing fleets trawling the waters between Greenland and the Faroe Islands. However, the fortuitous combination of advancements in information technology with innovations in financial instruments made Iceland's geographical isolation seemingly irrelevant. Financial globalization enabled this island nation with a population of roughly 320,000 to dramatically scale back its traditional dependence on fishing and aluminum smelting and make financial services its new leading sector. In less than a decade, the capital, Reykjavik (where much of Iceland's population resides), was transformed from a sleepy port city into a bustling cosmopolitan metropolis boasting all the amenities (and pleasures) offered by the likes of Paris, London, and New York. In 2005, the United Nations noted that Icelanders not only enjoyed the highest per capita incomes in the world, they had also bettered the perennial favorites, Norway, in human-development indicators such as education, health care, and life expectancy. Not surprisingly, Icelanders were said to be the happiest people in the world, and their country's success a model for others to emulate.

However, the Icelandic "miracle" was built on shaky foundations. Specifically, following the deregulation and privatization of the banking sector in the mid-1990s, Iceland's three largest banks (Kaupthing, Landsbanki, and Glitnir, which was then called Islandsbanki), came up with a novel, and at that time, eminently reasonable idea that Iceland's future prosperity demanded the country diversify away from its traditional bases in fisheries, farming, aluminum smelting, and geothermal power. The solution was ambitious: by drawing on its well-funded pension system and borrowing money on the international money markets, Iceland could become a leading center of global finance. The international capital markets, flush with funds, obliged (Wade and Sigurgeirsdottir 2012). Over the next few years the banks, along with the newly established stock market in Reykjavik, took advantage of the abundance of low-interest capital in international markets (Darvas 2011). They borrowed billions of dollars and euros to finance domestic investment and consumption and acquire foreign companies. The spending spree was unprecedented: banks and domestic enterprises not only snapped up large chunks of eastern Europe's telecommunications market, the United Kingdom's high-end stores like the House of Fraser, the iconic Hamley's toy store, and the West Ham soccer team, but also foreign-owned financial firms (especially in Britain and Scandinavia), besides investing aggressively in high-yielding securities, including subprime mortgages.

The resultant credit boom rapidly transformed Iceland's economy. The average family's wealth grew by 45 percent in five years (2000–05), and GDP accelerated to 6 percent a year. Like their banks, Icelanders (both individuals and businesses) used their newfound wealth to go on spending sprees, buying everything from BMWs to designer clothing to real estate both at home and abroad. To facilitate this, credit companies sprang up, offering 100 percent loans, many in foreign currencies. Foreigners hoping to cash in on Iceland's boom took large positions in its high-yielding currency (the krona), and foreign firms poured money into the country's numerous "sure-thing" projects.

In those heady times it seemed that Iceland had more than achieved its ambitious goal. Indeed, in less than five years, the three banks went from being almost entirely domestic lenders to major international financial intermediaries. The massive cash flows allowed these banks to earn huge dividends as they used short-term funding to invest in high-yielding securities. As hubris replaced prudence, investors, banks, and Iceland's government were assured by their own regulators, including U.S. rating agencies, among others, that the funds were well invested and that Icelandic banks were financially sound. Like the over-optimism surrounding the subprime mortgages, this assurance was quite misleading. The reality was that Iceland's banking sector had grown too big too fast. Following the privatization of the banking sector in 2003, the banks had increased their assets from slightly more than 100 percent of GDP to close to 1,000 percent of GDP. This audaciously oversized banking system now significantly outstripped the authorities' ability to act as a lender of last resort (if and when) the banks ran into trouble. In fact, so unprecedented was the borrowing binge that on the eve of the crisis, the foreign debts owned by Iceland's banks were more than nine times the country's GDP. More bluntly, Iceland's top three banks held foreign liabilities in excess of $120 billion, dwarfing the country's $14 billion GDP. For a small economy heavily dependent on imports, this was an unambiguous risk – indeed, the worst of all possible scenarios.

Predictably, this house of cards began to collapse when the "unexpected" happened. Spooked by the financial meltdown in the United States and a virulent contagion, the fickle foreign lenders demanded their money back. After all, if the subprime crisis had taught them anything, it was that risk should never be underestimated. However, Iceland's banks, which for all practical purposes were functioning more like hedge funds, were in no position to honor their obligations. When it finally dawned on investors that Iceland's banking system was far too big relative to the size of the economy and that it lacked tangible assets (not to mention that, with the onset of the crisis, the banks had been frozen out of the credit markets and therefore unable to make good on short-term payments), panic set in and a destructive bank run ensued. As investors rushed to pull their funds out, the contagion quickly spilled over, affecting the Icelandic krona. Within a week, the three banks collapsed, the krona's value dropped by more than 70 percent, and the country's stock market lost more than 80 percent of its value (Chand 2009). For both banks and lenders the problem was further compounded by a severe global credit crunch. Not only were foreign investors heading for the exit in droves, not even its brethren Nordic countries were prepared to come to the aid of the besieged island nation. Unlike the United States, which because of the sheer size of its economy, had countries like China and Japan prepared to pour billions of dollars into U.S. securities, Iceland, a bit player in the big-stake game of international finance, had no such benefactors.

Starved of liquidity (given the almost complete shutdown of inter-institution lending), Iceland's heavily exposed banks began falling like dominoes under the weight of debts incurred by the unrestrained lending and spending in the giddy boom times. This forced the Central Bank of Iceland to fix the value of the krona to 131 against the euro following a decline of more than 40 percent since the start of September 2008. With government bailout out of the question as Iceland's bank assets were more than 10 times greater than its GDP, a default became inevitable. Finally on October 5, Reykjavik used "emergency powers" rushed in by Parliament to place Landsbanki and Glitnir in receivership under the newly created Icelandic Supervisory Authority. The agency immediately began to restructure the bank, announcing plans to sell it to Finnish and Swedish businesses. The new powers also gave the government authority to dictate banking operations, including the ability to push through mergers or even force a bank to declare bankruptcy. On October 7, Iceland's government nationalized Landsbanki and Icesave (Landsbanki's Internet bank) and froze U.K. customer accounts.[10] In return, on October 8, the U.K. treasury froze the assets of Landsbanki in the U.K. and threatened legal action against Reykjavik. Yet even such drastic actions did not seem to quell market fears. On October 9, the Icelandic authorities took control of Kaupthing (the country's largest bank) and suspended trading on its stock exchange for two days. Again, it all seemed too little and too late. The bank collapses were already causing ripples throughout Europe as tens of thousands of people had accounts with subsidiaries of the Icelandic banks. When Reykjavik promised to guarantee only domestic depositors while reneging on guarantees to foreigners, especially the 300,000 account holders in the United Kingdom, such depositors rushed to Icesave to withdraw their deposits. The announcement also led to a diplomatic spat as U.K. Prime Minister Gordon Brown threatened to sue Iceland and use counterterrorist legislation to take over Icelandic bank assets and operation. True to his word, Brown used anti-terror legislation to seize billions of pounds of failed Icelandic banks' British assets and accused Reykjavik of "acting irresponsibly." Iceland's prime minister, Geir Haarde, in turn harshly criticized the British government, accusing Brown

[10]   Icesave was a high-interest, Internet-only savings bank launched by Landsbanki. It operated in Britain and the Netherlands under the EU's single-market rules (Iceland is a member of the European Economic Area). This meant that, when Landsbanki collapsed in October 2008, Icesave depositors were not covered by Dutch and British deposit insurance.

of "bullying a small neighbor." The financial crisis had veered into unfamiliar territory.[11]

The hard reality was that for all practical purposes, Iceland was "bankrupt" – it could no longer pay back its external debts and the krona had become essentially worthless in the rest of the world. It was a tragic turn for a country, which overnight literally went from being one of the lowest indebted countries in Europe to among the most indebted "advanced" country in Europe. The IMF warned that resolving Iceland's debt and banking sector problems could cost the public sector about 80 percent of the GDP. On October 13, Iceland swallowed its pride and officially requested assistance from the IMF to stave off bankruptcy (Chand 2009). On October 20, the announcement of an IMF-led rescue package of $6 billion indicated that the international community was ready to deal with Iceland's woes. On October 24, an IMF package totaling $2.1 billion was announced under the fund's fast-track emergency financing mechanism. On 19 November 19, the IMF made $827 million available to Iceland – the remainder to be paid in eight equal installments and subject to quarterly reviews. Even as Iceland moved to stabilize the krona and restore the interbank foreign-exchange market, its miseries were just beginning. Iceland now found itself facing a deep recession and an even longer recovery (Darvas 2011). Given the banking sector's relative size to the economy, Reykjavik finally informed a despondent public of the bad news: bank restructuring would be very expensive and resolving the country's unprecedented debt problems would require steadfastness.

Iceland's rapid rise and precipitous fall is a cautionary tale about the paradox of economic globalization – where small economies can experience big financial shocks. One way to understand how this potential shock can be transmitted is by examining a country's external balance sheet which comprises international assets (claims on nonresidents) and international liabilities (obligations toward nonresidents). The difference between the recorded value of international assets and liabilities defines the net international investment position, which can be either positive or negative. Within OECD economies, for example, the balance between international assets and liabilities varies substantially, ranging from net assets of more than 100 percent of GDP in Luxembourg and Switzerland to net liabilities of around 125 percent (if not higher) of GDP in Iceland. For small economies

---

[11] In August 2009, the Icelandic parliament finally voted in favor of repaying more than $5 billion to the governments of the United Kingdom and the Netherlands. The so-called Icesave bill will reimburse funds already paid by the two governments to compensate the estimated 400,000 people who lost their deposits when Icesave owner Landsbanki collapsed.

Table 3.4. *Current account versus public and private savings*

Region	Current account		Net public savings		Net private savings	
	1992–98	1999–07	1992–98	1999–07	1992–98	1999–07
South	−0.7	−6.8	−5.7	−2.1	5.0	−4.7
North	0.9	4.6	−3.3	−0.2	4.2	4.8

Note: Values expressed as percent of GDP.
Source: Holinski, Kool, and Muysken (2012, 6).

Table 3.5. *Current account decomposition as a percent of GDP*

Region	Current account		Trade balance	
	1992–98	1999–07	1992–98	1999–07
South	−0.7	−6.8	−0.9	−2.4
North	0.9	4.6	2.8	5.4

Source: Holinski, Kool, and Muysken (2012, 11).

with a negative position, the sustainability of a large stock of net international liabilities rests fundamentally on the willingness of international investors to hold claims. Iceland's experience revealed this reality in the most excruciating of ways.

The Eurozone's Sovereign Debt Problems

As noted, although it was believed that the wide economic variations among the eurozone members would converge over time, the opposite occurred: greater economic divergence. Holinski, Kool and Muysken (2012), drawing on evidence from four typical northern countries (Germany, Austria, Finland, and the Netherlands) and four typical southern countries (Greece, Portugal, Spain, and Ireland), illustrate this divergence with reference to the current account (Tables 3.4 and 3.5).

While northern economies such as Germany, Luxembourg, the Netherlands, Austria, and Finland built up impressive surpluses, the southern or peripheral economies such as Greece, Spain, Portugal, Ireland, and Italy accumulated large deficits. Although a combination of factors led to this divergence, domestic monetary and fiscal policy played a central role. Wage moderation coupled with significant productivity gains made the economies of Germany, Austria, and the Netherlands more competitive, whereas failure to adjust wages in line with lower productivity gains in Spain, Portugal, and Italy greatly impaired their competitiveness, resulting in a sharp erosion of their export base. For example, in 2007, "Greece saw wage increases of 6.2%, Spain 4.8%, Ireland 5.4% and Portugal 3.6%, compared to a eurozone average of 2.6 percent, and a rise of only 0.9% in Germany" (*Europe's World* 2011, 56). Accentuating this, the PIIGS's large external deficits and the core countries' equally large surpluses created persistent imbalances and led to the transfer of excess savings to the periphery. The massive credit expansion, especially mortgage loans, fueled a boom and later a bubble in the property market, especially in Ireland and Spain. Holinski, Kool, and Muysken (2012, 18) explain this by noting that the "*South* has been persistently borrowing from abroad to maintain its negative trade balance and pay the interest on its net debt. Particularly worrisome is the observation that *South* has not yet seemed able to convert its large inflow of foreign capital into a more a productive and competitive economy."

This explains why the heart of the eurozone's woes is a spiraling debt crisis, in particular, a sovereign-debt crisis that has stubbornly resisted all manner of fixes, including very expensive fixes. Although the crisis seemed to erupt suddenly, catching both market participants and policymakers by surprise, the root of the problems were years in the making and the symptoms of the malaise were evident for some time. In the case of Greece and Portugal, these symptoms included profligate governments spending beyond their means, and in the case of Ireland and Spain, an orgy of overconsumption and overinvestment by the private sector, especially banks and related financial institutions. In both Ireland and Spain, private debt quickly became public as their governments took over the debts of their overextended banking sectors. In Spain, the problem was further compounded because the debts of regional and local governments also become those of the central government. As will be discussed, each of these debtor peripherals could engage in such profligacy not only because of the low interest rates that Eurozone membership brought them, but also the adoption of the euro eliminated the exchange-rate risk. This in turn, unleashed unprecedented levels of cross-border lending (as noted, German and French banks were only too eager to lend), which resulted in the simultaneous buildup of large exposures among the banks in the lending countries and capricious debt buildup by banks and governments in the borrowing countries. The countries in the eurozone most impacted by the debt crisis had, for years, engaged in massive foreign borrowing. However, as in the United States, EU regulators had been asleep at the wheel and credit-rating agencies had submissively reported what their clients (the banks) wanted to hear. For their part, the credit markets caught in the enthusiasm and euphoria of irrational exuberance simply ignored the potential red flags signaled by mounting debts and current-account deficits. Greece's history of profligacy, chronic fiscal mismanagement, tax evasion, and poor public finances, Ireland's reckless private-sector bank borrowing and an unsustainable property boom that saw home prices in Dublin rise to levels far beyond those of similar homes in London or New York, Portugal's anemic growth and high labor cost, and Spain's sclerotic and increasingly uncompetitive economy and a property bubble to boot all failed to set off alarm bells.

The Making of a Greek Tragedy

In late April 2010, the spread between Greek and German ten-year bonds skyrocketed to 650 basis points. During the first week of May 2010, when the interest rate on Greek bonds jumped to a once-unimaginable 38 percent, default seemed imminent. In desperation, on May 10, after weeks of indecision, the EU finally unveiled a plan to deal with Greece's growing sovereign-debt crisis. As the *Economist* aptly noted, Eurozone leaders were forced into action when faced with their own "Lehman moment" – the frightening prospect of Greece defaulting and setting into motion an out-of-control sovereign-debt crisis that would engulf not only Portugal, Spain, and Ireland, but also a much larger economy such as Italy.[12] With their backs to the wall, eurozone negotiators put in long hours over the weekend of May 8 and 9 to produce an unprecedented "shock and awe" package of €750 billion (US$1 trillion) in the hopes of restoring confidence in the embattled euro and stemming the financial panic gripping the Continent.[13] The European Commission's president, José Manuel Barroso, proudly announced that the package confirmed that the eurozone would do "whatever it takes" to defend itself, and the fact that the IMF committed an additional $321 billion, and the world's leading central bank, the U.S. Federal Reserve, announced a joint intervention to make more dollars

---

[12] "The Euro: Emergency Repairs," *The Economist*, 13 May, 2010b; "The Euro and the Future of Europe," *The Economist*, 13 May, 2010c.

[13] The core of the loan package is a €440 billion (about $585 billion) mutual-support package backed by national guarantees that would buy distressed countries' bonds. In other words, this so-called "special-purpose vehicle" will guarantee loans to governments. In fact, to make the bonds attractive, Eurozone governments had to guarantee 120 percent of their value, while countries receiving the bailout agreed to deposit a certain portion of the loans they receive "as a cash buffer." The remaining €321 billion is provided by the European Commission and the IMF.

available for interbank lending, further underscored the commitment of the key players in the global community to ensure the eurozone's financial health. After all, President Obama, Chancellor Merkel, and President Sarkozy made it abundantly clear that they would leave no stone unturned to restore investor confidence in the eurozone.

The audacious $1 trillion "shock and awe" plan worked – or in Merkel's evocative phrase, the euro passed its "existential test." It seems that the markets desperately looking for a bold plan finally got their wish.[14] Just hours after the deal was announced, the Eureopan Central Bank (ECB) reversed its position and began to buy eurozone government and corporate debt.[15] In so doing, the ECB suspended its collateral standards to ensure that Greek debt remained eligible in its repurchase operations. This was a dramatic move as the ever-cautious ECB's bond-purchase plan would transfer Greece's risk (indeed, junk assets) from the private banks in Europe to the ECB.[16] Jean-Claude Trichet, ECB's president, tried to put the best spin on the situation by rejecting suggestions that the plan was the start of an expansive monetary policy, arguing instead that the decision confirmed the flexibility of the ECB to deal with contingencies and promised that the ECB's bond purchases were a short-term measure designed to prevent a possible debt crisis from spreading to the EU's banking system.[17] As the central banks began buying eurozone government bonds, the EU's financial system got a much-needed liquidity boost. In response, the risk premium on Greek and other government bonds plunged, and Greece's ten-year borrowing costs decreased by almost half. The beleaguered euro rallied against the dollar – climbing above the $1.30 mark for the first time in a week.

---

[14] Marcus Walker, Charles Forelle and David Gauthier-Villars, "Europe Bailout Lifts Gloom," *The Wall Street Journal*, 9 May, 2010. http://online.wsj.com/article/SB10001424052748704 879704575236602686084356.html (accessed July 15, 2010).

[15] Since its inception on January 1, 1999, the European Central Bank (ECB) has been responsible for conducting monetary policy for the Eurozone. The Eurozone came into being when responsibility for monetary policy was transferred from the national central banks of eleven EU member states to the ECB in January 1999. Greece joined in 2001, Slovenia in 2007, Cyprus and Malta in 2008, and Slovakia in 2009.

[16] As the *Economist* noted, "They [the EU] have committed an awesome €60 billion of EU-backed bonds, a €440 billion fund guaranteed by eurozone countries, and potentially up to €250 billion of IMF money. The ECB, a pillar of monetary orthodoxy, turned apostate and set about buying government bonds in order to lower the cost of borrowing for the euro zone's most troubled economies" ("The Euro and the Future of Europe," *The Economist*, 13 May, 2010c).

[17] "Interview with Jean-Claude Trichet, President of the ECB," conducted by Thomas Tuma and Christoph Pauly, *Der Spiegel*,13 May 2010. http://www.ecb.europa.eu/press/key/date/2010/html/sp100515.en.html

However, the calm was short-lived. Even Germany's bold decision to place a ban on the "naked short-selling" of eurozone government bonds and on the buying of sovereign credit-default swaps by investors who did not also buy the underlying bonds failed to have the desired effect. To the contrary, it only made it more difficult to sell government bonds. On May 17, despite the ECB's formidable $1 trillion bailout "guarantee," the euro fell to $1.22, its lowest level since April 2006. What explains the markets' abrupt volte-face? Why did the eurozone's unprecedented $1 trillion war chest fail to placate the markets? Why did the problems in Greece, a relatively small economy, so quickly morph into a broader crisis casting an ominous shadow over the entire eurozone and the EU?

Between January 1, 2001 (when Greece became the twelfth member of the EMU) and October 2009, the Greek economy looked more promising than it ever had. Economic growth and related macroeconomic indicators were robust (OECD 2009a). Greece, it seemed, had finally kicked its spendthrift ways to become a disciplined member of the eurozone. Then, in late October 2009, Athens dropped a bombshell. The newly elected prime minister, George Papandreou, announced that Greece's budget deficit was in fact 12.7 percent of GDP, not the 6 percent tabled by the previous government, and far more than the 3.7 percent of GDP Greek authorities had reported to the European Commission in early 2009.[18]

Clearly, Greece's previous government had not only deliberately fudged the data, the country's economic problems were far more serious than originally assumed. In addition to running a large budget deficit, Greece's government debt burden, at about 115 percent, was larger than its annual GDP (with the external debt burden totaling about 75 percent of GDP) at the end of 2009 (IMF 2010). As a result, credit-rating agencies such as Moody's and Standard & Poor's placed Greek debt on "negative watch" – an early warning of future downgrades. To the global financial markets still reeling from the subprime-mortgage-induced contagion, this news, coupled with awareness of Greece's large budget deficit and outstanding stock of debt raised grave doubts about Athens' ability to service its debt obligations. Although Greece represents just 2.4 percent of the eurozone economy, it is nevertheless deeply integrated within the EU, making the specter of another financial meltdown appear frighteningly imminent. The markets correctly feared that the headline shock alone of Greece's debt problems would have far-reaching, negative consequences for the entire EU.

---

[18] "Country Report: Greece," *Economist Intelligence Unit*, February 18, 2010; and "Greece Economy: An Austere Future," *Economist Intelligence Unit*, March 9, 2010.

As fear turned to panic, the contagion from Greece quickly began to spread to other eurozone countries. In a sense, Greece became the proverbial canary in the coal mine, delivering a rude wake-up call about the latent sovereign-debt problems within the EU. Indeed, as investors critically began to reassess other countries exhibiting Greece's macroeconomic characteristics, its woes hardly seemed unique. In fact, several of the eurozone countries, namely the PIIGS, shared many of Greece's structural problems. In particular, the PIIGS were burdened with large budget deficits and burdensome long-term debts, making them highly susceptible to a Greek-style meltdown. No doubt, large budget deficits, colossal debt levels, and uncompetitive cost structures signaled to nervous markets not only that a prolonged period of slow (possibly negative) growth was around the corner, but so was a high probability of sovereign-debt defaults. If these fears were realized, the euro would have to be restructured, resulting in a sharp lowering in the value of investors' bonds. As a result, the eurozone's fiscal problems resulted in a risk-averse "flight to quality," as investors shifted funds into seemingly safer assets such as the U.S. dollar and treasuries, including the yen as well as gold, silver, and other precious metals.

When the two major credit-rating agencies (Fitch and Standard & Poor's) sharply cut their rating on Greek bonds from A- to BBB+ and warned of further downgrades, a steep sell-off in the Greek (as well as Spanish and Portuguese) bond markets ensued, further adding to those countries' borrowing costs. Greece's deficit grew even larger as interest payments rose, further saddling Athens with a far more heavy debt burden. The eurozone's protracted negotiations and internal discord over how to deal with Greece's woes made a bad situation much worse. When Athens turned to the EU for assistance, the EU, in particular, the Germans, sent mixed signals, suggesting that Chancellor Merkel saw no upside to helping the profligate (and "deceptive") Greeks with hard-earned German taxpayers' money (Jones 2010). However, every day that passed without an orderly resolution of Greece's problems, only postponed the inevitable and added immeasurably to the cost of inaction. A broad agreement was finally reached (in late April 2010), under which the eurozone would provide Greece with €110 billion (including €30 billion from the IMF), only after Athens made a commitment to cut the national deficit to 7.6 percent in 2011, 6.5 percent in 2012, and less than 3 percent by 2014. Of course, all this was viewed by the bond markets as being too little too late (Garnham 2010).

Greece's problems were further exacerbated by the fact that Athens owed much money to a handful of German and French banks, which were backed by guarantees from their own governments. For over a decade, indeed, ever since Greece joined the eurozone, German and French financial institutions had flooded Greece with cheap credit (according to Barclays Capital, they together hold over $100 billion in Greek government bonds). During the early days of the crisis, these same banks, fully aware of the EU and the IMF's bailout plans, took advantage of this implicit "moral hazard" by deliberately allowing the problems to fester in hopes of getting the best deal for their imprudent investments. Similarly, speculators used credit-default swaps on Greek government debt to bet the country would default – thus forcing a bailout. As a result, short-selling of eurozone government debt and shares of major financial companies continued unabated during and after the announcement of the $1 trillion bailout. Indeed, Subramanian's (2010) charge that the bailout program imposed no losses ("haircuts") on banks that hold Greek debt, but simply placed undue burden of adjustment on both European and international taxpayers, has much merit.

In such an unpredictable and volatile environment, the chastened markets remained deeply wary of official pronouncements. Market participants were acutely aware that the EU, including several of the eurozone governments, had little room to maneuver. Having already used their "best" countermeasures (from massive stimulus spending and reduction in central bank interest rates) they were left with limited resources and even less policy flexibility. These limitations only exacerbated fears that heavily indebted eurozone countries such as Greece were in no position to meet their obligations. The markets naturally remained unsure if the bailout would actually work or was merely postponing the feared default. Even as the eurozone's massive $1 trillion bailout plan helped ease the financial pressure on its weaker members, the nervous markets remained deeply concerned about a possible sovereign-debt default. More worrisome was the fear that the global economy could succumb to a serious depression – a concern underscored by sinking global demand.

The markets were also cognizant of the fact that Greece had very few independent policy levers to address its mounting problems. Sovereign states always have the option of devaluing their currency to boost exports and thus rein in deficits. But as a member of the EMU, Athens no longer possessed this unilateral tool to gain a competitive advantage. The markets not only reached the unpalatable conclusion that Greece faced years of painful deflation and very low, if not negligible economic growth, but also that Athens had only one viable policy option: excruciatingly painful budget cuts to meet its adjustment requirements, despite financial concessions from the EU and the IMF. The markets also knew that even with this support, Greece faced a prolonged and painful period of deflation. The

IMF (2010a; 2010b) was already predicting that Greece's debt burden would increase to almost 150 percent of its GDP even under the best of scenarios – which would be if Greece successfully implemented a tough fiscal austerity program – an unlikely outcome given historical precedent. The markets were under no illusion about the difficulties involved in reforming Greece's notoriously inefficient public administration, fix the pervasive problem of tax evasion, or rein in the country's expensive health-care and pension systems. The organized (and often violent) protests by thousands of public-sector workers only reinforced perceptions that Athens, even if it wanted to enact painful spending cuts and steep tax increases, would bump up against insurmountable political headwinds that would, in the end, scuttle such reforms.

Eurozone policymakers also failed to adequately address Greece's Achilles heel: despite the massive bailout it was not always clear how the plan would address the underlying problems of systemic risk. As Greece's debt problem was one of insolvency and not illiquidity, markets were puzzled about how accumulating more debt could mitigate the problem of insolvency. El-Erian (2010, 1–2) provocatively notes this flaw:

As designed, the program is better at addressing liquidity rather than solvency problems. Consequently, Greece faces the risk of a "lost decade" similar to what Latin America experienced in the 1980s – and this for a simple reason, the program does little to address the debt overhang. As long as this overhang persists, high country risk will deter investments in Greece, be they financial or in the form of foreign direct investment.

Not only was there no mechanism to deal with Greece's massive debt problem, it was never made clear how Greece (and other EU countries with similar problems) would keep their promise to implement the necessary reforms in their financial sectors. Even as the ECB's decision was welcomed, analysts were aware that the ECB was now forced to print euros to buy worthless junk-rated debt. That is, simply monetizing the debts and thus raising the specter in the eurozone of debilitating inflation and low growth rates for the foreseeable future.

Why Ireland's Luck Ran Out

In the 1990s, the Republic of Ireland, long known affectionately as the Emerald Isle, acquired another moniker – one that signified strength and respect: the "Celtic Tiger." With its economy notching an average growth rate of more than 7 percent a year from 1997–2007 (the highest among the thirty OECD countries), the new name was seen as most apt. Then, it seems the proverbial luck of the Irish ran out. In short order, the Celtic Tiger became a whimpering house cat, forced to kneel down to the EU and the IMF for more than $100 billion to stave off even greater humiliation – defaulting on its debt. What went so wrong?

First, the Irish miracle was authentic. Several analysts, including Honohan (2009), Honohan and Walsh (2002), Kelly (2010), and Whelan (2010), among others, point out that Ireland's real GNP quadrupled during the "Celtic Tiger" period from 1990 to 2007 when it was among the most open and vibrant economy in Europe. Specifically, Ireland's GNP grew from 5 percent to an unparalleled 15 percent every year from 1991 to 2006. However, Ireland's remarkable growth was rooted in two very different, yet interrelated economic booms. First, beginning in the 1990s, was the sustained export-led boom. As Honohan (2009, 209) notes, banks were not "central to the financing" of the export boom period. Rather, a combination of Ireland's unfettered openness to the global economy, one of the lowest corporate tax rates in Europe, a sophisticated human capital base and unique comparative advantage, in particular, dramatic improvements in productivity and competitiveness, and the adoption of the euro in 1999 served as the catalyst behind the export boom.[19] Ireland became an attractive destination for blue-chip multinational corporations and high-tech businesses such as Microsoft, Intel, Google, Hewlett-Packard, and Pfizer, among others, and experienced a flood of foreign direct investment (FDI). Almost overnight, a largely foreign-owned manufacturing sector with concentration in information and communications technology, particularly computer software and financial services, including pharmaceuticals, took root and expanded, creating thousands of well-paid jobs and fueling exports.[20] However, the dot-com crash of 2001 served to significantly undermine Ireland's export-led growth as the U.S. information technology sector, including multinationals, sharply reduced both their investments and presence in the Irish republic.

However, this "bust" was quickly filled by another boom which was not unique to Ireland, but common in many OECD nations: spectacular

[19] Ireland's corporate tax structure at 12.5 percent is the lowest in the EU. For a good overview, see OECD (2005a); Owens (2005). Also see O'Hearn (1998), MacSharry and White (2000), and Ó Riain (2004). It should also be noted that Germany, France, and many European countries have long complained that Ireland's low corporate tax undermines open competition in the EU.

[20] It is estimated that "multinational corporations employ more than a quarter of a million people in Ireland. Google, for instance, established its European beachhead in Ireland in 2003.... About 70 percent of the nation's exports and 70 percent of business spending on research and development comes from foreign direct investment" Alderman (2010, B1).

expansion in the real-estate sector (both residential and commercial property) and domestic consumption. This second boom was financed by the banks, who supplemented their funds with massive foreign borrowings. For example, if at the end of 2003, net indebtedness of Irish banks to the rest of the world was just 10 percent of GDP; by 2007 it had skyrocketed to more than 50 percent (Kelly 2007). Why? As noted, membership in the eurozone meant that interest rates in Ireland remained low. This allowed Irish banks to borrow heavily and cheaply from other eurozone banks to finance the real-estate sector and domestic consumption. In the process Irish banks increased their assets in property-related lending eventually to unsustainable levels.[21] Thus, as in the United States, generous government subsidies and reckless bank lending fueled a building frenzy and speculation in real estate, not only in major cities, but throughout the country. This, in turn, led to grossly inflated land and house prices. At the boom's peak in 2006, a family home in Dublin cost as much as a similar home in London or New York. Kelly (2010, 1) notes that "as Ireland converged to average levels of western European income around 2000 it might have been expected that growth would fall to normal European levels. Instead growth continued at high rates until 2007 despite falling competitiveness, driven by a second boom in construction."

Why were such chronic excesses and bubbles allowed to occur unimpeded, or in Honohan's (2009, 216) pointed words, why did Ireland's traditionally conservative banks, known for their fiscal prudence, engage in "bank lending decisions [that had] begun to lose touch with reality"? There were several interrelated reasons: with low unemployment, rising wages, low-mortgage interest rates, rapid growth in immigrant labor, and above all, the easy availability of "cheap" capital due to the global savings glut and lack of exchange-rate risk for euro borrowing, major banks such as the Anglo Irish Bank engaged in an orgy of cheap borrowing to fuel the already booming real-estate sector. Left largely unregulated by policy makers, the banking sector in cohort with supplicant politicians and wealthy developers poured billions into real estate. Predictably, this overinvestment and overdevelopment triggered a massive property bubble (O'Sullivan and Kennedy 2010; O'Toole 2009). Whelan (2010, 233) vividly captures the outcome:

The result was an extraordinary construction boom. The total stock of dwellings – which had stood at 1.2 million homes in 1991 and had gradually increased to

---

[21] Honohan (2009, 209) notes that banks "began to increase the share of their assets in property-related lending from less than 40 percent before 2002 to over 60 percent by 2006."

1.4 million homes in 2000 – exploded to 1.9 million homes in 2008. As house completions went from 19,000 in 1990 to 50,000 in 2000 to a whopping 93,000 in 2006, construction became a dominant factor in the Irish economy. With the economy already at full employment, much of the labor employed in the construction boom came from the new EU member states in Eastern Europe, and the inward migration further fueled demand for housing. By 2007, construction accounted for 13.3 per cent of all employment, the highest share in the OECD.

As noted, massive bank lending underwrote this building frenzy. Kelly (2010, 1) aptly notes,

Ireland went from getting about 5% of its national income from house building in the 1990s – the usual level for a developed economy – to 15% at the peak of the boom in 2006–2007, with another 6% coming from other construction.... The international credit boom saw these economies experience a rapid rise in bank lending, with loans increasing to 100% of GDP on average by 2008. These rises were dwarfed, however, by Ireland, where bank lending grew to 200% of national income by 2008. Irish banks were lending 40% more in real terms to property developers alone in 2008 than they had been lending to everyone in Ireland in 2000, and 75% more to house buyers.

The global credit crisis and the resultant tightening of global liquidity and collapse of the property market had serious ramifications for Ireland's overleveraged banking sector. Unlike their U.S. counterparts, Irish banks had hardly issued complex mortgage or mortgage-related financial instruments, but they had issued loans to property developers generously and without much regulatory oversight. Those developers, in turn, invested in speculative real-estate ventures. Even more shocking, Irish banks, in particular, two of the country's largest banks, the Bank of Ireland and Allied Irish Banks (AIB) had financed much speculative real estate without asking for the requisite collateral. They now faced their moment of truth as the sharp drop in asset values depressed the balance sheets of these highly leveraged financial institutions.[22] As Ireland's real-estate boom went bust (housing prices fell by as much as 50 percent), the country's banking sector, burdened with an unprecedented volume of bad loans, saw its balance sheets deteriorate so rapidly that they faced simultaneously a solvency and a liquidity crisis.[23]

---

[22] Central Bank and Financial Services Authority of Ireland (CBFSAI). 2006. *Financial Stability Review*. http://www.centralbank.ie/fns_srep1.asp

[23] That is, Irish banks held assets that were not only worth far less than their liabilities, they were also so heavily leveraged that they lacked the ability to generate sufficient cash flow to service their creditors ("IMF Approves €22.5 Billion Loan For Ireland." *IMF Survey Magazine*, December 16, 2010. http://www.imf.org/external/pubs/ft/survey/so/2010/CAR121610A.htm)

Following the collapse of Lehman Brothers and at the height of the global credit crisis, Ireland found itself confronting heightened investor panic and depositor runs, and mounting fears of a total banking collapse, not to mention the potential of a humiliating sovereign default. In desperation, on September 30, 2008, Dublin approved a guarantee covering €400 billion ($530 billion) of liabilities of six of the largest Irish-owned banks – only to further increase that figure to €485 billion to cover foreign-owned banks with significant operations in Ireland.[24] In addition, on April 7, 2009, the non-performing property-based loans were transferred to Ireland's "bad-bank," the National Asset Management Agency (NAMA). Yet, these enticements proved inadequate to quell market concerns. The Irish government tried to calm the jittery markets by doing the unprecedented: guaranteeing the private sector's liabilities by providing a blanket guarantee to the deposit base of the country's entire banking sector for two years. That is, in a last-ditch attempt to restore confidence in the nation's financial system, Dublin took the bold gamble of providing an explicit guarantee to all bank deposits for two years. With this action, almost instantly, Ireland's essentially private-sector debt (worth three times the country's annual GDP) was transformed into public or sovereign debt. By nationalizing private debts (taking over the private losses of the banking system), Ireland saw its public debt jump from about 7 percent of GDP to more than 100 percent of GDP. Worse still, as a private-debt problem was converted into a sovereign-debt problem, private bondholders and other lenders who had skin in the game got off the hook as they were allowed to withdraw their funds, leaving the taxpayers to pick up the huge tab. Krugman (2010, A37) wryly captured this bitter irony:

Before the bank bust, Ireland had little public debt. But with taxpayers suddenly on the hook for gigantic bank losses, even as revenues plunged, the nation's creditworthiness was put in doubt. So Ireland tried to reassure the markets with a harsh program of spending cuts. Step back for a minute and think about that. These debts were incurred, not to pay for public programs, but by private wheeler-dealers seeking nothing but their own profit. Yet ordinary Irish citizens are now bearing the burden of those debts.

To be fair, the constraints of the situation didn't leave many other feasible options. For Dublin, simply walking away from the insolvent banks (and preventing a banking crisis from morphing into a sovereign-debt crisis) is easier said than done. Arguably, Dublin could have offered the holders of the senior debt of the major Irish banks more incentives (or read them the riot act)

---

[24] The Irish banks covered by the guarantee included the Allied Irish Bank, Bank of Ireland, Anglo Irish Bank, Irish Life and Permanent, Irish Nationwide Building Society, and the Educational Building Society.

in order to reschedule or restructure their debts. Of course, this could have triggered a destructive sell-off in the banking sector in the eurozone, besides negatively affecting bank ratings. Rather, the case of Ireland underscores that if a country has a banking/financial sector that is systemic or "too big to fail," the country or the sovereign often has little choice but to defend that sector as their fates are inextricably and intimately tied. Clearly the markets were cognizant of this. This partly explains why, contrary to expectations, the Irish government's gamble (and generosity) failed to satisfy the markets, in particular, its creditors (read: bondholders[25]). Given the massive volume of debt that Ireland was holding, foreign creditors began to doubt Dublin's ability to service its debt and continued to withdraw their funds from the banks.[26] By mid-2010 it was painfully clear that not only the yields and the prices of credit-default swaps for Irish government bonds were still increasing, but investors were still dumping the bonds of several of the peripheral eurozone members including Ireland, Greece, Portugal, and Spain or other countries that had run up massive debts and deficits. Despite massive infusion of capital, including the Irish government's decision to nationalize or take major equity stakes in five of the six insured banks at an estimated cost of €50 billion ($65 billion), Ireland's state-backed banks were still struggling to raise funds and becoming ever more dependent on the short-term loans provided by the EU. To the already nervous markets, this served to further exacerbate their fears regarding the possibility of an eventual bailout if not outright default.

Concerns about credit risk in Ireland (and other eurozone economies, including Portugal and Spain) remerged again in August 2010. This was most vividly reflected in the bonds issued by the Irish government which experienced a sharp widening (some 600 basis points) in the spread vis-à-vis the German Bunds – the widest margin since Ireland joined the eurozone. In turn, the bonds issued by the other peripheral eurozone countries (Greece, Portugal, Spain), and even Belgium and Italy also faced strong pressure. Indeed, the widening sovereign yield spreads between Germany and the vulnerable countries, including the rise in the cost of insuring eurozone debt against default, underscored growing market concerns about the deteriorating state of public finances and banking problems in Ireland and

---

[25] For example, on March 30, 2009, Standard & Poor's downgraded Ireland's credit rating from AAA to AA+, and on April 8, Fitch downgraded Ireland of its AAA credit rating to AA+.

[26] In 2010, Allied Irish Banks "admitted it was increasingly reliant on central bank funding after suffering €13 billion of outflows, matching the large loss of funds reported earlier by the country's largest bank, Bank of Ireland" (Inman and Treanor, 2010). Also, Honohan (2009, 207–8) notes that "by end-year (December 2008) the share price of three of the four listed banks were between 5 and 7 percent of their peak value reached in early 2007; the other one was trading at less than 1 percent."

weaker or peripheral members in the eurozone (ECB 2010). Market sentiment turned menacingly more negative when the rating agency Standard & Poor's further downgraded Ireland's sovereign debt in mid-August. Indeed, S&P's rather cold and unambiguous estimate that Ireland's blanket guarantee could potentially cost Dublin anywhere from €80 to €90 billion (or more than 50 percent of the country's GDP), and that its public debt level would likely hover around 130 percent of GDP by 2012 (similar to Greece in 2010) profoundly unsettled the markets.

In this highly unpredictable and charged environment, it did not take much to spook the already nervous investors. The chastened creditors became panicked once again and began selling off their peripheral euro bonds – and, in the process, triggering the Irish crisis on October 18 when the French and German finance ministries and Chancellor Merkel proposed that private creditors (specifically bondholders) be involved in any future "crisis resolution mechanism" – meaning that creditors also needed to take a "haircut" for their decisions. Although the vast majority of Irish citizens (as well as German citizens paying for the profligacy of the peripheral eurozone countries like Ireland, Greece, and Portugal) probably concurred with Merkel that foreign creditors who loaned billions to Ireland's banks without due diligence should share the cost of the bailout, such talk served only to further startle the jittery investors, sending shockwaves in the bond markets and pushing up yields in several of eurozone countries. The spreads widened further after the European Council on October 28, 2010 stated that other EU governments had agreed to the proposals to establish a crisis-resolution mechanism that could potentially impose losses on bondholders. Over the next two weeks, Irish spreads jumped by more than 200 basis points, despite adamant (if not obstinate) claims by the Irish *Taoiseach* (Prime Minister) Brian Cowen and Finance Minister Brian Lenihan that Ireland was "no Greece" – meaning that Ireland did not need a sovereign bailout, but rather banking-sector support.[27]

Yet it seems the damage was already done. As the contagion began to spread again with renewed vigor, a visibly angry Greek Prime Minister George Papandreou accused Germany for spooking the bond markets as Greece's massive debt came under intense pressure and the borrowing costs

---

[27] Greece and Ireland are very different cases. Greece's problem is rooted in the nation's massive public debt. Also, unlike Ireland's, the Greek economy is relatively closed and uncompetitive. On the other hand, Ireland's problem is rooted in the country's highly indebted banking system. This gives way to the argument that the Irish banking sector could be made whole again via reorganization (especially the imposition of a more robust supervisory system) and ample capitalization.

of Ireland and Portugal shot up. It seems that even if Merkel was correct in principle, her statements could not be more ill-timed, as they undermined already eroding confidence in the European debt markets. Shut off from the international capital markets and faced with escalating borrowing costs, Irish banks were forced to seek assistance or "emergency funding" from the ECB – further panicking investors and raising concerns in the other capitals of the eurozone (Faiola 2010). Eventually, this convinced Germany, France, and other European governments to push the beleaguered Irish government to formally seek assistance by accepting a bailout package offered jointly by the EU and the IMF. On November 28, 2010, Dublin finally received approval for an €85 billion ($113 billion) emergency-aid package of which some €45 billion would come from bilateral loans from the EU (in particular, the two EU rescue funds set up in spring 2010), €22.5 billion from the IMF, and €17.5 billion from its own pension reserves.

For its part, using the fund from its own pension reserves was just one of the bitter pills or "conditionality" Ireland had to swallow. Dublin, which in 2008 had already slashed spending and raised taxes to the tune of about €15 billion had to agree to an austerity plan that would, over the next four years, cut an additional €15 billion (€10 billion in spending cuts and €5 billion in tax and other revenue-generating measures), including sharp reductions in public-sector jobs, wages and benefits, and even more in property taxes from the already besieged homeowners. However, even these draconian cuts may not be enough to meet the government's (and the EU/IMF) target to bring Ireland's budget deficit down to about 2.8 percent of GDP by 2014 from the 12 percent in 2011.[28] Certainly, for the residents of Ireland, the future will be defined by a massive fiscal retrenchment – which means living with excruciatingly painful austerity measures and prolonged hard times.[29] Yet adding insult to injury, even as the cost of the massive bank bailout will remain a huge burden on Irish taxpayers for years to come, it is worth reiterating that the major banks from the other EU nations, including the United Kingdom, Germany, and France, which have large exposures to the Irish economy and are the beneficiaries of the Irish's government's blanket guarantee, will hardly feel the commensurate pain. Similarly, the EU/IMF package exempted senior bondholders (although subordinated-debt holders were not spared), who lent money to Irish banks from suffering any losses,

---

[28] Specifically, Dublin aimed to reduce the deficit to 9.1 percent of GDP in 2011, 7 percent in 2012, 5.5 percent in 2013, and to 2.8 percent by 2014. Nevertheless, a 2010 IMF report notes the problems in meeting these targets (IMF 2010c).

[29] Rogoff (2010, 2) has noted that "the so-called 'PIGS' (Portugal, Ireland, Greece, and Spain) face the prospect of a 'lost decade' much as Latin America experienced in the 1980's."

although the EU agreed that private investors will be held accountable for losses in future crises.[30] However, the EU did add an important caveat to this controversial measure. Specifically, beginning in 2013, eurozone bonds will include clauses requiring bondholders to accept debt-restructuring measures "on a case-by-case basis." This means that bondholders will be liable only if a country became "insolvent" and was about to default on its obligations (it is important to note that bondholders, including banks and hedge funds, were also protected in the Greek bailout).

Given this, it is hardly surprising that even as the Irish parliament approved the EU/IMF bailout package (on December 15, 2010), the opposition *Fine Gael* party threatened to renegotiate the agreement if it won the general elections set for mid-2011 with the aim to force senior bondholders in Irish banks to take their share of losses. Suffice it to note, if Ireland were to unilaterally renege on its responsibilities, the ramifications would be profoundly negative for the economy and Ireland's reputation. Regardless, the challenges for Ireland remain significant. For example, given the fact that the EU/IMF bailout package fails to strike an appropriate balance between revenue and spending measures, it is not clear how it will help Ireland reduce its public debt, which is estimated currently at around 130 percent of GDP. Clearly, in its current shape the package will add to Ireland's already high debt levels.

Reinhart and Rogoff (2009) argue that 90 percent of GDP is the highest sustainable level of public debt for a developed country. Ireland is estimated to accumulate a crippling 150 percent of GNP in debt by 2014 even if it carries out substantial domestic fiscal cuts. This means that Ireland may no longer be able to raise funds on financial markets without paying prohibitive interest rates. In turn, this raises questions about Ireland's long-term solvency. Not surprisingly, the markets know that a painful debt restructuring cannot be ruled out. Indeed, if the real task is to reduce the high debt ratios (rather than simply throwing more money at the problem), than giving the so-called haircuts, or write-downs and restructurings, sooner rather later makes more sense. Of course, this will mean some pain for the bondholders. Moreover, the average annual interest rate for the IMF/EU loans to Ireland set at 5.8 percent is rather high for a struggling economy. Ireland may not be able to service its debt. Under those circumstances the interest

---

[30] To be fair, Olli Rehn, the EU's commissioner for economic and monetary affairs, defended his position of "no haircut on senior debt" because he wanted to show the markets that the EU was serious when it said that only future bailout recipients could be forced to reduce bondholder returns – but only once the permanent mechanism came into force in 2013. See Chaffin (2010).

and principal will surely take more than chum change from the country's national income.[31] Given this, Ireland, like Greece, could very well need to devalue its currency if it hopes to restore competitiveness. Of course, that is not possible as long as Ireland remains in the eurozone.[32] As noted, debt restructuring is also an option, but this could precipitate a wider European banking crisis. In turn, such a crisis would negatively impact U.S. banks and the global financial markets, because Ireland's economy has deep financial ties to global markets – thereby making spillover risks significant. As an IMF study notes: "disorderly eruption of financial pressures in Ireland could have wider implications through foreign banks' exposure to Ireland."[33]

Portugal and Spain

Following in the footsteps of Greece and Ireland, Portugal became the third eurozone member to receive a bailout totaling €78 billion from the EU and the IMF. However, Portugal's problem did not stem from a Greece-style public profligacy or a housing market collapse like Ireland's. Rather, it stemmed from a fundamentally weak and uncompetitive economy whose

---

[31] Of course, the policy makers' assumptions that Ireland's economy will grow fast enough to enable it to service its mounting volumes of debt (both public and private) is based more on hope than on evidence.

[32] Eichengreen (2010, 1) notes,

The standard way to buffer the effects of austerity is to marry domestic cuts to devaluation of the currency. Devaluation renders exports more competitive, thus substituting external demand for the domestic demand that is being compressed. But, since none of these countries has a national currency to devalue, they must substitute internal devaluation for external devaluation. They have to cut wages, pensions, and other costs in order to achieve the same gain in competitiveness needed to substitute external demand for internal demand.

[33] The same IMF report (2010c, 6–7) notes

German and U.K. banks have the largest exposure to Ireland (€113 billion and €107 billion, respectively), followed by U.S. (€47 billion), French (€36 billion), and Belgian (€24 billion) banks. As a percent of home country banking system assets, banks from Belgium (2.2 percent), Germany (1.8 percent), and the U.K. (1.3 percent) are the most exposed. However, global banks' direct exposure to Irish sovereign debt remains very limited. Portfolio investments are another potential channel of financial contagion. The countries with the largest portfolio investments in Ireland are the U.K. (€134 billion), Germany (€112 billion), France (€95 billion), and the U.S. (€83 billion). Relative to home country GDP, the most exposed countries are Portugal (18.8 percent), the U.K. (8.9 percent), Belgium (8.1 percent), the Netherlands (6.2 percent), Switzerland (5.9 percent), France (5.2 percent), and Germany (4.8 percent). The largest part of foreign portfolio claims on Ireland is generally in the form of long-term debt securities, with the exception of the US, Switzerland and Sweden where equity securities are more important.

roots date back to a decade of anemic growth averaging a mere 0.7 percent a year (Sharma and Tam 2012). This outcome was primarily because despite integration in the EU, Portugal remained a closed and inexorably "statist" or heavily regulated economy, and for political reasons, Lisbon kept raising nominal wages even as productivity growth remained stagnant, if not actually declined. Artificial hikes in wages not only undermined Portugal's core comparative advantage in labor cost, it also led to superficial increases in asset values, which in turn, created an imbalance between real wealth and imagined wealth via misleading valuation. As Portugal's overpriced goods lost global market share, the country's economic growth was undermined. To compensate, Lisbon engaged in massive external borrowing (in the process amassing a huge deficit) to finance an investment and consumption binge.

Although Madrid did not seek EU/IMF assistance until June 2012, the Spanish economy remained highly vulnerable from the onset of the Greek crisis. During the period 1989–2006, "the Spanish economy grew at 4.7 percent annum, whereas output expanded by 3.8 percent per annum... there was scarcely any growth in productivity (Stein 2011 203; Bank of Spain 2011). Because expenditures were fast outstripping production, the economy not only lost competitiveness, but saw its external debt expand as borrowing by both the central and subnational governments was used to fill the shortfalls. Specifically, since 1975 (the end of Franco dictatorship) Spain went from being one of Western Europe's most centralized states to one of the most decentralized. However, fiscal decentralization has also meant a free rein on spending by subnational governments – whose proportion of total government expenditure is now among the highest in the OECD. Subnational governments engaged in massive expansionary fiscal policies during the post-2000 housing boom, exacerbating Madrid's budget deficits.

Nevertheless, the bulk of the borrowing was not by the public sector, but due to the reckless borrowing and spending by banks, businesses, and households. The private sector, in particular, the banks (which dominate the Spanish financial system and are large relative to the economy) borrowed "cheaply" in the international financial markets and invested much of it in the booming real-estate sector. For example, construction and real-estate loans grew from 10 percent of GDP in 1992 to 43 percent in 2009 (Bank of Spain 2009), and housing prices jumped "from an average rate of 1 percent per annum between 1995 and 1997 to 18 percent between 2003–04, or an average growth of 10 percent between 1995 and 2007" (Stein 2011, 203; also IMF 2011). Thomas and Minder (2012) vividly capture the boom times:

By any measure, the Spanish real estate boom was one of the headiest ever. Spurred by record-low interest rates Spaniards piled into holiday villas along the Costa Brava, gaudy apartments in Madrid and millions of starter homes throughout the country. But, since the frenzy drove Spanish home prices to a peak in 2007, they have fallen by at least one-fourth and the bottom seems nowhere in sight. With a rising portion of Spain's 663 billion euros, or $876 billion, in home mortgages [are] at risk of default.

However, when the housing bubble burst it exposed the fragility of the country's banking system, especially its saving banks, known as *cajas*. Madrid was forced to bail out the banks and pump generous volumes of liquidity in the economy. By taking over the banks' private debt, Madrid increased its overall (public) debt levels. The next chapter examines the ongoing efforts and challenges in dealing with the eurozone's problems.

FOUR

The Eurozone's Sovereign-Debt Crisis

Despite the unprecedented "bailout packages" for Greece, Ireland, and Portugal, and more recently Spain, and the EU's €750 billion ($1 trillion) war chest to quell the Eurozone's sovereign-debt crisis, the currency union's woes still remain intractable.[1] Greece continues to teeter on the brink of default and an ignominious exit from the eurozone, and the borrowing cost remains volatile in the eurozone's peripheral countries, Portugal, Ireland, Italy, Greece, and Spain (referred to uncharitably as the PIIGS). This reflects the market's deep concern about the sustainability of the PIIGS's public debts and fiscal policies, these countries' ability to stay within the eurozone, and the credibility of the eurozone's various crisis-resolution mechanisms.

The lingering fear is the contagion overwhelming the much larger economies like Spain and Italy with virulent spillovers into the much healthier economies in the seventeen-country, single-currency area, notably Germany and France. Markets know that if the volatility of Italian and Spanish bond yields are not stabilized it may become cost-prohibitive to roll over their already existing heavy debts at market rates. This could potentially force Rome and Madrid to seek bailouts that the eurozone cannot afford or sustain (Figures. 4.1, 4.2, and 4.3).

After all, this is what pushed Greece, Ireland, and Portugal over the cliff and forced them to seek bailouts from the EU and the IMF.[2] The nightmare scenario is the sovereign-debt crisis spreading to the eighth-largest economy in the world and the third-largest in Europe – Italy, which, as the cliché goes, "is too big to fail and too big to bail." Italy's level of public debt,

---

[1] Of course, official bailout packages consist of interest-bearing loans. These loans replace the maturing private debt. If grants were given, that would constitute a clear case of bailout.

[2] On July 12, 2011, Italian ten-year yields jumped more than 30 basis points rising above 6 percent for the first time since 1997. A 7 percent level is seen as unsustainable for Italy's borrowing needs.

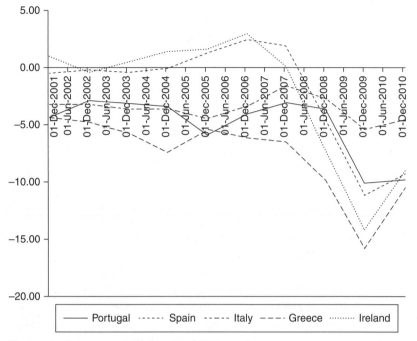

Figure 4.1. Government balance as % of GDP.
Source: Calculated from Eurostat.

estimated at more than $2.6 trillion or 119 percent of its total economic output, is nearly three times that of Greece, Portugal, and Ireland combined. This makes Italy the second-most indebted eurozone country after Greece in terms of debt-to-GDP ratio (Table 4.1; Figures 4.2, 4.3, 4.4; and Figure 3.1).

Italy's large debt-to-output ratio means that it could become more difficult for Rome to finance its expenditures with higher borrowing costs. On one hand, Italian banks and financial institutions as major purchasers of their country's sovereign debt has helped Italian bond yields remain lower than what the market expects; on the other, it has saddled banks with too much government debt (IMF 2011b). Falling bond prices and rising yields would act as a disincentive to banks from purchasing bonds, which would in turn push yields even higher. This would make the cost of servicing bank debts even more expensive and ultimately impossible. The problem is that Italy may be too big to save. If that were to happen the reverberations would be felt around the world. The resultant contagion would hit like a devastating tsunami, shaking the very foundations of Europe's banking and financial

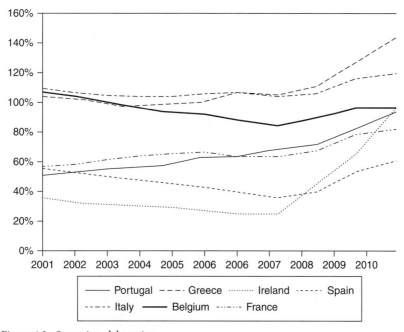

Figure 4.2. Sovereign-debt ratios.
Source: Calculated from Eurostat.

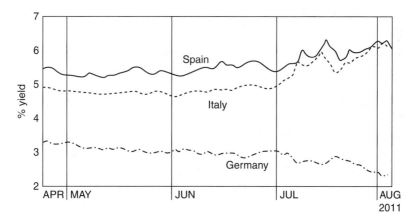

Figure 4.3. Yields on ten-year bonds for Spain, Italy, and Germany.
Source: Bloomberg.

Table 4.1. *Gross national debt in selected EU*
countries, 2010 (in U.S.$)

Country	Debt	% of GDP
Germany	3.0 trillion	83.2
Italy	2.6 trillion	119.0
France	2.3 trillion	81.7
United Kingdom	1.9 trillion	80.0
Spain	908.4 billion	60.1
Greece	467.3 billion	142.8
Portugal	228.2 billion	93.0
Ireland	210.6 billion	96.2
Belgium	485.0 billion	96.8
Austria	291.8 billion	72.3
Netherlands	527.7 billion	62.7
Finland	124.0 billion	48.4
Poland	228.2 billion	93.0
Sweden	208.2 billion	39.8
Denmark	145.2 billion	43.6
Hungary	111.3 billion	80.2
Latvia	11.4 billion	44.7
Estonia	1.4 billion	6.6

Source: Compiled from Eurostat.com.

sectors and triggering the mother of all liquidity crises, reminiscent of what happened after the fall of Lehman Brothers in September 2008. Hence, stabilizing the eurozone cannot be overstated.

Yet, despite the numerous predictions for its imminent demise, the eurozone, at least to date, has defied the odds. What explains this? Addressing this question requires a critical evaluation of a number of related questions, specifically: how has the so-called troika – the European Commission (EC), the European Central Bank (ECB), and the International Monetary Fund (IMF), including key member states, in particular, Germany and France, responded to the unprecedented crisis in its realm? What precisely has it done to keep the eurozone together? How effective has its efforts been? What can and should be done to save the union? Is there a way out of the crisis for the eurozone-distressed sovereigns? The following sections examine these interrelated issues by analyzing the EU and the troika's core initiatives beginning with the onset of Greece's crisis in late 2009 and concluding with the ECB's ambitious bond-buying plan or the "Outright Market Transactions" in September 2012 as well as the December 13, 2012 agreement to place eurozone banks under a single supervisor. However, given that the eurozone's

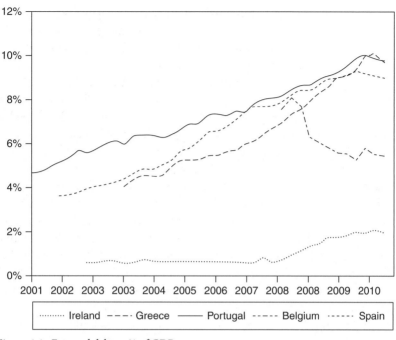

Figure 4.4. External debt as % of GDP.
Source: Calculated from Eurostat.

many woes are still unresolved the narrative too remains tentative as the ultimate fate of the currency union cannot be known.

Undoubtedly, there is much truth in the criticism that the troika's exasperatingly indecisive, inconsistent, piecemeal, and improvised approach to dealing with the eurozone's problems (aptly dubbed "kicking the can down the road") have served to exacerbate the monetary union's problems. But it is not entirely fair to lay all the blame on the troika and key eurozone governments, namely Germany (and France under Sarkozy), for playing the flute while the monetary union burns as much of the conventional commentary tends to. EU leaders know what is at stake. Indeed, German Chancellor Angela Merkel has often noted that "if the euro fails, then Europe too will fail" and that the EU leadership will do what it takes to keep the union intact. As noted, what is not always appreciated is that the governance structure of the EU and the eurozone makes arriving at expeditious and binding decisions extremely difficult. Despite this, the stark reality that their fates are inextricably intertwined has forced the EU (the fractious disagreements and acrimony notwithstanding), to continue to work together to keep the economic and monetary union intact.

Have the key players in this drama put in place the necessary policies and programs to pull the monetary union out of its seemingly unending crisis? Furthermore, have they shown the necessary flexibility and adjusted their efforts as circumstances have dictated? Admittedly, since the onset of the Greek crisis and for several months after, the troika remained convinced that the problem was Greece and that saving Greece was all that was needed to resolve the eurozone's problems. In their search for an easy fix (that is the most politically convenient and timid) – which they often arrived at in the eleventh hour – the troika has usually come up with a mixed bag of improvised, stop-gap, costly, sometimes imaginative and sometimes punitive measures that have allowed the eurozone to survive one crisis after another (at least at the time of this writing). Although the troika's efforts have fallen short of resolving the eurozone's fundamental woes, rather fortuitously, its punctuated measures have ended up creating a financial firewall around Greece. Arguably, even if this has made the eurozone better positioned to deal with a possible Greek exit,[3] it does not mean that the firewall will hold, and the potential contagion may not be contained and the collateral damage from a disorderly Greek exit may be unmanageable.

By mid-2012, following Spain's request for a €100 billion in bailout, the eurozone's problems had moved inexorably beyond Greece. The currency union is now confronting an existential crisis as the veritable financial firewall that markets assumed existed between small peripherals like Greece, Portugal, and Ireland and the much larger and systemic economies like Spain and Italy has been ominously breached. Seemingly reminiscent of the chronic developing country debtors of yesteryear, the eurozone is now facing a systemic crisis due to a loss of investor confidence. Indeed, the fear of a possible eurozone breakup has resulted in an ongoing repatriation of private capital from the peripheral countries to the core. This, in turn, has resulted in rising (and volatile) credit spreads on the peripheral countries' sovereign and bank borrowers.

The EU decision makers seem to have finally reached the unavoidable conclusion that their erstwhile, half-hearted, country-by-country firefighting efforts are no longer sufficient to assuage investor confidence and ultimately save the union. Rather, in order to ameliorate market concerns and end the wild roller-coaster ride the eurozone has endured over the past three years it must put in place unequivocal and emphatic measures, if not a coherent financial architecture for the union, to convince markets that it is

---

[3] It has also given the private sector time to prepare for a potential Greek exit. Banks and businesses have increasingly factored in losses in their balance sheets (and priced in the cost of a Greek default), including contingency plans in case of a disorderly Greek default.

genuinely committed to saving the monetary union. Undoubtedly, an efficiently functioning monetary union requires deep economic and financial
integration, in particular, political and fiscal union. However, this is not in
the cards, at least, not in the immediate future. This explains the widespread
pessimism regarding the troika and the EU's ability to ultimately save the
eurozone. However, without diminishing the many challenges ahead, this
chapter strikes a more optimistic note. It highlights the various measures
that the troika and the EU leadership has either agreed upon or put in place
over the past three years (which have been obscured by dithering and mixed
messages), in particular, a number of ambitious measures since the second
half of 2012. If further augmented with supporting institutions these measures have the potential to greatly mitigate market concerns and keep the
eurozone whole. Of course, whether the EU leadership and the troika prove
successful remain to be seen.

A New European Fiscal Compact

To show markets their steadfast commitment to deeper European economic
integration, on August 16, 2011, President Sarkozy and Chancellor Merkel
jointly announced their support for a "true European economic government." To show that their proposal was more than just on paper, both leaders stated that the new body, led initially by EU President Herman Van
Rompuy for a two-and-a-half-year term, will work to fast-track "a stronger
convergence in finance and economic policy within the eurozone," and meet
twice a year to oversee progress on economic integration. To show their
commitment, Germany and France pledged to harmonize their national
policies on corporate income taxes and establish a common tax on financial
transactions by 2013. In December 2011, eurozone member-states agreed to
deepen integration by requiring all members to enact legislation to constitu-
tionally bind their governments to maintain mandatory balanced budgets.
Deeper integration took an important step forward when on March 2, 2012
the leaders of twenty-five EU member countries (the United Kingdom and
the Czech Republic opted out) signed the Treaty on Stability, Coordination
and Governance in the Economic and Monetary Union. Also called the
"European Fiscal Compact," the agreement (already ratified by twelve of
the seventeen eurozone member states and in effect since January 1, 2013),
is designed to reinforce the "convergence criteria" – namely, that member
states' deficits should not exceed 0.5 percent of their annual GDP unless
they have a GDP-to-debt ratio of less than 60 percent. In other words, all
eurozone member countries will be required to follow Germany's example

and adopt a "debt brake" or a legal cap on the cyclically adjusted general government deficit of 0.5 percent of GDP. Clearly, the treaty's main goal is to limit government spending by placing strict new rules on deficits and debts. The supervision, to be carried out by eurozone member states (with each reviewing the others' budgets), is designed to mitigate the free-rider problem. Having learned a bitter and costly lesson from the "Greek irregularities," the European Court of Justice has been given the responsibility to make certain that every member abide by the rules of the court and the power to strike down a member's national laws if the country violates the established rules of fiscal discipline. In addition, the pact makes explicit that member states deviating from the Stability and Growth Pact's fiscal rules or who fail to meet the set targets will face tough sanctions in the form of a fine totaling up to 0.1 percent of their national GDP. The fiscal compact along with earlier measures to promote more effective cross-border surveillance to assess and manage systemic risks, macro-prudential supervision of financial institutions, and greater fiscal harmonization among the twenty-seven members of the EU are certainly long overdue and sorely needed to provide coherence to the union's fiscal policies – in particular, to serve as a buffer against the growth of unsustainable budgets.

Creation of EFSF and ESM and Expansion of the ECB

The eurozone now also has the makings of a supranational centralized fiscal entity designed to deliver funds to members facing economic shocks. On March 11, 2011, the twenty-seven member states of the EU agreed on a comprehensive plan to restore confidence in the banking sector and in the euro by permitting the European Financial Stability Facility (EFSF), established in June 2010, to lend the full €440 billion ($615 billion) at its disposal. Prior to this, the EFSF, because of strict credit-rating requirements, was able to lend only about €250 billion ($350 billion), raising legitimate concerns that the amount would be insufficient if a large economy such as Spain or Italy needed emergency funding. In addition, the EFSF funds can be used to buy bonds directly from governments via a buyback or a swap in which private owners of Greek government bonds, including banks and insurers, would accept cuts to the face value of their holdings. The EFSF is also allowed to purchase government bonds at a discount on the secondary market.[4] This also made it

---

[4] However, contrary to the EU's Executive Commission, including the ESB's request, Germany made it clear that the bailout funds used to buy bonds cannot be used to purchase debt in the open market or to finance debt buybacks.

possible to give Greece more time to repay its €110 billion bailout (approved on May 20, 2010) as the maturity on its loans were extended to 7.5 years and its interest burden reduced by 1 percentage point to about 4.2 percent.[5]

The eurozone leaders also agreed to replace the EFSF by a permanent "euro stability fund" called the European Stability Mechanism (ESM) with greater firepower (€500 billion) to be financed through a combination of credit guarantees and cash capital.[6] The ESM took effect on July 1, 2012 – a year earlier than originally planned – and has the blessings of Germany's Constitutional Court, which approved the country's participation in the ESM. By establishing the ESM, the eurozone has, in effect, created a new international financial institution like the IMF, although the ESM covers only eurozone member states. Like the IMF, the ESM's funding will be tied to strict conditions. Furthermore, ESM lending will require an 85 percent majority, ostensibly to limit a handful of countries to hold the institution hostage. Also, beginning in January 2013, all new eurozone government bonds with maturity above one year will include collective action clauses (CACs). This will go a long way to prevent individual creditors from blocking negotiations on debt restructuring, besides making it easier to enforce losses on bondholders in the case of default.

Despite the fact that the ECB has only the singular mandate to keep inflation at the target level (unlike the U.S. Federal Reserve's dual mandate to keep both inflation and unemployment in check), the ECB has nevertheless come to serve as the first line of defense against market instability and panic by helping to buttress Europe's payments system. In essence, the ECB has been functioning progressively as a de facto lender of last resort. For example, on October 8, 2008, the ECB and the Federal Reserve (with coordinated action with other major central banks) cut 50 basis points from their respective official interest rates. Since then the ECB has continued with the progressive easing of monetary policy. In its effort to improve liquidity, the ECB began in May 2009 a program to purchase covered bonds with an initial €60 billion. In summer 2009 the ECB extended €442 billion in one-year loans in a single liquidity operation to eurozone banks as emergency funding for a year. Starting in May 2010, the ECB has also been operating a new asset-purchase program called the Securities Markets Program

---

[5] It should be noted that the Greek bailout is not part of the EFSF, but a bilateral deal between Greece and the Eurozone. Also, Ireland, the other bailout recipient, did not receive equal treatment because of Dublin's refusal to raise its 12.5 percent corporate tax rate, much to the chagrin of France and Germany. See Crawford and Kennedy (2011).

[6] The EFSF and the much smaller European Financial Stability Mechanism (EFSM) were created as a "temporary measure" set to expire in 2013.

(SMP) via which it has been purchasing sovereign securities outright in the secondary market to help reduce the high spreads between the debt of the north and peripheral eurozone economies.[7]

On February 29, 2012, the ECB issued the second round of its long-term refinancing operation (LTRO), a massive, low-interest emergency loans for an unprecedented three years to the financial sector (to about 800 banks) totaling some €529.5 billion. This infusion was in addition to €489 billion in loans given to about 523 banks at the first offering on December 21, 2011. The brainchild of the newly appointed ECB president, Mario Draghi, the LTRO aims to prevent a Lehman-style banking collapse in Europe. Clearly, these efforts have paid off. The low-interest LTRO loans (averaging 1 percent), provided against collateral such as bonds and other forms of securities, has helped to ease the eurozone's debt problems by mitigating concerns about the banking sector, namely, that many European banks faced an imminent meltdown if they failed to meet their obligations (many upcoming soon) and provide relief to beleaguered governments, several of whom otherwise would have great difficulty in servicing or refinancing their debts at affordable rates. Indeed, the main reason the borrowing rates for Italy and Spain dropped (at least until June 2012) was because banks used LTRO loans to purchase bonds issued by these countries. Undoubtedly, the ECB's liquidity infusion helped to restore greater confidence in the financial sector – underscored by greater bank lending to one another and to businesses and households.

In early August 2012, when ECB's Draghi boldly announced that the central bank would do "whatever it takes to preserve the euro, and believe me, it will be enough," and that the currency union was "irreversible," global markets began their cautious watch and wait. On September 5, when Draghi unveiled the ECB's new bond-buying plan called the "Outright Monetary Transactions" (OMT), the stock markets rallied, and yields on government bonds across Europe fell – investors were clearly elated that Draghi was finally unleashing his long-promised "big bazooka."[8] To the markets, the ECB was finally taking aggressive action (like the U.S. Federal Reserve in 2008–09), with massive liquidity infusions to ease borrowing rates of struggling member states. Under the OMT, the ECB agreed to

---

[7]   The ECB argued that its actions did not amount to quantitative easing as it was sterilizing its purchases by collecting term deposits. Furthermore, the ECB defended itself by claiming that purchasing sovereign debt on the secondary markets was different from what the ECB treaty forbids: providing credit or purchasing sovereign debt from sovereigns. For details, see ECB (2011).

[8]   The OMTs will replace the ECB's Securities Market Program (SMP).

buy government bonds with maturities of one to three years on secondary markets with no limits to the amount of purchases to provide liquidity to sovereign-debt markets in the eurozone's periphery, provided countries receiving assistance accept strict conditionality and supervision. The ECB's twenty-three-member governing council approved the OMT plan, with a lone dissenter (Jens Weidmann of the Bundesbank), who has long argued the ECB should avoid direct financing of government deficits as it is prohibited by the EU. To placate Berlin, Draghi maintained that the OMT will not increase the money supply (and therefore, threat of inflation) because bond purchases will be "sterilized" in that for each euro the ECB spends on the OMT, the ECB will withdraw an equivalent amount from the financial system – thereby keeping the money supply constant. Second, member states seeking assistance must first ask the EFSF/ESM for financial assistance (that is, apply for a bailout), and accept the strict conditions and other sanctions set by the EFSF/ESM, including regular monitoring by the IMF as disbursements of assistance will be conditional on governments meeting agreed reform targets. Put bluntly, the ECB agreed to buy the bonds only of those member states who essentially agreed to submit to external review and control of their fiscal matters.

And, third, Draghi made a bold move by waiving the ECB senior creditor status on the bonds it purchased. This means that the ECB will have the same status as private creditors who hold bonds. Thus, unlike what happened during Greece's debt restructuring when the ECB's "preferred creditor" status protected it from taking a loss but subjected private investors to big write-downs, under the OMT private bond holders will not be first to receive haircuts. The central bank hopes that by removing private investors' concern about being paid back last in the event of a sovereign default, they will not head for the exits if the ECB intervenes and buys bonds. Draghi's bold gamble with the OMT has helped to reduce the short-term borrowing rates of peripheral countries, as well as the sovereign spreads between them, notably Spain and Italy. It has also helped to keep open access to international markets for the peripheral countries. Whether there will be enough time for these countries to put in place measures to restructure their debts and stimulate growth remains to be seen. If recent experience is any guide, the spreads on sovereign debt can quickly widen as markets remain deeply concerned that the austerity measures and stagnant growth will prevent fiscal targets from being met.

Nevertheless, adopting more lender of last resort functions carries costs. Specifically, the ECB's decision to buy unlimited amounts of government bonds issued by the peripheral eurozone countries and its extensive liquidity provision to rescue banks (in return for highly questionable types of paper as collateral for secure debt), has exposed it to risk and related moral hazard problems. Yet it is also important to note that without this intervention banks would not have any means of liquidity support, and therefore, would be in no position to strengthen their balance sheets. Cumulatively, the ECB's liquidity provisions, including the dollar credit from liquidity swaps, have helped to contain the contagion and lessen the overall negative impact of the crisis.[9]

Stress Testing the Banking Sector

According to the Bank for International Settlements (BIS), of the estimated $1.6 trillion of government debt and credit held by Greece, Portugal, Ireland, and Spain, the German and French banks hold some $1 trillion (Ewing 2010, B8). Uncertainty regarding the EU banks' exposure to shaky government bonds and which banks have underwritten credit-default swaps (CDS) have made insuring Greek debt a big source of volatility, and addressing these fears is essential to regain confidence and stability.[10] There is only one way to do this well: use a common risk-management tool, the "stress test" of the banking and financial sector to assess vulnerabilities and see if they can withstand another round of economic downturn without turning to the ECB for short-term loans to remain solvent. Such an industry-wide exercise in the United States (covering nineteen large banking groups) helped calm the markets during the height of the crisis. However, the EU leadership, in particular, Germany and France, kept delaying a U.S.-style stress test. The disagreement centered over which banks should be included in the test and the criteria to be used for assessing the banks' capital requirements, in particular, whether the balance sheets of the banks should be assessed for their holdings of the sovereign bonds of the PIIGS, especially those of Greece,

---

[9]   Nevertheless, it is important to note that the ECB's firepower has limits. As Nutting (2012) writes:

> The ECB's balance sheet has expanded to around €3 trillion... Against that €3 trillion, the ECB has €82 billion in capital and reserves. That's a capital ratio of about 36 to 1. (The Fed, by the way, has about $3 trillion in assets, backed by $55 billion of capital, for a capital ratio of about 54 to 1.) With such high leverage, it wouldn't take much of a decline in the value of the ECB's assets to eat through all of its capital. The ECB is not well-capitalized at all.

[10] Banks (both Greek and Eurozone) that have underwritten the CDSs would face massive liabilities if Greece failed to meet its obligations. Hence the reason the troika and Eurozone leaders want the Greek bond swap to be deemed "voluntary" – to avoid not only a massive CDS payout but also the vicious contagion that would spread to the EU's entire financial sector.

Ireland, and Portugal. The EU's previous stress test (in mid-2010) of large banks in the union proved not to be credible for a number of reasons. First, they were coordinated by the Committee of European Banking Supervisors (CEBS), an advisory body made up of representatives from the various national supervisory agencies with limited authority. Second, a sovereign default was not incorporated in the methodology despite market concerns about sovereign-debt sustainability of the PIIGS. Third, the chosen capital benchmark (a 6 percent Tier 1 capital ratio) was inconsistently defined by national supervisors – and thus easy for weak banks to pass. In fact, the criteria and findings were watered down and compromised (giving failing grades to only a handful of banks), even when it was widely acknowledged that several banks in terrible shape had received passing grades.[11] Indeed, market skepticism was vindicated when a number of banks (mostly Irish) that had passed collapsed just a week later.

To its credit, the EU seems to have learned its lesson by allowing the newly created European Banking Authority (EBA), to conduct the latest round of stress tests on ninety-one European banks representing about 65 percent of the EU's banking sector assets and a minimum of 50 percent of bank assets in each of the twenty-one participating countries. This test used a markedly more demanding and stricter matrix, including more realistic economic assumptions (such as requiring banks to show their survivability if the value of government bonds they are holding were marked down by 10 to 15 percent), preventing banks from relying on the worn-out survival strategy (proving viability by "creatively" shifting their business plan), and requiring banks to estimate their credit impairments, trading losses, and capital position under both a baseline and an adverse scenario for 2011–12. The result (released on 15 July 2011) showed that eight banks failed the test as they had insufficient reserves to maintain a core Tier 1 capital ratio of 5 percent in the event of an economic downturn and needed to raise a mere €2.5 billion to make up their capital shortfall. Such positive news helped to calm market concerns.[12] Nevertheless, a major flaw in the stress test was that the ECB did not review what would happen if Greece

---

[11] The 2010 stress test coordinated by the (CEBS) failed to generate sustained market confidence because its methodology failed to incorporate a "sovereign default scenario," despite growing concerns about the PIIGS's sovereign debt. Moreover, the capital benchmark selected (a 6 percent Tier 1 capital ratio) was inconsistently used by national supervisors and rather easy to pass.

[12] Among the banks that failed the tests, five were in Spain, two in Greece, and one in Austria. Sixteen banks narrowly passed the stress tests. However, all of the EU's biggest banks passed the test.

defaulted and proved unable to pay its mounting debt load.[13] This partly explains why banks remained generally hesitant to lend to each other and why they continue to depend so much on the ECB for funds. EU regulators are cognizant of this and know that they need to push weaker banks to raise new capital, merge with healthy banks, or restructure their portfolios. The ECB's candid admission and next steps have helped to instill greater confidence in the EU's financial sector.

Strengthening the Banking System

The European banking system's massive exposure to sovereign debt (that is, their holdings of government and corporate bonds from Greece, Ireland, Portugal, Italy, and Spain), have raised legitimate concerns about a credit squeeze and disorderly default. This is because when the banks originally purchased these bonds they were seen as secure risk-free investments. As a result they did not (nor were they required to) to put aside reserve funds in case the bonds lost their value. To the contrary, the banks often used these bonds as collateral to raise funds. With the bonds no longer seen as risk-free, markets have become worried that European banks burdened with huge debts would try to improve their balance sheets by refusing to lend. Compounding this, the massive write-off by EU banks (in particular, the French and German banks) of peripheral debt has made them much weaker. Markets know that the possibility of a contagion spreading from within the eurozone's banking sector is a real possibility. The trigger could be any of the troubled big banks. This explains why shares of major French banks, including Societe Generale, BNP Paribas, and Credit Agricole have plummeted, and why such giants as UniCredit in Italy and Santander and BBVA in Spain, which hold domestic bond portfolios (much of them issued by their governments) that far exceed their capital levels (deposits), are so shaky.[14] In the past these banks were able to borrow easily by using their home market government bonds as collateral as it was viewed as liquid, risk-free investments much like U.S. Treasury bonds. However, as the value of these bonds began their downward trend, the banks have had more difficulties financing their day-to-day operations, including their governments. As

---

[13] Critics have accused EBA regulators for failing to include a possible Greek default in the tests and for including only a 25 percent write-down on ten-year Greek government bonds held in banks' trading books even as the securities trade at about 51 cents on the euro.

[14] It is estimated that UniCredit's exposure to mostly Italian bonds is 121 percent of its core capital ratio, an alarming 193 percent for BBVA, and 76 percent for the global banking giant Santander.

a result, these banks have been forced to borrow directly from the ECB (because the cost of borrowing dollars in the open foreign-exchange market has shot up), but the markets also knew that this could not continue indefinitely as the EFSF simply does not have enough funds to recapitalize weak banks. The PIIGS's experience illustrates that if the interbank market (where banks lend to each other) refuse to accept these bonds or demand higher prices to reflect their lower value, these banks may no longer be able to access the financing necessary to run their operations. The fallout from this will be catastrophic.

As noted, to alleviate this potential catastrophe, the ECB has been steadily strengthening European banks by providing them with liquidity (as much as three-year funding at 1 percent interest) to roll over debts worth more than €250 billion. Also, the ECB's ambitious bank-recapitalization programs, including the LTROs, in which the ECB provided €500 billion in cheap long-term three year loans to banks in December 2011 plus a second installment of €530 billion in February 2012, have helped stabilize the banking sector by buffering it against losses stemming from sovereign-debt downgrades. Since the "no bailout" clause in the Maastricht treaty prevents the ECB from directly buying sovereign bonds from member countries, the ECB has advanced these funds via a creative backdoor method to strengthen the weak eurozone member states. These interventions have also provided much-needed breathing space to the major European banks, including Deutsche Bank, BNP Paribas, Banco Santander, and Société Générale, who have improved their liquidity positions by reducing leverage, selling assets, tightening credit terms, and sharply reducing their exposure to Greece and the other peripherals. Although the ECB's interventions have served to ease fears of a credit crisis, markets know that daunting longer-term challenges remain as European banks and sovereigns will continue to face new capital requirements – for example, Italy, with its crippling €1.9 trillion debt burden, plans to issue some €245 billion of bonds in 2012 – up from €223 billion in 2011.

Toward a Banking Union

In late June 2012, EU President Herman Van Rompuy, in collaboration with ECB President Mario Draghi, EC President Jose Barroso, and Luxembourg Prime Minister Jean-Claude Juncker (who is in charge of setting up eurozone finance ministers' meetings), released a proposal called "Towards a Genuine Economic and Monetary Union" to provide a road map for the establishment of a "common banking supervision and deposit insurance" and a "criteria-based and phased" step toward "joint debt issuance."[15] The group argued that banking supervision could be effectively carried out by ECB as existing treaties give it the power to regulate and oversee the seventeen independent national regulators. On September 12, 2012, the EC released a formal "blueprint" for unified bank supervision under the auspices of the ECB, which proposed that within a year (between January 2013 and January 2014) some 6,000 eurozone banks should be able to come under ECB's Single Supervisory Mechanism or SSM (Veron 2012). Beyond all expectations, on December 13, 2012, EU leaders reached an agreement to place eurozone banks under a single supervisor with the authority to monitor banks' operations and quickly intervene when a bank is in trouble. Under the deal, about 200 major banks (or banks that have more than €30 billion in assets or balance-sheets accounting for 20 percent or more of national GDP) will come under the direct oversight of the ECB by March 2014. Although thousands of smaller banks will continue to be under the supervision of national regulators, the agreement does give the ECB broad mandate to intervene if these smaller institutions face trouble. Moreover, EU countries outside the eurozone can choose to enter into "close co-operation arrangements" with the ECB.

A full-fledged banking union must have consolidated prudential supervision under a single entity, collective deposit insurance, shared bank-deposit guarantees (similar to the FDIC), a common resolution authority, and a common resolution fund. The creation of a single supervisor nevertheless marks a significant first step in controlling risk taking by banks and reducing regulatory capture – an endemic problem at the national level. Moreover, the fact that the EU is now considering establishing a genuine banking union (EU leaders have already directed the EC to complete a Recovery and Resolution Directive and a Deposit Guarantee Scheme Directive by June 2013), will only strengthen market confidence. After all, a European deposit guarantee would not only have served to limit deposit flight (what has been called a "bank jog" rather than a "bank run") from the peripheral economies to the north, it would have also prevented the gross imbalance within eurozone banks and cost the ECB far less to fund the bailouts for the PIIGS banking sector. Indeed, the EU leadership knows that it is the absence of an effective banking union that have made bank and sovereign funding costs in the periphery vary according to market perceptions of risk. After all, the

---

[15] Herman Van Rompuy (2012). "Towards a Genuine Economic and Monetary Union," Report by President of the European Council, Brussels, 26 June. consilium.europa.eu/uedocs/cms_data/docs/pressdata/.../131201.pdf

absence of a banking union created the vicious circle between banks and sovereigns – resulting in the transfer of debts from weak and collapsing banks to sovereign governments and placing the burden on fiscally prudent governments (Ireland and Spain) with huge debt loads.

However, before a genuine banking union can come into effect it will require the support of all the twenty-seven EU member countries. In other words, the agreement must first be approved by the European parliament and national legislatures before it can go into effect. Overcoming the political obstacles as it involves states giving up significant economic sovereignty will not be easy. Countries outside the eurozone have already raised concerns regarding the new powers to be granted to the ECB, in particular, the potential this has to put their banks at a competitive disadvantage if depositors outside the eurozone move their deposits to eurozone banks given the security provided by the ECB. Although non-eurozone members are free to join the banking union (but may not have full participation in supervisory decisions), and with Great Britain (London is Europe's biggest financial center) demanding a virtual veto (as a precaution against the ECB's potential power to shape EU-wide regulations) before it agrees to take part in the banking union, means that the path to a banking union is hardly assured. For their part, a number of core eurozone members, namely Germany, Finland, the Netherlands, and Luxembourg, have also expressed concerns regarding the granting of new powers to the ECB – leading them to push for greater powers for their national regulators when it comes to day-to-day oversight of their banks. Last, but not least, as long as Berlin remains opposed to the sharing of sovereign and bank liabilities, and above all, without a fiscal union that permits control over national budgets, it is hard to imagine that the proposed European banking union would be able to break the circular link between insolvent banks and indebted sovereigns. Similarly, establishing a unified or "single" deposit-guarantee scheme would be challenging as Berlin has made clear its opposition to any mutualization of eurozone debt. Nevertheless, by agreeing on a SSM the EU leaders have taken the first necessary step toward deeper banking integration.

Private Sector Burden-Sharing

Pervasive market uncertainty and volatility eventually forced the eurozone to coalesce around the taboo subject that "greater private investor involvement" (i.e., burden-sharing) was necessary to alleviate the intense pressures on Greece and the other peripherals. Private-sector involvement has been long and strenuously opposed by the credit-rating agencies and Jean-Claude

Trichet, the ECB's ever-cautious president. However, Chancellor Merkel, in her own faltering way, seems to have gradually warmed up to the idea that bondholders should do their part by swapping their existing Greek bonds for new seven-year obligations.[16] Yet her initial proposal to this effect was brushed aside without much consideration as it was deemed too onerous on bondholders. Actually, so intense was the opposition to burden-sharing that even the much milder French rollover plan, was not only summarily rejected by Standard & Poor's, the agency also threatened to declare "a technical default" if the French plan was adopted, despite the fact that the plan did not involve a reduction in the value of private sector holdings.[17] Yet this idea would not die – in large part because most policy makers and ordinary citizens intuitively felt that it was grossly unfair for private investors who made huge profits during the boom times expected taxpayers to pick up the tab to cover their losses. Similar sentiment was expressed by the IMF, which in an influential staff report (released on July 13, 2011), unambiguously noted that "given the scale of financing needs and the desirability of burden sharing," it was "appropriate" for private bondholders to share in any restructuring, or more bluntly, accept a reduction in the value of their assets (IMF 2011c).

Rather fortuitously, this issue was forced upon EU policymakers in early July 2011 – at the height of the turmoil in Italian bond markets as well as unexpected bad news from Dublin. On July 12, 2011, Moody's abruptly cut Ireland's debt rating to junk status, noting a "growing likelihood" that holders of Irish bonds may be forced into a restructuring of their securities to help deal with Dublin's debt burden. Stated more bluntly, according to Moody's, Ireland was in danger of default. Moody's decision reflected EU policymakers' "increasingly clear preference" to have private investors, namely bondholders, do their part either by rolling their bonds into longer-term securities or by agreeing to take an interest-rate cut. Aware that something drastic must be done to contain the crisis, Eurozone finance ministers seemed ready to consider what was once considered anathema: a structured default by Greece under which private bondholders would be encouraged to "voluntarily" help roll over some of Greece's debt.[18]

---

[16] The ECB has consistently opposed any plan that would be labeled a "selective default" by the credit-rating agencies. Their concern is that a selective default would increase the risk of the debt crisis spreading to Spain and Italy. Furthermore, a selective default would also sharply reduce the value of the sovereign bond holdings the ECB has already purchased or has accepted as collateral.

[17] "Selective or technical default" is default as defined by the credit-ratings agencies or the credit-default swap markets.

[18] "Private" investors and bondholders are mostly German and French banks (whose investments are government-guaranteed), as well as the IMF and the ECB. These four

In mid-July 2011, even as pressure intensified on Spain and Italy, the credit-rating agencies stuck to their guns by openly declaring that they would view any restructuring or rollover of Greek debt as a "selective default." However, gripped with the nightmarish fear that the contagion from Greece was engulfing Spain and Italy, EU policymakers had no time for theoretical debates as to what constituted a default. Arguably, for them, the day of reckoning had arrived, and now was time for action. But the road to Rome and Madrid began in Athens – as Greece, with a debilitating debt load at 160 percent of GDP, was near meltdown. Even if Greece notched double-digit growth (a near impossibility), Athens would still not be able to meet its debt obligations as it was insolvent and fast hurtling toward a disorderly and chaotic default.[19] If the eurozone could not get its act together to save a small economy like Greece, could one expect it to save trillion-dollar economies like Spain and Italy? But the question remained: how to save Greece? History and experience showed that some form of default or restructuring coupled with fiscal austerity is necessary to help highly indebted countries reduce their debt burdens. Thus, an orderly restructuring or default by Greece did not seem as dire as the credit-rating agencies were claiming. The following sections show that private investors have taken progressively bigger haircuts (in particular, under the bond-swap plan or the "Private Sector Involvement" to ease Greece's debt) – though to some, these haircuts are still not enough.

Saving Greece to Save the Eurozone

Greece's inability to meet its debt obligations or jumpstart its economy has served to accentuate the fear of contagion, besides contributing to the rise in sovereign-debt spreads. Fearful that a Greek default could further weaken Italy, Spain, and Portugal, the troika announced on May 10, 2010 the €750 billion rescue plan for the troubled eurozone economies, and on May 20, 2010, agreed to provide relief to Greece with a €110 billion bailout package. However, Greece's continued weakness and vulnerability forced the EU to call an emergency summit in mid-2011 ostensibly to prevent Greece's problems from spiraling out of control and engulfing the entire monetary union.

entities have the largest exposure to distressed sovereign debt, especially Greek debt. Also see, "The euro's real trouble: The crisis of the single currency is political as much as financial," *The Economist*, July 14, 2011.

[19] How else could one explain why the massive bailout and Athens's tough austerity measures failed to have a commensurate positive effect on Greek bond yields – with the two-year Greek yields still trading at 28 percent and ten-year yields at 17 percent in mid-July 2011.

In the late hours of July 21, 2011, the troika reached an accord to provide a second bailout of €109 billion in new financing for Greece, including a plan to radically write down the country's debt held by the private sector, made mostly of banks and insurers.[20] However, the troika made explicit that the loans would be available only after Athens put in place a broad privatization program and formally approved the new debt agreement with a written pledge from five officials: Prime Minister Papandreou, opposition leader Antonis Samaras, the head of Greece's central bank, the new prime minister, and the finance minister.

Long accused of making the eurozone's problems progressively worse by their procrastination and denial, in particular, their failure to come up with a credible plan to deal with the debt crisis, the scope of the troika's new measures exceeded market expectations, even if not all of the fine print was disclosed. The markets did know that in order to get "Madame Nein" or Chancellor Merkel on board, roughly a third of the new bailout loans had to come in the form of debt swaps or rollovers by private-sector bondholders, reminiscent of what the "Brady bond" debt relief did for insolvent Latin American governments in the late 1980s. Also, the ECB, which had long viewed the buying of bonds to bail out profligate governments as imprudent, faced its moment of truth when confronted with an unprecedented liquidity crisis – indeed, a potential systemic risk. Nevertheless, to persuade the cautious ECB president, Jean-Claude Trichet, to support the new plan, the EFSF agreed to provide compensation to the Central Bank for any losses it suffered on Greek bonds, and thereby allow the ECB to accept the bonds as collateral in loans to Greek banks.[21]

In addition, Greek's banks and private creditors agreed to "voluntarily" choose from a menu of four options to either restructure or roll over Greek bonds into longer-dated maturities or swap them for higher-rated securities. Although private creditors were to be provided with "credit enhancements" to encourage participation, they would not escape a haircut, as the bond exchange or securities would pay less than their original contracts because the principal amount of debt Greece had to repay was being reduced. Put bluntly, European banks (mainly German and French banks, who are the major holders of Greek debt) would have to write off billions of euros to give Greece the partial debt forgiveness it desperately needed. It was estimated

---

[20] Eurozone banks were also required to raise €108 billion in additional capital over nine months to cover potential losses.

[21] Of course, to rescue banks, the ECB has had to engage in extensive liquidity provision, and in the process accept highly problematic types of paper as collateral for secure debt. Without this support the banks would not have been able to strengthen their balance sheets.

that, on average, investors would take a 21 percent loss in the net present value of their current Greek bond holdings. The ECB made it clear that this provision would apply to Greece only.

Moreover, eurozone leaders agreed to lower interest rates on the bailout loans, not only for Greece, but also for Ireland and Portugal. Each country would have the obligation to pay about 3.5 percent interest – 2 percentage points less than the set 5.5 percent. As a result, these three countries could borrow at rates similar to those paid by Germany. For Ireland, this rate reduction amounted to a substantial savings of €900 million a year on interest payments alone.[22] To lessen the burden on these overleveraged sovereigns the accord agreed to generously extend the repayment schedules from 7.5 years to a minimum of 15 and a maximum of 30 years. Finally, the EFSF was granted sweeping new powers to assist "vulnerable eurozone economies" (or those not receiving bailout funds and are not insolvent), by extending them precautionary lines of credit to aid troubled banks and to allow the EFSF to buy bonds in the secondary market to ward off speculators – subject to ratification by individual eurozone governments and approval by the ECB.[23] As noted, this marked a sharp turnaround for the ECB from its earlier policy to lend only to countries facing imminent financial collapse.[24]

Although it took the troika what felt like forever, it and the ECB seem to have come to the unpalatable realization that Greece's problem was not one of temporary liquidity, but of insolvency. Through their actions, policy makers finally acknowledged that debt restructuring (which includes both a substantial commitment of additional official resources from the EU and the IMF as well as "voluntary" contributions from Greece's private creditors, primarily European banks) is pivotal to the resolution of Greece's debt crisis. The hope was that at a minimum, the reduction in interest rates and extension of maturities offered Greece the breathing space and a chance to return to solvency and growth.

---

[22] *The Economist*, "The euro crisis: bazooka or peashooter?" July 30, 2011.

[23] Implementation of the EFSF could take a while and is hardly guaranteed. In mid-September 2011, Finland demanded collateral for its share of Greek bailout loans, and in Austria political opposition forced Parliament to postpone a vote on the reforms. Further complicating matters, the Slovakian parliament announced that it will take up the issue only after all other EU members have ratified it.

[24] For details see "Statement by the Heads of State or Government of the Euro Area and EU Institutions," Council of the European Union, Brussels, 21 July 2011, http://www.consilium.europa.eu/uedocs/cms_data/docs/pressdata/en/ec/123978.pdf; also Spiegel, Peel, Jenkins, and Milne (2011); Kowsmann, Paris, and Fidler (2011); and *Spiegel* (2011).

However, there could be no guarantee that the restructuring of Greek debt, including fiscal transfers from the EU, would enable Athens to address the country's pervasive structural challenges, especially its eroding economic competitiveness. In fact, Greek goods and services are increasingly uncompetitive, not only within the eurozone, but also on world markets. The markets are cognizant of the fact that given Greece's current productivity levels, it cannot compete at the current value of the euro, and its high levels of indebtedness (relative to GDP) will take years to reduce. Furthermore, the new bailout package, by transferring additional risks to Germany, France, and other stronger eurozone economies (and their taxpayers), has the potential to weaken incentives for Greece and the other peripherals to implement the necessary fiscal and structural reforms. The plan suggested that if a country receiving bailout funds failed to implement the agreed-upon structural reform measures, the eurozone will have the power to impose the reforms. However, markets know that at the end of the day it will be up to Athens to deliver on its commitments to reform, including restructuring and privatizing its economy. Given the tough economic and political choices Athens has to make, they also know that such a commitment was hardly guaranteed. Finally, while Greece has communicated (by words and increasingly by deeds) that it is committed to a "sustainable budget path," footloose and yield-seeking investors rarely have the patience to wait for a recovery that could take years. As Reinhart and Rogoff (2009) show, private and public deleveraging (which applies to Greece) historically has been neither quick nor painless. Rather, in the three years following a severe financial crisis, government debts tend to almost double.

Markets also know that Greece's fate is not entirely in Athens's hand. For starters, markets realize that such a detailed and technically complex agreement will require time to implement as twenty-seven national parliaments must ratify the accord before it can be implemented. Exacerbating this, default and restructuring is difficult under the best of circumstances (when the debt is held by just a few banks and investors), but, as the experience of Latin America in the 1980s underscores, when there are legions of investors and creditors (as in the case of Greece and other peripherals), conflicts, including lawsuits, are common as stakeholders try to demand their "fair share" of the dwindling pie. Although the Institute for International Finance (an organization made up of the world's biggest banks), which negotiated the deal, hoped for 90 percent participation, it remained unclear what percentage of holders of Greek debt were prepared to voluntarily agree to the deal. Indeed, not every private investor was on board, and some international creditors demanded even more concessions from Greece. Adding to the uncertainty, parliamentary approval by EU member states was necessary before the EFSF's new powers became operational as the EFSF's enhanced powers were assumed, not guaranteed. Markets know that without the backing of the EFSF's deep pockets, the entire plan would go nowhere.

To many market participants, "restructuring" was tantamount to default. Not surprisingly, on July 22, 2011, Fitch claimed that because the plan involved getting bondholders to assume part of the cost, Greece constituted a "restricted default." Although Fitch assigned its new default ratings a "low speculative grade" (meaning that a restricted default is not too disruptive and will have no practical consequence as it is likely to be brief), it was still humiliating as Greece became the first country using the euro to default. Fitch and other rating agencies also warned that their ratings were not irrevocable and that future downgrades could not be ruled out. Much would depend on whether the new plan ameliorated investor concerns about debt sustainability in Greece and the other peripherals.

Markets Turn on the PIIGS

In the first week of August 2011, with the markets transfixed by the debt-ceiling drama in Washington D.C., concerns about the sovereign-debt problems in Europe took a backseat. However, with the U.S. debt-ceiling drama temporarily settled, the markets turned their attention back to Europe. Of course, the markets know that unlike the United States (which can meet its debt obligations by printing dollars and issuing common securities), the eurozone cannot issue a single debt instrument (like a eurobond). Although, individual governments can, the bond they offer would differ in risk, return, and liquidity.[25]

---

[25] On August 5, 2011, Standard & Poor's announced that it was reducing its credit rating for long-term U.S. government debt from AAA (the highest rating) to AA+. Yet despite the United States' huge deficits, it still collects enough tax dollars each month to stay current on its debt payments. Furthermore, the dollar's status as the world's reserve currency makes its relatively immune to market turmoil, and investors still consider U.S. Treasury bonds as among the safest and most liquid investable asset in the world. Also, S&P's downgrade had more to do with the political impasse in Washington, D.C. rather than fundamentals. After all, a number of countries with AAA-rated sovereign debts, including the United Kingdom and France, have higher debt loads than the United States. Nevertheless, it should be noted that the U.S. dollar notched up sharp gains vis-à-vis the euro because of the uncertain signals coming from the ECB and eurozone governments. In other words, given the United States' economic woes, the dollar's rally is not backed by economic fundamentals. Rather, with persistently high unemployment and the Federal Reserve's commitment to keep interest rates near zero for two years, the dollar's recent rally has more to do with investors' aversion to risks in the eurozone. Thus, this flight to safety to the

In an effort to keep the markets calm, ECB President Trichet announced (during the middle of his televised monthly news conference on August 4, 2011) that the ECB would restart its program of buying the sovereign debt of Irish and Portuguese securities, but not Spanish and Italian bonds. Trichet's remarks backfired as nervous investors concluded that Spanish and Italian bonds were mispriced and that the ECB had no real commitment or resources to deal with Spain and Italy. Predictably, yields on ten-year Italian and Spanish government bonds passed 6 percent – a threshold seen as unsustainable based on the overall weakness of both economies and the heavy debt loads each country already carried. Only after the ECB announced the next day that it was prepared to buy Italian and Spanish bonds (after the Italian prime minister committed his government to speeding up reforms and introducing a balanced-budget amendment by 2013, a year earlier than planned) did the stock markets temper their wild gyrations.[26]

On August 7, 2011, the ECB and the EFSF reiterated their commitment to buying Italian and Spanish bonds on the secondary market. However, given the massive size of the Spanish and Italian sovereign-debt markets, the ECB would have to buy many billions of euros of these bonds to have any real impact.[27] While this meant that the ECB would dramatically expand its balance sheet, it was still too early to predict if this seemingly desperate line of defense would bring and keep down Spanish and Italian bond spreads.[28] Nevertheless, the ECB's action did, at least in the short run, keep speculators at bay as they would have to think twice about selling or shorting Italian and Spanish bonds. Moreover, the downgrading of U.S. debt raised concerns over whether France could keep its AAA rating as its debt at 82 percent of GDP is among the highest of any AAA-rated country. Exacerbating this, the EU authorities suspected (with some justification) that traders were already spreading false information in an attempt to drive

---

dollar cannot be taken for granted. However, U.S. Treasuries bonds still remain the place to park capital in troubled times because there is no alternative to the security and liquidity they offer. Nevertheless, with the benchmark ten-year U.S. Treasury yields at record lows, investor dalliance with U.S. Treasury bonds may be temporary.

[26] In July 2011 Italy passed a €48 billion package that contained cuts in the funding for local governments, reduction in welfare payments, more fees for health services and reforms to the country's tax system. However, these measures were to be delayed until after elections in 2013. As Italian bond yields soared to fourteen-year highs, Prime Minister Berlusconi announced plans to speed up the reforms and balance the budget by 2013.

[27] Italy's bond market alone is estimated to be more than $1.6 trillion.

[28] In the ten weeks leading up to October 14, 2011, the ECB purchased an estimated €92.3 billion worth of eurozone bonds with no real impact as Italian and Spanish debt (estimated at around €2.3 trillion) is larger than the ECB's balance sheet.

the price of French bank stocks down in the hopes of then making a profit by short-selling. Thus, as a further precaution, the European Securities and Markets Authority imposed a temporary short-selling ban beginning on August 12, 2011 on bank stocks owned by France, Italy, Spain, and Belgium. The measure had the desired effect in calming market volatility and providing much-needed relief to European banks. Although the ban was necessary because unfounded rumors, reckless trading, and speculation (reflected in the rather unusual swings in financial stocks of French banks[29]) threatened the ability of several European banks to raise funds, such bans are hardly a long-term solution. In fact, short-selling bans, if enforced for too long, can lead to investor uncertainty – as in 2008 following the Lehman meltdown.

With no immediate resolution of the eurozone's problems in sight, investor confidence remained fickle, and the markets easily spooked. In this environment it is hardly surprising that in mid-September 2011, the eurozone once again came under threat as fears of yet another imminent Greek default pushed interest rates on the country's ten-year government bonds up to a new record of more than 24 percent. This new round of crisis was triggered after Merkel's deputy, Vice Chancellor Philipp Roesler, panicked markets with talk that an "orderly insolvency" of Greek debt (in other words, Greek bankruptcy) is a "possibility." Damage control by Merkel, Sarkozy, Greek Prime Minister Papandreou, and President Obama, as well as the decision by Germany's high court to uphold the country's participation in the bailout of Greece and the eurozone rescue fund helped calm markets and bolstered the euro. Investors nevertheless remained fearful that Greece was heading toward a chaotic default because putting together an "orderly default" is difficult, even in the best of circumstances.[30]

Under intense pressure, on October 27, 2011 the eurozone leaders reached a significant deal with private banks and insurers under which these creditors accepted a 50 percent loss on their Greek government bonds. In fact, private investors were "invited" to accept the loss under threat that their

---

[29] Gill (2011) notes that "French banks fell sharply midweek amid fears of a French downgrade, dragging down European shares. Société Générale plunged, hitting a 2½-year low and dropping 13.7 per cent over the week to €23.66. Other French banks also tumbled, with BNP Paribas falling 10.2 per cent to €35.45 and Crédit Agricole dropping 9.8 per cent to €6.46."

[30] The euro dropped to $1.3495 on September 12, 2011, the lowest level since mid-February. However, on September 14, the euro increased by 0.89 percent after the ECB announced that it would coordinate with the U.S. Federal Reserve and other central banks to conduct three-dollar liquidity operations to ensure banks have enough of the currency through year-end. This was important as European banks have had great difficulty to get funding for dollar assets after U.S. money market mutual funds cut short-term loans.

failure to agree could result in even larger losses. The write-downs were structured as a "voluntary exchange" of maturing Greek bonds for new bonds to avoid triggering the credit-default swaps (CDS). However, the EU could not bask in its glory for too long; rather inexplicably, on October 31, 2011, Prime Minister Papandreou, without consulting EU leaders, issued a call for a referendum on the bailout. Although he backed off a week later after pressure from exasperated EU leaders, the damage was done. The markets saw a lack of political will on Athens part and Greece hurtling inexorably toward default. As fears of a contagion grew, Italy's borrowing costs sharply rose with yields on ten-year Italian bonds trading as high as 7.48 percent in early November 2011 – their highest since the adoption of the euro in 1999. This run-up on Italian bond yields came despite valiant buying by the ECB to keep those yields below 6 percent. Breaching the 7 percent threshold was deemed akin to crossing the Rubicon because it was the line Ireland and Portugal crossed before receiving bailouts from the EU and the IMF. In late November 2011, with the credit-rating agencies warning of further government downgrades, the extremely secure ten-year German bund yield rose by 12 basis points (or 0.12 percentage point), to 2.26 percent, the highest since October 28. For France, Finland, the Netherlands, and Austria the impact was immediate: they would have to pay more interest on their bonds. Frantic EU leaders came up with yet another plan. As noted, on December 9, 2011, the EU (with the exception of the United Kingdom), endorsed a new balanced budget pact for more effective region-wide oversight of government spending and agreed to raise an additional $270 billion to assist indebted member governments meet their obligations.

As 2011 came to a close, markets seemed to have come to terms with the reality that fundamental reforms such as issuing common debt in the form of eurobonds would have to wait. This was good news to Merkel who steadfastly maintained that there will be no joint eurozone borrowing (bonds) or an expansion in the ECB's role. Rather, the focus must be on debt reduction and closer economic coordination between the seventeen eurozone members. On January 13, 2012, Standard & Poor's cut its ratings for Cyprus, Italy, Portugal, and Spain by two notches and lowered the ratings of Austria, France, Malta, Slovakia, and Slovenia by one notch, leaving Germany as the only eurozone member with an AAA rating. Stripping France, the eurozone's second largest economy, of the AAA ratings made it much more expensive for the eurozone's bailout fund to assist the truly beleaguered economies because the bailout fund's own rating depends on those of its members. Hardly surprisingly, Merkel used the downgrade to implore the eurozone to accelerate efforts to implement a more centralized currency union and to get the union's permanent bailout facility, the ESM, to begin its operations sooner than the scheduled July 1, 2012 date.

More Carrots and Sticks to Save Greece

To the markets, the eurozone's Achilles heel remained Greece. Despite massive bailouts and several months of punitive austerity, Athens continued to fall behind with the implementation of the agreed fiscal and structural reforms, and the country's financial situation remained precarious. To the markets, this only reinforced the view that a disorderly default by Greece was a real possibility.[31] Without a meaningful resolution of Greece's problem, the EU's problem was not going to go away. In February 2012 the troika, along with Berlin and Paris, came up with a radical plan that struck a chord with the financial markets. The plan came in the form of (a) an extension of the second bailout package from €109 billion to €130 billion to help Athens avoid a potential default on a €14.5 billion bond redemption due on March 20, 2012 and (b) a bond-swap plan (called the Private Sector Involvement or PSI) to ease Greece's debt burden by cutting the real value of private-sector investors' bond holdings by some 70 percent (the ECB and other central banks were to be exempt). In practice, this would mean that private creditors such as banks (including Greece's six largest banks) and investment funds (including Greece's social security and pensions funds[32]) would have to exchange their old Greek bonds for new ones with half the face value and with new thirty-year maturity from the original seven years, besides reducing the average interest rates from around 4.8 percent to 3.65 percent.[33] The PSI deal was deemed critical as without it Athens could

---

[31] It was reported that on September 18, 2011, the German finance minister, Schäuble, "repeated warnings that Greece will not receive any more aid unless it keeps promises it made to the International Monetary Fund, the European Commission, and the European Central Bank to cut government spending and improve the economy" (Ewing 2011, A1). Of course, the troika did not require Athens to adopt additional austerity measures but to implement those already agreed to. These include further reductions in the number of state employees, cuts in state salaries and pensions, reductions in health spending, closure of loss-making state enterprises, fast-track on privatizations, and increases on heating-oil tax.

[32] According to the Institute of International Finance, an estimated €17.5 billion in bonds owned by Greek social security funds and managed by the central bank will be part of the swap.

[33] Private creditors will get a haircut of 53.5 percent of the nominal value of Greek bonds, including a reduction in the coupon for new bonds – starting at 2 percent and rising to 4.3 percent from 2020. This translates to a loss of net present value of about 70 to 75 percent – a sharp increase from the 21 percent originally agreed upon in July 2011.

not secure the second bailout funds. If agreed to, cumulatively, the bailout and bond-swap deal would help write off half Greece's privately held debt and reduce the country's debt load by €100 billion.

However, the deal came with tough preconditions. The troika demanded a series of non-negotiable guarantees from Greece in exchange for the bailout funds.[34] Specifically, the troika made clear that there would be "no disbursement before implementation" – meaning that the Greek parliament had to first approve a reform program that clearly identified an additional €325 million worth of "structural expenditure reductions" to ensure that its fiscal targets were achievable. Given that public-sector wages and pensions constitute some 75 percent of total public spending in Greece, the bulk of these reductions had to come from further cuts to the minimum wage by some 22 percent, elimination of an additional 15,000 civil-service jobs, and further reductions in the pensions of public-sector workers (IMF 2011e). The troika also made it explicit that the Greek parliament had to provide written commitment that the agreed reforms would be implemented in a timely manner, regardless of whichever political party (or parties) formed the next government following national elections scheduled in April 2012.

With Greece's economic future seemingly hanging in the balance, Prime Minister Lucas Papademos urged lawmakers to do their "patriotic duty" and approve the additional measures "without delay," because the alternative, "a disastrous default" – that is, a humiliating bankruptcy and departure from the eurozone, would be far worse. Even as thousands in opposition to the proposed agreement rioted in the streets (with a large frenzied mob battling police and burning down buildings), Greek lawmakers, in the wee hours of February 13, grudgingly approved the tough austerity package. Out of the 300 members of the parliament, 199 voted yes, 74 voted no, 5 voted present, and 22 were absent.

Nevertheless, this was still not enough for Athens's frustrated paymasters. Further underscoring the deep distrust that had grown between Athens and the EU, the troika upped the ante by stating that before the second bailout could be delivered, the Greek parliament "must" provide more "clarity" regarding its implementation plans. The euro working group, comprising

---

[34] In January 2012, Germany's economic minister, Phillip Roesler, advised Greece to surrender control of its budget policy to outside institutions if it cannot implement the agreed-to reforms. Roesler was hardly alone in calling for an outside institution taking control of Greece's economic-policy decisions. In fact, several eurozone member states suggested that the bailout funds be placed in an escrow account and disbursed only as Greece delivers on the fiscal and structural reform benchmarks over the next three years.

the finance ministry officials from all seventeen eurozone member states, drew up a list of demands Athens had to accept before the deal was approved. These included details on how the Greek government planned to meet its missed debt-reduction targets, clarification on how it intended to further reduce labor costs, and reassurance that all political leaders would back the deal – especially after Antonis Samaras, head of the center-right New Democracy Party and the country's presumptive next prime minister, publicly announced that he may try to renegotiate the agreement following the April elections.

In the pre-dawn hours of February 21, after months of tense negotiations, eurozone finance ministers finally approved the €130 billion bailout ($172 billion) for Greece. Although eurozone leaders agreed to further lower the interest rates on the loans on the first bailout, a number of additional conditions were also added. First, before any funds could be released Athens had to implement its agreed €3 billion in spending cuts.[35] Second, Athens had to pass within the next two months a new law that gave priority to "debt servicing payments" over any other government funding. However, in the meantime it had to set up a "segregated account" (that is, an escrow account to be managed separately from its main budget) to ensure that priority was given to debt servicing. The account must also have enough funds to enable Greece to service its debts for the next three months. Third, in an unprecedented move in the fiscal affairs of a sovereign state, the troika announced that it was going to place permanent monitors in Athens to carry out "enhanced and permanent" monitoring and ensure timely implementation.[36] And, fourth, second bailout funds could be made available only after a bond swap between Athens and private investors was concluded by March 9, 2012.

---

[35] The Associated Press notes:

> Legislation tabled in [the Greek] Parliament late Tuesday [February 21, 2012] outlines a total €3.2 billion ($4.2 billion) in extra budget cuts this year agreed by the Cabinet last week. The measures include nearly €400 million ($530 million) in cuts to already depleted pensions. Health and education spending will be reduced by more than €170 million ($225 million), subsidies to the state health care system will be cut by €500 million ($661 million), and health care spending on medicine will fall by €570 million ($754 million). And some €400 million ($529 million) will be lopped off defense spending – three quarters of which will come from purchases. ("Greek Parliament to discuss austerity, bond swap deal as unions plan protest rally," *Associated Press*, Wednesday, February 22, 2012. http://www.washingtonpost.com/business/markets/greek-lawmakers-set-to-discuss-private-debt-relief-deal-as-unions-plan-anti-austerity-protest/2012/02/22/gIQANusk

[36] IMF. 2012. "Euro-Group Statement," February 20. http://www.consilium.europa.eu/uedocs/cms_Data/docs/pressdata/en/ecofin/128075.pdf

Although the troika made every effort to ensure that their restructuring of Greek debt qualified as "voluntary," there was no way of knowing what percentage of private creditors would be willing participate in the bond swap. In order for Athens to secure the bailout funds, however, private creditors, which included insurer Allianz, large banks such as BNP Paribas, Commerzbank and Deutsche Bank, as well as Greece's own Eurobank EFG and National Bank of Greece, had to approve the plan before March 9, 2012. Athens only muddied the waters when it passed legislation to retroactively include collective action clauses (CACs) in the contracts that govern Greek government bonds.[37] This gave Athens the power to force recalcitrant bondholders to accept the terms provided a majority (67 percent) agree voluntarily – rather than the 75 percent required for the exchange to be "voluntary." Under the rules of the International Swaps and Derivatives Association, credit default swap contracts are triggered when a debtor coerces a creditor, the association nevertheless declared Athens's move as a "non-event." However, Standard & Poor's was not so forgiving, and on February 28, the agency cut Greece's credit rating to "selective default" after it concluded that the CAC constituted "a de facto restructuring and thus a default." For its part, Athens repeatedly stated that it preferred PSI participation of 90 percent before it proceeded with the bond swap. Finance minister Evangelos Venizelos further complicated matters by stating that if participation fell short, Athens would not hesitate to use CACs to bring reluctant creditors on board.

Just hours before the March 9 deadline passed, a significant majority of private creditors (85.8 percent) voluntarily agreed to the bond-swap deal. This cleared the way for Athens to meet its €14.5 billion bond repayment due on March 20, which meant accessing the €130 billion bailout funds. Athens also informed the Eurogroup (made up of eurozone finance ministers) that it planned to activate the CACs applicable to bonds governed by Greek law to impose the exchange on the remaining holdouts and bring the participation rate to 96 percent.[38] This move was anticipated as the troika and eurozone leaders emphatically opposed payouts on Greek CDSs because they feared that payouts would encourage speculators to bet against vulnerable eurozone member states and further exacerbate the region's debt crisis. Athens use of CACs forced investors to take losses on their CDS

---

[37] For an overview of CACs, see Sharma (2004).

[38] To holders of foreign law and government-guaranteed bonds (about 4.3 percent of the total), Athens extended the offer to come on board by March 23. It made clear that after the deadline, the holdouts would not receive any benefits such as the 15 percent in cash-like securities.

contracts.[39] However, since the outstanding CDS contracts were small, it only constituted payout on only about $3 billion.[40] It seems that caught between a rock and a hard place and facing the choice of getting nothing if the deal failed and Greece was forced to undergo a disorderly default, private creditors reluctantly agreed to take a significant haircut by swapping their Greek bonds for new bonds with a face value of less than half (53.5 percent) the previous securities, besides accepting much lower interest rates and longer maturities. Under the biggest sovereign-debt restructuring in history investors agreed to write down more than half of the value of their Greek bond holdings, and in a bold sweep cut more than €100 billion from Greece's public debt. It also marked for the first time a reduction in Greece's debt load.

Although the bailout and debt relief helped to relieve Athens of its immediate financing needs, avert an imminent bankruptcy, and allow Greece to remain in the eurozone, no one could guarantee if the agreement would jumpstart the moribund Greek economy – or at least generate enough revenue to meet its obligations. Indeed, the €130 billion question was whether growth would return, or would the new austerity further cripple the economy by deepening an already devastating recession, and in the process set Greece for yet another debt restructuring and making its survival contingent upon even more external support. To the markets, Greece faced such

---

[39] The International Swaps & Derivatives Association's determinations committee ruled the use of CACs as a "restructuring credit event" (Moses 2012). However, this is not likely to be the end of the story as CDS holders, especially hedge-fund investors, can file lawsuits against Athens. As the experience of Argentina shows, litigation can be arduous, bitter, and costly.

[40] Not only is the market for CDS contracts on Greek debt relatively small, given that investors have long known of a potential Greek default they have already priced that into the market – unlike the subprime mortgage collapse, which caught markets by surprise. Cumulatively, these developments helped to allay fears that a Greek default could trigger a run on Europe's banking system. Indeed, if in the past two years foreign investors have adjusted their portfolios to minimize exposure to Greece, many Greek citizens have likewise pulled an estimated €40 billion from their banks (Landon 2012). This means a run on Greece's bank would be less harmful then would have been the case a year ago. Taylor (2012) notes

The correlation between spreads on risk-sensitive Greek credit default swaps and spreads on default swaps on sovereign debt elsewhere in Europe has declined... the anticipated orderly write-down will be far less damaging than a sudden default. Even if it triggers default-swap payments, those should be manageable, since the outstanding credit default swaps on Greek debt total only about $3 billion.

The International Securities and Derivatives Association which oversees CDS has also reported that the actual payouts on CDSs linked to Greek bonds will be less than $3.2 billion.

a Herculean challenge that there was no guarantee that the bailout coupled with a significant debt-relief package would be enough to reduce the nation's debt from 160 percent of GDP to 120 percent of economic output by 2020 – a figure that both the IMF and foreign creditors perceive as sustainable. Further, there could be no guarantee that Athens would follow through with the deeply unpopular austerity program after elections or be able to implement reforms at the pace envisioned by the troika. Under such circumstances, a disorderly default by Greece is a real possibility, as is Greece choosing to unilaterally declare a debt moratorium and leaving the euro.

Nevertheless, as the *Economist* has noted, following the Greek bailout deal, the eurozone's sovereign-debt crisis moved from the "acute phase" to the "chronic" and more "stable phase."[41] By gradually quarantining Greece, the eurozone has been able to mitigate the pervasive fear of a virulent contagion spreading from Greece. In fact, the reason a relatively small economy like Greece (representing just 2.4 percent of the total eurozone economy), stood like the sword of Damocles over the entire monetary union (and beyond), was because there was no meaningful financial firewall between Greece and the rest of the eurozone. Hence, if Greece defaulted on its debts, it could unleash potentially devastating shockwaves to the other peripherals, the rest of the eurozone, and beyond.

Furthermore, with the passage of time the markets have formed a more nuanced understanding of the Greek economy, namely that Greece is an exception rather than the rule in the eurozone. Although lumped together in the PIIGS, there are, nevertheless, important differences between Greece and the other peripherals. For starters, on the eve of the eurozone crisis, Greece's economy was in far worse shape. This partly explains why reforms have not worked as well as those implemented in Ireland and Portugal and why Greece's current account imbalances have failed to move downward – unlike those of Ireland and Portugal. The passage of time has also rehabilitated the reputations of the EU leadership and the troika. This is because they began to stop kicking the proverbial can down the road and address Greece's problems in a more realistic manner. For example (and as discussed earlier), when in early 2010 the EU leadership claimed that domestic structural reforms would be enough to jumpstart the Greek economy and arrogantly dismissed the idea that Athens needed financial support, the markets remained unconvinced. In July 2011 when the leadership argued that debt restructuring was unnecessary as the problem was one of illiquidity rather than insolvency, the markets were still unconvinced. In October 2011 when the eurozone leaders suggested that

---

[41] "Europe and the euro: a way out of the woods," *The Economist*, 2012. February 18.

only a modest reduction in private debt would be enough to overcome Greece travails, the markets still disagreed. Only when the EU leaders, in particular the German and French leaders, the troika, and the representatives of private creditors, finally stopped their procrastination and denial and did what they should have done much earlier – that is, restructure Greece's massive debt burden via a meaningful write-down of Greek bonds, were the markets buoyed. The fact that the negotiations showed that the troika can manage complex large-scale debt restructuring without destabilizing markets has been an additional feather in the cap of the EU leadership.

Finally, what prompted the EU and the troika into action was arguably the realization that the eurozone's problems are their own. In other words, the cavalry (United States or China) may not come galloping to their rescue, and it is up to the Europeans to solve their problems. The United States has repeatedly urged the EU to commit more of its own money to crisis management before increasing the IMF's crisis resources or looking for help from the United States. In similar fashion, China, which has an estimated 25 percent of its $3.2 trillion foreign exchange reserves in euro-denominated assets, has not fundamentally altered its investment structure, nor has Beijing made any firm financial commitments to the eurozone such as buying more eurozone debt. For its part, the G-20 has reiterated its position that the EU must do more to deal with its financial problem before the body considers the EU's request and commits an additional $500 billion in new funding to the EU via the IMF. To the G-20 the "do more" means a further enhancing the "financial firewall" by effectively combining the temporary EFSF with the permanent ESM, and to increase the ESM's lending power.[42]

The Crisis Becomes Systemic

In the second week of April 2012 the markets reacted negatively on concerns regarding the Spanish economy. On April 10, Spain's ten-year bond yields (an indicator of the interest rate Spain has to pay to borrow on international debt markets) rose above the 6 percent mark for the first time since December 2011. Two related concerns seem to have triggered market fears:

---

[42] Italian Prime Minister Mario Monti has also urged the Eurozone leaders to double the ESM's funds to €1 trillion, while ECB President Mario Draghi and the IMF's managing director, Christine Lagarde, have called for a larger firewall. However, Germany, the ESM's largest contributor, is opposed to expanding the ESM's €500 billion lending capacity either via a pooling of the remaining €250 billion in the EFSF temporary bailout fund with the ESM or for the ESM and the EFSF to operate simultaneously.

First, the dismal state of the Spanish economy reeling under an unemployment rate of 23 percent and second, prediction by the Bank of Spain (the country's central bank) that the nation's economy would further contract by 1.7 percent by year end 2012. Under these difficult recessionary conditions, Madrid is under tremendous pressure to carry out a difficult juggling act: simultaneously jumpstart its moribund economy and carry out sharp budget cuts. Prime Minister Rajoy publicly committed to an ambitious goal of reducing the budget deficit from 8.5 percent of GDP to 5.3 percent by end 2012 and 3 percent by end 2013. Needless to say, markets remained deeply skeptical if such ambitious deficit reductions could be achieved and whether enough economic growth would occur under such unforgiving conditions for Spain (and the other peripherals) to reduce their debts to sustainable levels. Exacerbating Madrid's challenges, the country's semi-autonomous regional governments (all of whom have high debt loads), have not shown the fiscal discipline to rein in their debt problems. Spanish banks' huge volumes of nonperforming loans as a result of the collapse of the real-estate market in 2008 have not recovered, and there was mounting concern that Madrid will have to inject even more capital to save the banks from collapsing. Markets know that if Spain, which makes up about 11 percent of the eurozone's GDP (compared to Greece's 2 percent), is unable to achieve its goals, it will be forced to turn to the ECB for a bailout. However, the real fear is that the ECB's firewall will not be strong enough to contain Madrid's problems and thus a real potential of a virulent contagion engulfing Italy.

As if concerns about Spain were not enough, on May 5, 2012 Europe witnessed two major political shakeups: French voters elected their first socialist president in seventeen years, François Hollande, and angry voters in Greece severely punished the socialist Pasok and the conservative New Democracy Party candidate (both of which were part of a unity government that agreed to the second EU-IMF bailout) by giving them a combined total of about 35 percent of the vote. Worse still, roughly two-thirds of the Greek electorate voted for antibailout parties, including those of the radical left and far right. Given that the EU/IMF had made clear that any breach by Athens of the second austerity and reform plan would lead to an immediate halt of its rescue funds, this election outcome raised concerns about the future of bailout agreement and Greece's place in the eurozone.[43] The only glimmer of hope was that since none

---

[43] In a public statement, Klaus Regling, the head of the eurozone's rescue fund, noted that Athens has to agree with international lenders on the terms for financial aid before any more funds are released after June 2012. However, the EFSF agreed on May 9, 2012 to release the latest €4.2 billion aid as Greeks sort out who will form the next government.

of Greece's parties had received an outright majority, soul-searching and fresh elections (scheduled for June 17) might deliver a favorable outcome – that is, a pro-reform and pro-eurozone result.

Hollande's statement that "at the moment when the result was proclaimed, I am sure that in many countries of Europe there was relief and hope: finally austerity is no longer destiny" (*The Economist* 2012) raised concerns about the future of Franco-German unity essential to the functioning of the eurozone. With his proclamation, Hollande put the spotlight on the long-festering debate regarding growth versus austerity. On one hand, the troika and the eurozone's paymaster, Germany, remain convinced that austerity measures (such as spending cuts and higher taxes) is essential to reduce the massive levels of government debt and that failure to do so will eventually force markets to severely punish any country that fails to cut its deficits and reform its economy. On the other hand, the seemingly endless austerity that directly and immediately impacts individual lives – cuts to public services, reduced public-sector wages and pensions, and higher taxes and retirement ages – are hugely unpopular, as underscored by the Greek and French electoral verdicts. With Hollande's victory, the narrative that punitive austerity stifles growth because it further pushes beleaguered economies struggling to recover from recession back into recession finally had traction. Not surprisingly, Hollande's proposal that a "growth pact," including a financial-transactions tax and infrastructure investments to boost job creation, found sympathetic ears. To support his position, Hollande repeatedly pointed to the United States, which has made modest spending cuts but notched higher growth than the United Kingdom, which has made deep cuts without any growth or reduction in unemployment levels. To Hollande, a growth pact underpinned by eurobonds issued by the ECB to provide for the debt-refinancing for all eurozone member states is essential. Of course, this is anathema to Merkel, who, like most Germans, sees converting profligate member states' debt burden onto mainly German taxpayers as unjust and irresponsible. Unfortunately, in hard times, striking the right balance between cutting debt and stimulating growth is rarely an option. Despite all the efforts and modest gains, it seemed that the eurozone's problems remained as intractable as over.

Indeed, Spain's woes came to the forefront again when it became evident that BFA-Bankia (BKIA), the country's fourth-largest bank, established in 2010 by the merger of seven troubled savings banks, continued to lose its share price even after it was nationalized on May 9, 2012. On May 25, 2012, BKIA requested €19 billion in capital injections from the Spanish government. Two more banks followed with a request of €9 billion two days later.

On June 5, even as Madrid acknowledged that its banks needed assistance, it successfully auctioned about €2 billion worth of debt to show investors that it could still tap credit markets. However, this "success" was mainly due to Spain paying investors high rates (slightly more than 6 percent) and the country's own banks purchasing the bulk of its ten-year bonds. Clearly unimpressed, Fitch downgraded Spain's credit rating from A to BBB (just two notches above junk), and on June 7 warned of further downgrades. Fitch also revised its earlier assessment that only €30 billion was needed to save Spain's banks to €100 billion. Although, to its credit, Madrid has reduced the number of troubled banks through mergers and capital injections (unlike Ireland, Madrid refused to create a bad bank to absorb the toxic debt from banks' balance sheets), but the country's banking sector remains mired in bad debts. The Bank of Spain's claim that the banks are burdened with about €175 billion in bad loans may be too optimistic as it is well-known that the savings banks or *cajas*, including Spain's two largest banks, Banco Santander SA and Banco Bilbao Vizcaya Argentaria SA, have enormous volumes of bad assets and nonperforming loans on their books, not to mention that Spain's banks own a huge volume of government bonds. This means that rescuing the banking sector by issuing bonds would entail a huge cost and could turn Spain's banking crisis into a full-blown sovereign-debt crisis like Ireland's. This explains Madrid's request that the EU's "assistance" be given directly to banks for the explicit purpose of bank recapitalization and not to the government – something Madrid feels is justified as Spain was not fiscally profligate like Greece.

Needless to say, this did not sit well with Europe's paymaster, Germany, for it knew that such a transfer would leave the EU little powers of oversight, in particular, limited authority to require Madrid to implement the necessary banking-sector reforms. On June 9, 2012, the IMF released its report on Spain's financial sector three days ahead of schedule, noting that Spanish banks needed at least €40 billion in recapitalization funds. On the same day, Madrid finally conceded that it needed assistance and formally asked the EU for €100 billion in aid to stabilize its banking sector. In a preemptive move, eurozone policy makers, anxious to dampen market concerns and stabilize Spain's position before the June 17 elections in Greece, expeditiously approved Madrid's request. Since "aid" or what Prime Minister Rajoy called "a line of credit" does not equate to "rescue" or "bailout," Madrid claimed that Spain would not face the obtrusive conditions imposed on Greece, Ireland, and Portugal by the troika.[44] Furthermore, Rajoy stressed that the interest rates on

---

[44] The troika subjects countries under its program to rigorous quarterly inspections by the EU and the IMF, besides requiring recipients of its aid to sign an extensive memorandum

the "line of credit" would be much lower than the 7 percent Madrid has been forced to pay on the international debt markets – a rate that eventually forced Ireland and Portugal to seek bailouts.

Although Rajoy hoped to separate his government from the banks (thereby limiting the public debt load), by urging the EU to transfer the aid directly to the troubled banks and not channel it through his government, the vague mechanics of the transfer process created uncertainty. This is because the eurozone's two rescue funds the temporary European Financial Stability Facility (EFSF) and the permanent European Stability Mechanism (ESM) do not permit such transfers. In the end it was agreed that the EU would lend the funds directly to Madrid to buy stakes in the mostly insolvent banks. More specifically, the funds would be placed in Spain's own bank bailout fund (the Fondo de Reestructuracion Ordenada Bancaria, or FROB) and directed to the shaky financial institutions.

However, neither the convoluted lending mechanism nor the "bailout lite" could obfuscate the fact that the €100 billion, which totals some 10 percent of Spain's GDP, would sharply increase Spain's debt-to-GDP ratio, raise the deficit (currently at 9 percent of GDP), and add to Spain's burgeoning public debt which has already doubled since 2008. According to the Bank of Spain, the national debt stood at 72 percent of GDP in mid-2012, but this is expected to increase to 80 percent by year's end after the cost of the new bailout is added. Although Spain's debt burden is relatively modest compared to Greece's (165 percent) or Italy's (120 percent), markets are concerned that Madrid may not be able to meet its obligations given Spain's sharp economic contraction and uncertainty about its fragile banking sector. Exacerbating this, the lack of clarity in the lending mechanism, in particular, where the aid funds would come from, made the already worried bondholders even more nervous. Germany unhelpfully sent mixed messages, on one hand stating that it is not for Berlin to decide whether the ESM or the EFSF funds were tapped, and on the other, expressing a clear preference for the ESM.[45] Bondholders know too well that the ESM is a

---

of understanding in order to hold them responsible for meeting agreed-upon targets covering spending and structural reforms.

[45] Crook (2012) notes:

Both dangers were recognized before the deal was put together. Why then did the EU design the rescue this way? Why not simply extend direct EU support to Spain's banks? The answer is Germany. Chancellor Merkel and her parliamentary allies insisted that Spain should bear responsibility for the rescue. German taxpayers should not be directly exposed to the costs of helping Spain's banks. On the same reasoning, Merkel has said that the Spanish rescue funds should come from Europe's new permanent lending facility, the European Stability Mechanism, on terms that would make the new debt senior....

senior creditor and has to be paid back first if Spain were to default on its debts.[46] That is, if the funds were to come from the ESM, payment to euro-zone members would take precedence over private lenders such as bond-holders who are subordinate creditors. Put bluntly, bondholders would be forced to take a considerable haircut – as Greece's experience showed.

Not surprisingly, relief soon gave way to concern. On June 12, 2012 the yield on ten-year Spanish bonds rose to 6.83 percent, the highest level since the euro's introduction in 1999. Two days later, after Moody's downgraded Spain's bond rating, the yield on Spain's ten-year bond breached the 7 per-cent mark – the threshold at which bailout assistance seemingly becomes necessary and the same level that triggered the bailouts for Greece, Ireland, and Portugal. Perhaps more ominous, yields on Italy's ten-year government bonds reached 6.2 percent on June 13. In no uncertain terms, the markets were signaling that they saw no real difference between the problems faced by the sovereign and its banking sector. In other words, investors were cor-rectly concluding that because the cost of recapitalizing the banking sec-tor would ultimately fall on Spain, the "negative feedback loop" that occurs when governments take on large debt to bail out their banks would further exacerbate the government's debt problems and eventually force it to seek a bailout.

Even the victory of Greece's New Democracy Party (which promised to honor the bailout commitments) in the country's parliamentary elections on June 17 brought the eurozone only a fleeting respite. Although the elections tempered fears of an imminent sovereign default and a disorderly departure of Greece from the monetary union, markets understood that Greece, in its fifth straight year of a biting recession, could still default and exit the euro. More ominously, the markets' wild swings from bouts of optimism and pes-simism seemed to confirm that the eurozone was facing a systemic crisis due to loss of investor confidence. The case of Spain, in which relief quickly gave way to despair, despite the massive bailout and positive news from Greek, underscore how deeply worried markets are about the future of the single-currency system. Indeed, if just a few months before, a €100 billon in support to clean up Spanish banks would have been cheered by the mar-kets and greatly eased investor concerns, by June, such country-by-country

---

Germany's government is in a horrible political bind. Even allowing for this, the country's response to the crisis now borders on the unintelligible.

[46] This explains Madrid's preference for aid channeled through the EFSF (the temporary rescue fund), which does not hold preferred creditor status. Nevertheless, the EFSF would require Spain to meet Finland's demand for collateral to guarantee its loan portion.

firefighting efforts were seen as too little too late, and apparently no longer enough to assuage worried investors.

The rapidly deteriorating confidence in the monetary union forced the leaders of the eurozone's four largest economies (Germany, France, Italy, and Spain) to hold an emergency mini-summit on June 22, 2012. In a show of solidarity the leaders endorsed a €130 billion stimulus package (equal to about 1 percent of the eurozone's GDP) to jumpstart growth. This was a significant step given Chancellor Merkel's opposition to using fiscal stimulus to boost growth. However, Merkel resisted pressure to back the call by France, Italy, and Spain to fast-track the eurozone toward a fiscal union, including issuing some form of collective debt, preferably in the form of eurobonds. Rather, Merkel maintained her long-held view that the eurozone must first transfer control over national budget and economic policies to Brussels before Germany would consider issuing a common bond. Nevertheless, in their attempt alleviate pressure on Madrid, the leaders agreed that the ECB could relax its collateral rules to allow financial institutions to pledge a wider range of assets (meaning collateral of a lower quality, including certain mortgage-backed securities and car loans) totaling some €100 billion in exchange for ECB funds. Spanish banks, which have held large volumes of mortgage-backed securities and related assets since the country's real-estate bubble burst, are the clear beneficiaries. Not surprisingly, the Spanish bonds rallied following the announcement. However, the ECB's decision to ease its collateral rules (after the first such action six months ago) further weakens its balance sheet which is already burdened with the more than €1 trillion it has pumped into the monetary union's shaky banking system. This is much to the concern of the Bundesbank worried by the growing risks taken on by the ECB, namely, that the continued deterioration of the ECB's balance sheet could limit its ability to respond to new challenges. On the other hand, without the ECB's intervention, the eurozone's banking sector would face a serious credit crunch.

The EU leaders came to their annual summit in late June as divided as ever on how to resolve the eurozone's continuing debt crisis. With borrowing costs skyrocketing and the crisis showing signs of going from bad to worse, Hollande, along with Italian Prime Minister Mario Monti and the European Commission, called for the issuance of eurobonds to revive growth. To underscore his country's desperate situation, Rajoy bluntly stated that Madrid could not afford to finance itself for much longer at current bond rates (Spanish ten-year government bonds had been trading at yields above 6.8 percent for about two weeks). The normally quiet Monti even warned that "if Italians become discouraged that their efforts aren't helping, it could unleash political forces which say 'let European integration, let the euro, let this or that large country go to hell', which would be a disaster for the whole of the European Union" (Charlton 2012, 1). However, Merkel, reluctant to expose Germany to new risk, stood her ground.

But under relentless pressure, Merkel was finally outflanked. In a dramatic act of brinkmanship, Hollande refused to endorse the treaty on deficits, and Monti and Rajoy refused to approve the stimulus package until Germany approved measures to "calm" the Italian and Spanish bonds markets by allowing eurozone rescue funds to buy their government bonds and support their banks. This, the three leaders argued, was critical to break the "vicious circle" of convergence between banking and sovereign debt. Finally, "Frau Nein" made concessions that seemed impossible just hours earlier. She agreed that the EFSF and then the ESM (once it came into force on July 1, 2012) would be allowed to directly recapitalize Spanish banks and to purchase Italian sovereign bonds. To make this possible, the ESM rules had to be significantly relaxed to make its loans to Spanish banks (and if need be to Italian banks) from not having "seniority status." In other words, official lenders (taxpayers) would not receive preferred creditor status, and private-sector bondholders would be given the same rights when it came to repayment in case of a default (as noted earlier, giving preferred status to official lenders pushed private bondholders to demand higher interest rates). It also meant that (a) Spain (and, if need be, Italy) could recapitalize its shaky banking sector without increasing sovereign-debt load, (b) access to ECB and ESM funds would enable Italy and Spain to sharply reduce borrowing costs as they would pay much lower interest rates than available on the open market, and (c) EU member states that meet debt and deficit targets would be allowed to apply for bailouts without having to adopt the stringent austerity measures.

Although the deal exposes German taxpayers to risky assets of Spanish and Italian financial institutions, Merkel seemingly found comfort in the fact that she did not budge on the core issue: the sharing of debt via eurobonds. Moreover, she claimed that the ESM funds can be made available only under strict rules or after the eurozone has in place a single bank supervisory body or "bank regulator" to replace the ineffective hodgepodge of the current seventeen.[47] She also claimed that no new funds were allocated to enhance the buying power of the EFSF and the ESM (which hold

---

[47] The European Banking Authority (EBA) was established in 2010. However, it lacks powers to effectively do its job, in particular, conduct effective stress tests on eurozone banks as it does not have a mandate to carry out direct on-site supervision. The proposed regulator will work closely with the ECB and have authority over eurozone banks to prevent systemic problems from developing. Of course, it remains to be seen if it will have the necessary

about €500 billion), apart from some €100 billion to recapitalize Spanish banks. Although markets know that this sum is paltry compared to the needs of Spain and Italy (both have €2.5 trillion in outstanding sovereign bonds), they rallied arguably because the summit exceeded all expectations by delivering a "comprehensive package" to deal with the eurozone's challenges. The new deal helped calm investor concerns – although concerns lingered about whether the summit, like the previous one, would prove to be a short-term palliative.[48]

With the E.U. caught in a vicious grip of a systemic crisis and facing a potential "lost decade," even such a bold step is insufficient to regain investor confidence and ultimately save the eurozone. The EU decision makers must move beyond gradual and temporary fixes and put in place more comprehensive measures that will convince markets that the leaders are serious about structural reforms and deeper fiscal and financial integration of the monetary union. They must consider even bolder measures – from issuing joint eurobonds to fundamentally correcting the deficiencies in the eurozone's fiscal architecture. Certainly, these options are not going to be easy or come quickly. Yet, as the following illustrates, with some innovation, each offers possibilities. Moreover, both options are far more desirable than an exit or a default – which, for all practical purposes, will destroy the eurozone and the unique project it represents.

United States of Europe?

As noted in Chapter 3, the eurozone has a peculiar governance system. On one hand, the ECB conducts monetary policy for the entire zone, on

---

powers to be effective. Also, Merkel informed Germany's lower house of parliament in Berlin on June 29 that establishing a eurozone bank supervisor before the ESM funds can be used to recapitalize banks could take "several months or perhaps a year." It is important to note that before the ESM can purchase bonds in secondary markets all eurozone members must formally approve this – although the "get-out clause" in the ESM's rules does allow the ECB and the EC to act with an 85 percent majority if they believe that the monetary union's existence is under threat.

[48] On July 20, 2012, seventeen eurozone finance ministers unanimously approved the terms of a bailout for Spanish banks. They agreed to provide up to €100 billion in assistance with an initial €30 billion in emergency funds to be disbursed by the end of July. However, this failed to reduce the yields on ten-year Spanish government bonds, which stood at 7.28 percent. Apparently the markets spooked after Madrid's announcement that the national economy would remain in recession through 2013 and the Valencia region's request for more official financing in order to meet its debt-refinancing obligations and pay for basic services. Two days later, when the Spanish media reported that up to six autonomous regions (out of seventeen) may be seeking aid, the yields on Spanish bonds jumped to more than 7.5 percent.

the other, individual member states have autonomy vis-à-vis their fiscal policies. Given this, it has been long argued that the eurozone cannot have a monetary union without also having a fiscal union. Krugman (2010b) has lucidly highlighted the anomaly that besets the eurozone and has outlined a possible solution. He notes that the impact of any financial crisis is never uniform but is felt differently in different parts of the country. However, a continental economy like the United States is able to mitigate the regional imbalances and distortions because it is also a political union. Specifically, in the United States, the free movement of people from economically depressed and weaker regions to more vibrant economic regions helps promote adjustment over the medium term while the federal fiscal transfers helps reduce the negative impact on the depressed areas. However, in Europe, although labor mobility has greatly increased over the past decade, it still lags far behind the cross-border movement of trade and capital. Europe's policy makers are well aware that the portability of pensions and health care would speed up labor mobility, but they are also cognizant of the political difficulties in achieving this goal. Unlike the United States and other federal systems, federal fiscal transfers do not really exist in the EU – with huge negative implications for depressed areas. To Krugman, if the eurozone is to remain a viable entity, it must have a mechanism to keep in check the fiscal deficits in its countries.

In a similar vein, Feldstein (2010, A19) has argued:

The structure of the EMU that created the euro actually encourages members to run large deficits. A country with its own currency would see that currency deteriorate and its interest rates rise if it sold large amounts of debt to global investors. But because EMU countries share a currency, there has been no market feedback to warn when a country's deficit is getting dangerously high. Since Greek bonds were regarded as a close substitute for the euro bonds of other countries, the interest rate on Greek debt did not rise as the country increased its borrowing – until the market began to fear default.

To Feldstein (2010, A19; also see Feldstein 2012), Europe must become more the United States, at least in its political structure. He notes:

There may be something to learn from the United States. Although the 50 states share a currency and each sets its own spending and tax policies, state deficits remain very low. Even California has a deficit of only about 1 percent of the state's GDP and total general obligation debt of less than 4 percent of state GDP. The basic reason for these small deficits is that each state's constitution prohibits borrowing for operating purposes. States can issue debt to finance infrastructure but not salaries, services, transfer payments or other operating expenses.... If the EMU governments were to adopt similar constitutional rules, the interest rates on their bonds would fall.

The creation of a federal-style fiscal transfer union similar to the system in the United States will take time. Even if some sort of a halfway fiscal union is agreed to, at a minimum, it will require a new treaty with unanimous approval of all seventeen members. If current pace of progress is any indication, that could take years – time the eurozone does not have. However, a quick way to reduce the widening productivity gap between the northern and southern eurozone economies is via exchange-rate adjustments. Lumping highly disparate economies in a monetary union without giving them a viable tool to adjust to one another's exchange rates has exacerbated divisions as it has left the southern economies with an unpalatable option: the reliance on very painful "internal devaluation" to rebalance their economies. In lieu of a U.S.-style fiscal union (which everyone agrees is years away), northern economies, and Germany in particular, can greatly alleviate the pressure (and suffering) in the periphery by allowing its central bank to loosen monetary policy and tolerate a much higher level of inflation than the north (especially Germany) is used to. The resultant changes in relative real wages could boost growth in the south by making their exports more competitive. Over time it would also reduce the south's dependence on bailout and subsidies that are currently paid by northern taxpayers. Moreover, as Krugman points out, greater labor mobility (i.e., allowing workers to move to high-growth countries) within the EU can help to quickly alleviate the problem of unemployment in the south.

Exit or Default

Why is exit or default not a good option? To the euro-skeptics, the cost of having a common currency clearly outweighs the benefits, and therefore the beleaguered eurozone countries have only one viable choice: quit the eurozone. Indeed, it is no longer heretical to say that given the onerous demands placed on countries like Greece, Ireland, and Portugal, it makes sense for them to altogether abandon the euro. Feldstein (2010) argues that it would be to Greece's advantage to leave the euro because it would allow the devaluation needed to promote exports and so mitigate the impact of the tough austerity measures. Feldstein (2010, A19) notes

If Greece reverts to the drachma and floats the currency, it would probably achieve a devaluation of about 30%. That would make its products and services much more competitive, boosting economic activity and employment. Although the value of its external euro-denominated debts would rise by a similar percentage when stated in drachma that would be largely offset in the debt restructuring that is virtually inevitable in Greece.

Similarly, Krugman (2012, A19) points out, "If the peripheral nations still had their own currencies, they could and would use devaluation to quickly restore competitiveness. But they don't, which means that they are in for a long period of mass unemployment and slow, grinding deflation." Chief executive of Pimco Mohamed El-Erian (2011) has argued that a temporary Greek exit, or what he calls "a sabbatical from the eurozone – but not the European Union," is the only way Athens can "regain the policy flexibility needed to restore competitiveness." Similarly, Rogoff (in Pressley, 2010, 2) argues that the EU needs a mechanism to allow countries such as Greece to temporarily exit the euro and re-enter it at a later date, after they have successfully restructured their debt.[49] Suffice it to note, if outright exit is the only option, the suggestions by El-Erian and Rogoff are nonstarters.

Because Athens cannot engage in currency devaluation or depreciation under the euro, any competitive gains require deep and painful wage cuts and deflation if Greece is to export itself out of a recession. Certainly, the reintroduction of the drachma would allow Athens to engage in a massive nominal and real depreciation of its currency to boost competitiveness and growth – at least relative to countries in the eurozone. Although this may solve some of Greece's woes, it will also create new problems. Wyplosz points out that Greece's euro-denominated debts, if converted into new drachma, would skyrocket, resulting in defaults by both the government and private borrowers. He notes "at this stage, it is very difficult to see an exit from the euro area as a panacea."[50] It is important to reiterate that even if Greece (and the other peripherals) exited the euro they would still have their euro-denominated debt. Therefore, a depreciated drachma would dramatically raise the cost of holding foreign-denominated debt, triggering an immediate default. Second, Greece may not be able to just export its way out of its current predicament because it has an anemic export base that is fast losing competitiveness. Athens's big foreign-currency earner is tourism, not exports. Third, if Greece were to leave, the bank "jog" could potentially become a full-scale bank run or even a stampede on domestic banks in the peripheral economies as everyone with euro funds would immediately transfer or repatriate their remaining euro-denominated savings and assets. Undoubtedly, the banking sectors would cease to function, and the EU economy come to a grinding halt. Aslund (2012, 1) warns:

I argue that a Greek exit would not be merely a devaluation for Greece but would unleash a domino effect of international bank runs and disrupt the EMU payments

---

[49] James Pressley, 2010. "Harvard's Rogoff Says EU's Bazooka Won't Prevent Defaults," *Bloomberg*, May 18.
[50] For details, see http://www.economist.com/debate/days/view/526.

mechanism, which would lead to a serious, presumably mortal, disintegration of the EMU. It would inflict immense harm not only on Greece but also on other countries in the European Union and the world at large.

Not surprisingly, when *Der Spiegel* (on May 6, 2011) reported that Greece was considering leaving the eurozone, German finance minister Wolfgang Schäuble stated that an exit would be "economic suicide." Athens angrily described the report as "borderline criminal."

Why should default not be an option? After all, individuals and businesses frequently default and recover, as do sovereign states. While sovereign default and bankruptcy is always humiliating and carries onerous burdens such as being shut out of global markets and paying exorbitant interest rates for loans, it nevertheless allows debtors and debt-weary governments to effectively restructure their debt, rather than just rolling it over or receiving a new extension on repayment. Meaningful restructuring will also alleviate the successive rounds of ever more painful austerity which is already facing stiff opposition as the combination of massive expenditure cuts, layoffs, and tax increases are putting significant pressure on businesses and households. Indeed, some have suggested a "controlled default" as a way out for Greece. The problem is that there is never any guarantee that bankruptcy proceedings will occur in a controlled manner. If Greece's default turns out to be disorderly, it will spook markets even more, resulting in panic and chaos reminiscent of what happened following Lehman's bankruptcy. The contagion and meltdown that would follow would be hard to contain. Hence, the eurozone's visceral fear of any form of default.

What about Eurobonds?

The eurozone has a large and vibrant government debt market, but as debts are issued by individual governments, they differ in their risk, returns, and liquidity. Would mutualizing the eurozone's sovereign debts into a common "eurobond" by allowing financially weak members to pool their credit standing with the stronger ones alleviate the region's problems? Financier George Soros (2011) has long argued that eurobonds can help to immediately resolve the crisis. He notes:

Europe needs eurobonds. The introduction of the euro was supposed to reinforce convergence; in fact it created divergences, with widely differing levels of indebtedness and competitiveness. If heavily indebted countries have to pay heavy risk premiums, their debt becomes unsustainable. That is now happening. The solution is obvious: deficit countries must be allowed to refinance their debt on the same terms as surplus countries. This is best accomplished through eurobonds, which would be jointly guaranteed by all the member states.

Similarly, Barry Eichengreen (2011, 96) has argued that the EU should relax the rules governing ESM loans after it comes into existence in 2013. In particular, the ESM should be authorized "to issue E-bonds – bonds backed by the full faith and credit of the entire group of EU member states, including Germany – and allow troubled members like Greece and Ireland to exchange their existing sovereign debt for E-bonds up to some limit (say, 60 percent of GDP)."

Although, Germany, the EU's paymaster, in a show of common resolve, has stated its broad support for some type of pooling of budgets and jointly issuing debt instruments to enable the indebted countries to borrow at cheaper rates, Merkel has also explicitly stated that eurobonds are not a subject of discussion as long as the fiscal policies of eurozone member states remain in the hands of individual national governments and the current debt problems remain unresolved.[51] Berlin is reluctant to issue common or joint eurobonds because it views this option as a disguised form of "transfer union" designed to move funds from the healthy and "responsible" northern countries to the weak and profligate peripheral economies. This view is justified because if the eurozone issues bonds collectively, then each member must also accept joint liability for the outstanding debt. Moreover, there is valid concern that the issuance of joint eurobonds would not only push up Germany's borrowing cost, it would also reduce incentives for the peripheral countries to implement the reforms their inefficient and mismanaged economies so urgently need. Arguably, if the backing of joint eurobonds had been in place, Greece, Ireland, and Portugal may not have found the political will to agree to enact tough (but long-needed) reforms such as liberalizing their labor markets, cutting their bloated governmental bureaucracies, privatizing moribund state-run enterprises, ending generous (and unaffordable) entitlements for government workers, cracking down on tax evaders, and slashing budgets to reduce their fiscal deficits to the EMU's 3 percent maximum within the next three years. Greece, for example, agreed to reduce its fiscal deficit only because it could no longer avoid such drastic reforms. Even more risky, a default on eurobonds by Greece or the other peripherals could potentially wreck the economies of the core countries. Not surprisingly, echoing Germany's concern, Jens Weidmann, president

---

[51] German Finance Minister Wolfgang Schaeuble summed up his country's position on eurobonds nicely when he reiterated that they "provide totally the wrong incentive" and that they "would not promote fiscal discipline, but the opposite. We're ready to talk openly about any proposal. But we're not going to do the opposite of what will solve [the eurozone's] problems" (*EU business*. 2012. "Germany digs heels in on Eurobonds" 23 May. http://www.eubusiness.com/news-eu/finance-public-debt.gmv).

of the Bundesbank, has often stated that it is not the ECB's role to act as a lender of last resort to eurozone governments – which he argues is both illegal and wrong as it introduces a significant moral hazard. Moreover, he says, the ECB should end its current (and limited) bond-purchase program. To Weidmann, the only viable way for countries like Italy and Greece to restore investor confidence is for them to continue to enact bold market-friendly structural reforms.

No doubt, if the eurozone governments agree to issue joint bonds and thereby accept collective responsibility for sovereign debt, it will send an unequivocal message that they are committed to keeping the union whole. Indeed, given the EU's limited policy options, the issuance of common eurobonds or similar forms of debt mutualization is the most powerful weapon the EU has in its arsenal. This is because eurobonds in providing for a common sovereign borrowing with shared liability and risk can serve as a substitute for the eurozone Achilles heel – the lack of a fiscal union. Furthermore, by breaking the banking-sovereign feedback loop, a common bond could dramatically reduce market volatility in sovereign borrowing costs and the debt burdens of the peripherals by allowing them to borrow at affordable rates. But how can eurobonds be made more palatable to Berlin?

As proponents often note, the trick is to design politically palatable sovereign bonds. After all, EFSF/EFSM/ESM bonds are a form of eurobonds – albeit not the most efficient types. In other words, the problems associated in the joint issuance of eurobonds can be mitigated by designing a hybrid version. To this effect, several options have been floated. Of course, the most effective, at least in terms of sharply and quickly lowering the borrowing costs of peripheral member states would be a "full eurobond" that covers the sovereign financing of the entire eurozone. However, this is not in the cards. Drawing on an idea articulated by Delpla and Weizsäcker (2010), some have proposed a "partial eurobond" or the so-called "blue bond proposal", which would replace 60 percent of GDP of national debt with blue bonds and the remaining 40 percent of the debt with the remaining national or "red" bonds. This means that once a member state has issued 60 percent of its senior debt, further borrowing must be in the form of its own nonguaranteed bonds, with procedures in place for an orderly default. Suffice it to note, for the peripheral countries, the yield on the 40 percent would be higher – giving them an incentive to keep their borrowing under control. However, the problem with this proposal is how to preserve the credibility of the blue bond once the ceiling is exhausted – which could happen very quickly. Some have suggested an even more modest "euro-bills" proposal, designed to introduce common debt issuances with a short-term maturity (one year at most), covering about 10 percent of a country's GDP. Again, this would not be very effective in assuring markets. The same applies to the proposal of issuing common bonds under which each member country's liability could be based on the size of its participation. This would mean that even if countries like Germany would have to accept higher interest rates, they would be exempted from assuming any liability risks. Furthermore, the common bonds would be issued with strict rules regarding borrowing and spending by member countries, including compliance with EU's fiscal rules. However, this proposal lacks the firepower to calm markets.

Not be outdone, in November 2011, the EC released a green paper exploring the feasibility of common issuance of sovereign bonds called stability bonds. Stability bonds would pool all eurozone sovereign issuance, but unlike in previous proposals, each country would be liable for its own and others' eurozone debt. The trade-off: in exchange for having their debt guaranteed, the weaker peripheral member states would have to pay a premium to the stronger northern member states. A member state's premium would be linked to a risk metric, in particular, its ratio of debt to GDP. Thus, eurozone countries with high debt levels would pay higher premiums to compensate for the risk undertaken by stronger member countries. Since the issuance of stability bonds would mean shared fiscal sovereignty among the member states, it will take time before this can be put in practice.

A proposal that better takes into account the political factors is outlined in a November 2011 report by the German Council of Economic Experts, which proposed a quasi-eurobond called the European Redemption Pact and an associated European Redemption Fund.[52] Like eurobonds, this would be a common debt vehicle, but unlike eurobonds, they would be temporary. The report proposes that

1. Eurozone member countries that have not received a bailout could pool their debts into a European Redemption Fund to issue common guaranteed bonds on debts for each country beyond 60 percent of their GDP, the threshold specified in the Maastricht and SGP criteria;

---

[52] Bofinger, Peter, Lars P. Feld, Wolfgang Franz, Christoph Schmidt and Beatrice Weder di Mauro, 2011. "A European Redemption Pact," 9 November. http://voxeu.org/index.php?q=node/7253

2. These bonds would be backed by the member states €2.3 trillion in gold reserves;
3. Recipients of the fund must adhere to specific spending and economic measures;
4. Recipients of the fund must also adhere to a European Redemption Pact detailing how they will lower their gross public debt to 60 percent of GDP over the next 25 years – the life of the pact and fund.

Overall, this proposal is not only compatible with the EU Treaty's no-bailout clause but is also similar to bonds issued by the EFSF. In other words, this type of eurobond can be introduced without the need to reopen treaties or with only minor modifications to the treaties.

Undoubtedly, before some form of eurobonds become reality, an effective supranational agency capable of enforcing budgetary discipline and preventing the buildup of imbalances, including the power to impose punitive sanctions (such as the freezing of EU funds and the suspension of a country's voting rights in EU ministerial councils), must first be put into place. Merkel has repeatedly stated that eurobonds are not subject to discussion as long as the fiscal policies of eurozone members remain in the hands of individual national governments. In other words, the powers of the EC must be substantially strengthened, for example, the EC must be allowed to thoroughly examine the national budgets of each country, before eurobonds can be approved.[53] It is important to reiterate that Merkel (and other northern governments) have not completely ruled out issuing common government debt in the form of eurobonds. Former French president Sarkozy used to say that "eurobonds can be imagined one day, but at the end of the European integration process not at the beginning" (Clark 2011). Although Merkel's view that fiscal centralization is essential if there is to be a viable monetary union does not sit well with some members, namely peripheral states who see this as a ploy to centralize power within the EMU and Germany and allow excessive intrusion by Germany in the affairs of sovereign states, clearly they do not have leverage to oppose it. It remains to be seen if the PIIGS are willing to cede some of their sovereignty for the privilege of having a common eurozone debt.

---

[53] Council of the European Union. 2010. "Council conclusions on crisis prevention, management and resolution," 3015 Economic and Financial Affairs Council meeting Brussels, 18 May. The fact that Germany (in 2009) enshrined in its constitution a law forbidding the federal government from running a deficit of more than 0.35 per cent of GDP by 2016 should be a model for others to emulate.

Table 4.2. *Eurozone's struggling economies 2011–2012*

	Q4 2011	Q1 2012	Q2 2012	Q3 2012
Eurozone	−0.3	0	−0.2	−0.1
Germany	−0.1	0.5	0.3	0.2
France	0	0	−0.1	0.2
Italy	−0.7	−0.8	−0.7	−0.2
Spain	−0.5	−0.3	−0.4	−0.3
Netherlands	−0.6	0.2	0.1	−1.1
Portugal	−1.4	−0.1	−1.1	−0.8
Greece	−7.9	−6.7	−6.3	−7.2

Source: Eurostat, 2012 (% change as compared with the previous quarter).

Concluding Reflections

At the time of this writing (mid-December 2012), the agreement to place eurozone banks under a single supervisor, the ability of the ECB under its "Outright Monetary Transactions" facility to carry out unlimited intervention (or purchase bonds of troubled eurozone countries), progress in the restructuring, resolution and recapitalization of the Spanish banking sector, and the disbursement to funds to Greece by the EFSF (after receiving a clear commitment by Athens to reduce its debt-level to less than 110 percent of GDP by 2022), have all helped to improve market confidence as reflected in reduced borrowing costs and decreased financial-market volatility. Yet the Eurozone's woes are far from over (Table 4.2). Debt levels are still too high for many member states. For example, although debt swaps have substantially reduced Greece's outstanding debt to private creditors, Athens still owes official sector creditors – a burden that will continue to increase with more borrowing for deficit financing and bank-recapitalization costs. Given that the eurozone's economy remains caught in the grips of deep contraction, a "lost decade" is a real possibility.

Not surprisingly, the fear of a possible disorderly eurozone breakup remains palpable. This explains the steady repatriation of private capital from the peripheral countries to the core. The IMF (2012, 27–29) reports

Both Spain and Italy have suffered large-scale capital outflows in the 12 months to June [2012] – on the order of €296 billion (27 percent of 2011 GDP) for Spain and €235 billion (15 percent of GDP) for Italy. Foreign investors retreating from periphery bond markets drove a large share of these flows... adding strains are the continued deposit outflows from periphery banks which reflect a combination of waning confidence and economic contraction.

Moreover, with banks from the eurozone's core member states sharply scaling their exposure to the peripheral countries, the "currency union is becoming increasingly fragmented between the periphery and the core." This balkanization, in turn, has led to rising credit spreads on the peripheral countries' sovereign and bank borrowers.

Undoubtedly, the greatest challenge facing the eurozone is to jumpstart its stalled economic engine. Although confidence has improved (that is, risk aversion has been tempered) since the ECB offered to buy the bonds of struggling economies, namely Spain and Italy, the bloc must continue to improve investor confidence by aggressively pursuing and building on the gains of the past three years. At a minimum this means augmenting the embryonic banking union and moving expeditiously toward deeper fiscal integration. Put bluntly, markets are no longer going to be satisfied with half measures. They are demanding a meaningful banking, fiscal, and monetary union with the ability to resolutely respond to challenges. This in the end will help jumpstart the eurozone's moribund economy and help alleviate its debt problems and the tough austerity measures that citizens in Greece, Spain, and other peripherals have been forced to endure.

FIVE

Russia

Not an Exceptional Country

Even as country after country in Eastern Europe, including in the former Soviet states, were succumbing to the financial contagion, Russia was deemed to be an exception to the rule. Hailed as an "economic miracle" (after notching impressive growth rates between 2000 and 2007), Russia was believed to have real immunity from the malaise plaguing its neighbors (Aslund, Guriev, and Kuchins 2010). Indeed, in September 2008, Prime Minister Vladimir Putin called Russia a "safe haven." However, the notion of Russia's immunity proved to be false after its economy contracted by some 7.8 percent. Why did the Russian economy succumb so quickly to the financial contagion? What does it tell us about the Russian economy – despite some two decades of market reforms? How can Russia better insulate itself from the vagaries of the global financial markets? The following sections address these interrelated questions.

Russia Is Not Like Eastern Europe

Many countries in Eastern Europe, including the former Soviet republics, began to feel the effects of the financial contagion long before Russia. This is because the markets woke up to the reality that these countries (like Iceland, Europe's first victim of the crisis) were also living beyond their means. Like Iceland, Eastern Europe's problems began with easy access to credit – the result of many countries, including Estonia, Latvia, Lithuania, Belarus, Ukraine, and Bulgaria, having pegged exchange rates. This attracted large inflows of short-term lending from Western European banks, which began to flood the region starting in 2004 (Martin 2010; Brixiova et al., 2010; Darvas 2011). By 2008, the thirteen former Soviet-bloc countries had accumulated a collective debt to foreign banks or in foreign currencies of more than U.S.$1 trillion (IMF 2009a; 2009b). The biggest lenders were Western European banks, in particular, Austrian and Italian banks (IMF 2008b; 2008c).

Because much of these borrowed funds went into consumption, including speculative ventures such as real estate, Eastern Europe soon had its own homegrown bubble problem. Here it is important to underscore that domestic policy and Western European banks were equally responsible for creating this problem. The foreign banks not only engaged in reckless lending (the loans by Austrian banks to Eastern European countries are equivalent to almost 70 percent of Austria's GDP), they also failed to assess the creditworthiness of their borrowers and actively encouraged borrowing in foreign currencies. Both Eastern European governments and their private sectors obliged because, in addition to being able to borrow at lower rates, with local currencies appreciating, their payments would actually go down over time. Not surprisingly, more than two-thirds of mortgages in Hungary and Poland were denominated in Swiss francs (László 2009). However, when the global credit crunch hit, these countries with large debt denominated in foreign currencies simply could not meet their obligations.

Iceland's rapid meltdown only heightened concerns about other countries with similar problems. What many Eastern European countries had in common with Iceland was excess credit, large and rising current account deficits and businesses and households that borrowed heavily in foreign currency. While these problems were most pronounced in the Baltic countries, Romania, Bulgaria, Hungary, and the Ukraine suffered from the same fatal flaws (Marer 2010; Martin 2010). On their part, Western European banks, reminiscent of their operations in Iceland, by deepening their links with the emerging Eastern European economies, had built huge exposure to these economies, both directly and through local subsidiaries. Perhaps the most notorious were the Austrian banks, namely the Erste Bank and Raiffeisen International, which had more than $295 billion exposure to Eastern Europe, or roughly 68 percent of the Austrian GDP, while the Swedish banks and their subsidiaries lent recklessly to Latvia's construction industry, including to Latvian banks involved in not much else apart from financing consumer loans (Darvas 2011; Kasjanovs and Kasjanova 2011). As troubles mounted, it did not take long for the transition economies in Eastern Europe and Central Asia to feel the negative effects of the growing financial turbulence (Mitra 2010).

As economic difficulties in Western Europe led to a decline in global liquidity and an increase in risk aversion, investors began to quickly abandon emerging markets. Ukraine and Hungary were among the first countries to suffer the fallout of the expanding crisis. The highly vulnerable Ukrainian economy, with its high short-term external debt relative to reserves, and the high exposure of banks to foreign funding, including balance sheet mismatches and a weak underlying fiscal position, was hit particularly hard (Zettelmeyer et al., 2010). Similarly, Hungary's high external debt levels (which amounted to 97 percent of GDP at end-2007) and significant balance sheet mismatches negatively affected investor interest for Hungarian assets. As a result, Hungary was hit hard by the global deleveraging (IMF 2008c; Marer 2010). However, this was just the beginning of the maelstrom. Next in line were countries whose recent economic boom was fueled, in part, by large-scale public and private borrowing from Western European banks and easy access to foreign-currency-denominated loans. As it turned out, these included most of the transition economies in Eastern Europe and Central Asia, which

received shocks through several channels simultaneously. In the capital markets, external financing continued to decline, with total gross capital inflows (syndicated bank lending, bond issuance, and equity initial public offerings) plummeting from $56.6 billion in the second quarter of 2008 to a meager $3.9 billion in the first quarter of 2009. At the same time, spreads for government borrowing on international markets, a key measure of credit risk, widened to unprecedented levels. Between September 2008 and March 2009, spreads on sovereign five-year credit-default swaps increased from a range of 68 to 270 basis points to 381 to 1,100 basis points. (World Bank 2009a, 111)

The economies of Eastern Europe and Central Asia were not only burdened with high levels of public debt in euros, they also had low levels of savings. For example, in mid-2008 Eastern European borrowers owed about $400 billion to Western European banks. This was equivalent to about one-third of the region's GDP. As credit dried up, these countries mounting debt problem further worsened as their currencies were in free fall against the euro. It was soon clear that many had little ability to meet their payment obligations. By the end of October 2008, the Polish zloty has lost 48 percent against the euro, the Hungarian forint had lost 30 percent, and the Czech Krona had fallen about 23 percent, making payment of their euro-denominated debt exceedingly difficult, it not impossible. In fact, there was recognition, that if pushed, most of these economies (and their financial institutions) would default on loans without outside assistance. Exacerbating this, the economic slowdown in Western Europe sharply reduced the demand for exports from these transition economies, particularly those with growing trade with the fifteen original EU member countries. Ukraine, for example, highly dependent on steel exports, was negatively impacted as the price for steel literally plummeted overnight. By mid-January 2009, the IMF had approved

Table 5.1. *Russia: internal economic indicators, 1999–2008 (% growth from previous year)*

Year	Real GDP growth	Consumer price index	Average real wages	Real personal disposable income	Unemployment rate
1999	6.4	85.7	−23.2	−8.8	12.6
2000	10.0	20.8	18.0	11.3	10.5
2001	5.1	21.5	19.9	8.7	9.0
2002	4.7	15.8	16.2	9.7	8.1
2003	7.3	13.7	9.8	13.5	8.6
2004	7.2	10.9	10.3	8.6	8.2
2005	6.4	12.7	12.6	11.5	7.6
2006	6.7	9.7	14.4	10.2	7.2
2007	8.1	9.0	16.2	12.0	6.2
2008	5.6	14.1	10.3	2.7	6.3

Source: Cooper (2009, 6).

emergency loans for Hungary, Ukraine, Iceland, Belarus, and Latvia totaling over $39 billion, with requests for more assistance from a number of other countries.

Is Russia Like Eastern Europe?

Unlike its neighbors, Russia had strong economic fundamentals that were widely seen to make the country immune to the crisis. Between 2000 and 2007, Russia's real GDP per capita grew on average by about 7 percent a year, along with improvements in living standards (Table 5.1), and Russia's nominal GDP increased five-fold since 2002 with GDP per capita increasing to $12,000 in 2008 (World Bank in Russia 2008; OECD 2009b).

Thanks to its export revenues based on hydrocarbons (oil and gas) and vital precious metals such as titanium, platinum, and related raw materials used in aerospace industries, electronics, and automotive production, Russia enjoyed a healthy current account balance and a huge external surplus (Table 5.2), strong indicators that Moscow would ride out the storm relatively unscathed.[1]

---

[1] For Russia, oil and gas revenues are a significant source of foreign exchange and government revenue. According to Goldsworthy and Zakharova (2010, 3), "In 2008, oil and gas exports accounted for two-thirds of all Russian exports by value, while oil and gas revenue amounted to a third of general government revenue."

Table 5.2. *Russia's external economic indicators (in billions of U.S.$)*

Year	Exports flows	Imports	Current account balance	Foreign-exchange reserves	Foreign direct investment
1999	75.5	39.5	24.6	12.5	3.3
2000	105.0	44.9	46.8	28.0	2.7
2001	101.9	53.8	33.9	36.6	2.7
2002	107.3	61.0	29.1	47.5	3.4
2003	135.9	76.1	35.4	76.9	8.0
2004	183.2	97.4	59.0	124.5	15.4
2005	243.6	125.3	83.3	182.2	12.9
2006	304.5	163.9	94.4	303.7	30.8
2007	355.5	223.4	76.2	476.4	55.0
2008	471.6	291.9	102.3	427.1	60.0

Source: Cooper (2009, 8).

Furthermore, and unlike its neighbors, although Russia was a major holder of fixed income securities issued by government-backed mortgage lenders in the United States, its banking system did not have direct exposure to subprime mortgage-backed securities and was better supervised with healthy fiscal and external account surpluses. Russia's financial system is not only small by international standards, it is also dominated by domestic banks.

Total assets of banks were 54 percent of GDP at end-2007, compared with over 200 percent in France, Germany, and Japan.... The banking system is dominated by state-owned banks (Table 5.3). State-owned banks – accounting for over one third of total banking assets and nearly 60 percent of household deposits – are dominated by six large banks.... Foreign-controlled banks account for about 17 percent of banking assets and have a low share of deposits and finance their credit expansion with foreign borrowing. (IMF 2010d, 11)

In addition, the Russian government's Reserve Fund and National Welfare Fund held the equivalent of $162 billion, and its hard currency and gold reserves totaled about $597–$600 billion – the third-largest reserves in the world after China and Japan.[2] To its credit, Russia had prudently saved its oil and gas revenues in the Oil Stabilization Fund and had created a sovereign wealth fund, the surpluses of which were invested abroad.[3] Russia's

[2]   Gaddy and Ickes (2010, 288) note that "Russia's currency reserves grew by $55 billion in 2005, $120 billion in 2006, and $170 billion in 2007, bringing the total to nearly $600 billion by mid-2008." Also see IMF (2010e, 48–50), and Cohen and Szaszdi 2009).

[3]   In 2004, Russia set up the Oil Stabilization Fund to set aside part of the country's oil revenues. This was later split into the Reserve Fund and the National Wealth Fund. By early

Table 5.3. *Russia's bank and assets*

Bank	% of total banking assets	Ownership
Sberbank	23.7	State
VTB	8.0	State
Gazprornbank	4.7	State
Rosselhozbank	2.9	State
Bank of Moscow	2.8	State
Alfa-bank	2.5	Private domestic
UniCredit Bank	2.1	Foreign
Raiffeisenbank	2.1	Foreign
VTB-24	2.0	State
Rosbank	1.7	Foreign

Source: OECD. 2009. *Economic Survey of Russia 2009: Stabilization and Renewed Growth: Key Challenges.* Paris: Organization for Economic Co-operation and Development.

large and robust stock of foreign reserves was seen as a bulwark against any currency or financial crisis as the central bank could easily withstand even a run on ruble-denominated deposits in the banks, while in terms of coverage of foreign refinancing or repayments, international reserves were quite robust and healthy. With the price of hydrocarbons at an all-time high, coupled with important post-1998 era reforms in the banking and financial sector (which helped Russia achieve large fiscal and external account surpluses and low levels of debt[4]), investors viewed Russia as a safe haven in troubled economic times. Yet, despite these cushions, Russia could not escape the financial contagion. In fact, by October 2008, its fearsome waves had reached Russia and soon engulfed the economy (Figure 5.1).

What explains this? For starters, the tightening global credit markets resulted in an acute liquidity crisis around the world with a particularly negative impact on all emerging-market economies, including Russia's. Specifically, in the case of Russia, total gross capital inflows declined to

2009, the Oil Stabilization Fund had accumulated $225 billion – amounting to 17 percent of GDP. Goldsworthy and Zakharova (2010).

[4] In fact, by early 2005, Russia had paid off its sovereign debt. Gaddy and Ickes (2010, 288) note that when Putin came to office,

The first priority, however, was to decease Russia's sovereign debt. They inherited a foreign debt of over $130 billion, which they began to reducing as soon as Putin entered office. But, it was the boom in oil prices that began in early 2004 that allowed them to in effect fully retire the government's foreign debt. In January 2005, Russia paid off the entire balance of its debt to the IMF – three and one-half years ahead of schedule.

Percent, year-on-year　　　　　　　　　　　　　　　　Index, 0 = neutral

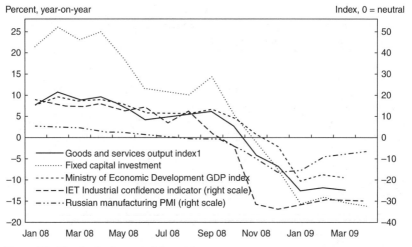

Figure 5.1. Russia: the impact of the crisis.

Note: Estimated on the basis of data on change of physical volume of production in agriculture, mining and quarrying, manufacturing, electricity, gas and water supply, construction, transportation, wholesale, and retail trade.

Source: OECD. 2009. *Economic Survey of Russia 2009: Stabilization and Renewed Growth: Key Challenges.* Paris: Organization for Economic Co-operation and Development.

$75 billion in the third quarter of 2008, down 40 percent from the same period in 2007. Russia's problems were further exacerbated by the severity of the global recession, which led to a sharp decline in the demand for raw materials and other primary commodities. Russia's oil and gas export revenues (key drivers of the economy) fell to less than one-third of their peak value by September 2008.[5] To the markets these "twin shocks" may have seemed erringly like a repeat of the crisis Russia faced in August 1998 when Moscow was forced to devalue the ruble by some 75 percent, default of its GKOs (treasury bills denominated in rubles) valued at about $60 billion, and froze international bank transactions for 90 days (Gilman 2010). After all, the common denominator between 1998 and 2008 was the global economic slowdown and the sharp decline in the price of its major export commodities, oil and gas (Belousov 2010). However, if in 1998, Russia was burdened with a fiscal deficit, high levels of public debt, low reserves, and mounting interest payments, in contrast, in 2008, Russia's macroeconomic vulnerability was much lower and its huge foreign currency reserves made

---

[5]　Crude-oil prices fell dramatically from U.S.$144 a barrel in July 2008 to below U.S.$55 a barrel in mid-November 2008. For details, see IMF (2009b).

it well prepared to deal with the shocks arising from the global markets – or so it seemed.

However, there were two big differences between 1998 and 2008. First, despite a decade of impressive growth rates, the Russian economy not only had failed to diversify away from hydrocarbons, it had actually become even more resource-dependent. If before the 1998 crisis,

oil and gas accounted for almost half of Russia's export revenues and directly for one-fifth of federal government revenues, in 2008 the share of oil and gas in export receipts had reached 68 percent, and natural resources directly accounted for half of federal government revenues. Extraction industries accounted for more than 10 percent of the total value added, and their true contribution to GDP was much higher, because about 60 percent of industrial production was concentrated in closely related sectors such as oil refining and fertilizer and metal production. (Berglof, Plekhanov, and Rousso 2009, 16).

Given this, the sharp drop in commodity prices, especially hydrocarbons, severely eroded Russia's fiscal and external account surpluses, including its international reserve. This eventually impacted Russia's GDP, which experienced a 10 percent drop between mid-2008 and mid-2009 (World Bank in Russia 2009). Overall, the Russian economy contracted by 7.9 percent in 2009 (IMF 2010d; 2010e; Central Bank of Russian Federation 2010).

Second, although government debt was negligible in 2008, the private sector had accumulated a substantial volume of short-term debt in part because the policy of controlled appreciation of the ruble contributed to excessive foreign-currency borrowing (Hanson 2011; Sapir 2008). Given that private-capital inflows were mostly in the form of loans to corporates and commercial banks, many of the commercial banks were heavily indebted as they had borrowed from abroad at low interest rates. Therefore, even as the Russian government was accumulating an impressive volume of foreign exchange, Russian corporations and private companies (in particular, the "big four," Gazprom, Rosneft, LUKoil, and Rostekhnologii), and banks were borrowing lavishly from abroad because dollar interest rates were much lower than ruble rates.[6] As Morse notes,

While prices were rising, Russian firms used their unfettered access to Western credit markets to borrow capital with few strings attached. This was particularly the case for the state-owned energy giant Gazprom, which has borrowed tens of billions of U.S. dollars in Western markets since 2004 without any requirements

---

[6] The ruble floated against a basket comprising roughly 55 percent U.S. dollars and 45 percent euros. Between 2002 and mid-2008, when world oil prices were rising and the balance of payment surpluses robust, the ruble gained roughly 36 percent against the dollar. This encouraged foreign borrowing.

that it reinvest in new energy supplies – or any other conditions. Gazprom used the money to buy assets in the very countries where the credits were issued, and without any monitoring. (Morse 2009, 50)

Yet this was not the worst. The most reckless were the powerful oligarchs who with explicit support of the Russian government used their company shares in oil and gas as collateral for foreign loans. In the process they accumulated an equally "impressive" foreign debt and in particular, a potential short-term debt problem. According to an IMF study, Russian banks' external borrowing totaled some "($200 billion as of end-September 2008), largely in the form of syndicated loans or credit lines from foreign parent banks. Large firms have also been actively tapping into international financial markets and accumulated about $300 billion in external debt. Between end-2000 and the third quarter of 2008, banks' loan books grew at an average annualized rate of more than 50 percent, almost as fast as in Ukraine" (Berglof, Plekhanov and Rousso 2009, 17). This meant that despite Russia's huge reserves, its external (mostly corporate) debt was much higher. As refinancing external liabilities became extremely difficult due to the global credit crunch, Russian corporate borrowers found it exceedingly difficult to meet their obligations.[7] Although the government dipped generously into the accumulated reserves to meet public debt obligations and bail out well-connected oligarchs, the many medium and small firms that relied on easy bank credit found it impossible to continue operations (Mauldin 2008).

As the impact of the twin shocks spread through the financial sector and the real economy, the Russian economy was hit by simultaneous shocks, including a sharp decline in export earnings, over-leveraged corporate balance sheets, a deep and painful credit crunch and banking failures, mortgage defaults from the collapse of the real-estate sector, and capital flight (Sestanovich 2008). No doubt, Russia's invasion of Georgia on August 8, 2008, and what Hanson (2011, 459–61) described as "an all-too-acute apprehension about the behavior in adversity of the Russian state… the general unpredictability of the Russian business environment," and in particular, "fear of expropriation," further exacerbated the economic problems. The concerns about political instability and prolonged conflict made jittery and risk-averse market participants pull out of Russia en masse, putting

---

[7]   The IMF (2010d, 15) notes that "the increase in global risk aversion since mid-2007 slowed the flow and raised the cost of foreign funding to the banking system, exposing some banks to potential refinancing difficulties. Since mid-2007, access to the Eurobond market has remained limited and domestic bond market volume has decreased in late 2007 and early 2008."

tremendous pressure on the stock market and the ruble.[8] Not only did the Russian Federal Financial Market Service impose a blanket ban on short-selling, on September 17, 2008 it was forced to close the country's stock exchange for two days to prevent the total collapse of the stock market. Despite this, Russia's stock markets declined by nearly 70 percent in 2008, losing two-thirds of their value in less than five months (World Bank in Russia 2008, 4; also Stoner-Weiss 2009), and "the country spent one-third of its gold and foreign currency reserves – or US\$216 billion – defending the ruble."[9]

The Russian leadership's policy response in 2008 was in sharp contrast to that in 1998 when authorities hastily devalued the ruble by some 75 percent, defaulted on their debt obligations, valued at around \$60 billion, and froze international bank transactions for three months (Aslund 2007). In 2008, both the government and the Central Bank of Russia (CBR) responded quickly by boosting liquidity and providing capital injections to the banking system, besides ensuring timely repayment of external obligations. For example, in order to boost liquidity and confidence in the interbank market, the CBR lowered the reserve requirements for all bank liabilities by 4 basis points (thereby pumping an additional 300 billion ruble in the economy), quickly provided emergency liquidity assistance by offering guarantees for interbank lending to qualifying banks, agreed to accept a wide range of collateral, including nonmarketable collateral, and announced that it would compensate those banks with a rating of above BB-/Ba3 for losses they incurred on the interbank market (IMF 2011e, 8–10). Also, not only were the majority of personal deposits secured in the state-owned Sberbank, the CBR also provided Sberbank with an unsecured loan of 500 billion ruble in the hopes of increasing liquidity in the banking and financial system. On September 29, 2008, the Russian parliament adopted a law to provide banks and businesses the funds to help them repay their foreign loans, aptly called "On additional measures to support the financial system of the Russian Federation."

In order to maintain the stability of the ruble, the CBR used its considerable reserves to support a "gradual and predictable" depreciation by allowing the private sector to hedge its foreign-exchange exposures and to prevent 1998-style panicked deposit runs (IMF 2011e, 9–10). Although Kremlin's

---

[8] Of course, while capital flight was related to the much-anticipated fall in the value of the ruble, the invasion made the situation worse.

[9] CNN. 2009. "Russia Admits Financial Mistakes," March 4. http://edition.cnn.com/2009/BUSINESS/03/02/russia.economy/index.html#cnnSTCText. See also Naumov, Igor, 2009. "The Country Has No Need for Metal," *Nezavisimaya Gazeta*, 13 March.

gradual devaluation (rather than a sudden, one-time devaluation) of the ruble gave banks and businesses more time to adjust and prevented a financial panic, it also proved very costly as the authorities spent billions in order to instill confidence in the ruble and stabilize the banking system. Also, these measures had little effect. After all, Russia's reserves were designed to offset the temporary declines in the oil price rather than maintain the ruble at an artificial level. Not surprisingly, by the end of 2008, the ruble had depreciated by around 15 percent against the dollar-euro basket. Stott (2008) aptly notes:

> In a country where few hold shares but most watch the price of dollars, the fate of the rouble was of huge significance. Ordinary Russians, who have suspected for some weeks that the real economic picture may be less rosy than the official one painted by state-controlled television, have been quietly withdrawing large amounts of roubles from banks to buy dollars. The central bank announced... it had spent $57.5 billion of reserves in the past two months selling dollars to prop up the rouble and... over the same period savers had withdrawn a quarter of all their deposits.[10]

By December 5, 2008, Russia's foreign currency and gold reserves were down to $437 billion. The country had lost $31 billion in one week (October 17 to 24) and $17.9 billion in the week of December 5.

Russia's painful reversal of fortune further heightened the country's political and social tensions. Living standards were severely impacted by rising inflation, unemployment levels at more than 10 percent (or much higher, according to unofficial figures), and the fact that many of the unemployed lack access to formal safety nets (Gidadhubli 2010). Economic contraction in 2009 resulted in an increase in the number of poor and a shrinking of the middle class. The World Bank estimates that "the number of poor people in Russia will likely reach 24.6 million, an increase by 7.45 million." Moreover, the "crisis has significantly worsened not only poverty but also income distribution in Russia... The share of vulnerable population has increased to 20.9 percent in comparison to 18.3 percent previously (an increase of 3.6 million people). And the Russian middle class is likely to shrink – by about 10 percent – from 55.6 to 51.2 percent (a decline of 6.2 million people)" (World Bank in Russia 2009, 13–14). Rising unemployment and social dislocation also fueled widespread protest and civil unrest, including attacks on the millions of *gastarbeiters*, or guest workers. The vast majority of these workers came from Caucasia or Central Asia (and provided labor

---

[10] Stott, Michael. 2008. "Russia Acknowledges Financial Crisis Has Hit Hard," Reuters, November 21. http://www.reuters.com/article/idUSTRE4AK4L620081121

during the boom years. Most left either voluntarily or by force – exacerbating problems in their home countries.[11]

The economic contraction in Russia also resulted in negative regional spillovers. Central Asian countries, namely Kazakhstan, Tajikistan, the Kyrgyz Republic, and Uzbekistan, with a total population of around 60 million, are deeply linked to Russia through trade, financial flows, and remittances (IMF 2009b). Each has been affected negatively by the slowdown in Russian economy. For example, the significant depreciation of the Russian ruble vis-à-vis the dollar during 2008–09 also forced many of Russia's trading partners to devalue their currencies as well. During the height of the crisis, Armenia, Kazakhstan, the Kyrgyz Republic, and Tajikistan devalued their currencies by some 25 percent, leaving their financial sectors vulnerable to volatile exchange-rate movements and severe "haircuts" for unhedged borrowers (Alturki et al., 2009). Kazakhstan, a major oil exporter, saw a sharp drop in the revenue from its oil exports, although the drop has helped the Kyrgyz Republic and Tajikistan, both energy importers. On the other hand, over the past decade, several Central Asian countries, in particular, the Kyrgyz Republic and Tajikistan, have become increasingly dependent on money sent home by their citizens working abroad. For example, in 2008, remittances accounted for 47 percent of Tajikistan's GDP. Overall, remittances from Russia to the Commonwealth of Independent States fell by more than 30 percent in 2009 (IMF 2011d). However, as noted, worsening unemployment in host countries like Russia has forced many migrants to return, putting added pressure on the already spartan and stretched domestic social services.

Lessons for Russia

Both the crisis of 1998 and 2008 underscore that Russia has to do much more to diversify its economy away from oil and gas (Aslund, Guriev, and Kuchins 2010). Clearly, previous efforts have not produced the desired results. As noted earlier, Russia depends more on oil and gas revenue now than it did a decade ago. Hence, it still remains a "petro-state." In addition, the Russian authorities must strengthen the country's legal, economic, and political infrastructure to support business and enterprise (Petrakov 2010). The crisis has underscored that Russia's banking and financial sectors need

---

[11] Lowe, Christian. 2009. "Financial Crisis Hits Migrant Workers in Russia," *The New York Times*, January 14. http://www.nytimes.com/2009/01/14/business/worldbusiness/14iht wages.4.19358424.html

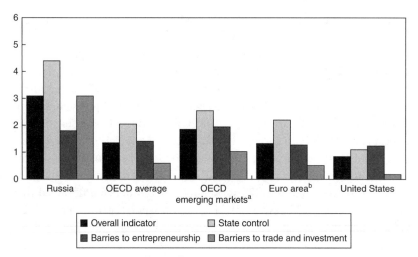

Figure 5.2. Barriers to entrepreneurship.
a. Czech Republic, Hungary, Korea, Mexico, Poland, Turkey.
b. Austria, Belgium, Finland, France, Germany, Italy, Luxembourg, Netherlands, Portugal, Spain.
Note: Index scale of 0–6 from least to most restrictive.
Source: OECD. 2009. *Economic Survey of Russia 2009: Stabilization and Renewed Growth: Key Challenges*. Paris: Organization for Economic Co-operation and Development.

to be modernized to better intermediate capital and investments and to stimulate more productive lending. Specifically, the limited diversification of the Russian banking sector, its excessive reliance on short-term funding, and its weak corporate governance and flawed supervisory framework will continue to act as a break on growth (IMF 2010d). Similarly, the business environment needs significant improvement in areas like property rights and rule of law (IMF 2010d). Among the 181 countries surveyed by the World Bank for ease of doing business, Russia occupies the 120th position, below Nigeria. An OECD study reveals a similar pattern (Figure 5.2).

No doubt, such constraints are not conducive to domestic entrepreneurship, especially the expansion of small and medium businesses so essential to sustained economic growth and diversification, nor to Russia's ambition to function as the economic hub for the region. This weakness explains why, despite Russia's oil wealth, the bulk of investments have come in the form of short-term loans rather than long-term foreign direct investment. Finally, to mitigate the social and economic impact, especially on the weak and vulnerable, it is essential for the government to increase its social safety outlays. Unlike Western Europe's expansive welfare programs(guaranteed health insurance and generous unemployment benefits), which have helped to mitigate the negative effects of the crisis, Russia does not have these "automatic stabilizers." In addition, over the longer term, Russia needs to raise its productivity growth. Despite gains in productivity growth following the 1998 crisis, the absolute level of productivity is still below the average productivity level in manufacturing sector in OECD countries. This makes Russia less competitive in global markets. Of course, it is hard to improve productivity without commensurate improvements in human capital. Therefore, Russia, indeed Eastern Europe, must invest more in human capital via the provision of better education and health services to be competitive in the global economy.

SIX

China

Crisis Management to Rebalancing

Even as the global economy was gripped in the throes of a financial crisis following the collapse of Lehman Brothers in September 2008, China was among a handful of economies that conspicuously remained an outlier. Not only was the Chinese economy booming – notching an impressive 9.3 percent growth in GDP in 2008, Beijing's top priority was to dampen the inflationary pressures and prevent the economy from overheating. To many analysts, the starkly divergent trajectories of the world's largest and second largest economies could be explained by a single fact: the Chinese economy had tangibly "decoupled" from the American economy. More specifically, the China-centered trade integration in Asia and the massive ability within China's economy to generate a domestically driven demand meant that the Chinese economy's business cycle had become less synchronized with that of the advanced economies, notably the United States and Western Europe.[1] Predictably, this led observers to conclude that China was immune from an economic slowdown emanating from the United States and Europe.

To others, China's immunity was due to the "cushion" Beijing enjoyed because of its substantial foreign-exchange reserves. Beijing's holdings of U.S. Treasury debt skyrocketed from about $46 billion in 1998 to $587 billion by 2008.[2] According to the U.S. Treasury, China's investment in

---

[1] Decoupling was always understood to mean a loosening, not a full elimination, of the relationships between the business cycle. Akin and Kose (2007) argue that decoupling is part of the process of globalization. Drawing on data from 106 countries (which they divide into developed, emerging, and low-income), they measure how the correlation between economies has shifted over time even as cross-border flows have expanded. They find that even as growth has become more synchronized among the developed and emerging economies, over the past two decades, economic activity in emerging economies has decoupled from that of the developed economies.

[2] Office of Management and Budget. 2008. Mid-Session Review, Budget of the U.S. Government, Fiscal Year 2009, July 2008. See www.whitehouse.gov/omb/budget/fy2009/pdf/09msr.pdf.

Table 6.1. *Foreign holders of U.S. treasury securities*
(September 2008)

	$ (Billions)	Percent of debt held by the public
China	587.0	10.1
Japan	573.2	9.8
United Kingdom	338.3	5.8
Caribbean Banking Centers [a]	185.3	3.2
Oil Exporters [b]	182.1	3.1
Brazil	141.9	2.4
All Other	852.9	14.6
Total	2,860.7	49.0

a. Caribbean banking centers include Bahamas, Bermuda, Cayman Islands, Netherlands Antilles, Panama, and the British Virgin Islands.
b. Oil exporters include Ecuador, Venezuela, Indonesia, Bahrain, Iran, Iraq, Kuwait, Oman, Qatar, Saudi Arabia, the United Arab Emirates, Algeria, Gabon, Libya, and Nigeria.
Source: U.S. Treasury. 2009. *Treasury Bulletin*, Table OFS-1.

Treasury bonds totaled some $585 billion in September 2008, compared to Japan's, which totaled $573.2 billion (Table 6.1). Moreover, in mid-2008, Beijing held the world's largest cash reserve of roughly $2 trillion.[3] This figure did not include an additional $800 billion in U.S. debt that Beijing purchased through third countries (such purchases are not recorded by the U.S. Treasury as being held by China). This meant that on the eve of the crisis China owned $1 out of every $10 of U.S. public debt. This made Beijing the largest foreign holder of U.S. government debt – indeed, the U.S. government's leading foreign creditor – and the world's leading creditor nation, while the United States became the world's largest debtor.

Rather ironically, if China's reserves had been vilified for creating the "global savings glut" seen as responsible for the crash of 2008, Beijing's formidable reserves were now seen as a source of much-needed global liquidity in an increasingly capital-scarce world.[4] Not surprisingly, it was suggested

---

[3] At the end of 2010, China held an estimated $2.85 trillion worth of foreign reserves. This is equivalent to 48 percent of China's 2010 GDP.

[4] Specifically, before the crisis broke, in an important speech titled "The Global Saving Glut and the U.S. Current Account Deficit," Ben Bernanke, the U.S. Federal Reserve chair, offered a novel explanation for the rapid rise of the U.S. trade deficit in recent years. To Bernanke, the source of the problem was not America, but Asia – especially China and the booming economies of East and Southeast Asia. He argued that in the mid-1990s, these economies were significant importers of capital by borrowing abroad to finance their ambitious development. However, in the aftermath of the Asian financial crisis of 1997–98, they made a sharp volte-face. Cognizant of the fact that absence of foreign hard

that the well-endowed and booming Chinese economy could serve as a potential "shock absorber" and "locomotive" to help drive the global economy out of its deep malaise (Dobson 2009, 10).

Others were upbeat because China (like the other major Asian economies of Japan, India, and South Korea) had only modest exposure to the toxic subprime loans and structured credit products originating in the United States, including the fact that; the Chinese financial sector does not trade much in derivatives (Lardy 2010). The claim by the People's Bank of China (PBC, the country's central bank) that none of its $2 trillion foreign reserves was invested in subprime debt was just a slight exaggeration – that a large percentage of China's reserves are invested in long-term U.S. securities is well known. It is estimated that the Bank of China held about $8.9 billion of securities backed by U.S. subprime loans, whereas the exposure reported by the Industrial and Commercial Bank of China and by the China Construction Bank was about two billion dollars each (Caijing 2009; also Lee and Park 2009, 17). Suffice it to note, these are extremely small debts. That is, even if the three Chinese banks' exposure to risky subprime assets totaled $12.9 billion, that was still a mere 6 percent of the $199 billion in private foreign securities.

Furthermore, since China's banks rely extensively on deposits rather than on wholesale funding and because they fund their loans through deposits rather than capital markets, they were better insulated from the global credit crunch than Western banks – indeed, banks in much of the world.[5] Beijing's limited reliance on foreign capital to finance growth gave it a further shield, and the country's corporate and banking-sector balance sheets were relatively robust.[6] The ambitious and wide-ranging banking reforms of early 2000, which included bank recapitalization, the strengthening of corporate supervision, and greater compliance with international best practices, had not only helped remove a large portion of the nonperforming loans of the banking sector (Table 6.2), but also led to higher risk-weighted capital adequacy ratios.[7]

This made China's once-moribund banking system more solvent. Indeed, the major banks capital positions were strong on the eve of the crisis (Kwong 2011; Riedel, Jin, and Gao 2007), and this explains why no

---

currency reserves had made them vulnerable, they began to protect themselves (upon the IMF's advice) against future crisis by amassing huge war chests of foreign assets. Amid a global economic downturn, these savings provided a source of stability.

[5] In fact, China did not experience a credit crunch.

[6] In 2007, China was the largest next exporter of capital with some 21 percent of all exported capital. (IMF, 2008d, 169).

[7] In 1998, the central government issued some 270 billion yuan of treasury bonds to recapitalize the large state banks, in addition to creating four asset-management companies or "bad banks" for these banks to transfer their nonperforming loans to (Ma 2007).

Table 6.2. *Nonperforming loans (% of commercial bank loans)*

	1998	2003	2004	2005	2006	2007[a]
China[c]	28.5[b]	17.8	13.2	8.6	7.1	6.2
Hong Kong[d]	5.3	3.9	2.3	1.4	1.1	0.9
Germany	3.0	5.2	4.9	4.0	3.4	n/a
Japan	5.4	5.2	2.9	1.8	1.5	1.5
United States	1.0	1.1	0.8	0.7	0.8	1.1

[a] Data for Hong Kong, China, Rep. of Korea, Japan, Singapore, and the United States as of September 2007.
[b] Figure refers to 1999 data.
[c] 1999–2001 data are for state-owned commercial banks only.
[d] Reported nonperforming loans are gross classified loan ratio of retail banks.
Source: Lee and Park (2009, 19).

financial institutions failed during the height of the crisis in 2008–09 (Woo and Zhang 2011).

Equally important, China's low budget deficits, modest level of public debt (about 18 percent of GDP in 2007 compared to nearly 40 percent for the United States), and a largely closed capital account served as critical buffers to external shocks. More specifically, these factors meant that not only would the spillover effects into the Chinese economy be minimal, but also easier to contain. Although it was well-known that Beijing had a potential housing-bubble problem, it was also felt that China's banks were far better prepared to withstand falling house prices than their U.S. counterparts because Chinese buyers (unlike their American counterparts) are required to put down a minimum deposit of 20 to 30 percent as a down payment and as much as 40 percent on second homes.

Also, rather counterintuitively, although the Chinese economy has become deeply enmeshed into the global economy, it is still not fully integrated into the global financial system (Yao and Wu 2011). In particular, China is still a minor player in the *global financial system*. For example, Chinese banks, some of which are large by global standards based on market capitalization and the size of their balance sheets, have only modest international presence. Furthermore, the renminbi (RMB[8]) debt market is shallow, and the Chinese currency plays a relatively minor role in the global foreign-exchange market. In fact, the RMB is hardly used outside China, except for a modest amount in Hong Kong, and Chinese capital markets

[8] The RMB is also known as the yuan. Hence, the term RMB and the yuan are used interchangeably.

are not a major source of financing for foreign borrowers. Overall, China's capital market is small relative to the size of the domestic economy and relies heavily on FDI rather than securities investment and other forms of capital flows to access international capital markets.[9] Although there has been gradual liberalization, Beijing continues to heavily regulate many cross-border transactions and subjects portfolio capital flows to various restrictions. A cautious approach to financial-sector liberalization has meant that portfolio flows are still largely channeled through large institutional investors via the QFII (Qualified Foreign Institutional Investors) and QDII (Qualified Domestic Institutional Investors) programs established in 2002. The QFII program is restricted to funds-management and securities companies with at least $10 billion in assets, including the world's top 100 commercial banks. In addition, the securities regulator of the QFII's home country must sign a "Memorandum of Understanding" and have a track record of good relations with the China Securities Regulatory Commission (CSRC). The QDIIs must have assets of over 5 billion RMB.[10]

Finally, since the crisis was seen as related to factors specific to the U.S. economy, especially problems associated with expansionary monetary policy that had kept U.S. interest rates low for some years and led to a real-estate bubble (rather than to systemic factors such as an oil shock or adverse trade relations), it was believed that the economic fallout would be mainly limited to the United States and that U.S. authorities would, in short order, contain the crisis.

The Contagion Hits

China did not remain immune long – but it has fared far better than most. In early December 2008, the RMB experienced its largest weekly decline against the U.S. dollar since July 2005 (when the RMB's peg to the dollar was lifted), and China's foreign exchange notched a modest decline largely through valuation changes. It is important to note that the contagion caused a *slowdown* in China's economic growth – the Chinese economy never actually *contracted*. China's quarterly growth rate in 2008 was 10.6 percent, 10 percent, 9 percent, and 6.8 percent – an average of 9.3 percent. Given its perceived immunity, how and why was China impacted? In particular, through what channels did the contagion spread into the Chinese economy? How did Beijing respond

---

[9] Beijing is also quite selective about FDI and encourages foreign companies to invest in China using the so-called Greenfield FDI.

[10] The CSRC is the executive arm of the State Council Securities Committee which was established in 1992 to regulate China's securities and futures market.

to the economic and sociopolitical challenges unleashed by the crisis, how effective has the response been, and what can Beijing do over the long term to rebalance its economy and make it less vulnerable to external shocks?

At the outset it should be noted that contagion stemming from a financial crisis can be transmitted simultaneously via several channels – both broad and specific. Broadly, the rapid global spread of the crisis unambiguously underscores that in today's interconnected world no country is an island. Closely integrated financial and banking systems and deepening trade inter-dependence has meant that even countries not directly exposed to the toxic subprime assets originating from the United States are extremely vulner-able to the financial contagion. This is in part because economic globaliza-tion creates not only deep and entwining linkages between economies, but also convergence among them. As such, troubles in one part, especially the largest part (the United States) will inevitably send waves that may become ripples in some places (China) and a tsunami in other places (Iceland).

Furthermore, global economic integration has generated unprecedented levels of capital flows. These funds now cross national borders, often at will, despite attempts by governments to control and regulate their move-ment. Such financially integrated markets also mean more rapid and powerful spillover across economies through both traditional and newer types of channels. Although spillovers through the traditional trade chan-nel remains a central transmission mechanism (even though global trade patterns have become more diversified), financial spillovers have become more pronounced as the rising correlation of global equity prices and the potential for sudden capital-flow reversals mean that shocks at the core can be transmitted rapidly throughout the entire global financial system. For example, China's stock markets are particularly vulnerable to swings in investor sentiment. Heightened anxiety over growing losses led foreign institutional investors (FIIs) to sell billions of their investment in Chinese companies to cover losses accrued in their home markets. As a result the stock exchanges took a beating –the Shanghai stock market fell by 48 per-cent between May and November 2008 (De Haan 2010, 761).

Decoupling did not mean that a downturn in the U.S. economy would not have an impact on emerging market economies like China. Rather, as articulated by the IMF and Akin and Kose (2007), in more nuanced versions of the decoupling thesis did distinguish between the effects of a "moderate" slowdown in the U.S. to a "sharp slowdown or recession":

Most countries should be in a position to "decouple" from the U.S. economy and sus-tain strong growth if the U.S. slowdown remains as moderate as expected, although countries with strong trade linkages with the United States in specific sectors may experience some drag on their growth. However, if the U.S. economy experienced a sharper slowdown because of a broader-than-expected impact of the housing sector difficulties, the spillover effects into other economies would be larger, and decoupling would be more difficult. (IMF 2007b, 148)

As the crisis became more severe, especially after the collapse of Lehman Brothers, decoupling no longer guaranteed immunity.

China's integration into the global economy, exemplified by its export-led growth strategy, has proven to be remarkably successful in producing an unprecedented 10 percent annual growth for the past three decades (Lin 2012). During this period, China has seen its share of world GDP rise to 13 percent in 2010 from less than 2 percent in 1980 – even as its share of the world's population declined from 25 percent to 20 percent. Equally impressive, with real GDP per head increasing almost thirty-fold, hundreds of millions of people have been lifted out of abject poverty. On the eve of China's economic reforms in 1978, incidence of poverty in China was among the highest in the world. However, over the past three decades, the proportion of people living in extreme poverty fell from some 53 percent to less than 5 percent. This means that across China, the number of people living in extreme poverty has fallen by more than 500 million since 1978 (IMF 2012; Lin, Cai, and Li 2003; World Bank 2009). Few countries have grown so quickly over such an extended period of time or reduced the incidence of poverty so sharply. However, with the onset of the crisis, China's heavy dependence on exports of goods and services has become a liability.

As Table 6.3 shows, China's exports of goods and services as a share of GDP rose sharply, from 9.1 percent in 1985 to 37.8 percent in 2008.

In fact, in 2007, China not only replaced the United States to become the world's second-largest exporter of merchandise goods (after the EU), its net exports (exports minus imports) contributed to a whopping one-third of its overall GDP growth in 2007. Most of the export industries were direct beneficiaries of foreign direct investment (FDI), which totaled some $92.4 billion in 2008 – making China the third largest recipient of FDI after the EU and the United States (Xing 2010). Also, according to Chinese government estimates, in 2007 more than 80 million people depended on the "foreign trade sector" for employment – with some 28 million employed directly in enterprises engaged in exports. Therefore, on one hand, rapid and unprecedented changes in the structure of the Chinese economy have generated sustained economic growth, but on the other, it has made growth highly dependent on the continuation of robust external trade and

Table 6.3. *China's exports of goods
and services (as % of GDP)*

Year	Percentage of exports
1985	9.1
1990	14.2
1995	19.5
2000	23.4
2005	36.5
2008	37.8

Source: Economist Intelligence Unit.

external capital flows (Arora and Cardarelli 2011). This also means that a global slowdown in demand would rapidly translate into a corresponding negative impact on economic growth.

As the United States, the European Union, and the Middle East account for a significant portion of China's exports, the sharp deterioration in demand with the onset of the financial crisis saw the value of China's exports fall by 16.7 percent between October 2008 and November 2009 (IMF 2010g; OECD 2010). According to a World Bank study, "Since the onset of the crisis, exports shifted from 20 percent annual growth to an annualized contraction of more than 25 percent in early 2009" (Vincelette 2010, 13). The most severely impacted have been the technology and capital-intensive exports, forcing several companies (both domestic and foreign) in these key sectors to shut down their factories and businesses. Such sharp export contraction also led to equally sharp declines in FDI, which "plunged to −35.52% in November 2008. The period of negative FDI growth lasted for nine months until September 2009" (Woo and Zhang 2010, 354).

Cumulatively, these had a deleterious impact on the highly export-dependent Chinese economy. Indeed, with demand for Chinese exports evaporating, some "67,000 small and medium-sized companies across China were forced to shut down in 2008" (Yang and Lim 2010, 27). In Guangdong province, some 6.7 million jobs were lost (De Haan 2010, 763), and in China's key industrial provinces, an estimated "20 million workers lost their jobs" (Overholt 2010, 28). In addition, as many as 26 million of China's estimated 130 million migrant workers were left unemployed (Yingzi and Dingding 2009). No doubt, the authorities are cognizant of the fact that after years of double-digit growth anything less than 8 percent annual growth could lead to further unemployment and social tensions. Indeed, Overholt (2010, 28) notes:

The loss of tens of millions of jobs supplemented another domestic trend, namely the rapid rise over the years in the number of the so-called "mass incidents," or popular demonstrations. According to official statistics, these had risen from 8,700 in 1993 to about 40,000 in the year 2000, compounded by increasing size, violence, and effectiveness of the protests, with a further rise to 74,000 in 2004. Official statistics do not yet reveal the scale of the additional impact of the financial crisis, but there have been many widely publicized protests by workers losing their jobs.

Beijing's Ambitious Response

The global financial crisis of 2007–08, which saw an abrupt and sharp shrinkage in external demand, the rise of protectionism in the advanced economies, and a growing chorus of criticism of China's economic policies from U.S. lawmakers in both houses of Congress and the White House, only underscored what Beijing had already come to recognize: that excessive dependence on exports was not a sustainable economic strategy. That is, China's investment-driven and export-oriented development model, with exports accounting for 40 percent of GDP, was becoming increasingly difficult to maintain (Morrison and Labonte 2008). In fact, Lardy (2006, 1) points out that Chinese authorities have been increasingly concerned about the country's economic trajectory and as early as 2004, "China's top political leadership agreed to fundamentally alter the country's growth strategy by rebalancing the sources of economic growth."

This is because China has developed two forms of macroeconomic imbalance: a domestic or internal imbalance due to high investment (hence, "investment-led growth") combined with very low household consumption, and an external imbalance due to the country's export-led development strategy that relies heavily on exchange-rate undervaluation and intervention in the foreign exchange-rate markets to promote exports (Figures 6.1 and 6.2). The internal imbalance has resulted in rapid and massive capital accumulation, imbalances between expenditure and production, and the overall income gains not percolating to the Chinese people in line with the growth in the country's GDP.[11] On the other hand, the external imbalance has generated a massive surplus in the current account of the balance of payments.

[11] That is, although overall the living standard of the masses has greatly improved, it has not improved in line with the growth of China's GDP.

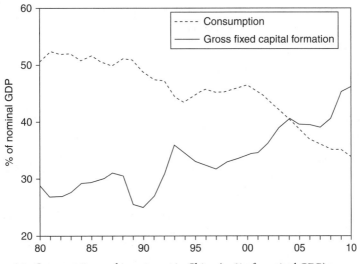

Figure 6.1. Consumption and investment in China (as % of nominal GDP). *Source*: Fukumoto and Muto (2011, 4).

Former Premier Wen Jiabao, (whose tenure ended in March 2013) a strong proponent of macroeconomic rebalancing, repeated the imperatives of rebalancing at every opportunity. At the influential National People's Congress in March 2007, Wen noted that "the biggest problem with China's economy is that the growth is unstable, unbalanced, uncoordinated and unsustainable." Again, in a keynote speech to the National People's Congress in March 2010, Wen unambiguously noted that a development strategy based on investments to facilitate exports cannot be sustained indefinitely. Rather, he pointed out that "unleashing domestic demand holds the key to long-term and steady development of China's economy." Wen noted that "expanding domestic demand is a… basic standpoint of China's economic development as well as a fundamental means and an internal requirement for promoting balanced economic development."[12] In other words, Wen declared a transition or rebalancing away from exports and investment-driven growth toward "consumption-driven growth" essential to the long-term dynamism of the Chinese economy. To guide this transition, or in Wen's words, "put China's economy quickly on the path of endogenous growth," he pledged that billions of renminbi would be invested in "human and social services" – especially affordable housing, expanding educational opportunities, and delivering a more comprehensive health and social-welfare system.

[12] Wen Jiabao, 2010. "Consolidate the upward momentum and promote sustained growth," 13 September, available at www.ccchina.gov.cn/en/NewsInfo.asp?NewsId=25436.

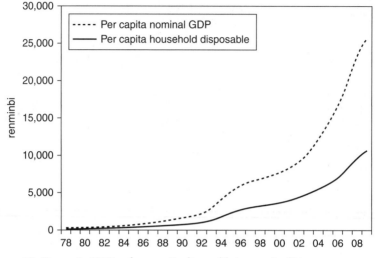

Figure 6.2. Per capita GDP and per capita disposable income in China.
Source: Fukumoto and Muto (2011, 5).

Beijing, which had maintained a contractionary fiscal policy from 2001–07[13] found itself in a good fiscal position (the fiscal balance as percentage of GDP in early 2008 was 0.7, and the debt-to-GDP ratio was only 20 percent) to stimulate the economy (IMF 2008c, 46; World Bank 2009a). Coupled with this, Beijing's formidable war chest of cash reserves totaling more than $2 trillion gave it unprecedented policy flexibility – especially fiscal policy – by giving it the ability to boost the economy if it began to slow down.[14] As the strong headwinds emanating from the global contagion began to make their deleterious impact felt, Beijing did precisely this. On November 11, 2008, the authorities announced a massive 4 trillion RMB ($586 billion) "*duiying guoji jinrong jinggi weiji de yilanzi jihua*" or "investment plan to counter the negative effects of global financial crisis" over the next two years (Table 6.4). Totaling some 14 percent of China's GDP in 2008, it was arguably the biggest peacetime stimulus ever.

As Table 6.4 shows, the stimulus package targeted seven core spending areas. General infrastructure included construction and expansion projects

[13] According to the World Bank (2008c, 12), "During 2001–07, when growth was high and rising, fiscal policy was appropriately contractionary. In 2005, the fiscal policy stance was officially adjusted to 'prudent.' In 2006 and 2007, fiscal contraction was particularly sizable."

[14] Office of Management and Budget. 2008. Mid-Session Review, Budget of the U.S. Government, Fiscal Year 2009, July 2008. See www.whitehouse.gov/omb/budget/fy2009/pdf/09msr.pdf.

Table 6.4. *China's stimulus package*
(total: 4 trillion RMB)

Infrastructure	2.87
General infrastructure	1.50
Reconstruction of Sichuan earthquake area	1.00
Rural area infrastructure	0.37
Technology and environment	0.58
Technology and structural adjustment	0.37
Energy savings and emissions reductions	0.21
Social measures	0.55
Construction and renovation of cheap houses	0.40
Social security and health	0.15

Source: National Development and Reform Commission (NDRC 2009).
http://www.ndrc.gov.cn

of high-speed railways, new expressways and highways, airports, city subways, and nuclear power plants. Through targeted social spending, the authorities hoped to further increase investment in the public health-care system, education, and subsidized housing, as well as to raise benefits for the unemployed and other welfare programs. To generate employment, the authorities announced plans to reform the value-added taxes (VAT) system, including increasing VAT rebates for export industries and replacing other cumbersome taxation with a more simple corporate income tax.[15] The stimulus funds could be made available almost immediately, because as Woo and Zhang (2011, 679) note, unlike in the United States or the UK, where the expansion of the monetary base was used to repair the "balance sheets of commercial banks... the expansion of the monetary base in China replaced export demand and externally financed investment demand with internally generated demand." Hence, Naughton (2009, 278) notes:

Disbursement began almost immediately. The Chinese government and Communist Party sent an emergency directive to government departments at all levels, emphasizing the need to prop up domestic demand and start new construction projects. Literally within weeks, local governments throughout China were meeting to compile lists of shovel-ready projects that complied with central government directives.

---

[15] China uses both the business tax (BT) and value added tax (VAT) in its turnover tax system. The VAT applies to the sale of goods, and the BT is primarily levied on taxable services. This leads to the double-taxing of some industries. In October 2011, Beijing announced that the VAT would eventually replace the BT, and pilot programs to this effect were launched on January 1, 2012 for selected industries in Shanghai.

As a result, resources began flowing through the pipeline by the end of 2008, and expanded government investment began to have a discernible impact on the economy during the first quarter of 2009.

However, to many observers, Beijing's expectations for its massive stimulus to generate a much-needed domestic consumption, and thereby rebalance the economy, were puzzling because "social measures" represented a mere 5 percent of the package. This was correctly viewed as insufficient to stimulate domestic consumption. Moreover, the stimulus package was seen as contradictory in that it subsidized exports and targeted infrastructure despite the fact that China already has overcapacity in industrial production and infrastructure (De Haan 2010; McKissack and Xu 2011). Given this, the concern was that the multiplier effects of the stimulus would be much lower than expected. Indeed, it was suggested that a more prudent way to stimulate domestic consumption would have been to send tax rebates directly to mid- and low-income families because these rebates would produce faster and targeted results. Equally perplexing, the stimulus package did little to improve the social safety net – which stands at less than 1 percent of GDP. Chinese citizens are prodigious savers because they are justly concerned about the prohibitively high medical, education, and housing costs as well as the lack of social security and other safety nets when they retire (Ma and Yi 2011). This is particularly true for poorer households, who try their best to save because they fear the consequences of serious illness, unemployment, and old age in a country lacking effective government safety nets.[16]

In order to discourage precautionary savings and boost consumption, on January 21, 2009, Beijing announced additional spending of some 850 billion RMB over three years. This was designed to improve health-care provisions by initially covering some 200 million uninsured citizens with the goal of achieving universal coverage by 2020 and improving access to primary health care in underserviced areas. Also, beginning in February 2009, a pension plan for rural workers was initiated and the level of pensions to the elderly poor modestly increased. To encourage spending by rural households, the authorities unveiled the "household appliances going to the countryside" (*jiadian xia xiang*) and "exchanging old for new" (*yi xiu huan xin*) programs. Under these initiatives, rural residents would receive subsidies and rebates on purchases of goods such as refrigerators, TVs, and

---

[16] Furthermore, the absence of sophisticated financial intermediation contributes to a high level of savings. For example, private companies are forced to save a significant proportion of their earnings to finance future investment because access to bank lending can be unpredictable. Also, the relative lack of consumer credit fosters precautionary savings.

washing machines for four years. Furthermore, to help the struggling property sector, the minimum down payment was reduced to 20 percent of a home's value, from 30–40 percent, and the transaction tax waived for properties held for at least two years. The Twelfth Five Year Plan (2011–16) further committed to construct 36 million low-income housing units by 2016. However, a recent IMF study (Ahuja et al., 2012, 12), notes that "There are few signs in the data that the initiatives to build out the social safety net and increase the provision of social housing have led precautionary savings to decline or have created sufficient momentum for household consumption to reverse the secular decline as a share of GDP that has been seen over the past several years."

Arguably, without effective privatization of state and collective-owned land and state assets, the stimulus efforts may be a one-time boost only. As noted, spending by Chinese households as a percentage of GDP remains significantly below private spending levels in other emerging economies. China's private consumption has failed to grow, not because Chinese consumers do not like to purchase goods and spend on vacations, but because most do not own property and collateral assets. Most households are wage-earners who have not felt enough of the "wealth effect" to boost their consumption levels. Unless these concerns are effectively dealt with, consumers will not be spending their rainy-day savings anytime soon. It also means that financial stimulus is a one-time shot designed to alleviate immediate problems in the economy by giving it a boost. More sustained growth must come less from government-backed capital infusion and more from balanced growth, including productivity growth.

Between 2001 and 2007, Beijing maintained a fairly contractionary or tight monetary policy to control inflation and cool the asset-price bubbles (World Bank 2008). However, once the contagion spread to China, the PBC quickly adopted what it called a "moderately loose" (but in reality, a highly expansionary) monetary policy to support their highly expansionary fiscal policy. Specifically, beginning in the fourth quarter of 2008, the central bank began to pump substantial volumes of liquidity into the banking system, and the lending limits of commercial banks were scrapped in early November 2008 to provide even more loans. These easy-credit policies had predictable results – massive credit expansion. As Table 6.5 shows, broad money (M2) grew 28.4 percent in the second quarter of 2009 – a significant increase over the end of 2008. Yu (2009, 10) notes that "in the first half of 2009, bank credit increased by 7.3 trillion RMB, which was above the official target for the full year... In contrast, the annual increases in bank credit in 2006 and 2007 were 3.18 trillion Yuan and 3.63 trillion Yuan respectively."

Table 6.5. *Monetary indicators (2008–2009)*

	2008				2009	
	Q1	Q2	Q3	Q4	Q1	Q2
M1	18.0	14.0	9.2	9.0	17.0	24.8
M2	16.2	17.3	15.2	17.8	25.4	28.4
Bank Loans	14.8	14.1	14.5	18.8	29.8	34.4

Note: M1=money supply; M2=M1 plus quasi money.
Source: Vincelette et al., World Bank Study (2010, 16).

In addition, to ease bank lending, the deposit reserve requirement ratio (RRR, which is the amount of bank reserves over the sum of deposits and notes) was lowered four times in 2008 – from 17.5 percent to 14 percent – giving banks more funds to lend. The central bank cut the benchmark interest rate on a five-year loan from 7.47 percent in September 2008 to 5.31 percent in December 2008, where it remained until June 2010. In similar fashion, rates for mortgage loans were sharply reduced. Lardy (2010, 2) estimates that:

The combined effect of a reduction in the benchmark five-year loan rate and the adjustment in the mortgage factor meant that the interest rate a potential home buyer would pay on a mortgage with a term of five or more years was reduced by two-fifths, from 6.66 to 4.16 percent. This meant that the monthly payment on a 20-year mortgage was reduced by 18.6 percent. For property investors the 40 percent minimum down-payment on a mortgage, introduced in the fall of 2007, was scaled back to 20 percent. And the compulsory penalty interest rate that applied to property investors, which had been set at 1.1 times the benchmark rate starting in September 2007, was eliminated.

Not surprisingly, such an aggressive easing of credit led to a massive increase in bank lending – totaling some 30 percent of GDP in 2009 (Figure 6.3).

The Outcomes: Intended and Unintended

China's massive fiscal program, complemented by accommodative monetary policies and unprecedented bank lending, played an essential role in helping the economy emerge from the crisis relatively quickly. A dynamic, computable general-equilibrium model developed by Diao, Zhang, and Chen (2012) to assess the impact of the 4 trillion yuan stimulus package on China's economic growth shows that GDP growth rate in 2009 could have fallen to 2.9 percent without the stimulus mainly as a

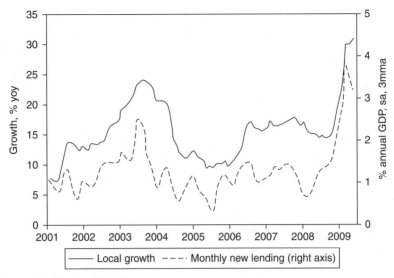

Figure 6.3. New bank lending.

Note: mma = monthly moving average, sa = seasonally adjusted.
Source: Vincelette et al., World Bank Study (2010, 17).

result of the sharp decline in exports of manufactured goods. The revitalization of domestic demand not only helped GDP to recover by the second quarter of 2009, but also to boost intraregional trade. Yet China's credit expansion during 2009–10 was one of the highest in the world. The fact that bank-financed investment has resulted in massive credit growth (some 9.95 trillion yuan in lending was granted in 2009 alone), carries inherent risks.

China experienced this explosive bank financed credit boom, in large part, because of the peculiar nature of the country's political institutional arrangements. For example, the central government financed only about 29 percent (or 1.18 trillion yuan) of the stimulus by issuing central government bonds. The bulk was financed by local governments borrowing from commercial banks, the corporate bond market, and via local financing vehicles (LFVs). Created by local governments (by pooling public assets, such as land, and using these as a vehicle to raise capital), the LFVs were explicitly designed to circumvent the no-borrowing constraint imposed on local governments by Beijing in 2006. However, lacking the necessary checks and balances to ensure prudent borrowing, the LFVs have amassed huge debts (Shih 2010). Moreover, although reforms in the banking sector have weakened the monopoly of state banks, and non-state banks have

Table 6.6. *China's banking sector*

	Total assets in RMB (billions)	State ownership (percent)
Five Big Banks		
1. Industrial and Commercial Bank of China	9,757.2	51
2. China Construction Bank	7,555.5	48
3. Agricultural Bank of China	7,100.0	100
4. Bank of China	6,951.7	70
5. Bank of Communications	268.3	26
Three Policy Banks		
1. China Development Bank	3,821.2	100
2. Agricultural Development Bank of China	1,354.7	100
3. Export-Import Bank of China	566.7	100

Source: Chinese Banking Regulatory Commission (CBRC), Annual Report, 2008.

increased in both number and the range of services they offer, the "big four" state-owned commercial banks[17] still dominate (Table 6.6) and direct the bulk of the credit to state-owned enterprises at very low cost. In addition, the government also holds significant equity stakes in the remaining shareholding commercial banks, including the rural cooperative banks and credit societies (which are technically not state-owned). Beijing still maintains tight control over the banking sector, while regional banks are effectively controlled by local governments as they tend to be major shareholders. Such pervasive state presence gives it tremendous clout, and predictably, bank lending is still very much based on government directives rather than purely economic considerations.[18]

Moreover, like the central government, provincial/municipal and local governments can also raise funds via off-balance sheet vehicles such as the credit-related wealth management products (CWMPs), credit-related trust products (CTPs), and as noted, via the newly allowed bond issuance backed by central government credit) to finance stimulus and related spending programs. In fact, the central government clearly stipulated that only 1.18

[17] China's "big four" state-owned banks include the Industrial and Commercial Bank of China (ICBC), China Construction Bank (CCB), Bank of China (BOC), and the Agricultural Bank of China (ABC). Geiger (2008) notes that these four banks control some 80 percent of the entire banking sector's assets, have around 70 percent of the total deposits, and provide more than 80 percent of the total lending.

[18] This is a remarkable transformation from the one-time Soviet-style mono-bank system, under which the PBC controlled almost four-fifths of all bank deposits and provided 93 percent of all loans (Sharma 1999).

trillion RMB (out of the 4 trillion RMB) of stimulus spending would be funded by Beijing. In other words, local governments had to fund the bulk of the spending. Local governments usually do this with Beijing's backing – which instructs state-owned banks to provide loans "guaranteed" by local governments. This explains why state-run banks lend so generously and without delay and local governments borrow so generously and often. Yet, as we know from the 2008 global crisis, placing loans off the books into off-balance sheet vehicles does not eliminate counterparty risk from the system. Rather, it just places it elsewhere – in this case, on the central government.

As Yu (2009, 12) notes, this is, in part, because "local governments have an insatiable appetite for grandiose investment projects. Investment led by local governments is likely to lead to a sub-optimal allocation of resources." In fact, in early 2012, the National Audit Office announced that "it had uncovered 531 billion yuan ($83.8 billion) in irregularities involving local government debt, which amounted to 10.7 trillion yuan as of the end of 2010."[19] Similarly, Naughton (2009, 280) points out

In order to move such a huge volume of credit, banks have inevitably turned to large, especially state-run companies to take up the loans. State firms enjoy implicit government guarantees for these loans.... The result is that the share going to China's private sector, already low, has dropped further. Loans to households for all purposes – consumption as well as household business – made up only 15 percent of the increased lending in the first half of 2009, down from a 2007 peak of nearly one-third of all lending.... The long-term objective of creating a more diverse and resilient economy, less dependent on large state-run firms, has been seriously set back.

Indeed, a number of analysts including Naughton (2009), Bremmer (2010), and Huang (2011) have noted that China's stimulus program may have inadvertently served to further enhance the role of the state in the economy at the expense of the private sector. Hence, there are legitimate concerns about the commercial viability and soundness of many of these investments. If economic conditions deteriorate and these investments fail and put the repayment of the underlying debt in doubt, China will once again face the specter of sizable nonperforming loans problem in the banking sector, unsustainable asset-price inflation (especially in real estate and equity markets), and excess capacity. Indeed, the IMF (2011c) has correctly

[19] http://www.forbes.com/sites/kenrapoza/2012/01/31/china-debt-burden-safe-sound-says-wen/ Kenneth Rapoza, 2012. "China Muni Debt Safe and Sound, Says Wen," *Forbes*, January 31.

warned that such rapid and massive credit expansion also carries the real potential to distort and exacerbate the country's already skewed growth patterns – that is, further imbalance the growth pattern.

The Imperative of Rebalancing

There are no guarantees that the normal business cycle can fundamentally rebalance China's economy. During the Asian financial crisis, robust growth and demand in the advanced economies helped support Asia's recovery. However, this time, the United States, Japan, and Western Europe are in recession, if not difficult economic times, and their business confidence and consumption, on which China and other Asian countries (indeed, the world) depend, are still reeling from massive deleveraging, crashing equity prices, and tight credit markets. The precipitous fall in asset prices (equity, bond, and housing markets) has dramatically eroded the net worth of households in the advanced economies. According to an IMF study:

During the first three quarters of 2008 alone, the value of household financial assets decreased by about 8 percent in the United States and the United Kingdom, by close to 6 percent in the euro area, and by 5 percent in Japan. As global equity markets plunged in the last quarter of 2008, household financial wealth declined further – for example, by an additional 10 percent in the United States. At the same time, the value of housing assets also deteriorated in line with falling house prices, especially in the United States and the United Kingdom. (Brooks, 2009, 1)

More precisely, "the losses in household wealth during 2008 were about $11 trillion in the United States ($8.5 trillion in financial assets and $2.5 trillion in housing assets) and were estimated at $1.5 trillion in the United Kingdom ($0.6 trillion in financial assets and $0.9 trillion in housing assets)" (Brooks 2009, 1–2). Such unprecedented loss of household wealth coupled with growing financial liabilities in the advanced economies will inevitably force many households to deleverage their balance sheets and engage in more precautionary savings. This means that U.S. consumers who have long served as the locomotive – not only for the U.S. economy, but for the global economy – will not be able to serve in that role. In addition, the further winding down of government support for consumer spending will further depress consumption.

Table 6.7 illustrates that as consumers in the advanced economies abruptly cut back on spending in 2008, demand for exports sharply fell. Sales of both labor-intensive manufacturing products as well as higher value-added goods such as computers and related equipment and automobiles have fallen since September 2008 in all Asian countries for which data are available.

Table 6.7. *Collapse of exports (value, % change)*

Country	2007	2008				2009a
		Q1	Q2	Q3	Q4	Q1
World	**15.1**	**22.1**	**25.2**	**21.0**	**−9.5**	**−29.1**
China	25.7	21.4	22.4	23.0	4.3	−19.7
India	21.5	37.6	37.1	25.5	−12.8	−24.1
Malaysia	2.7	9.9	20.8	16.8	−7.5	−22.2
Thailand	7.4	13.5	16.5	23.7	−9.7	−16.2
Philippines	6.4	2.8	5.5	4.1	−22.3	−39.9
Vietnam	23.8	28.7	31.8	37.6	5.7	3.4
Cambodia	14.1	97.2	45.8	5.3	−3.3	—
Lao PDR	12.1	36.2	15.7	42.7	4.9	—
Bangladesh	11.1	17.5	8.6	19.3	12.5	10.6
Pakistan	2.9	20.9	25.9	19.0	1.7	−17.9
Sri Lanka	18.0	9.3	6.8	5.4	−3.5	−10.7

Note: First-quarter figures are estimates using latest available data. Data for PRC are actual values. "—" indicates data not available.

Source: Asian Development Bank (ABD). 2009. *Report to the Second Global Review on Aid for Trade: Aid for Trade in the Asia and the Pacific: An Update*. June, Asian Development Bank: the Philippines, p. 3.

If these current trends are any indication of the potential long-term trends, export-dependent economies are at risk of a structural decline in demand from the advanced economies. In other words, the era of easy credit to finance consumer durables may be over, and the overleveraged households in the United States and elsewhere in the rich economies are saving more (Feldstein 2008). If these "course corrections" hold, export growth could be structurally lower, and China's (and Asia's) export-led growth strategy may no longer be as critical as in the past. If global demand for Chinese-produced goods remains suppressed for the foreseeable future, China and the Asian region's longer-term recovery will mean that its traditional reliance on export promotion as the driver for growth will have to diminish.[20] This means rebalancing growth away from exports and toward domestic demand in order to adjust to the structural shifts taking place in the global economy. For export-dependent economies like China, a boost in global demand is essential for recovery, but domestic-policy reorientation

[20] China's dependence on exports was vividly illustrated in May 2009 when Beijing introduced a "buy Chinese clause" that discriminates against foreign businesses.

is also essential for long-term sustainability. As noted earlier, this could be partly achieved by building stronger social safety systems that would reduce the need for precautionary health, education, and retirement-related savings. Beijing, by effectively reducing imbalances, can significantly aid in the recovery of the global economy as well as push the Chinese economy toward a more sustainable path.

Over three years from 2007–09, China's current account surplus (a broad measure of its international trade in goods and services) was reduced by half. By end-2011, the current account surplus fell to 2.8 percent of GDP from 10 percent in 2007. Beijing also posted a $31.5 billion trade deficit in February 2012. What explains this? Is it because China's economy is rebalancing externally and domestic consumption is expanding? No doubt, there is some evidence that domestic demand is rising relative to exports – but to what extent is unclear. However, internal or domestic rebalancing remains static as China still has very low household consumption-to-GDP (about 30 percent in 2011). According to the data compiled by the IMF (see Ahuja et al., 2012, 20), the decline in China's external surplus is not "due to consumption rising as a share of GDP or national savings falling." Rather, it is due to a combination of factors, including a much weaker global demand, very high levels of domestic investment, and a sharp increase in commodity prices relative to Chinese-manufactured goods. Stated bluntly, the Chinese economy is still overly dependent on exports and large-scale infrastructure investment.

It is worth reiterating that Beijing has viewed rebalancing away from exports and investment and toward domestic consumption as a long-term goal, and in all fairness, such structural changes take time. Nonetheless, Beijing must make domestic rebalancing a top priority. Indeed, the crash of 2008, and the fact that China's two largest export destinations (the United States and the eurozone) are already in various stages of a massive deleveraging underscores the fact that a growth strategy based on exports cannot be sustained indefinitely. It is in Beijing's interest to move expeditiously toward rebalancing focused on domestic consumption. Failure to do so could very well determine China's economic "landing" – whether its economy will slow gradually or decline abruptly and sharply after the stimulus-fueled growth of the past three years begins to run out its course. Of course, an immediate action Beijing can take to facilitate rebalancing toward domestic consumption is to adopt a sustained policy of external rebalancing by allowing its undervalued currency to appreciate faster. As the next section argues, revaluation of the RMB to rebalance U.S.-China trade is essential for sustained global recovery.

Rebalancing through Currency Reforms

Since a close relationship exists between monetary policy and international trade, domestic monetary stimulus and central bank interventions in foreign-exchange markets can help boost exports. To this end, Beijing has regularly intervened in international exchange markets to prevent the RMB from appreciating relative to other currencies, particularly, the U.S. dollar. Certainly, Beijing's maintenance of an artificially low exchange rate is tantamount to erecting import tariffs and maintaining export subsidies –at least, as far as the trade account is concerned. In turn, this policy has enabled Beijing to accumulate large global and bilateral trade surpluses. However, this strategy has also angered Beijing's trading partners, namely the United States, which has long claimed that Beijing deliberately "manipulates its currency" and engages in "mercantilist" practices to give itself an unfair advantage in global trade.

It is useful to reiterate that to the United States, the origins and persistence of its massive trade deficit with China are due to Beijing's mercantilist economic policies (Tables 6.8 and 6.9). The U.S. contention regarding China's mercantile behavior is rather straightforward: Beijing engages in gratuitously unfair trade practices via outright protectionism, most perniciously, by deliberately manipulating its currency. Specifically, in maintaining an undervalued exchange rate, Beijing has been able to dramatically increase its export growth and pile up large current account surpluses – the latter by aggressively intervening in foreign-exchange markets to keep its currency from appreciating. This in turn has resulted in a massive build-up of foreign-exchange reserves (Goldstein and Lardy 2005). However, if Beijing allowed market forces to determine the value of its currency, its current account surpluses would be much lower and U.S. trade balances much healthier.

Not surprisingly, U.S. manufacturers, with the backing of lawmakers in Congress, have long argued that the artificially low yuan has placed U.S. companies at a huge competitive disadvantage *inter alia*, contributing to the bankruptcy of U.S. companies and the loss of tens of thousands of U.S. jobs.[21] The contention is that the yuan is so undervalued (by some accounts as much

---

[21] From its peak in early 1998, the United States has lost more than 3.3 million manufacturing jobs. While not all of the job loss can be attributed to China, the U.S. manufacturing sector, despite significant productivity growth, could not overcome the huge trade advantage China gained by having an undervalued currency. The decline in manufacturing employment has led both Democratic and Republican senators to threaten the Chinese with substantial tariffs on Chinese imports to offset the Chinese currency advantage. For details, see Hufbauer and Wong (2004).

Table 6.8. *U.S. merchandise trade with China: 1980–2007*
(in billions of U.S.$)

Year	U.S. exports	U.S. imports	U.S. trade balance
1980	3.8	1.1	2.7
1985	3.9	3.9	0
1990	4.8	15.2	−10.4
1995	11.7	45.6	−33.8
2000	16.3	100.1	−83.8
2001	19.2	102.3	−83.1
2002	22.1	125.2	−103.1
2003	28.4	152.4	−124.0
2004	34.7	196.7	−162.0
2005	41.8	243.5	−201.6
2006	55.2	287.8	−232.5
2007	65.2	321.5	−256.3

Source: U.S. Congressional Research Service (2008, 2) in Morrison (2008a).

Table 6.9. *U.S. merchandise trade balances with major trading partners: 2007 (in billions of U.S.$)*

Country/ trading group	U.S. trade balance
World	−791.0
China	−256.3
European Union (EU27)	−107.4
Organization of Petroleum Exporting Countries (OPEC)	−127.4
Japan	−82.8
Canada	−64.7
Mexico	−74.3
Association of Southeast Asian Nations (ASEAN)	−50.6

Source: U.S. Congressional Research Service (2008, 2) in Morrison (2008a).

as 40 percent) that it amounts to an unfair trade subsidy. This unfair advantage permits a flood of cheap Chinese-made goods into the United States and makes U.S. products expensive in China.[22] Thus, it is claimed that if the yuan

[22] Some economists claim that the yuan is anywhere from 15 percent to 40 percent undervalued against the dollar, making Chinese exports to the United States cheaper and contributing to China's trade surplus with the United States. Of course, no one really knows the true extent of the undervaluation. When the market does not decide a currency's value, the nominal exchange rate (the number of units of one currency you can get for one unit of another) is essentially made up. It is whatever the government chooses it to be, so long

were traded at its true market worth, the bilateral imbalance between the two countries would be substantially reduced, if not altogether eliminated. This is because China's exports to the United States would become more expensive in dollars and would therefore decrease, while China's imports from the United States would become less expensive in yuan and therefore increase. To make matters worse, China's unwillingness to allow the yuan to appreciate has, in turn, made other Asian Pacific Rim countries reluctant to allow their currencies to appreciate because of their fear of losing further export sales to China.[23] As the U.S. trade deficit with China soared to record levels in first-quarter 2005, the Bush administration came under intense pressure to take unilateral action to address the problems associated with the artificial undervaluation of the yuan. U.S. Treasury Secretary John Snow called for an immediate Chinese exchange-rate adjustment, but many other lawmakers called for punitive tariffs on cheaply priced Chinese imports unless China sharply revalued its currency.

In May 2005, the U.S. Senate voted, by a margin of 67 to 33, to consider a proposal to impose a 27.5 percent tariff on all imports from China unless Beijing stopped inflating its currency. In May 2005, the United States decided to reimpose quotas on seven categories of clothing imports from China, limiting their growth to no more than 7.5 percent over a twelve-month period. On June 23, 2005, the Bush administration, which until then had insisted that diplomacy was working in getting China to allow the yuan's value to be set by currency markets rather than controlled by the government, finally warned China that it could be cited as a "currency manipulator" and face economic sanctions unless it switched to a flexible exchange system. Labeling China's currency policies "highly distortionary," the Bush administration warned that it was going to closely monitor China's progress toward adopting a flexible exchange system.

It seems that the unrelenting pressure worked. On July 21, 2005, Beijing made its biggest monetary shift in more than a decade by revaluing the yuan and dropping the currency's peg to the U.S. dollar. Chinese leaders announced that the yuan's exchange rate would become "adjustable, based on market supply and demand with reference to exchange rate movements

---

as the regime can be feasibly maintained. For a good overview, see Keidel (2011), Lardy (2005), Subramanian (2010a), and Makin (2007). For a dissenting view, see Lin, Dinh, and Im (2010).

[23] Indeed, following the Chinese revaluation, Malaysia responded by shifting its own currency regime from a dollar peg to a basket peg. However, given the very small initial change in the yuan's value, most countries in the region seem to be waiting for a more substantial yuan revaluation before taking action.

of currencies in a basket" (Morrison and Labonte 2011, 2), composed of the dollar, the yen, and the euro, among a few other key currencies.[24] This was an important, albeit modest shift. From 1994 to July 2005, the value of the yuan was pegged to the U.S. dollar at a rate determined by the People's Bank of China. The yuan traded within the range of 8.27 to 8.28 to the dollar because the People's Bank maintained this peg by buying dollar-denominated assets in exchange for the yuan in order to reduce excess demand for the yuan. As a result, the exchange rate between the yuan and the dollar remained largely the same despite changing market conditions. When Beijing abandoned the peg by moving to a system that linked the value of the yuan to a basket of currencies, it effectively raised the yuan's value by 2.1 percent.[25] This meant that prior to the revaluation, US$1 bought 8.28 yuan, and following revaluation US$1 would buy roughly 8.11 yuan. Beijing made it clear that it had set tight parameters on how much the yuan could rise. Clearly, the aim was to make sure that the yuan did not float by a big margin, but appreciate[26] by a modest 2 percent by moving within a tight range of 0.3 percent against a group of foreign currencies belonging to China's top trading partners.[27] Thus, unlike a true floating exchange rate, the yuan was allowed to fluctuate by only 0.3 percent on a daily basis against the basket. However, this modest and gradual appreciation (called a "managed float") allowed China to continue to accumulate foreign reserves – implying that if the yuan was allowed to free float, it would appreciate much more rapidly – by some accounts by another 20 to 30 percent. Critics were barely placated by the fact that from

[24] Revaluation is the resetting of the fixed value of a currency at a higher level.

[25] Both flexible and floating exchange rates have distinct advantages, but no single exchange-rate regime is appropriate for all countries in all circumstances. A fixed exchange rate that pegs the value of a currency to a stronger foreign currency like the U.S. dollar or the euro has advantages for developing countries seeking to build confidence in their economic policies. On the other hand, countries with fixed exchange rates are seemingly more vulnerable to currency crises. As economies mature and become more closely aligned with the international financial markets, exchange-rate flexibility seems more advantageous.

[26] When a currency increases in value, it experiences appreciation. When it falls in value and is worth fewer U.S. dollars, it undergoes depreciation. Thus, when a country's currency appreciates (rises in value relative to other currencies), the country's goods abroad become more expensive, and foreign goods in that country become cheaper. Conversely, when a country's currency depreciates, its goods abroad become cheaper, and foreign goods in that country become more expensive.

[27] Both the central bank governor, Zhou Xiaochuan, and Premier Wen Jiabao noted that the revaluation should be viewed as the first in what is expected to be a series of steps over years to shift the yuan toward even greater flexibility as China increases its participation in the world trading system. See People's Bank of China. 2005. "Public Announcement of the People's Bank of China on Reforming the RMB Exchange Rate Regime," July 21. http://www.pbc.gov.cn/english/detail.asp?col=6500&id=82.

July 2005 to June 2008 the yuan appreciated by 14.4 percent relative to the U.S. dollar (or from 8.35 to 6.6 to the dollar) because in effective terms it was much less because most other major currencies have appreciated against the dollar, despite China's large and growing trade surplus.

However, in July 2008, in the midst of a global financial meltdown, Beijing resumed its earlier practice of pegging the RMB (or in other words, suspending its policy of allowing the yuan to strengthen), to revive its faltering export-dependent economy. From September 2008 to June 2010, Beijing kept the RMB stable against the dollar at 6.83 yuan to the dollar – in effect, preventing the renminbi from appreciating by putting in place a de-facto peg against the U.S. dollar. During the height of the global recession the voices of the critics of China's currency became muted, because among other things, the artificially low yuan allowed the United States and other cash-strapped countries, to borrow large sums from China to stimulate their economies. In fact, rather ironically, Beijing's currency and trade policy actually helped to stimulate the United States', and indeed, the global economy. Specifically, by purchasing U.S. securities (in particular, Treasuries), Beijing was indirectly helping the United States to fund its massive budget deficits and skyrocketing debts. High demand from China not only boosts the value of fixed-income securities (and thereby keeps U.S. interest rates low), it also makes it much cheaper for Washington to borrow – and in the process keep its domestic mortgage and related consumer-loan rates rather low.

By 2010, with the global economy on the mend (but job growth in advanced economies still stagnant), calls for China to let its currency float more freely grew again. Nobel laureate Paul Krugman (2010a), who had kept his powder dry during the depth of the crisis, fired the first salvo when he scathingly noted that "China has become a major financial and trade power. But it doesn't act like other big economies. Instead, it follows a mercantilist policy, keeping its trade surplus artificially high. And in today's depressed world, that policy is, to put it bluntly, predatory." According to Krugman's "back-of-the-envelope" calculations, China's weak-yuan policy cost 1.4 million U.S. manufacturing jobs. Of course, the United States is not alone in its criticism. Beijing's policy has also resulted in a large depreciation of the yuan against the euro – making it extremely hard for the beleaguered eurozone countries to compete with Chinese exporters.

On April 3, 2010, the Obama administration announced that it would delay publication of the semiannual exchange-rate report to Congress (due on April 15), containing the international economic and exchange-rate policies of the United States' major trading partners. The report was eagerly awaited because it would officially state the Obama administration's position on China's exchange-rate policy, in particular, whether Treasury Secretary Timothy Geithner would declare China a "currency manipulator." Instead, striking a measured tone, Geithner tactfully noted that "China's inflexible exchange rate has made it difficult for other emerging market economies to let their currencies appreciate. A move by China to a more market-oriented exchange rate will make an essential contribution to global rebalancing." Geithner noted that "the best avenue for advancing U.S. interests at this time" is via discussions in multilateral and bilateral forums, including that of the G-20 finance ministers and central bank governors in late April; the semiannual Strategic and Economic Dialogue between the United States and China in May; and during the meeting of G-20 leaders and finance ministers in June.[28] To further assuage Beijing, on April 7, Geithner made an impromptu seventy-five-minute stopover at the VIP terminal of Beijing airport (on his trip to India) to meet with Vice Premier Wang Qishan (China's leading finance official) to "exchange views on U.S.-China economic relations and the global economy."[29]

No doubt, the Treasury's conciliatory message was intended to deescalate tensions that had been brewing for months between Beijing and Washington. In fact, this round of the war of words began during Geithner's confirmation hearing in January 2009 for Treasury Secretary when he bluntly stated that both he and "President Obama – backed by the conclusions of a broad range of economists – believe that China is manipulating its currency."[30] Geithner's tough rhetoric brought nods of approval from the members of

---

[28] "Statement of Treasury Secretary Geithner on the Report to Congress on International Economic and Exchange Rate Policies," April 3, 2010, United States Department of the Treasury, no, TG-627, http://www.ustreas.gov/press/releases/tg627.htm.

[29] Bill Powell. 2010. "Why Geithner Made A Surprise Stop in Beijing." *Time*, April 8 http://www.time.com/time/world/article/0,8599,1978666,00.html?xid=rss-fullworld-yahoo, and Keith Bradsher, 2010. "China Seems Set to Loosen Hold on Its Currency," April 8, *The New York Times*, http://www.nytimes.com/2010/04/09/business/global/09yuan.html?ref=business&src=me&pagewanted=print.

[30] In his written statement to the Senate panel, Geithner noted then-Senator Obama's support for "tough legislation to overhaul the U.S. process for determining currency manipulation and authorizing new enforcement measures so countries like China cannot continue to get a free pass for undermining fair trade principles." However, the Obama administration quickly backtracked from Geithner's statement and declined to label China a currency manipulator. Rather, the administration noted that while it still believes that the yuan is undervalued, it also recognizes that China has taken steps to rebalance its economy and enhance exchange-rate flexibility. See Lori Montgomery and Anthony Faiola. 2009. "Geithner Says China Manipulates Its Currency," *The Washington Post*, January 23, p. A08. http://www.washingtonpost.com/wpdyn/content/article/2009/01/22/AR2009012203796.html. Also see "Statement by Treasury Secretary Timothy Geithner on Release of

the Senate Finance Committee – many of whom have long rallied against Beijing's alleged malpractice and were hoping for a firm stance against China from the new Obama administration. However, to the markets, Geithner's tone signaled a potential confrontation between the world's two largest economies. The already jittery markets responded almost immediately as investors became concerned that China would scale back its purchase of U.S. debt if the new administration pushed Beijing to further revalue its currency. The dollar promptly fell, the price of gold jumped by $40, and the price of U.S. Treasury debt was driven further down.[31] Although Geithner tried to gloss over his remarks by stating that what he actually meant was for China to adopt "market exchange rates," he brought only a short respite to this response.

Rather abruptly, on June 19, 2010, Beijing relaxed its exchange-rate policy by making the yuan a bit more flexible. The People's Bank ruled out any large one-time revaluations. Not surprisingly, by early August 2011, the yuan-dollar exchange rate was 6.44 – a modest appreciation. Clearly, it would be prudent for Beijing to adopt a much more flexible exchange rate. After all, China's emphasis on exchange-rate stability in the face of rising current account surpluses has not only generated intense protectionist pressures in the United States and elsewhere, it has also forced the People's Bank to accumulate massive foreign-exchange reserves with negative domestic consequences.

Specifically, keeping the RMB from rising against the U.S. dollar means not only that China's central bank has to print more money to keep interest rates low, but also such a strategy can exacerbate inflationary pressures if more money ends up chasing too few goods. It also means that China has fallen into a "dollar trap" – borrowing at higher cost and lending the money back to the United States for low to zero return. Because the bulk of these securities has been (and are) purchased when interest rates were (are) at historically low rates, they will lose value when rates eventually increases. It also means that Beijing is exposed to large capital losses on its foreign reserve holdings (which are mostly in U.S. dollars) as the RMB appreciates. Inflation would further exacerbate this problem. Indeed, there is broad consensus that if the U.S. Federal Reserve continues to print money (and thereby further debases the dollar) to pay down its debt, inflationary

Semi-Annual Report to U.S. Congress on International Economic and Exchange Rate Policies," April 15, 2009. http://www.treas.gov/press/releases.tg90.htm.

[31] Treasury securities (or Treasuries) are the debt-financing instruments of the U.S. government. There are four types of marketable treasury securities: Treasury bills, Treasury notes, Treasury bonds, and Treasury Inflation Protected Securities (TIPS).

pressures would become a pervasive problem. This would mean that Beijing would have paid a "premium" for U.S. securities, but will be paid back with dollars that are worth far less. Although Beijing is now prudently moving more of its reserves into securities with shorter maturities (which are less vulnerable to rising interest rates and inflation), the fact is that the bulk of their reserves would lose value.

Rather than locking such huge foreign currency reserves (the fruit of years of hard work and sacrifice by the Chinese people) in investments like Treasury securities (arguably to finance consumption by ungrateful foreigners), Beijing would be better off utilizing these resources to improve the living conditions of its people by investing in education, health care, housing, social security, and other human needs. Domestic exchange-rate appreciation can greatly facilitate this as it will provide price incentives to shift resources toward production for domestic use and by raising real household income. Indeed, a meaningful appreciation of the exchange rate would immediately spur domestic consumption as it would give Chinese consumers real purchasing power – something China needs to expand and sustain. Finally, if Beijing's oft-stated goal of making the RMB a global reserve currency (or even more modestly, increase the use of the RMB in international trade and finance), is to be realized, a meaningful loosening of foreign-exchange controls, especially in the capital account, and allowing the RMB to be freely traded (in effect, revaluation), is essential. Of course, the United States should be cautious regarding its wishes. After all, China could strengthen its currency by reducing its currency reserves. This would mean reducing or "unloading" its huge stockpile of U.S. securities. This, in turn, would drive down the price of securities and sharply increase interest rates, making it more costly for the United States to finance its deficit and debt, not to mention that the borrowing rates of U.S. consumers could also see a sharp spike.

Postscript

By early 2012, pressures for the yuan to appreciate eased substantially after China's trade became more balanced – that is, the once-huge trade surpluses have dwindled. In a surprise move, Beijing announced that, effective April 16, 2012, the central bank would allow the yuan to rise or fall by 1 percent instead of the previous limit of 0.5 percent. Certainly, doubling the size of the yuan's trading band against the dollar moved China a step away from its investment and export-based growth model. However, such a timid step will hardly make consumption the key driver of growth anytime soon.

Rather, pressure on the yuan to appreciate has been reduced as China's trade surplus and capital inflows have shrunk with the yuan approaching a seemingly equilibrium level against the dollar.[32] It is important to note that even as the central bank allows the market to play more of a role in the yuan's daily movements, such a modest widening of the trading band will greatly limit how much the yuan can rise and fall from the official rate set by the central bank each day. Also, this does not mean that Beijing will necessarily allow faster appreciation of the yuan in the coming weeks or allow the yuan to eventually float freely.[33] Indeed, in late May 2012, the renminbi dropped further against the U.S. dollar than in any other time since it was allowed to appreciate in 2005. Visibly upset, the Obama administration released a report two days later criticizing Beijing's decision and demanding that the Chinese authorities release data on the scale of its foreign-exchange market interventions (U.S. Department of Treasury 2012). Although the report did not explicitly label China as a "currency manipulator," Mitt Romney, the Republican presidential nominee, made it clear that if he were elected president, he would label China a currency manipulator on his first day in office. Clearly, unless Beijing fundamentally reforms its currency policy, the issue will remain a thorn in Sino-U.S. relations. Of course, there is hope that China's ambitious Twelfth Five Year Plan is committed (at least on paper) to dramatically rebalancing the domestic economy by raising household income, expanding social services, and boosting consumption. This is in the interest of both the Chinese and the global economies.

[32] As noted, China's current account surplus dropped sharply from about 10 percent of GDP in 2007 to around 2.8 percent in 2011. A surplus between 2.5 and 4 percent of GDP is widely seen as when a currency has reached its fair value or "equilibrium."

[33] This is because the daily trading band limits intraday fluctuations, and the central bank is not constrained on how it sets the daily official exchange rate.

SEVEN

Japan, South Korea, and India

Impact and Recovery

When the financial crisis erupted in the United States with the collapse of Lehman Brothers, it was widely believed that the fallout would be largely limited to the United States and that authorities there would eventually contain the crisis. After all, Asia was not the epicenter of the crisis, and the roots of the crisis were related to factors specific to the U.S. economy, especially problems associated with expansionary monetary policy that had kept U.S. interest rates low for some years and led to a real-estate bubble, rather than to systemic external factors such as an oil shock or adverse trade relations. As noted in the previous chapter, this view was prevalent not only in China, but also in Asia's other major economies: Japan, South Korea (hereafter Korea), and India. In fact, one of Japan's senior ministers dismissively stated that the crisis "would have no more effect than a bee sting" (Kojima 2009, 16).

This optimism was not based on wishful thinking. Since Japan, Korea, and India, like China, had little exposure to the so-called toxic subprime securities and loans originating in the United States, they were assumed to be relatively immune because the spillover effects into their economies would be minimal.[1] In addition, Japan, the world's second largest economy, with its substantial foreign-exchange reserves, was deemed to not only have the wherewithal to withstand the crisis, but also to serve as a source of much-needed global liquidity in an increasingly capital-scarce world. Finally, blessed with healthy corporate and banking-sector balance sheets (especially low volume of nonperforming loans, Table 7.1) and widely seen as increasingly decoupled from Western economies (that is, economic growth

---

[1] Japanese financial institutions' losses totaled some $4.1 billion. Meanwhile, "Woori Bank of Korea reported a loss of $445 million out of $491 million in assets linked to subprime loans and collateralized debt obligations" (Lee and Park 2009, 17).

Table 7.1. *Nonperforming loans (% of commercial bank loans)*

	1998	2003	2004	2005	2006	2007[a]
India	14.4	9.1	7.2	4.9	3.5	2.7
Japan	5.4	5.2	2.9	1.8	1.5	1.5
South Korea	7.6	2.2	1.7	1.1	0.8	0.7
Germany	3.0	5.2	4.9	4.0	3.4	n/a
U.S.	1.0	1.1	0.8	0.7	0.8	1.1

[a] Data for Japan, Korea and U.S. are as of Sept. 2007. The data for India and Germany are as of end-2007.
Source: Lee and Park (2009, 19).

in Asia was becoming more independent of the United States and Western Europe), Asian economies, it was concluded, were not as vulnerable to an economic slowdown emanating from the United States and Europe. Indeed, conventional thinking assumed that Asia's resilient economies could serve as both "shock absorbers" and as the world's "locomotive" – and thereby help to pull the U.S. and the global economy out of its malaise.

In hindsight, these predictions turned out to be unduly optimistic. Like China, the East Asian and Indian economies after showing initial buoyancy and resilience succumbed to the crisis – although Japan and Korea were impacted far more severely than India. As Table 7.2 shows, India (like China) was moderately impacted, whereas Japan and Korea were hit particularly hard. Japan experienced negative economic growth in 2008, and both countries experienced further sharp economic contraction in 2009. Takatoshi Kato (2009, 1) noted:

The intensity of the downturn took everybody by surprise and was much larger than what could have been anticipated based on historic correlations of growth between the Asian and the advanced western economies. In the fourth quarter of 2008, GDP in Asia (excluding China and India) plummeted by close to 15 percent on a seasonally adjusted annualized basis. This was a much steeper downturn than in other regions, including those at the epicenter of the crisis.

What explains why East Asia was impacted more severely than India? What were each country's sources of resilience as well as vulnerabilities? What explains Korea's "exceptionalism" – which, despite experiencing a deep and wrenching economic contraction in the fourth quarter of 2008 made a phenomenal V-shaped recovery by the second half of 2010? How have authorities in the three countries responded to the unprecedented challenges unleashed by the crisis, and what each must do to better insulate their economies from the vagaries of economic globalization? This chapter

Table 7.2. *GDP growth, 2007–2009*

	2007	2008	2009
China	13.0	9.0	7.5
India	9.0	7.1	6.0
Japan	2.4	−0.7	−2.5
South Korea	5.0	2.5	−1.5

Source: Calculated from IMF. 2008. International Financial Statistics (CD-ROM), Washington, D.C.: the IMF; and the World Bank. 2009 and *Global Development Finance* 2009. Washington, D.C.: The World Bank.

highlight the point that each country was impacted via its own specific vulnerabilities as well as through broad transmission channels. Clearly, the Asian region is far less insulated from the global financial markets than earlier assumed. Although Asian banks were not exposed directly to subprime loans, the strong indirect effects of the global financial contagion underscore the region's growing global integration. Indeed, the Asian region experienced a "sudden stop" of capital flows, including net outflows from the equity markets. Furthermore, given the region's tightly integrated supply chain, the contagion also spread with rapid speed and dramatic impact on intraregional trade.

Furthermore, because East Asia is heavily export-dependent and is closely integrated into the global economy (especially the U.S. economy), the impact of the global economic crisis on Japan and Korea was swifter and deeper despite the region's relatively strong macroeconomic fundamentals. In other words, East Asia's growing financial linkages with the rest of the world exposed it to the forces of global deleveraging. This explains why East Asia suffered a double whammy – a loss of export markets and tightening credit due to the global credit crunch. In addition, the collapse of external demand from the advanced economies severely impacted the region's tightly integrated supply chain with negative effects on intraregional trade. Heavily export-dependent economies, including Japan, Korea, China, and Asia's newly industrialized economies (Thailand, Malaysia, Vietnam, and the Philippines) were impacted particularly hard. Although India's relatively low dependence on exports helped it to better contain the transmission of the global demand shock, India was nevertheless affected because the country's investment growth in recent years has relied on favorable international credit conditions. As external financing tightened, it negatively impacted investment growth with the resultant slowdown in overall GDP growth. Nevertheless, the experience of Korea also underscores the notion that the problems inherent to global integration can be mitigated through sound domestic macroeconomic policies, including prudential regulations.

The Case of India

From 2004 to the mid-2008, India enjoyed a growth rate of 9 percent per annum. This was the fastest in its history and almost on par with that of the world's star performer, China. Even in the midst of the global financial meltdown, India's GDP grew by 5.8 percent in the fourth quarter of 2008 (Ahluwalia 2011; IMF 2009e). Such sustained growth rates enabled the country to weather the global recession better than most. Nevertheless, growth rates are only part of the explanation. According to Subramanian (2009, 2), India's approach to globalization (which he colorfully terms "Goldilocks globalization"), a strategy that "relies neither too much on foreign finance nor too much on exports" explains India's remarkable economic resilience during these hard economic times. Subramanian (2009, 2) notes that because "India has not been a gung-ho globalizer," the two channels via which a financial crisis is transmitted – finance and trade – only modestly impacted India. Indeed, an IMF (2009g, 15) report underscores the limited spillovers through trade by noting that "a 1 percent downturn in global growth is estimated to trim only 0.3 percentage points from India's growth." On the other hand, countries that depend heavily on capital inflows or recklessly borrowed large amounts of foreign capital have experienced major disruptions to their exchange rates, asset prices and financial systems as capital inflows stopped or "fled to safety." Similarly, countries that rely heavily on exports have suffered as a result of the collapse in external demand.

India was resilient against the contagion's impact because its financial sector was not exposed to the U.S. subprime mortgages securities (RBI 2009; 2009a; 2008; Reddy 2009; Pat 2009). The so-called "conservative approach" coupled with active policy interventions in both the monetary and financial sectors adopted by the central bank, the Reserve Bank of India (RB1), kept the banking sector "protected" from the global financial markets.[2] Specifically, the Indian financial sector is relatively insulated as none of the major Indian banks have much exposure to U.S. subprime mortgage debt,

---

[2] The former governor of the Reserve Bank of India, Y.V. Reddy (2009), notes that it was not only the RBI's conservative approach but also the active policy interventions in both the monetary and financial sectors that have helped India weather the storm.

Table 7.3. *India's banking system as of March 31, 2008*

	Public sector	New private sector[a]	Old private sector	Foreign
Number of Banks	28	8	15	28
Number of Offices	53,338	3,623	4,642	280
Share of Assets (%)	69.8	17.2	4.5	8.4

[a] Banks created since 1993.
Source: Reserve Bank of India (2009).

including, limited off-balance sheet activities, or securitized assets.[3] Indian banks did not have toxic assets because credit-default swaps are not permitted in the country (Patil 2010). The State Bank of India, the ICICI Bank (the country's largest private bank), the Bank of Baroda, and Bank of India have exposure to international securitized debt in the form of collateralized debt obligations (CDOs) for only around $3 billion.[4] This is miniscule in comparison to ICICI's $100 billion balance sheet. Overall, when the contagion struck, India's banks (both public and private) were financially sound with strong balance sheets, well capitalized with low nonperforming assets and reasonably well regulated (Patil 2010). At 12.5 percent, the capital-to-risk weighted assets ratio of Indian banks was above the regulatory norm of 9 percent and well above the Basel Accord norm of 8 percent (IMF 2009i, 24). India's banking sector was further protected from the worst of the global banking crises because India's state-owned banks still hold about 70 percent of the nation's banking assets (Table 7.3). Therefore, rather ironically, India's financial protectionism inadvertently translated into foreign banks controlling only a small share (8.4 percent) of the country's banking assets, and furthermore preventing foreign banks from fleeing with their assets as they did elsewhere during the onset of the crisis.

Implicit in Subramanian's (2009) notion of "goldilocks globalization" is the paradox that some parts of the Indian economy are fully integrated into the global economy whereas other parts are barely integrated. This is because India is still a minor player in the global financial system. Indian

[3] The IMF (2009i, 25) citing the RBI, notes that "India has virtually no exposure to U.S. subprime mortgage assets or to other structured credit products. The total exposure to five troubled global institutions is reported at US$1 billion (0.1 percent of system's assets). While these exposures are small compared to earnings and capital, they are fairly concentrated."

[4] Shriya Bubna and Abhijit Lele. 2008. "Subprime Crisis to Hit 4 Big Banks' Profits," January 7. http://www.rediff.com///money/2008/jan/07sub.htm.

banks, some of which are large by global standards, based on market capitalization and the size of their balance sheets, have only modest international presence. The rupee is not fully convertible (and hardly used outside India), and its capital markets are small relative to the size of the domestic economy. Furthermore, India relies heavily on FDI (foreign direct investment) rather than securities investment and other forms of capital flows to access international capital markets. In other words, there has been only gradual liberalization as India still subjects portfolio capital flow to various restrictions.[5] Complementing these, India's recent growth has been driven predominantly by domestic consumption and investment. External demand, as measured by merchandise exports, accounts for less than 15 percent of the country's GDP, giving India relative insulation from the vagaries of global trade. Finally, unlike during the 1991 economic crisis, India in 2008 enjoyed healthy reserves (Rajan and Gopalan 2010). Although India's total reserve assets declined by about 7 percent to US$274 billion from August 2008 to the second week of October 2008, its foreign-currency reserves were still more than adequate to cover its debt obligations.[6] Cumulatively, these strengths served to calm market jitters and mitigate a potentially destructive financial panic.

India's Vulnerabilities

Given these buffers, what explains India's vulnerabilities, and what were the channels via which the Indian economy was impacted by the contagion? The answer: in this era of globalization, it is almost impossible for any country to remain completely immune, especially if the contagion is emanating from the world's largest economy. Economic globalization not only creates deep and entwining linkages between economies, but also "convergence" among them. Indeed, Jayaram, Patnaik, and Shah (2009, 115) find strong "evidence that business cycles in India are coupled with those in industrial countries and that this coupling has been increasing with India's greater globalization."

[5] Mohan (2008, 3) notes, "India, while encouraging foreign investment flows, especially direct investment inflows, a more cautious, nuanced approach has been adopted in regard to debt flows. Debt flows in the form of external commercial borrowings are subject to ceilings and some end-use restrictions... Similarly, portfolio investment in government securities and corporate bonds are also subject to macro ceilings."

[6] As Rajan and Gopalan (2010, 1) point out, "The reserve buildup in India has certainly been impressive, rising from around US$5–6 million in 1991, to nearly US$300 billion in mid 2008."

In the specific case of India, what were gentle ripples when the subprime crisis broke in mid-2007 became larger waves by the fourth quarter of 2008. There are two major reasons for this. First, the country's stock market is particularly vulnerable to swings in investor sentiment. In India (and elsewhere) banks and foreign institutional investors (FIIs) sold billions of their investment in Indian companies to cover losses accrued in their home markets, including limiting their exposure, and in the process undermining investment activity. As a result, the Indian stock exchanges took a beating. Acharya and Kulkarni (2012, 20–21) point out that the Indian stock market lost "more than 60 percent of its peak valuation... Index prices fell from a peak of 6,288 in January 2008 to 2,524 in October 2008... another market index – the BSE index – similarly fell nearly 59 percent from 20,873 in January 2008 to 8,510 in October 2008" (also see IMF 2009j). Similarly, Rajan and Gopalan (2009, 6) note that "massive FII infusions in the previous few years had propelled India's Bombay Stock Exchange (BSE) to a high of almost 20,000 points in end-2007 when it was less than 14,000 points a year earlier (January 2007)." In turn, this led to an intense liquidity crisis (a consequence of the global liquidity squeeze), due to the tightening of global credit markets and the rapid withdrawal of FIIs. India's financial markets, including equity markets, money markets, foreign-exchange (forex) markets, and credit markets all came under intense pressure. According to the IMF (2009i, 8), an estimated $9–$10 billion was withdrawn from the Indian market by foreign portfolio investors between April and December 2008 – with some $4 billion in outflows in October alone (also Acharya and Kulkarni 2012, 20). Rajan and Gopalan (2009, 6–8) note that "while net FII inflows were just over US$20 billion in 2007–08 (April–March), there was a net withdrawal of over US$11 billion between January and October 2008. This, in turn, pushed down the BSE index sharply to just below 14,000 points by October 2008, effectively giving back all the gains since January 2007." Similarly, FDI inflows "fell from 4.6 percent of gross domestic investment in the third quarter of 2008 to only 0.7 percent during the fourth quarter" (World Bank 2009a, 133).

The credit squeeze forced Indian banks to shift their credit demand to the domestic banking sector, and as the forex market came under pressure (due to reversal of capital flows as part of global deleveraging), businesses were forced to convert domestic funds into foreign currency to meet their external obligations. In turn, this placed downward pressure on the rupee – which depreciated from about Rs 39 to $1 in January 2008 to Rs 49 to $1 in October 2008 (Acharya and Kulkarni 2012). The Reserve Bank's intervention in the forex market to manage the volatility in the rupee resulted only in further tightening of liquidity. To help fill the gap left by a sharp decline in foreign investment, the Reserve Bank made more funds available by reducing its benchmark interest rates. Yet, the interest rates Indian banks charged were still higher than what was once charged by foreign institutions, not to mention that domestic lenders were reluctant to extend credit in an uncertain and highly volatile market. The impact was painful: as commercial credit from foreign banks dried up, it was replaced with credit lines from domestic banks. However, as noted, because domestic banks charged higher interest rates, this caused the rupee to depreciate, raising the cost of businesses' existing foreign loans.

Second, as the Indian economy opened up to the world in recent years, its structure has undergone significant changes. In particular, the importance of external trade and external capital flows in the overall economy has sharply increased. For example, India's two-way trade (merchandise exports plus imports) as a proportion of GDP has grown from 21.2 percent in 1997–98 to 40.6 percent in 2008–09 (RBI 2009a). Since India's external trade in merchandise and services accounts for a significant portion of its economy, a global slowdown in demand inevitably had a negatively impact. Coupled with this, tighter credit conditions and investor uncertainty slowed investment growth. As the United States, the EU, and the Middle East account for some three-quarters of India's goods and services trade, a slowdown in these economies impacted India's exports. Nevertheless, it is important to note that because India's economic performance is driven by domestic consumption it is less export-dependent than China and other East Asian countries. The main drivers of aggregate demand in the Indian economy remain domestic consumption and investment. That is not to say that exports are not important, but rather in terms of the macro aggregate demand, India still remains a home-market-driven economy.

Also, in recent years, India's services sector has become a major part of the economy, with GDP share of over 50 percent. The country is now an important hub for exporting IT services (Panagariya 2009; Ratanpal 2008). Not surprisingly, India's outsourcing industry and export-dependent IT sector quickly felt the pain of declining revenues – not only due to a slowdown in global demand, but also because of the rise in the value of the rupee against the U.S. dollar. In fact, tightening credit and the declining value of the dollar impacted India's IT companies rather severely because the industry derives more than 60 percent of its revenues from the United States. Furthermore, some 30 percent of business that use Indian outsourcers are projects from U.S. banking, insurance, and the financial-services sector, and a sharp slowdown in demand negatively impacted these businesses. For example, Infosys and Wipro, two well-known outsourcing companies, laid off their workers on the expectation of a sharp drop in earnings as their customers in the United States and Europe cut back spending. India's service-sector exports will continue to face challenges as financial services firms in the advanced economies, who are the major users of outsourcing services, are restructured and consolidated.[7]

India's export-oriented labor-intensive textile and garment sectors, already facing stiff competition from China and other low-income country producers, were also severely impacted. The sector, which employs hundreds of thousands of people, was negatively hit by slowing exports and the rising costs of capital. The small and medium-sized enterprises (SMEs) that employ the bulk of workers in the labor-intensive manufacturing sector were particularly affected as they face greater difficulty in attracting funding due to their modest profitability and limited collateral base. For many SMEs, the credit crunch meant either sharp scaling bank or bankruptcy. As these businesses cut back production, millions of workers were laid off or given shorter working hours and lower wages. Of course, job losses in this sector also have a negative-multiplier effect because they adversely impact domestic suppliers and the vast informal services sector the suppliers support. The absence of a social safety net in India has put millions of people at risk of falling back into poverty. Finally, another channel via which the job market and the broader economy came under pressure was due to the return of thousands of migrant workers. In 2008, migrant remittance flows to developing countries totaled $338 billion, with India as the top receiver at $52 billion (Ratha, Mohapatra, and Silwal 2009). However, the sharp decline in remittances sent home each year by some 6 million Indians working abroad (mostly in the Gulf States) placed undue hardship on many households. The bad news is that remittance

---

[7]   On May 4, 2009, President Obama unveiled plans to reform the rules on taxing the foreign earnings of U.S. firms by fixing a "broken tax system that rewarded firms for creating jobs in Bangalore rather than Buffalo, New York." To this effect, Obama promised tighter rules on the taxation of businesses' foreign earnings and a crackdown on the use of tax havens. He argued that this will make it much more difficult for U.S. firms to shift income to subsidiaries in low-tax countries and limit how much these firms can defer tax payments on their foreign earnings. These measures, if enacted, will directly impact many U.S companies (in particular, those in pharmaceutical, technology, financial, and consumer-goods companies) as these companies have millions of employees in India in wholly-owned subsidiaries (for example, India's information-technology and outsourcing companies employ about 2.5 million workers, and U.S. companies account for about 60 percent of their business). Of course, the full extent of the impact remains to be seen. Some argue that a tax disincentive to discourage outsourcing to countries like India will not be very effective because companies move jobs to India not because of the lower tax rate, but because of the availability of highly skilled labor at low cost.

from migrant workers is expected to further decline as the oil-producing Middle Eastern countries retrench and the advanced economies cut back on consumption.

Because foreign-portfolio investment added buoyancy to the Indian capital markets, Indian corporations were engaged in aggressive acquisition overseas (resulting in the high volume of outbound direct-investment flows). That is, during the good times between 2000 and 2008, Indian firms bought more than 1,000 international mergers or acquisitions worth over $72 billion. Among the high profile, Tata Steel borrowed extensively to buy Corus in 2007, while Hindalco, India's biggest aluminum company, borrowed $3 billion to buy Novelis, a Canadian manufacturer of aluminum products. However, the bulk of these purchases was financed by foreign borrowing. Many of these firms were saddled with huge debts, in part because some of the purchases turned out to be dubious. Tata's purchase of Jaguar Land Rover in 2008, for instance,

saddled Tata Motors with a prestigious brand, prodigious losses and a $3 billion loan, the last $1 billion of which it managed to refinance on May 27th, days before it fell due. It has had to call on the help of the Tata Group's holding company, which underwrote its faltering rights issue last year, and the indulgence of India's biggest state bank, which guaranteed an $840m bond it floated in May.[8]

Not surprisingly, Tata's "corporate profit growth fell to 9 percent in April–June quarter from about 25 percent in 2007" (IMG 2009i, 12).

Finally, the depreciation of the rupee has not had a favorable impact on export growth because of weak external demand and because "some importers and firms with large foreign exchange liabilities, incurred partly to finance overseas acquisitions are also suffering from the rupee depreciation" (IMF 2009i, 12; also Ahluwalia 2011). Suffice it to note that continued depreciation can negatively affect those businesses that have borrowed in foreign exchange without hedging. Moreover, the depreciation of the U.S. dollar has not only increased uncertainties associated with capital movement but also by driving up the prices of commodities in dollar terms it has exerted imported inflation. Indeed, this poses a real threat as global external shocks can generate runaway inflation – for example, a sharp hike in food prices can quickly erode the gains made in economic development, especially poverty reduction.

As noted, the subprime-induced general tightening of the global credit markets and the resultant "credit crunch" have reduced capital flows. This

[8] *The Economist*. 2009. "Gone Shopping: Indian Firms' Foreign Purchases," May 28. http://www.economist.com/business/PrinterFriendly.cfm?story_id=13751556

is reflected in the capital account. Between March and September 2008 central-bank data showed heavy portfolio investment net outflows of $5.5 billion compared to net inflows of $18.4 billion from the same period in the previous year. Over the short term, this may not be a serious problem as India still has a fair amount of liquidity in its domestic economy. However, if the problem persists over time, the credit crunch could have a negative impact. For example, an impact on the business sector's ability to raise funds from international sources can impede investment growth as these businesses would have to rely more on costlier domestic sources of financing, including bank credit. This could, in turn, put upward pressure on domestic interest rates.

Policy Responses and Challenges

New Delhi responded to the crisis with fiscal stimulus and monetary policies to contain the contagion and stimulate the domestic economy. Specifically, policy makers put in place fiscal stimulus measures between December 2008 and February 2009 to boost domestic demand, including sector-specific relief packages for housing, textiles, and infrastructure. The fiscal stimulus packages totaled some 3 percent of GDP (IMF 2009i). In addition, the authorities adopted measures to provide liquidity, strengthen the capital of financial institutions, protect savings and deposits, address the regulatory deficiencies, and unfreeze credit markets, as well as putting in place measures to keep the domestic money and credit markets functioning normally and limit insolvency due to liquidity stresses (Ram 2009). For example, on December 6, 2008, the RB1 cut key interest rates by 1 percentage point amid signs of slowing economic growth and eroding investor confidence following the terrorist attacks in Mumbai. The cut brought the benchmark repo rate (at which the central bank makes short-term loans to commercial banks) from 7.5 percent to 6.5 percent. The reverse repurchase rate (the rate at which it borrows from commercial banks) was lowered from 6 percent to 5 percent to increase the access to credit and encourage banks to lend more to consumers, especially to large firms and the state governments. Between October 2008 and April 2009, the repo rate was reduced by 425 basis points or from 9 percent in August 2008 to 4.75 percent in May 2009; the reverse repo rate was reduced by 275 basis points or 6 percent in November 2008 to 3.25 percent in April 2009, and the cash reserve ratio (CRR) was reduced by a cumulative 400 basis points, or from 9 percent in August 2008 to 5 percent in January 2009 (RBI 2009). In addition, the RBI also announced measures to ease credit to small businesses, exporters, the real-estate sector, and others hit hard by the economic downturn. Access to credit from foreign sources was also eased by lifting some of the constraints on external commercial borrowing. For example, the ceiling on FII investment in rupee-denominated corporate bonds was doubled. These were in addition to the fact that since mid-September, the Reserve Bank has plowed an estimated 3 trillion rupees ($60.2 billion) into the financial system.[9]

Overall, these measures helped to unfreeze liquidity, albeit only modestly. This was (and is) because of the prevailing uncertainties and concerns about further economic slowdown and because banks (both Indian and foreign) have become more risk-averse. In such an environment, interest-rate reduction by itself cannot overcome the basic problem of tightened access to credit. It should be noted that a Keynesian-style strong fiscal stimulus to jump-start the economy (a strategy adopted by China, the United States, and other Western governments) is not a long-term option for India. This is because there is not much more the authorities can do as India already has a very large fiscal deficit (the combined fiscal deficit of the central and state governments in the fiscal year 2009–10 increased to around 12 percent of GDP) on top of a debt-to-GDP ratio of more than 80 percent. Indeed, India's high fiscal deficit has led Standard & Poor's to downgrade India's "long-term sovereign debt outlook" from "stable" to "negative." While few will dispute that fiscal stimulus was necessary to prop up economic activity in face of an unprecedented crisis, in the case of India, more government spending has the potential to only make this problem even worse as any further increase in fiscal deficit to GDP ratio could result in a further downgrading of India's credit rating and a loss of business confidence. Policy makers' recognition of the urgency to reduce the nation's deficit was reflected in a relatively small fiscal package of less than 0.5 percent of GDP for public spending in 2009. Policy makers have also appropriately stressed that making the financial system efficient at intermediating capital and directing it to the most productive investments is critical to India's long-term growth (Subbarao 2009).

The Case of Japan

Japan, the world's third largest economy, was widely viewed as a source of global stability and liquidity when the crisis first broke. Japan's banks,

---

[9]   Erika Kinetz. 2008. "India's Central Bank Cuts Key Interest Rates," *USA Today*, December 6. http://www.usatoday.com/money/economy/2008-12-06-363760723_x.htm.
      It is important to note that India's exchange-rate policy has been more flexible and variable (in both nominal and real terms) than China's. While this variability may not be huge (and the Reserve Bank of India does indeed intervene), India's exchange-rate policy and outcomes have greater flexibility than China's. As a result, India does not face the challenges China does.

Table 7.4. *Japan: near-term projections*

	2008	2009	2010
(Calendar Year, Growth Rate)			
Real GDP	−0.6	−6.2	0.5
Total Domestic Demand	−0.8	−2.9	0.5
Net Exports (Contribution)	0.1	−3.6	0.0
CPI Inflation	1.4	−1.0	−0.6
Current Account Balance (in Billions of U.S. Dollars)	157.1	76.4	56.0
In Percent of GDP	3.2	1.5	1.2
General Government Balance[a]	−6.3	−11.2	−8.9
Structural Balance[a]	−4.9	−7.9	−5.6
Primary Balance Excluding Social Security[a]	−3.6	−7.8	−5.2

[a] In percent of GDP. Fiscal year basis.
Source: IMF. 2009. "Article IV Consultation with Japan: Concluding Statement of the IMF Mission," May 20. http://www.imf.org/external/np/ms/2009/052009.htm

particularly the so-called mega-banks that had overcome the problems that plagued them in the 1990s (the "lost decade"), were much more robust with sound economic fundamentals.[10] The banks were not overexposed to investment banking or structured finance and had reasonably strong capital positions with massive deposit bases. As a result, Japanese banks were not only expected to weather the subprime crisis but also to serve as a source of liquid global capital. However, the crisis highlights Japan's particularly close integration with the global economy. Such integration means that a collapse in external demand and financial spillovers can quickly plunge even a sound economy into recession (Cargill and Sakamoto 2008). The severity of the financial meltdown in the United States and the resultant sharp drop in the equities market caused severe losses in Japanese banks' equity holdings, especially their Tier 1 capital, forcing them to raise new capital. Despite attempts by the authorities to ease the fallout (the Bank of Japan reduced its policy rate in November 2008) through fiscal stimulus, it failed to stop the contagion (Table 7.4).

The first signs of a slowdown in economic activity were anemic domestic spending and a decrease in exports, particularly to the United States and Europe. In October 2008, Japan's global exports of autos and electronics sharply declined, while exports to other Asian countries, especially China,

---

[10] There is a vast literature on Japan's "lost decade" and its lessons. For a good overview, see Cargill, Hutchison and Ito (2000); Hoshi and Kashyap (1999); Kuttner and Posen (2001); Motonishi and Yoshikawa (1999); Syed, Kang and Tokuoka (2009).

plunged for the first time in almost seven years (IMF 2009k). In November 2008, exports were down by 26.8 percent and in December by 35 percent. The decline rate reached 49.4 percent in February 2009 (Kojima 2009, 16). As Sommer (2009, 2) notes, "Most of the drop in Japan's exports was caused by a sharp retrenchment in overseas demand for motor vehicles, information technology (IT), and capital goods.... Japan's car exports fell by 65 percent since September 2008, with shipments to the United States plunging almost 75 percent." Although the export decline was not unique to Japan as other countries also experienced significant fall in external demand, Japan was particularly vulnerable for two reasons. First, Japan's reliance on foreign trade has grown in recent years. Kazuo Ueda (2009, 49–50) notes:

In 2007 [Japan's] exports to GDP ratio was 16%. This is much higher than the U.S., where the number was 8.4%.... Japan has depended much more on exports recently. During the economic upturn of 2003–07 the contribution of exports to growth was stunningly high at 67%. In previous upturns the ratio was usually less than 50%. In the late 1980s, Japan's "bubble" years, it was less than 10%. More formally, the correlation between export growth and real GDP growth was surprisingly absent before 1990; the correlation coefficient between the two was minus 0.03 during 1970–90. It rose to 0.61 during 1991–2008. It is higher at 0.73 during the last 10 years. In other words, in the post-bubble period Japan has failed to deliver a domestic demand-led growth and become increasingly exposed to economic fluctuations in the rest of the world.

Second, as Kawai and Takagi (2009, 1) have compellingly argued, the structural changes in Japan's export base, where "over 90 percent of Japan's exports consist of highly income-elastic industrial supplies, capital goods, and consumer durables" made Japan extremely vulnerable to a drop in external demand.

With the export base rapidly deteriorating, the manufacturing and industrial sectors, dominated by export-oriented industries, including autos, electronics, and machinery were adversely impacted. Japanese manufacturers were forced to cut output by 9.6 percent in December 2008. Such massive fallout quickly rippled through the job market, with companies announcing massive job cuts and greater reliance on temporary workers. Japan, which has long prided itself on full employment, saw the unemployment rate rise from 3.8 percent in October 2008 to 5 percent in April 2009 (IMF 2009k, 6). As Ueda (2009, 50) notes, "Japan's manufacturing firms' domestic procurement rate for parts and materials is fairly high, while American firms rely more on imports for parts and materials supply. Thus, a given demand shock, say, a decrease in exports, generates larger spill-over effects in Japan."

So fast and deep was the contagion that Japan's economy contracted for two consecutive quarters of 2008 for the first time since 2001. According to the IMF (2009l), from October to December 2008, Japan's real GDP shrank at an annual rate of 12.7 percent – the worst record in 35 years. It was the steepest drop since the 13.1 percent fall in January–March 1974 when the nation was reeling from the effects of the first oil crisis. Japan's economy deteriorated further during January–March 2009, notching a decline at the annualized rate of 15.2 percent. In contrast, the U.S. economy fell by an annualized 6.1 percent during the first quarter of 2009, and Italy's declined by 9.4 percent. Like Japan, Germany's trade-dependent economy shrank by a record 14.4 percent. However, the slowdown of Japan's export-driven economy was only part of the problem. Unlike other major currencies, the yen has been appreciating. This was largely due to the unwinding of the so-called carry trade, as investors who borrowed in cheap yen to invest in high-yield currencies began reducing their positions abroad,[11] and also because the yen usually tends to "benefit" from its perceived safe-haven appeal in times of economic uncertainty. Yet it is always the yen's rise, or more appropriately, its volatility that generates concern. This is because a rising yen can not only stall growth in one of the world's largest economies, but also the entire global financial sector is vulnerable because of the carry trade. That is, investors who took out massive loans in hitherto low-interest-rate currencies (like the yen), exchanged the money to higher-interest-rate currencies (like the dollar or the euro), and then re-loaned it. They made money from the interest on the second loan, which was higher than what they had paid on the first one. This strategy worked as long as interest rates and currency valuations remained steady. However, in the midst of the crisis, with the U.S. Federal Reserve and European Central Bank cutting their benchmark interest rates, carry traders, including many large financial institutions, faced potentially huge losses.

Moreover, Japan, which used to run a massive trade surplus, due in part to its prodigious savers, is seeing that era come to an end. Japanese households now save far less of their income not so much because they have become more spendthrift, but mainly because of life-cycle changes (Sheard 2009). As the ratio of Japanese aged over 65 to those of working age rises

[11] The "yen carry trade" refers to the act of borrowing at low interest rates in yen and using the loan to buy higher-yielding assets elsewhere. Borrowers can exploit the gap between the U.S. and Japanese yields by borrowing for next to nothing in yen and then putting the money into U.S. Treasuries and benefitting from an interest-rate difference of more than 3 percentage points from the dollar's rise against the yen. Investors make their profit when they reverse the trade and pay back the yen loan.

(from 14 percent in 1980 to an estimated 34 percent in 2008, and possibly 49 percent by 2020), consumption patterns have been changing. Retired people tend to live off their savings and save less. This trend, coupled with the slump in global demand and a strengthening yen, has pushed the country's trade balance into a deficit. From July 2008 to January 2009, Japan's annualized trade deficit jumped to ¥4 trillion ($39 billion), compared with a surplus of almost ¥11 trillion a year earlier.[12] In addition, Japan's foreign-investment income has also been shrinking because of lower dividends and interest rates. As a result, its total current-account surplus dropped to only ¥125 billion in December 2008 (92 percent less than a year ago) – in other words from "a record 4.8 percent of GDP in 2007 to an annualized 1.4 percent of GDP in the Q1 (first-quarter) of 2009" (IMF 2009k, 6).

The Case of South Korea

Four years after the crisis many countries are still living with the adverse effects of the "great recession." The world's leading economies, including the United States, the eurozone, and Japan, which were hit hard by the crisis, have not fully recovered. The U.S. economy continues to languish under low growth and high unemployment, while the eurozone is facing an existential crisis that could potentially lead to the breakup of the monetary union. According to a vast body of scholarship, such tepid recovery or even stagnation, is to be expected. Reinhart and Rogoff (2009) claim that the aftermaths of systemic financial crises are characterized by long, deep recessions with very low growth and high unemployment. Just as it was with the Great Depression of the 1930s (when it took economies on average more than a full decade to regain their former per-capita GDP), it will again take time before per-capita GDP and unemployment rates return to their pre-crisis levels. Reinhart and Rogoff show that in ten of fifteen severe post–World War II financial crises, unemployment did not return to pre-crisis levels even after a decade, and double-dip recessions occurred in seven of the fifteen financial crises, indicating that, if history is any guide, meaningful recovery is still some years away.

How, then, did Korea, the world's fifteenth-largest economy, buck this trend? Despite experiencing a deep and wrenching economic contraction in the fourth quarter of 2008, the Korean economy made a remarkable V-shaped recovery by the second half of 2010, notching an impressive 6.2

---

[12] *The Economist*. 2009. "Japan's economy: Rebalancing act," March 5. http://www.economist.com/finance/displaystory.cfm?story_id=13240636

percent growth in 2010 and prompting the ever-cautious IMF to announce that "Korea's rapid recovery from the global downturn has transitioned into a full-fledged expansion" (IMF 2011g, 4). Although growth slowed in late 2011 and in 2012 (due to an overall slowdown in the world economy), Korea's economy grew at around 3.0 percent in 2012. This is impressive given continued global economic turmoil and uncertainty. What explains Korea's phenomenal rebound? As the following sections illustrate, although the combination of revival and growth in external demand, coupled with expansionary fiscal and monetary policies, made an important difference. Often unacknowledged are the implementation of wide-ranging structural and financial-sector reforms, some under IMF tutelage, forced by the Asian financial crisis of 1997–98.[13] These reforms, including more effective regulation and supervision of financial institutions and better management of foreign-exchange reserves, have made the Korean banking and financial sectors more resilient to devastating exogenous shocks, leaving these sectors with an enhanced ability to absorb shocks and to recover quickly from a deep economic contraction. The Korean experience vividly underscores that a healthy financial sector is sine qua non in this age of rapid global economic integration. Absent such financial health, not only will economies be highly vulnerable to all manner of exogenous shocks, but measures to mitigate these shocks, including costly stimulus packages, will only be partially effective.

Korea's Deep Structural Reforms

Arguably, the singular reason behind Korea's fall from grace, or why the Korean economy succumbed so easily to the 1997 crisis, was because of "crony capitalism" rooted in the ubiquitously corrupt relationship between the country's *chaebols* (or large-industrial conglomerates), the banking sector, and the state (Sharma 2003). Ironically, it is also "crony" and "casino" capitalism in the United States – vividly manifest in profligate bank lending, irresponsible borrowing, ineffective regulation, and an incestuous relationship between Wall Street and Washington, D.C. – that is widely seen as responsible for the subprime meltdown that eventually ushered in the global financial crisis (Johnson and Kwak 2010).

However, the difference has been official response to these systemic structural problems. In the midst of the Asian crisis, confronted with a

---

[13] During the 1997–98 Asian financial crisis, the Korean economy experienced a free-fall as real GDP growth rate plunged to −6.7 percent in 1998 from the pre-crisis average of 8 percent. The government was forced to seek a $60 billion credit line from the IMF. For details see Sharma (2003).

debilitating and humiliating economic collapse (in which citizens were reduced to donating their valuables to the national coffer to help it pay the national debt), Korean authorities embarked on a broad and ambitious goal to radically clean up their economy. Unlike their U.S., European, and Japanese counterparts, who have been only too happy to kick the proverbial can down the road or buy time via massive stimulus spending, the Korean authorities showed purpose and resolve and opted to implement painful-yet-necessary structural reforms. In lockstep with the recommendations of the 1997 Presidential Commission on Financial Reform, the Korean authorities promptly closed a number of problem banks and restructured twelve of the thirty-two largest banks through mergers and recapitalization; increased the existing banks' capital requirements; strengthened the viable banks' balance -sheets by providing them much-needed liquidity in order to get them to restart lending; established the Financial Supervisory Commission (FSC) in 1998 and the Financial Supervisory Service (FSS) in 1999 to enhance prudential regulation; established the Korea Deposit Insurance Corporation (KDIC) in 1996 to insure bank deposits, including deposits in securities companies, insurance companies, merchant banks, and savings banks to limit the problems arising from systemic risk; created a publicly funded corporation (the Korea Asset Management Corporation, or KAMCO) to purchase nonperforming loans; and enhanced the Bank of Korea's financial and regulatory powers to improve transparency and oversight and reduce political influence. Additionally, swift adjustments in fiscal and monetary policies, including prudent depreciation of the real exchange rates, helped boost recovery (Lee and Rhee 2007).

These reforms were accompanied by wide-ranging industrial restructuring designed to rein in the *chaebols,* in particular, reducing these giant conglomerates' control over financial institutions and allocating them credit based on their performance. *Chaebols* who failed to measure up or were deemed beyond repair, such as the once all-powerful Daewoo Group, were forced to undergo humiliating bankruptcy and restructuring in 1999. The dissolution of the Daewoo Group (the fourth largest *chaebol* in Korea), was a stern warning to others that no company was "too big to fail." Finally, painful-yet-necessary labor-market reforms were implemented to raise productivity and to make Korean exports more competitive internationally. By tackling the economy's structural problems head on (rather than engaging in quick fixes), Korean authorities set the economy on the path to rapid economic growth by late 1998. As the next sections show, these measures also played a considerable role in preparing Korea to better weather and recover from the global financial crisis of 2008.

Korea amid the 2008 Crisis

Like Japan, South Korea was viewed as well positioned to weather the global economic turmoil (Cho 2009). The country was blessed with strong macroeconomic fundamentals (from 2005–2007, real GDP grew at 4.75 percent on average and the unemployment rate was at 3.5 percent). The current account was healthy and the international reserves large enough to provide the "self-insurance" against sudden stops and panic deleveraging. Second, the balance sheets of banks were strong because Korean financial institutions were not heavily exposed to U.S. mortgage debt and related securitized products.[14] In 2008, Korean banks' aggregate nonperforming loan ratio was 0.8 percent, compared to 6.0 percent before the Asian financial crisis, and their Basel capital ratios a respectable 11 percent – up from 7 percent in 1997. Third, the corporate sector was robust. The highly leveraged *chaebols* of yesteryear were in much stronger financial shape. In 1997 the debt-to-equity ratio of the corporate sector was 426 percent, but in 2008 it stood at 131 percent (Jun-kyu 2010, 10). Fourth, apparently having learned the bitter lessons from the Asian crisis (when the inflow of dollars dried up and Korea's economy spiraled into a recession), Seoul had built up huge reserves of dollars and euros, in part by restricting much of its borrowing in the domestic markets. On the eve of the Asian crisis, Korea's foreign reserves amounted to only $8.4 billion, but by end-2007, that number had grown to a robust $260 billion (Park 2009, 1), and the total ratio of external debt to foreign reserves in 2008 was a manageable 173 percent. Fifth, although the Korean economy remains fundamentally export-dependent, its rapidly expanding intraregional trade linkages with Asia were seen to provide it much greater protection. That is, over the past decade, Korea has diversified its export markets. In 2008, North America and the EU constituted only 13.3 and 15.1 percent of the Korean export market, while China, ASEAN, Japan, and other markets constituted 22.1, 10.4, 7.1, and 19.1 percent, respectively, of the Korean export market. Clearly, by all key measures, the economic fundamentals of the Korean economy seemed sound in 2008 (IMF 2008c; 2008e; World Bank 2008).

Despite these obvious strengths, the spillover from the financial contagion proved more severe than anticipated. The Korean economy was hit

---

[14] According to the IMF (2008e), "Holdings by Korean banks of subprime-related RMBS and CDOs is reported to be around $660 million, and net exposure to structured investments around $2 billion (or 2 percent of banks' equity). Reported exposure of Korean banks and insurance companies to securities issued by Fannie Mae and Freddie Mac is also small, at around $550 million."

rather hard, contracting by 5.1 percent in the last quarter of 2008 from the previous three months. The capital account recorded a deficit of $42.6 billion in the fourth quarter of 2008, which was roughly equivalent to 20 percent of GDP. Thus, according to the IMF, Korea's was "among the sharpest contractions worldwide."[15] Why did Korea experience such an unusually high degree of financial instability despite strong macroeconomic fundamentals, while other Asian economies with comparable fundamentals showed far greater resilience during the height of the financial turbulence? A key factor was Korea's adoption of open-capital account liberalization.

Unlike every other major economy in Asia, Korea placed almost no restrictions on foreign residents' purchase and sale of domestic equities. Similarly, no limits were placed on domestic financial institutions' foreign borrowing. Thus, the liquidity of Korea's bond and equity markets not only meant that foreign investors could easily unwind their holdings during times of stress and uncertainty, it also meant that Korean banks could easily borrow. Not surprisingly, many had exceptionally large exposure to short-term foreign loans. When the rollover rate on those loans fell due to the worsening global credit crunch it resulted in repayment pressures (as the banks' weakened balance sheets fueled capital flight) and an eventual downturn in real economic activity. The experience of Korea demonstrates that unrestricted cross-border capital flows provide rewards of greater financial depth to the recipient country, but they also carry potential risks (as foreign investors and domestic residents can quickly withdraw their funds from the local financial markets). These risks are greatly magnified if the domestic banking sector becomes excessively exposed to short-term foreign loans. In times of economic uncertainty, the risk and dangers of financial contagion become amplified.

An unintended outcome of this policy was that many Korean households and SMEs became heavily indebted as Korean banks with access to cheap credit funneled funds to the SMEs and households. Kang (2009, 6) notes that "for the past decade, gross foreign debt has increased about 2.3 times – from $163.8 billion to $380.5 billion in 2008. During the same period, short-term foreign debt has increased from $39.5 billion to $151.0 billion, and its proportion in the gross external debt has also increased." According to the OECD (2008, 4), Korea's short-term foreign debt... soared from $66 billion

[15] See IMF (2009n). However, according to a senior policy maker at the IMF, Korea's economy, based on "preliminary data, the economy contracted by 5.6 percent in the last quarter of 2008, over the previous quarter" (Anoop Singh, 2009). "Korea, Navigating through the Global Headwinds," *Yonhap News Agency*, February 2. http://www.imf.org/external/np/vc/2009/020209.htm

at the end of 2005 to $189 billion in September 2008." And because much of the borrowed money failed to go into productive investments, Korean households and SMEs were facing huge debt:

In just over two decades, the household savings rate in Korea has plummeted from a world-beating 25 percent to a projected 3.2 percent in 2010 – the lowest among OECD countries. If the projections are accurate, South Koreans will soon be saving roughly half the amount that Americans do. In the face of the financial crisis, as banks limit access to credit, there is likely to be a rise in personal and small business bankruptcies (IMF 2009o, 1-2).

Korean financially institutions were severely impacted by global risk-aversion and the resultant drop in capital flows due to global deleveraging following the collapse of Lehman. As everywhere else, the global credit crunch made it very hard for local banks to acquire dollars and other foreign currencies needed to refinance activities such as foreign-denominated loans to the domestic SMEs. Korean banks, which had accumulated substantial short-term foreign-currency debt and had a high loan-to-deposit ratio (about 120 percent) in the banking sector to boot were hit particularly hard by the external shocks as both domestic and foreign-exchange liquidity tightened for banks with large financing needs.

Moreover, as foreign investors began to retrench from Korea and with dollar assets leaving the country (and the global credit markets freezing up during the peak of the crisis), asset prices dropped sharply, and Korean banks found it exceedingly difficult to access dollars to repay maturing dollar loans.[16] As the dollar liquidity strains spilled over into the local currency markets, banks became even more cautious about extending loans on concerns of worsening asset quality and fears about counterparty risk. At the peak of the crisis, as foreign investors withdrew funds en masse from domestic equity and bond markets (due to heightened risk-aversion), the resultant foreign-capital outflows not only caused a steep decline in the stock market but also led to a substantial depreciation of the exchange rate (with the Korean won depreciating by some 40 percent) and a sharp increase in premiums on credit-default swaps. In early October 2008, the won fell to 1,484.90 to the dollar, its weakest rate since the Asian crisis in 1997 (IMF

---

[16] Kang (2009, 4–5) notes

The Korean financial markets have also been heavily hit by foreign investors' retreating from their portfolio investment to Korea.... In 2008 more than $50 billion of investment flowed outward from Korea. This massive withdrawal occurred in every type of foreign investment: foreign direct investment (FDI), portfolio investment, financial derivatives, and in the category of other investments.... In 2008, $225 billion was withdrawn from the Korean financial markets.

2009n, 6–7). The derivatives, originally put in circulation to reduce risks caused by a rise of won versus the U.S. dollar, became a liability as the won's sharp depreciation against the dollar only increased the cost of servicing foreign debt.

As one of the world's most open economies, Korea is extremely vulnerable to the contraction in global demand. The traditional trade channel became a huge problem for Korea as global demand sharply dropped. The country's trade deficit, having been in the black since the end of the Asian financial crisis, recorded a deficit of $12.3 billion in August 2008 largely due to the sharp rise in crude-oil prices.[17] However, the sharp contraction in global trade made this problem much worse as Korea is a heavily export-dependent economy. Park (2009, 5–6) points out that "in 2007, 57 percent of total exports were shipped out by four industries – automobiles, ship building, electronics and chemicals." Lacking a "diversified mix of export products," and "with a heavy concentration in a limited number of manufactured export goods, which are highly cyclical" made the Korean economy highly vulnerable. On top of this, as Kang (2009, 2–3) notes, "exports to four major regions and countries – China, Japan, the EU, and the United States – make up more than 60 percent of Korean exports. Therefore, if these economies suffer, Korean exports will decrease, and the Korean economy will suffer." As a result, Korea experienced "its largest drop in exports on record and at the low point in January 2009, exports were down 35 percent from the previous year" (IMF 2009o, 1). The precipitous decline in global consumption weighed heavily on manufacturers of big-ticket items, in particular, the nation's carmakers. According to the Korean Ministry of Commerce, Hyundai Motors, Kia Motors, GM Daewoo, Renault Samsung, and SsangYong Motors reported a combined 13.1 percent year-on-year reduction in sales for December 2008. Overall, exports declined sharply with plummeting global demand, a problem further complicated by weaker domestic consumption and investment. At end-2008, exports dropped by 9.8 percent while domestic sales plummeted by 23.2 percent. Although Korean exports jumped 17 percent in January 2008, led by oil products, flat panels, machinery, and mobile-phone handsets, it later declined due to apprehensions about the U.S. economic slowdown. Indeed, the country's broadest measure of trade (the current account) recorded an annual deficit for the first time in a decade, meaning Korea was spending more on goods, services, and investments from overseas than it was selling abroad.

---

[17] South Korea is the world's fifth-largest oil importer.

Response to the Crisis

Japan and South Korea responded to the crisis with expansionary fiscal stimulus and monetary policies to both contain the contagion and stimulate their economies. Among other things, they introduced measures to provide liquidity, strengthen the capital of financial institutions, protect savings and deposits, address regulatory deficiencies, and unfreeze credit markets, including measures to keep their domestic money and credit markets functioning normally and limit insolvency due to liquidity stresses.

The Bank of Japan's policy rate cuts and measures to facilitate corporate financing certainly helped to ease credit conditions (Kawai and Takagi 2009). However, the reality is that Japan's policy options are limited given its already extremely low interest rates (the Bank of Japan cut its policy interest rate from 0.5 per cent to 0.3 per cent in October 2008) and highly indebted public finance. In May 2009, Japan also put in place a 13.9 trillion yen "extra budget" to stimulate its economy badly battered by two quarters of double-digit decline (OECD 2009). Again, on December 1, 2009, the Bank of Japan announced a 10 trillion yen ($115 billion) short-term lending facility, with a fixed 0.1 percent interest rate, to boost liquidity and reverse deflation. However, this facility, worth just 2 percent of GDP, had modest impact.[18] As noted, the room for fiscal stimulus is constrained by Japan's already high level of public indebtedness.[19] Given this, the Japanese government's two stimulus packages to boost economic growth offer no guarantees. Indeed, some two decades of stimulus spending have failed to bring the sclerotic Japanese economy to life. Rather, it has only added to the public debt estimated to be twice the size of Japan's $5 trillion economy. Finally, hanging on top like the sword of Damocles is the perennial fear of deflation – a problem exacerbated by a fast rising yen. Unlike their Korean counterparts, Japanese policy makers have not shown the decisiveness to deal with their country's problems, underscored by the fact that the Japanese economy has failed to emerge from the deflation that it fell into in the 1990s. The great recession of 2008 has only exacerbated Japan's never-ending deflation.

[18] *The Economist*. 2009. "Battling Deflation in Japan: Waking up to Reality," December 3. http://www.economist.com/node/15022473/print

[19] Based on current projections, the OECD (2009) estimates that the stimulus packages could boost Japan's budget deficit to 10 percent of GDP in 2010 and the gross public debt to 200 percent.

The Korean government, including the Bank of Korea, responded aggressively to the crisis through use of diverse policy instruments.[20] With the onset of the crisis, and especially following the collapse of Lehman Brothers in September 2008, Seoul implemented a fiscal-stimulus package equivalent to 1.2 percent of its GDP, or $11 billion dollars. In March 2009, the government announced a 28.9 trillion won supplementary budget (equal to around 3 percent of GDP) to boost the domestic economy. The government's two fiscal packages, including the original budget and supplementary budget, totaled 3.6 percent of GDP – among the largest fiscal expansion among G-20 countries (IMF 2009n). Moreover, the Korean authorities created a 20 trillion won Bank Recapitalization Fund to assist banks in shoring up their capital base by purchasing their subordinated bonds, hybrid bonds, and preferred stocks. Further, in October 2008, the government announced that it would guarantee banks' external liabilities up to a total of $100 billion (OECD 2008). For their part, these banks were expected to use part of the credit to support activities in the real economy, including extending credit to businesses, in particular, SMEs. In fact, to prevent potentially large-scale bankruptcies by SMEs, credit guarantees by two public entities, the Korea Credit Guarantee Fund (KODIT) and the Korea Technology Finance Corporation (KOTEC), increased their funding dramatically – reaching some 59.4 trillion won (5.6 percent of GDP) in 2009 (BOK 2009).

The Bank of Korea also eased monetary policy by bringing down its base policy rate from 5.25 percent to 2 percent between October 2008 and February 2009, besides lowering the interest rate on its loans from 3.5 percent to 1.25 percent (OECD 2008). In order to encourage flows of funds into the money and bond markets (which were reeling under the credit crunch), the central bank widened the scope of eligible securities and eligible financial institution counterparties for its open-market operations and provided liquidity (of up to 5 trillion won) to support financial institutions subscribing to its "Bond Market Stabilization Fund." Last but not least, to facilitate the supply of credit through banks, the Bank of Korea not only raised its aggregate credit ceiling (from 2.5 trillion won in November 2008 to 9.0 trillion in March 2009) and paid banks interest on their required reserve deposits, it also helped the banking sector build its capital base in order to give banks incentive to lend to businesses, especially small and medium enterprises.[21]

---

[20] The data is based on: The Bank of Korea. 2009. "Policy Response to Financial Turmoil." http://eng.bok.or.kr. For a good analysis and review, see Eskesen (2009).

[21] Of course, paying interest on required reserve deposits rather than simply lowering banks' reserve requirement ratios has the quick policy effect of improving the bank balance sheets.

As cross-border lending became tight, especially from September–December 2008, Korean banks faced serious difficulty in rolling over their external debt. This forced the central bank to step in with foreign-exchange swaps to alleviate funding pressures and stabilize the won. Specifically, the central bank put aside $55 billion in foreign-exchange reserves to provide as swaps or loans to banks and trade-related businesses (Alp, Elekdag, and Lall 2011). In addition, the Bank of Korea entered into swap arrangements with central banks of its major trading partners, including a $30 billion bilateral swap arrangement with the U.S. Federal Reserve on October 30, 2008, and on December 12, 2008, the Bank of Korea entered into a 180 billion yuan or 38 trillion won (about US$26 billion) swap arrangement with the People's Bank of China, besides expanding the ceiling of an existing currency arrangement with the Bank of Japan from US$3 billion to US$20 billion.[22] Last, but not least, the central bank provided foreign currency liquidity totaling some $26.6 billion to domestic financial institutions experiencing difficulties raising foreign capital and introduced a $10 billion Foreign Currency Loans Secured by Export Bills Purchased in late 2008 to provide finance to domestic SMEs (OECD 2008).

Cumulatively, these measures helped to limit the impact on Korea's real economy besides helping the country maintain its international credibility. Government actions, most notably currency swaps, brought a measure of stability to the foreign-exchange market, especially in late 2008 and early 2009. Indeed, the rollover of Korean banks' external liabilities improved substantially by the end of January 2009. Also, as Alp, Elekgad, and Lall (2011, 2), point out, the Bank of Korea's proactive monetary policy, namely, allowing the exchange rate to depreciate as capital flowed out of the country, including cutting policy rate by 325 basis points, reduced the depth of the economic contraction. They correctly note

Were it not for an inflation targeting framework underpinned by a flexible exchange rate regime... the actual outcome of a −2.1 percent contraction, the outturn would have been −2.9 percent if the BOK [Bank of Korea] had not implemented countercyclical and discretionary interest rate cuts. Furthermore, had a fixed exchange rate regime been in place... output would have contracted by −7.5 percent.... In other words, exchange rate flexibility and the interest rate cuts implemented by the BOK helped substantially soften the impact of the global financial crisis on the Korean economy.

---

[22] This is separate from the existing currency swap already entered into under the Chiang Mai Initiative, which was set up as a set of bilateral currency swap lines in the wake of the 1997–98 financial crisis. Specifically, the initiative was designed to prevent a sudden run on financial assets that wreaked havoc on Asian economies in the late 1990s.

Nevertheless, given the depth of the crisis, government actions, regardless how ambitious, could not limit all fallout. In the case of Korea, despite valiant efforts, between June and October 2008, the country's foreign-exchange reserves fell by $46 billion, and the won continued to depreciate – by about 26 percent in trade-weighted terms between July and November of 2008. As Park and Song (2011, 7) note, "The nominal exchange rate, which had remained below 1,000 won per US dollar during the first quarter of 2008, began a sharp depreciation in April to reach a high of 1,513 won per US dollar on 24 November. Among the East Asian currencies, the Korean won lost most in value vis-à-vis the US dollar that year." Clearly, given the large volume of bonds held by foreigners, especially the large volume coming up for renewal in the first quarter of 2009, the swap arrangement failed to convince markets about Korea's ability to service its foreign debt. Thus, although, the Korean government's policy measures helped to soften the negative impact of the crisis, they came at a heavy cost.

Lessons and Challenges

Chastened by the 1997–98 Asian financial crisis, Korea's wide-ranging structural and financial-sector reforms enabled it to absorb the shocks and to recover far more quickly from the 2008 global crisis than most countries. Yet, as an open export-dependent economy, Korea remains highly vulnerable to the potentially destabilizing effects of volatile international capital flows. This explains why accumulating, if not hoarding, foreign-currency reserves is seen as an effective "self-insurance" strategy – the first line of defense against externally induced volatility. No doubt, during the 2008 crisis, countries with sufficient reserves avoided sharp drops in output and consumption. Korea's large foreign-currency reserves enabled it to stabilize the domestic market by intervening directly in the foreign-exchange market and to supply desperately needed dollars to financial institutions and to establish a $30 billion swap line with the United States. Of course, holding huge reserves is not cost-free for the domestic economy, and it exacerbates the problem of macroeconomic imbalances and the resultant "global savings glut" that U.S. Fed Chair Ben Bernanke has identified as the number one culprit of the global crisis. However, what constitutes an adequate level of reserves will always vary greatly from country to country because financial crises impact countries differently, with some experiencing panicked withdrawal of foreign capital by both foreigners and domestic residents, to some experiencing a sharp loss of export income. Arguably, given Korea's strong economic fundamentals and sound macro-prudential regulations, it could manage with much lower levels of reserves – but that is something Seoul in cooperation with international institutions will have to work out.[23] Experience informs that for an export-dependent economy with an open-capital account, the most effective defense against external shocks is a flexible exchange rate and continually deepening foreign-exchange markets, but the reality is more complex. Although Korea officially maintains a market-determined exchange rate, during the crisis the authorities intervened extensively to smooth volatility. Excessive intervention should not become a habit, and Korea will be better off by maintaining more exchange-rate flexibility. In the end, strong macroeconomic fundamentals are the best protection against the vagaries of global capitalism.

Finally, the road out of the Asian financial crisis – robust growth and demand in the advanced economies – is now filled with many potholes. With the United States, Japan, and Western Europe reeling from massive deleveraging, volatile equity prices, high-debt burdens, and tight credit markets, not to mention that the precipitous fall in asset prices (equity, bond, and housing markets) has dramatically eroded the net worth of households, excessive reliance on external demand is fraught with dangers. Like China, South Korea must decisively rebalance its economy toward domestic demand to reduce its vulnerability to external shocks. However, as the preceding discussion has shown, given that Korean households are already burdened with a high level of debt and have very low savings, rebalancing in Korea will not be as straightforward as in China. Rather, boosting the incomes of lower-income households is a prerequisite for boosting domestic demand. How to do this in the most efficacious manner is an important challenge for the Korean authorities. Finally, Korea (including other Asian economies such as India and China) should not slow their integration into the global economy. Although international trade and openness to global capital markets were the channels via which the contagion traveled, these are the same channels that have enabled these economies to grow – and for Korea to recover so quickly. Rather, the experience of Korea confirms that strong domestic macroeconomic fundamental is key to navigating through the violent storms the global economy occasionally unleashes.

---

[23] The "rules of thumb" measure used by the IMF to determine "reserve adequacy" suggest that countries should hold reserves covering 100 percent of short-term debt or the equivalent of three months' worth of imports.

EIGHT

The Middle East amid the Global Financial Crisis

When the financial crisis first broke, the prevailing view was that the Middle East, or MENA, an economically diverse region that includes the oil-rich economies in the Persian Gulf and the resource-poor countries such as Egypt, Morocco, Syria, and Yemen[1], was either going to successfully weather the impact of the crisis or altogether escape it. The reasons for the region's supposed immunity varied. The oil-rich Gulf Cooperation Council (GCC) states[2], which together control 45 percent of the world's oil reserves and 18 percent of the natural gas reserves, were awash with liquidity from skyrocketing oil prices (much of it invested in their "sovereign wealth funds" (SWFs), seemed well-sheltered from the fast-spreading contagion. Well-endowed SWFs such as the Kuwait Investment Authority (KIA) and the Qatar Investment Authority (QIA) were seen as having the capacity to continually boost liquidity and confidence in both the domestic and the regional economy.[3] In fact, the GCC nations

---

[1] The MENA region includes Algeria, Bahrain, Djibouti, Egypt, Iran, Iraq, Israel, Jordan, Kuwait, Lebanon, Libya, Malta, Morocco, Oman, Qatar, Saudi Arabia, Syria, Tunisia, United Arab Emirates, West Bank and Gaza, and Yemen.

[2] The GCC countries include the UAE, Oman, Bahrain, Kuwait, Qatar, and Saudi Arabia.

[3] While there is no agreed-upon definition of SWFs, the U.S. Department of Treasury defines SWFs as government-investment vehicles funded by foreign-exchange assets that are managed separately from official reserves. More broadly, SWFs are investment funds controlled by governments. They are state-owned investment funds composed of financial assets such as stocks, bonds, real estate, or other financial instruments funded by foreign exchange assets. SWFs can be structured as a fund or as a reserve investment corporation. The types of acceptable investments included in each SWF vary from country to country. For example, countries with liquidity concerns limit investments to only very liquid public debt instruments. A number of countries have created SWF to diversify their revenue streams. For example, the funding for the Norwegian Government Pension Fund comes from oil revenues, the Singapore Investment Corporation is funded through foreign exchange reserves, and the UAE relies on its oil exports for its wealth. As a result, UAE devotes a portion of its reserves in an SWF that invests in assets that can act as a shield

Table 8.1. *Real GDP (%) for selected Middle Eastern economies*

	2007	2008	2009	2010[b]
Middle East	6.3	5.9	2.5	3.5
Oil Exporters[a]	6.2	5.6	2.2	3.7
Iran	7.8	4.5	3.2	3.0
Saudi Arabia	3.5	4.6	−0.9	2.9
United Arab Emirates	6.3	7.4	−0.6	1.6
Kuwait	2.5	6.3	−1.1	2.4
Mashreq	6.7	6.9	3.4	3.1
Egypt	7.1	7.2	3.6	3.0
Syria	4.2	5.2	3.0	2.8
Jordan	6.6	6.0	3.0	4.0
Lebanon	7.5	8.5	3.0	4.0

[a] Includes Bahrain, Iran, Kuwait, Libya, Oman, Qatar, Saudi Arabia, United Arab Emirates, and Yemen.
[b] 2010 figures are estimates.
Source: (IMF 2009d, 92).

were seen as possible "shock absorbers" and "stabilizers" – their exceptionally strong economic positions giving them the ability to serve as both a potential cushion against the global downturn and as an engine pulling cash-starved economies from recession by providing desperately needed liquidity and supporting global demand. On the other hand, the economic backwardness and relative isolation of the hydrocarbon-poor countries from the global financial and capital markets (without the oil industry, the Arab world accounts for only 2.5 percent of world economic growth), was seen as their saving grace, a shield against the vagaries of global financial turmoil.

However, as Table 8.1 shows, after an initial period of calm and seeming resilience, the economic turbulence reached both the oil-rich and oil-poor MENA economies. Real GDP growth declined across the region, although, the forces behind the contagion and the impact were varied and uneven.

Despite the adoption of highly expansionary policies (the central banks provided stimulus packages, liquidity, and deposit guarantees and lowered

against oil-related risk. The amount of money in SWFs is substantial. The estimated value of all SWFs is estimated to be $3.6 trillion – and if current trend holds they are projected to reach $10 trillion by 2012 (IMF. 2008. "Sovereign Wealth Funds – A Work Agenda," Washington, D.C., February 28, www.imf.org/external/np/pp/eng/2008/022908.pdf.

reserve requirements and interest rates) to mitigate the adverse economic shocks, the region nevertheless saw economic growth contract from 6 percent in 2008 to 2.5 percent in 2009. The slowdown proved broadly similar in oil-producing and non-oil-producing countries. However, the socioeconomic impact and the authorities' response to the challenges have been quite varied.

For example, Kuwait, in keeping with global trends, saw its stock-exchange index fall by 50 percent in October 2008. However, news that a Kuwaiti bank had suffered significant losses in late 2008 from trading in currency derivatives further spooked the markets and saw the country's third-largest bank lose $1.4 billion, forcing the Kuwaiti authorities to guarantee customer deposits at local banks. When, in December 2008, Kuwait's largest investment company defaulted on most of its $3 billion debt obligations and was forced to negotiate a debt restructuring, Kuwait quickly passed a financial-stability law to provide financial-sector guarantees, and set up a stock-market stabilization fund totaling some 3 percent of GDP. However, the impact on the real economy has been modest because Kuwait (like other oil-rich GCC countries) have a comfortable financial cushion to mitigate negative socioeconomic impacts. On the other hand, the impact on the resource-poor MENA countries has been severe. The GCC is a key source of investment financing (through FDI and other flows) and remittances for these economies, and thus the abrupt decline in income and investment flows adversely impacted growth and living standards. Hardest hit have been the 69 million people in the Middle East and North Africa who draw subsistence on less than $2 a day.[4]

The following sections highlight the various transmission channels through which the contagion spread to the MENA countries, the overall socioeconomic impact of the crisis, and short and potential long-term economic implications. This chapter also examines how the governments and regional bodies have responded to the challenges posed by the unprecedented crisis in their midst, and how the MENA countries, especially the poorest, can better insulate their economies from the vagaries of the global financial markets. Detailed reference to MENA countries: Egypt, Yemen, and the United Arab Emirates (UAE) are used to illustrate these interrelated issues.[5]

---

[4] http://go.worldbank.org/7UEP77ZCB0

[5] The United Arab Emirates (UAE) is a federation of seven states situated in the southeast of the Arabian Peninsula. They include Abu Dhabi, Ajman, Dubai, Fujairah, Ras al-Khaimah, Sharjah, and Umm al-Quwain.

Table 8.2. *Trade openness of Arab countries in 2004 (%)*

Country	(Exports/GDP)	(Imports/GDP)	(Trade/GDP)
Algeria	40.6	23.1	63.7
Bahrain	72.1	63.2	135.2
Egypt	10.6	17.9	28.6
Jordan	35.8	75.1	110.9
Kuwait	47.4	22.8	70.3
Lebanon	8.0	46.5	54.5
Morocco	20.1	36.1	56.2
Oman	57.7	35.3	93.0
Qatar	70.6	22.6	93.3
Saudi Arabia	49.9	17.5	67.5
Sudan	16.5	19.6	36.1
Syria	22.3	29.2	51.6
Tunisia	33.6	44.1	77.7
UAE	46.2	40.3	86.6
Yemen	30.8	28.5	59.3

Source: Economic and Social Commission for Western Asia (ESCWA) (2009, 16).

Transmission Channels

For the MENA region, spillovers through the trade channel remain the central transmission mechanism. As Table 8.2 shows, MENA countries are quite open in terms of trade; the trade openness index of thirteen Arab countries averages around 71.3 percent. Of course, the oil-exporting countries register the highest indices, reflecting the weight of oil and gas in their exports, as well as the importance of imports in their economies.[6]

Over the past decade, but particularly during 2002–07, the GCC countries invested a significant portion of their earnings from the record-high oil revenues into a large portfolio of financial and equity investments in the G-7 countries, especially the United States and Europe. Hydrocarbon-poor countries like Egypt, Morocco, and Jordan, which had liberalized their financial markets, including stock markets and the banking sector, also benefitted from foreign investment inflows from both the GCC and G-7 countries. However, deeper financial integration also meant the possibility of more rapid spillover across economies through newer types of financial channels.[7] As previous chapters have shown, financial spillovers

---

[6] The "trade openness index" is the ratio of the sum of exports and imports to GDP.
[7] Of course, the trade and financial channels of crisis transmission tend to interact because the availability of trade credit is linked to trade volume.

have become more pronounced as the rising correlation of global equity prices and the potential for sudden capital-flow reversals mean that shocks at the core can be transmitted rapidly throughout the entire global financial system. Indeed, a significant volume of withdrawals from emerging economies, including the GCC equity and debt funds, confirm that investors in the advanced economies began to retract from emerging economies to "safe havens" like U.S. Treasuries around October 2008.

Leading the charge were cash-strapped U.S. financial institutions, which began to "deleverage" by either selling or repatriating their assets to raise cash to strengthen their balance sheets back home (this was vividly reflected in the volatility experienced by regional stock markets). In turn, this led to sharp drops in stock prices around the world, the relative increases in the value of the U.S. dollar against all currencies, a reversal in capital flows, a shortage of liquid foreign reserves, and tighter restrictions on credit availability. In the GCC the problems were most evident in a widening of sovereign risk spreads and a sharp downturn in stock markets, especially for real-estate companies as they are among the largest publicly listed companies in the region (IMF 2009h). In the GCC, stock-market capitalization "fell dramatically by 41 percent ($400 billion) between the collapse of Lehman Brothers in September 2008 and end-2008 – and volatility increased" (IMF 2010h, 16).

The sharp decline in stock prices, in turn, negatively impacted banks, which suffered extensive loan defaults and asset-value losses. Since a significant percentage of the GCC's SWF were invested in equities and real estate they also suffered huge losses. These problems were further compounded by expectations of an appreciation of the dirham vis-à-vis the U.S. dollar. The hard economic times in the GCC also contributed to a sharp drop in their investments in the MENA region, including Egypt, Morocco, and Jordan, which had become increasingly dependent on these investment flows. Finally, even MENA economies with limited or no exposure to toxic subprime assets were impacted because of the links between their financial sectors and new hybrid products, including derivatives, sovereign credit-default swaps, collateralized debt obligations, and new forms of mortgage-backed securities.

Some Evidence from Egypt and Yemen

Between 2007 and mid-2008, the Egyptian economy grew at an unprecedented rate of about 7 percent (IMF 2010i). The unemployment rate dropped from 11 to 8 percent and the seemingly unchangeable poverty levels were finally on the decline. The country's financial sector, especially the banks and investment companies, were not large holders of subprime mortgage-backed securities (the so-called toxic assets), and banking sector reforms, especially in the area of bank supervision and consolidation of nonperforming loans (NPLs) had made the banking sector more resilient. Just as important, Egypt's net international reserves stood at a robust $35 billion in October 2008 (IMF 2009p). However, these robust fundamentals hardly made the Egyptian economy immune to the contagion emanating from the advanced economies. The MENA countries that do not export oil, such as Egypt, but also Yemen, Morocco, Tunisia, Jordan, and Lebanon, heavily depend on external assistance, foreign-direct investment flows, exports, tourism, and remittance receipts from workers abroad (mainly from Western Europe and the GCC countries). In Egypt, the revenue generated by tourism and remittances account for a substantial proportion of its GDP. As a result, the country is extremely susceptible to exogenous economic shocks as a decline in these revenue streams (both in absolute terms and as a share of GDP) can have immediate negative consequences for economic growth and development.

Indeed, Egypt's real GDP growth fell by 2 percentage points in 2008 and early 2009, and by a further 4.5 percent in the remainder of 2009 (IMF 2009p). The Egyptian economy has been impacted by broad transmission channels, including global deleveraging and a drop in export revenues, as well as country-specific channels such as the contraction in merchandize exports and tourism and sharp reductions in Suez Canal tolls and remittances from expatriate workers. More specifically, the sharp decline in the merchandise exports to key external markets (notably Europe and the GCC) resulted in declines in foreign revenue and contraction in the domestic labor market (World Bank 2010, 27–8). Tourism, which is the country's major foreign-exchange earner (bringing in some $11 billion dollars in 2007 and contributing 8.5 percent of Egypt's GDP), experienced a significant decline between mid-2008–2010 with ramifications for the domestic economy as tourism has many multiplier effects, notably on employment (World Bank 2010, 29). According to the Egyptian Ministry of Economic Development, "each tourist dollar spent ultimately generates $4 or $5 in income," which shows that there exists a strong correlation between income and tourism (Mohieldin 2008, 40–42). Because Egypt (and other oil-poor MENA countries) depend heavily on tourism for foreign exchange and for creating service-sector employment, the impact of the regional and global downturns have been serious (Khalil 2009). Similarly, in fiscal 2007–08 (end of June 2008), remittances from Egyptian expatriate workers (the vast majority work in the oil-rich Gulf countries) sent about $8.56 billion to the home country.[8] However, the regional economic downturn resulted in major retrenchment of labor and capital with the most expendable, the emigrant workers, facing massive layoffs. In fact, by end-2008, thousands of workers from Egypt, Yemen, and the West Bank and Gaza (among other countries) began to return "home" en masse from the Gulf, further adding to the ranks of the unemployed. Of course, already high and rising unemployment is a huge challenge not only for Egypt, but all MENA countries as they are characterized by large and rapidly growing working populations due to a demographic bulge of 16–24-year-olds.

Exacerbating Egypt's woes was the loss of revenue from the Suez Canal. Despite concerns about pirates off the Somali coast, the waterway earned a record $5.2 billion in 2007. However, the sharp shrinkage in global trade and the resultant drop in the numbers of ships using the canal led to a sharp drop in toll revenue (which stood at $301.8 million in February 2009), a 25 percent decline from the $408 million in January 2008. In mid-2008, Egypt experienced an abrupt reversal of portfolio flows as foreign investors pulled out of the equity and government bond markets.

The IMF (2010i, 6) notes that "following the Lehman shock, foreign investors withdrew from Egypt's equity and government debt markets, with foreign T-bill holdings declining by over 80 percent by April 2009." The central bank responded by running down its foreign-currency deposits with commercial banks. The sharp decline in external liquidity raised the cost of debt servicing and put pressure on the current account balance (IMF 2009n), and the stock-market "decline continued through February 2009, with losses reaching 70 percent relative to the April 2008 peak" (IMF 2010i, 6).

The experience of Yemen illustrates how countries lacking in oil wealth and depended on exports, foreign-direct investment, tourism, and remittances are not only hit hard during downturns, but find it much more difficult to get their economies back on track when recovery eventually takes hold. Yemen is among the poorest countries in the MENA. Its economy has been stagnating, with an estimated 35 percent of its population living below the poverty line. As MENA is the world's largest net food-importing region, Yemen, like a large number of countries in the region, suffered heavily from the food and fuel crisis which preceded the onset of the global financial crisis. With food (and oil) prices skyrocketing to record levels from 2006 to

---

[8]   World Bank (2009d, 15) finds that remittances totaled $6.3 billion in 2007 – up 25 percent over 2006 levels.

mid-2008, the terms of trade for food and oil-importing countries, including Yemen, Morocco, Tunisia, Lebanon, Jordan, and Egypt, among others, plummeted, with rising inflation (around 17 percent in Yemen) having an adverse effect on the poor (IMF 2008g).

When the financial crisis broke, one of its unintended blessings was that it also contributed to declines (sometimes sharp) of food and oil prices. This provided some relief to countries reeling under its inflationary impact. Yemen's isolation from the global economy was also seen as a blessing. Like most resource-poor MENA countries, Yemen is insulated from global financial markets. Yemeni banks have low exposure to private foreign lending, and portfolio investment is almost nonexistent given the absence of a domestic stock market or commercial credit market (IMF 2009r). Yet, these were not enough to insulate Yemen as the country is also highly vulnerable to commodity price shocks because it is a major importer of food and inputs and depends heavily on remittances from workers in the GCC and on official aid, categorized here as FDI (in fact, the case of Yemen confirms the empirical evidence that aid is procyclical with donor incomes). Moreover, domestic financial institutions have limited deposits and liquidity. The loss of revenue from expatriate workers placed great pressures on government finances, as have declines in donor assistance and tighter external financing conditions. This has translated into ballooning fiscal deficits, pressures on account balances, and overall worsening of the country's budgetary position. However, unlike its resource-rich neighbors, Yemen does not have the wherewithal to meet revenue shortfalls. This has meant that Yemen has been unable to put in place a vigorous fiscal stimulus to respond to the economic downturn. As a result, the crisis hit Yemen particularly hard with poverty levels in both rural and urban areas notching sharp increases in 2008 (Breisinger et al., 2010).

Case of the UAE

The experience of the United Arab Emirates, in particular, some of the federation's member-states, underscores the fact that wealth is not necessarily a protection against financial crises. Rather, misallocation of resources can make even wealthy states extremely vulnerable to a severe contagion. When the crisis began, the UAE was assumed to be well insulated from the global financial turbulence despite the fact that its economy is among the most globally integrated in the world.[9] The UAE is an important participant in

---

[9] Over the past decade the UAE has pursued ambitious free-market policies to diversify its economy away from a dependence on fossil fuel. In 2004, the United States and the UAE

global capital markets through several "blue-chip" investment institutions, including, the Abu Dhabi Investment Council, the Dubai Ports and Free Zone World, Dubai Holding, and the Abu Dhabi International Petroleum Investment Company (IPIC). In addition, the Dubai Financial Market, Abu Dhabi Securities Exchange, Nasdaq Dubai, and the Saudi Stock Exchange are an integral part of the global financial markets. The UAE's banking sector, awash with "windfall" liquidity from record oil prices, was seen as healthy. In fact, the UAE's banking system was not only well capitalized, but also highly profitable as the "banks' assets and profits increased sharply in 2007 and the capital adequacy ratio stood at 13.3 percent by mid-2008, above the regulatory minimum of 10 percent."[10]

An unintended outcome of the punitive investment restrictions imposed by the United States (especially on several Middle Eastern countries) after September 2001 was that the GCC was forced diversify its massive foreign-exchange surpluses regionally. That is, instead of investing the bulk of its revenues in U.S. Treasury bills or in Eurodollar accounts at multinational banks, the GCC governments began to aggressively build up their SWFs, including investing in a variety of domestic state-controlled institutions. The UAE, which began devoting a significant portion of its oil revenues in the SWFs, was able to build up a colossal war chest worth more than $875 billion by May 2007. This massive accumulated wealth (at least, relative to its GDP) was seen as a bulwark that could be used to mitigate the effect of oil price cyclicality and support continued investments to sustain growth. Finally, since the federation's write-downs from subprime assets were minimal, it was seen as immune to the crisis.

Nevertheless, in the oil-producing countries where export of hydrocarbons is the single most important determinant of economic success, the rather abrupt drop in oil prices (from $147 per barrel in July 2008 to $38.60 per barrel in December 2008) was an ominous sign. According to the World Bank, "For the GCC in aggregate, oil and gas revenues dropped from $670 billion in 2008 to an estimated $280 billion during 2009 – a massive decline equivalent to 38 percent of the group's GDP" (World Bank 2009a, 126). In the UAE, the sharp decline in the price of oil heightened concerns that since

entered into a Trade and Investment Framework Agreement (TIFA) that established a formal dialogue to promote increased trade and investment between the two countries.

[10] By end-2008, only a few Gulf banks had exposure to subprime loans: Abu Dhabi Commercial Bank with $272 million, Bahrain's Arab Banking Corporation with $1.2 billion, the Kuwait-based Gulf Investment Corporation with $446 million, and Bahrain's Gulf International Bank, which was downgraded by Moody's because of its holdings of U.S. mortgage-backed securities. It had to make provisions for $966 million and raise additional capital (IMF 2009s; Woertz 2008, 8).

the oil sector accounts for about 37 percent of the Emirates' GDP, the country could now face deflation as the era of cheap credit was over and that the federation would not be able to generate the considerable fiscal surpluses to meet its ambitious (and costly) spending targets.[11] Even SWF investments were not foolproof as a number of these funds suffered heavy losses on equity investments following the sharp slide in stock markets in 2008. The Abu Dhabi Investment Authority (ADIA) is believed to have lost an estimated $125 billion in 2008 after the credit crisis sharply cut asset prices. According to Setser and Ziemba (2009), the SWFs and foreign-currency funds of the GCC lost about 27 percent of their assets – some $350 billion – in 2008 alone.

Exacerbating this was the potential exposure of the Emirates' (and especially Dubai's) real-estate sector to global markets. In April 2008, "the six members of the GCC … announced or began projects worth $1.9 trillion."[12] Specifically, soon after the Dubai International Financial Centre (DIFC) free zone opened in 2004, it became the world's fastest growing financial center, boasting the presence of hundreds of banks and insurance companies from around the world.[13] Because foreign financial institutions did not have to pay any tax on profits and faced no restrictions on foreign exchange or repatriation of capital, they expanded rapidly via franchising their operations throughout the region and lending to the Emirate's booming real-estate and construction sectors. However, foreign banks were not the only willing lenders. UAE banks and financial institutions in partnership with foreign subsidiaries also engaged in rampant speculative lending in real estate. Indeed, the UAE, via its quasi-government companies (including Nakheel, Emaar, and Dubai Properties), invested billions in its property sector in an effort to diversify its economy and reduce dependence on the oil industry.

As a result the UAE experienced a boom in property development. It boasts more glittering skyscrapers than Manhattan, and with prices to match. The lid came off the real-estate sector following Dubai's decision to allow foreign investors to buy property in designated areas on a freehold basis in 2002. The red-hot property market exploded with skyrocketing property values, rampant speculation, and round-the-clock construction to

---

[11] Abu Dhabi accounts for 94 percent of the UAE's crude-oil output. Not surprisingly, it is the wealthiest of the seven members of the Emirates with more than half of the country's GDP.

[12] *The Economist*, 2008. "How to Spend it," April 20–May 2, p. 37.

[13] In fact, Dubai came to rival Bahrain, the major financial centre in the region for more than four decades.

meet insatiable demand, not only in Dubai, but throughout the Emirates. The most ambitious were the mega-projects, including the three Palm Islands and Burj Dubai, which, at 688 meters, is the world's tallest building. However, what was not well known was the extent of the banks' (both foreign and domestic) exposure to the real-estate sector via loans to developers – namely, whether these loans were backed by strong collateral. This uncertainty generated palpable fear that a sharp reversal in the UAE's real-estate and property market could (like in the United States) implode with devastating effect.

In October 2008, one of the Emirate's big three land developers, Nakheel, in addition to the companies directly controlled by Dubai's bullish ruler, Sheikh Muhammad bin Rashid al-Maktoum, such as Dubai World, Investment Corporation of Dubai, and Dubai Holding, announced that they were scaling back dredging work on the massive artificial-island projects, Palm Deira, the largest of the three Palm Island archipelagos, audaciously named "the World" (the island was designed as replica of the world) Nakheel boasted that the World would house more than one million "highly selective" residents who would have access to state-of-the-art conveniences, including luxury complexes personally designed by no other than the irrepressible Donald Trump himself, but also the world's largest indoor ski slopes featuring fresh powder year round.

This news about Nakheel served as a wake-up call, finally underscoring that Dubai's real-estate bubble, built on the backs of borrowed cash and speculative investment, was finally unraveling. Intensified global deleveraging led to a large contraction in liquidity and severe tightening of credit conditions, particularly in regions that were seen to be highly leveraged and dependent on foreign lines of credit such as Dubai. Soon this resulted in distressed sales of Dubai property, including of the high-end Palm Jumeirah, which saw prices plummet as investors rushed to offload homes and other property. Among the casualties was the exquisite tower that Donald Trump had promised would be "the ultimate in luxury," and a $100 billion beachfront resort complex. By early November 2008, property prices had fallen by 4 percent in Dubai and by 5 percent in Abu Dhabi for the first time since 2002.[14] This was just the beginning. By the end of November, prices had

---

[14] According to the *Wall Street Journal*, the average asking price for homes in Dubai fell 4 percent in October from September 2008, and prices for the upscale Dubai "villas" fell by 19 percent. In next-door emirate Abu Dhabi, average home prices fell by 5 percent. http://online.wsj.com/article/SB122649558637520553.html?mod=googlenews_wsj#printMode. Chip Cummins. 2008. "Dubai Faces Hit as Property Boom Fades," *The Wall Street Journal*, November 13

dropped by 25 percent. Sensing further losses, the large foreign banks that had been financing much of the UAE's and particularly Dubai's real-estate boom quickly began to pull out. The burden now fell squarely upon local banks and financial institutions, most of which were simply ill-equipped to deal with the unprecedented burden. Abu Dhabi's largest mortgage lender, Amlak Finance, shocked investors when it announced in early November that it was temporarily halting new home loans. A few days later the UAE's biggest bank, Emirates NBD, announced its decision to stop lending to foreigners who work for Dubai's property firms. Other banks followed suit. Worried about the health of their loan-to-value ratios, banks either lent less or refused to lend at all. By end of 2008, the UAE's once-booming property sector lay moribund, facing not just a major slowdown in loan growth and real-estate activity, but potential collapse. Only the UAE could provide the desperately needed liquidity.[15]

With an estimated $1.8 to $2 trillion in foreign assets (by end-2008), of which roughly 60 percent was in U.S. dollars, it was only a matter of time before the GCC would experience asset depreciation (Woertz 2008). This was soon felt on the Emirates stock markets as stock and asset values plunged and the sovereign wealth funds took their share of losses, especially funds with a high allocation in equities. The World Bank (2009a, 126–7) noted:

GCC sovereign wealth funds lost 27 percent of their value in the 12 months ending December 2008, with losses as high as 40 percent among those funds heavily allocated to emerging markets and private equity placements. GCC equity prices in dollar terms dropped by some 58 percent between September 15, 2008 and March 12, 2009 (a period during which virtually all bourses registered sharp declines). Over the same period, equity prices in UAE plummeted by 70 percent, contrasted with a decline of 55 percent for all emerging markets.

On November 16, the Dubai Financial Market (DFM) index closed at 1,981.44 points, falling by 68.51 percent from the year's peak of 6,291.87 points on January 15 with a loss of 4.67 billion dirhams ($1.27 billion) in market value. On the same day, the Abu Dhabi Securities Exchange (ADX) also fell to its lowest point of the year, with its general index hitting 2,755.62, down 46.48 percent from 5,148.49 points on June 11 with a loss of 1.52 billion dirhams.

The UAE's Central Bank responded vigorously (and preemptively) to mitigate the adverse economic developments, in particular, the drying-up

---

[15] On May 11, 2009, Nakheel confirmed it would be receiving funds from the Dubai government to meet its outstanding obligations. In 2009, Dubai sold US$10 billion of bonds to the UAE Central Bank to raise funds to support cash-strapped state-linked companies and announced plans to issue another US$10 billion in bonds later this year.

of liquidity following the outflow of foreign deposits. On September 22, 2008, the Central Bank announced the establishment of an emergency lending facility totaling some 50 billion dirhams to provide liquidity for the banking sector, including guaranteeing all deposits and local interbank loans. On October 8 it announced a 2 percentage-point cut in its lending rate (to 3 percent) to generate liquidity of local banks. On October 8, the Central Bank lowered the rate on its repurchase of certificate of deposit (REPO) from 2 percent to 1.5 percent. The Kuwait Investment Authority (KIA) and the Abu Dhabi Investment Authority also repatriated part of their foreign assets and deposited them in domestic banks to provide liquidity (IMF 2010h). In addition, SWFs' resources were used to invest in local equity markets, and the Qatar Investment Authority and the KIA purchased domestic bank shares to help enhance bank capitalization. Equally significant, to prevent spillovers from the global turmoil and to boost confidence in the economy, the central banks in a number of countries (UAE, Kuwait, and Saudi Arabia) announced that they would provide a three-year blanket guarantee to deposits and savings in all national banks and foreign banks with "significant operations" in the federation, including a guarantee to all interbank lending operations between banks (Khamis and Senhadji 2010). It also made a commitment to inject liquidity in the financial system if and when necessary. The government's decision to inject an addition 70 billion dirhams into the banking system in late October 2008 under an "emergency liquidity support fund" (in the form of interest-yielding government deposits) to provide banks with long-term funding relief underscored the UAE's willingness to restore liquidity to the markets and rebuild confidence in the Emirates' financial sector (IMF 2009t).

The policy response, including the purchase in February 2009 by UAE's central bank of $10 billion of Dubai's bonds, provided some respite but failed to stop the panic or the financial bleeding. This is because, although the global financial turmoil in the Emirates' (and the GCC countries') banking sector has been uneven, all experienced a reduction in their profitability due to reduced growth in business volumes, tighter interest-rate margins, increased credit costs, and direct and indirect exposure to the increasingly volatile local stock and property markets. For states like Dubai, which, unlike oil-rich Abu Dhabi, rely on debt and equity finance raised in the international markets to support their overly ambitious plans, access to credit became a huge problem. The fact that UAE's central bank quietly purchased half a $20 billion five-year bond issued by Dubai was seen as proof that the latter was having trouble meeting its $80 billion debt obligation. Not surprisingly, property prices, which had fallen by about 25 percent in the last quarter of 2008, fell by the same amount in the first quarter of 2009. According to the *Economist*, in March 2009, "UAE developers had postponed $335 billion worth of construction projects. One two-year project was proceeding so slowly that it would take 20 years to complete." Similarly, "The debt of Dubai's government and government-controlled companies is about $80 billion. Almost $11 billion comes due this year (including interest) and $12.4 billion next. Nakheel alone must refinance a $3.52 billion bond in December and another worth 3.6 billion dirhams ($980 million) five months later."[16]

Making the grave situation even worse was the report by the IMF that the decline in oil prices coupled with OPEC's production cuts would reduce oil export revenues by almost 50 percent in 2009, or a loss of some $300 billion compared to 2008. "As a result, oil exporters' current account surplus of around US$400 billion in 2008 [was] expected to turn into a deficit of US$30 billion in 2009" (IMF 2009u). The impact was almost immediate for the 1.5 million foreigners working in the GCC countries, in particular, workers from South Asia, who make the largest expatriate community and work mostly as contract laborers – often on perilous construction sites earning as little as $150 a month. The grounding halt of the once-booming construction industry hit these workers particularly hard, because among other restrictions, employees who lose work in the UAE and other states automatically have their visa rescinded, generally giving them about 30 days to leave the Emirates. This was unfortunate as the large expatriate community, even unemployed, could have helped support domestic demand to stimulate growth in the non-oil GDP.

On November 25, 2009, the Dubai government was forced to ask its creditors for a six-month payment standstill on an estimated $60 billion of liabilities owed by one of its own flagship conglomerates, Dubai World.[17] Coming at a time when many felt the worst of the crisis was over sent shockwaves in the global financial and stock markets. The situation was further compounded when a senior government official (the director general of Dubai's department of finance) stated that the Emirate did not believe it was under any obligation to stand behind the debts of Dubai World forever,

---

[16] *The Economist*. 2009. "Dubai: A New World," April 23 (online edition) http://www.economist.com/finance/displaystory.cfm?story_id=13527891

[17] It is estimated that the total debt Dubai owes is about $80 billion – with Dubai World shouldering the bulk. Dubai World, an investment company, is owned by the government of Dubai. It is one of the three main state-owned enterprises in Dubai, along with the Investment Corporation of Dubai and Dubai Holdings (which "owns" the Jumeirah Hotel Group, including the seven-star Burj Al Arab).

and that creditors should take their share of the responsibility. Investors who had long been under the assumption of a blanket guarantee provided by the federation were clearly shocked and unnerved. Panicked investors, fearing a possible bank run, and the worst-case scenario, a sovereign default (as the Dubai government felt no responsibility to guarantee the debts of a state-owned company), began to flee by retreating to the traditional safe haven: the U.S. dollar. The panic subsided only after the Central Bank of UAE promised to "stand behind" the region's banks by providing more emergency liquidity. Although fears have since receded, the inability and unwillingness of the Dubai government to refinance the debt of its own company, Dubai World, was a rude wake-up call for investors around the world. Investors could no longer take for granted the explicit backing governments have traditionally given to state-owned companies against insolvency. The reality is that governments around the world have responded to the financial crisis by taking on unsustainable levels of debt, and many are simply no longer in a position to provide more finance – Dubai is just one case in point. Finally, the manner in which the government of Dubai handled (or mishandled) this issue has done damage to its credibility and put a big stain on its once-stellar reputation as the premier place to do business in the Arab world. Dubai's ruler, Sheik Mohammed bin Rashid Al Maktoum, who once had investors fawning over his every utterance, now cannot seem to reassure them despite giving several public statements. Clearly, regaining the Midas touch will take time.

Responding to the Challenges

As noted, the governments of the MENA countries utilized monetary and fiscal stimulus, including strengthening macro-prudential regulation and supervision of their financial sector, to respond to the crisis. Of course, the extent and depth of these measures varied depending on a country's economic endowments. For example, Kuwait, Saudi Arabia, and the UAE increased stimulus spending to boost economic activity. In fact, Saudi Arabia's $400 billion investment plan is the highest in the G-20 in terms of share of GDP (IMF 2010h, 29). MENA countries also shored-up their banking sectors by offering deposit guarantees, Qatar and the UAE pumped generous volumes of liquidity into their banking systems totaling up to 2 percent and 7.3 percent of GDP (the Qatari government spent some 6 percent of its GDP to purchase banks' holdings of equity and real-estate assets), and Kuwait passed a financial-stability law to provide financial-sector guarantees (Khamis and Senhadji 2010, 51–52). For the oil-poor MENA countries, given the magnitude of the regional and global downturn, restoration of the global financial markets, in particular, the unclogging of credit markets and the revitalization of demand in the United States, the EU, and the GCC, is essential for sustained economic recovery.

What more can the MENA countries do in the near term to preserve the region's financial stability and cushion against the lasting impact of the global slowdown? Of course, the external environment is something they cannot control. Recession or the break-up of the eurozone, anemic "recovery" in the United States, and volatility in the price of oil and gas could very well result in further deterioration in the balance sheets of financial institutions in the GCC, besides adversely impacting investor and consumer confidence.

Moreover, further corrections in asset prices cannot be ruled out. As noted earlier, the sharp downturn in asset prices in 2008 translated into losses for the SWFs. Given this, prudence dictates a review of the SWFs' long-term strategy for individual countries and the region. In particular, SWFs, in addition to playing a greater role in supporting domestic macroeconomic and financial stability, must also pursue profitable investment opportunities in the region.

The MENA countries, especially the economically vulnerable economies, need more targeted fiscal-stimulus packages to mitigate the negative impacts of the crisis. Specifically, these packages must be geared toward job creation, investment in infrastructure, including properly targeted safety-net programs to alleviate the suffering of those most adversely affected by the crisis.[18] Moreover, the stimulus packages must be well coordinated across countries so the outcomes can be reinforcing across the region. Both the oil-rich MENA countries (who, despite their own difficulties, have greater fiscal space and are in a stronger position to help) as well as multilateral financial institutions like the World Bank and the IMF must help fund the stimulus packages for the region's poorer nations. The reality is that for the low-income MENA countries, an increase in donor financing will be necessary to maintain aggregate demand and enhance social safety nets.

Finally, one of the lessons of the Great Depression was that lack of cooperation and retreat into protectionism exacerbated the situation. Clearly, UAE President Sheikh Khalifa bin Zayed Al- Nahayan understands this and has embraced multilateralism and a cooperative approach to solve economic

---

[18]   In fact, job creation is very critical as unemployment in the region is high. On average, 14 percent of the labor force is unemployed – the world average is 6.7 percent. Unemployment is particularly acute among youths and women.

and financial challenges in the region. No doubt, the UAE, along with the other GCC countries, have been working together to stem the economic problems. Apart from adopting the expansionist policies discussed in this chapter, the other item on the top of their agenda in the immediate aftermath of the crisis was to put in place a long-planned pact to issue a single currency before a self-imposed 2010 deadline for monetary union. Of course, this raises the thorny question regarding the dollar peg. Specifically, even as the U.S. dollar has been depreciating against major currencies (and central banks around the world have been gradually moving away from the U.S. dollar in an effort to stem losses from the declining dollar-exchange rate), the UAE and the GCC have long stated that they would not unpeg their currency from the dollar as the dollar peg had served them well for decades.[19] The five GCC members (Saudi Arabia, the UAE, Qatar, Oman, and Bahrain) peg their currencies to the dollar, thereby setting an official reference rate at which central banks buy and sell. The only exception is Kuwait, which in 2007 abandoned its peg and now links its currency to a currency basket that includes the dollar, the euro, the yen, and the pound sterling. The five GCC members have long maintained that the peg strengthens economic cooperation in the region, reduces speculative pressure on regional currencies, prevents capital flight in UAE banks toward foreign-denominated accounts, and that continuing the peg is an important requirement for issuing a common currency by 2010.[20] However, as the dollar has further plummeted, member states, most notably Dubai (including business interests in the region) have urged the member states to rethink the peg and the region's broader monetary policy – namely, for the GCC to peg against a basket of currencies. They claim that such a policy would not only take into account the region's growing trade with the eurozone and Asia, but curb the region's growing inflation problem.[21] Dubai and other states of the UAE (the UAE is one of the world's main holders of dollar-denominated assets), is also concerned that the dollar's decline is preventing expatriates (both professionals and ordinary workers) from taking jobs in Dubai and other UAE states.

---

[19] The dirham was adopted as the UAE's official currency in 1973 when it was pegged to the dollar at the rate of 3.9474. In 1978, the dirham was de-pegged. The dirham's exchange rate against the dollar was raised to 3.671, and in 1998, the exchange rate was adjusted to 3.672.

[20] Only Oman has ruled out revaluing its currency, arguing that a weaker rial helps attract foreign investment and makes exports more competitive – and, in the process, offsets inflation. It has also ruled out joining the plan to create a single currency. Oman also dropped out of the proposed monetary union in 2006.

[21] An undervalued dirham imports inflation into the UAE because exports are priced in U.S. dollars and the bulk of imports in other currencies.

In early 2008, the UAE Central Bank set up a task force to study a possible unpegging or revaluation of the dirham from the dollar. The study concluded that the dollar was a reliable peg for the Gulf currencies and that the GCC's planned common currency would remain linked to the dollar. Evidently, this strong endorsement helped reserve the large private capital inflows that were driven by expectations of an appreciation of the dirham vis-à-vis the U.S. dollar. Indeed, currency futures indicate that markets no longer doubt the peg. Moreover, the fact that countries with pegged exchange rates (Bahrain, Kuwait, Libya, Oman, Qatar, Saudi Arabia, Syria, and the UAE) have benefited from the continued monetary easing in the United States seems to have vindicated the Central Bank's decision. Nevertheless, it is certain that in the near future the GCC will need a new monetary regime with a single currency set against a basket of currencies and interest rates that are appropriate to the domestic economy. In that sense, revaluation should be seen as the first step toward a GCC single currency. No doubt, even as the debate on merits and demerits of the peg will continue (currently the only alternative given serious consideration is repegging the dirham to a stronger basket of currencies), deeper intraregional trade among MENA countries should be accelerated as it can act as a buffer against global downturns. Currently, the region is more integrated through labor mobility than through trade and investment. Although regional integration from FDI and portfolio investments have risen in many MENA countries, the extent of intraregional trade still remains lower than in all other regions of the world except for South Asia. Intraregional integration via freer movement of goods, services, labor, and capital, including harmonization of regulatory and supervision standards, can help improve the competitiveness and resilience of the region.

NINE

The Great Recession and the World's Poorest

In an ironic and cruel twist the global economic crisis emanated from the world's largest and most advanced economy (the United States) rather than from the profligacy and mismanagement typically associated with the emerging-market and developing countries. In fact, when the subprime-induced global crisis broke out in the United States in mid-2007, the macroeconomic positions of most developing countries, including the large emerging market economies such as China, India, Brazil, as well as many of the world's least-developed countries[1] (LDCs) were robust (AfDB 2010; World Bank 2007). The economic prospects for sub-Saharan Africa had never looked brighter (World Bank 2008b). For the first time in decades the region's GDP was growing at a comparable rate with the rest of the developing world – except China and India (Tables 9.1 and 9.2). Private-capital flows to Africa totaled an unprecedented $55 billion by the end of 2007 (World Bank 2008a; Ezekwesili 2009). Similarly, FDI flows to LDCs saw dramatic expansion – a sixfold increase between 2000 and 2008. On the eve of the crisis FDI flows exceeded $32 billion (UNCTAD 2010, 7). Coupled with extensive debt relief (mostly in the form of debt write-offs) under the HIPC (Heavily Indebted Poor Countries Initiative) and the Multilateral Debt Relief Initiative (MDRI) and adoption of prudent policies, many LDCs were finally able to reduce their external debt burdens and improve the living standards of their citizens.[2]

An earlier version of this chapter was published in Sharma and Imparato (2009).

[1] Some forty-nine countries are recognized as LDCs by the United Nations. Of these, thirty-three are in Africa, ten in Asia, five in the Pacific, and one in the Caribbean.

[2] These two multilaterally funded initiatives have helped to substantially reduce the debt-to-GDP and debt-to-export ratios in the LDCs. Freeing funds (that would otherwise have gone into debt servicing) have enabled these countries to fund much-needed social programs. For details, see Sharma (2007).

Table 9.1. *GDP growth 2006–2009 (in %)*

	2006	2007	2008	2009
World	5.1	5.0	3.1	−1.4
Advanced Economies	3.0	2.7	0.8	−3.8
United States	2.9	2.2	1.1	−2.6
Euro Area	2.8	2.6	0.8	−4.8
Japan	2.4	2.1	−0.7	−6.0
United Kingdom	2.9	3.1	0.7	−4.2
Canada	3.1	2.7	0.4	−2.3
China	11.6	11.9	9.0	7.5
India	9.8	9.3	7.3	5.4
Emerging and Developing Economies[a]	7.9	8.0	6.0	1.5
Sub-Saharan Africa	5.1	6.9	5.5	1.5

[a] Includes the African continent; Central and Eastern Europe, and the Commonwealth of Independent States.

Source: 2006–07 figures from (IMF 2008g; 2009h); 2008–09 figures from (IMF 2009e).

Table 9.2. *GDP growth in LDCs (2007–2010)*

Year	Real GDP growth (%)	Real GDP/capita growth (%)
2007	8.6	5.6
2008	6.5	4.1
2009	4.6	2.3
2010	5.7	3.4

Source: *World Development Indicators* (World Bank, 2011).

Equally impressive, a decade of relative sustained growth and more effective banking supervision and regulation had not only allowed a number of sub-Saharan countries to build up their monetary reserves (providing a cushion against short-term difficulties such as the boom and bust associated with commodity price volatility), but also much stronger bank balance sheets. Because an appreciable segment of the African continents' banks fund their operations with domestic deposits and relatively secure investments (most LDC banks have traditionally funded their lending mainly through local deposits than through foreign borrowing), they had limited exposure to derivatives and related toxic U.S. subprime mortgages securities (Kasekende et al., 2009). Not surprisingly, the LDCs were seen as quite immune to the global financial turmoil swirling in their midst and were expected to ride out the crisis with only minimal impact.[3]

Unfortunately, such optimism proved to be misplaced. The crisis unambiguously and painfully has shown that in today's interconnected world, no country is an island. Furthermore, the collateral damage is far more destructive if the crisis and the contagion emanate from the advanced economies (Reinhart and Rogoff 2009). The ferocious contagion began to hit the developing countries in the last quarter of 2008, and by early 2009 much of the world was feeling the effects, with the LDCs bearing the brunt of the impact.[4] As Table 9.1 shows, growth in the "advanced" or high-income countries declined from 2.7 percent in 2007 to 0.8 percent in 2008 and −3.8 percent in 2009. Growth in the emerging and developing economies dropped to 1.5 percent in 2009 from a robust 6.9 percent in 2007, and in sub-Saharan Africa (home to the majority of LDCs), from 6.9 percent in 2007 to 1.5 percent in 2009. As Table 9.2 shows, overall GDP growth in the LDCs declined from 8.6 percent in 2007 to 4.6 percent in 2009. However, such aggregate macroeconomic data do not tell the whole story. The LDCs were impacted disproportionately and far more severely because their fragile and limited economic endowments, high levels of poverty, and absence of safety nets mean that even small economic shocks have deleterious socioeconomic repercussions.

The following sections examine a number of interrelated issues, namely: why and how were the LDCs impacted? What has been the impact on human development? How have these countries responded to the crisis? What programs and policies have been put forward by the world's rich nations, including the G-20, and the multilateral financial institutions to assist the world's poorest nations, and how effective have they been? Finally, what can the international community and LDCs do to better insulate their economies from the vagaries of the international economic system?

---

[3] Of course, a number of low-income countries have a high share of foreign ownership in their banking systems. If the parent banks become capital constrained there is the potential that they will withdraw capital from subsidiaries in developing countries. To some extent this has already happened. The result has been that banks in these countries have difficulty servicing their debts.

[4] Because all LDCs are highly dependent on a few key exports they were negatively impacted by the crisis. However, some were impacted more severely than others. Exporters of primary commodities such as oil and mineral products bore the brunt of the crisis, followed by exporters of agricultural products. A handful of LDCs, such as Bangladesh and Cambodia, that export textile and clothing also experienced a decline in exports. In 2008, LDCs accounted for only 1.1 percent of world merchandise trade.

Transmission Channels and the Impact of the Crisis

According to the WTO (2009), LDCs' merchandise exports fell by 26 percent or from $176 billion to $126 billion between 2008 and 2009. Thus, the LDCs were impacted mainly through the trade channel. Increasingly, LDCs are an integral part of the international supply chain as exporters of raw materials and basic commodities. Manufacturing exports specialization is confined to a few Asian LDCs such as Bangladesh and Cambodia. Yet, even here roughly 70 percent of exports are made up of labor-intensive manufactures such as textiles, clothing, and footwear. The vast majority of LDCs, especially in sub-Saharan Africa, depend heavily on commodity exports (raw materials and minerals). Overall, primary commodity exports account for more than 90 percent of their merchandize exports. As a result, the LDCs are highly vulnerable to exogenous shocks and were adversely impacted from the sharp downturn in global demand.[5]

The severe economic contraction, if not recession, in some of the advanced economies resulted in sharp deceleration in export growth in the LDCs and other developing nations. Many LDCs not only saw their export markets shrink overnight, the prices paid for their exports also plunged to historic lows, resulting in a deterioration of trade and current account balances. Among the LDCs, Cambodia experienced perhaps the most severe economic contraction. Its real GDP growth rate plunged from 10 percent per annum during the period 2002–07 to −2.5 percent in 2009 largely as the result of a steep 20 percent fall in international demand for its garment exports in the first nine months of 2009 when compared with the same period of 2008. Factory closure, in turn, led to a sharp 35 percent decline in FDI in 2009. The human impact was devastating as the forced "closure of at least 50 factories and the temporary closure of many more [resulted] in the laying off of more than 62,000 full-time workers (18 percent of the total workforce in the garment sector)" (UNCTAD 2010, 26).

Similarly, in sub-Saharan Africa, no commodity exporter (agricultural or mineral) has been spared (AfDB 2010; UN-ESCAP 2009). For example, the sharp drop in the price of diamonds in Botswana forced the country's major operator of diamond mines to suspend operations in 2008. Botswana

---

[5]   According to UNCTAD (2010, 17),

An overwhelming majority of LDCs (32 out of the 47 for which data were available) experienced a growth slowdown in 2009 compared to the boom period, and GDP per capita declined in 19 of them. This slowdown was quite severe in a third of LDCs, including most countries that had grown rapidly during the boom period, namely the oil and mineral exporters, as well as some Asian and Island LDCs.

(the world's biggest diamond producer), where the gem accounts for more than one-third of GDP and between 70 and 80 percent of export earnings, experienced a major economic setback. Similarly, in South Africa (Africa's largest economy) diamond mining giant De Beers saw prices of the precious stone fall by 30 percent in the fourth quarter of 2008. In early 2009, the company was forced to implement an extended leave period for skilled workers, besides letting go thousands of miners. In Zambia, when the price of copper dropped from a high $9,000 per ton in early 2008 to less than $4,000 in early 2009, the country's foreign earnings receipts, heavily dependent on copper exports, suffered a catastrophic decline (Ezekwesili 2009a). In a scenario familiar to other mineral exporters, Zambia closed two of its major mines in 2008 and scaled back production in others, besides putting thousands of workers out of work.

A combination of commodity price shock in terms of plunging cotton prices and the appreciation of the euro (to which the region's CFA franc is pegged) against the dollar severely impacted Burkina Faso's cotton-dependent economy. Cotton makes up some 60 percent of the exports and is the main source of foreign exchange for Burkina Faso, Africa's biggest cotton producer. This important sector also provides about 700,000 jobs. In fact, "the expansion of cotton growing has stimulated production of cereals, mainly because fertilizer financed with cotton credit can also be used for other crops. As a result, poverty has been reduced by one-quarter in cotton-growing areas" (Adenauer 2009, 16). However, falling international cotton prices have eroded the gains Burkina Faso made in recent years. Other major commodity producers such as the Democratic Republic of Congo, South Africa, Nigeria, Angola, and Gabon, among others, have been similarly affected. The April 2009 issue of the *Economist* vividly documents the impact:

The slump in demand for Congo's bountiful minerals has been painful. In Katanga province, 300,000-odd miners lost their jobs virtually overnight last year, as copper and cobalt exports plummeted. In December, Congo slashed its estimate for this year's cobalt exports by more than half. The reality may be worse. Fewer people want diamonds. Direct foreign investment to Congo this year is likely to fall by more than two-thirds. The country's GDP growth may dive from 8% last year to less than 3%. The local currency has lost more than a third of its value since last year.

These problems have been compounded by the combination of tight credit in the advanced economies and sharply reduced investment flows to the developing countries, especially the LDCs. Foreign direct investment flows, including private portfolio and bank-lending flows, have all declined rather abruptly in response to weakened global growth and investor risk aversion.[6] In turn, this has contributed to significant declines in stock prices and currency depreciation, besides increasing the external borrowing costs for both sovereign and private-sector borrowers. In sub-Saharan Africa, private capital flows, which in 2007 had surged to some $55 billion (and for the first time exceeded foreign aid) declined by almost 50 percent in 2009. African stock markets, like Uganda's, fell by more than 40 percent in 2009 and has still not fully recovered, while Ghana and Kenya were forced to postpone sovereign bond offerings worth more than $800 million to finance much-needed infrastructure projects (Devarajan 2009).

Earnings from tourism and workers' remittances, which make up a substantial (and in some LDCs the largest) portion of financial flows, also fell sharply. In 2007, recorded remittances to developing countries were larger than revenues from the most important commodity export in twenty-eight countries. In thirty-six countries they were larger than private and public capital inflows. According to the World Bank, remittance flows to developing countries totaled some $304 billion in 2009 – down from an estimated $328 billion in 2008. Sub-Saharan Africa experienced a −8.3 percent slowdown in its remittance flows with significant socioeconomic repercussions as remittances provide a lifeline to many poor families.[7] The challenges facing LDCs have been further exacerbated by declines in official development assistance (ODA) as donor economies, facing constrained budgets, have reduced their aid allocations. This, coupled with the swing toward more protectionist and inward-looking economic policies in the OECD countries, has further constrained market access. Overall, the experiences of the LDCs confirm that an absence of deep integration into the global financial system is not sufficient to keep a country or region immune from global financial market turmoil as indirect channels such as slower global growth and credit tightening can have just as severe an impact on investment flows, export demand, commodity prices, and the exchange rate.

The Impact on the World's Poorest

In 2007, an estimated 53 percent of the population of LDCs was living in "extreme poverty," or on less than $1.25 a day. Approximately 78 percent was living on less than $2 a day. Overall, some 421 million people were living in extreme poverty in LDCs before the crisis struck (UNCTAD 2010,

---

[6] FDI flows in 2010 totaled $26.39 billion – a $6 billion decline from 2008, when FDI accounted for $32.35 billion (UNCTAD 2011, 16).

[7] For details see www.worldbank.org/prospects/migrationandremittances.

31–35). However, contrary to expectations, the World Bank's (2012a) latest findings indicate that despite the sharp negative impacts of the financial crisis on vulnerable populations, and despite the slowdown in the rate of poverty reduction in some countries, overall global poverty rates have kept falling.[8] Most notable, the proportion of people living in extreme poverty in sub-Saharan Africa fell to less than 50 percent (to 47 percent) for the first time since 1981 – with 9 million fewer people living in extreme poverty in 2008 than 2005.[9] These findings corroborate the World Bank's earlier finding that in every region of the developing world, the percentage of people living on less than \$1.25 a day and the number of poor declined between the years 2005 and 2008 (Chen and Ravallion 2008). That is, "an estimated 1.29 billion people in 2008 lived below \$1.25 a day, equivalent to 22 percent of the population of the developing world. By contrast, in 1981, 1.94 billion people were living in extreme poverty."

No doubt, such broad-based progress in fighting global poverty is good news. However, as the World Bank study notes, the two most critical factors behind these gains in poverty reduction have been the unprecedented levels of poverty reduction in China (where the bulk of reduction has taken place) and strong growth in the BRIC countries (Brazil, Russia, India, and especially China), which, in turn, has greatly helped commodity exporters in Africa and elsewhere.[10] Of course, the sobering reality is that no one can be certain that the reduction can be sustained. Indeed, the World Bank (2012a) warns that the greatest threat to continuing poverty reduction would be further global economic contraction as this could effectively erode the many hard-won gains made toward reducing poverty. It is worth reiterating that despite progress, some 43 percent of the world's population still survives on less than \$2 a day. This means that vast numbers of people can easily slip back into extreme poverty. In the case of sub-Saharan Africa, "Some 33 percent of the middle class (\$2–\$20) remain vulnerable to slipping back in to poverty in the event of exogenous shocks, because the bulk of these households have per

---

[8] The discrepancy in the figures is mainly due to the dataset used. UNCTAD and the FAO use an international poverty line of \$1 a day based on 1993 cost-of-living data. The World Bank uses the revised international poverty line of \$1.25 a day in 2005 prices. This is a more reliable for assessing "extreme poverty" because it is the average of the national poverty lines for the world's poorest countries.

[9] Africa's poverty headcount rose at every three-year interval between 1981 and 2005. Poverty levels almost doubled from 205 million in 1981 to 395 million in 2005.

[10] For example, China's share of imports from sub-Saharan Africa increased from about 5 percent in 2002 to 19 percent in 2010, and "for the first seven months of 2011, growth in exports destined for China from Sub-Saharan Africa was 10 percentage points higher than those destined for high-income countries" (World Bank 2012b, 2).

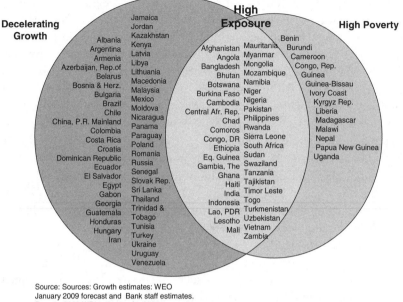

Figure 9.1. Financial crisis and countries' exposure to poverty risks.
Source: http://siteresources.worldbank.org/NEWS/Resources/WBGVulnerableCountries
Brief.pdf.

capita incomes just above the $2 poverty line (between $2 and $4)" (World Bank 2012b, 6). As Figure 9.1 shows, almost 40 percent of the 107 developing countries are highly exposed to the poverty effects of the global economic downturn, and many are extremely vulnerable to decelerating growth and widening poverty levels. Hence, now is not the time for complacency.

Given the poor's already precarious existence (low income, zero or negligible savings, absence of social safety nets, low levels of nutrition, and poor health), poor households in the developing world (and particularly in the LDCs) are vulnerable to even the most minor of economic shocks. Specifically, their extremely low threshold means that even a minor negative shock can quickly and irrevocably reduce poor families to destitution or what Jeffrey Sachs (2005) has termed the "poverty trap" – a vicious cycle under which poverty begets even more poverty, making a poor country and its people simply too impoverished to achieve sustained economic growth. Sachs (2005, 56–57) eloquently notes,

When poverty is extreme, the poor do not have the ability by themselves to get out of the mess.... When people are poor, but not entirely destitute, they may be able to save. When they are utterly destitute, they need their entire income, or more, just to survive. There is no margin of income above survival that can be invested in the future. This is the main reason why the poorest of the poor are most prone to becoming trapped with low or negative economic growth rates. They are too poor to save for the future, and thereby, accumulate the capital that could pull them out of their current misery.

Research confirms that among the most destructive action poor households are forced to take in their desperate attempts to protect their living conditions is to cut back on their consumption and pull their children out of school to add to the family's income (Ravallion 2009). Poor nutrition for children, especially in their early years, retards their physical and cognitive abilities for life, and school dropouts earn far less as adults – making poverty a vicious cycle.

The financial crisis also came on the heels of the global food crisis that was already having a negative impact on food security in many developing countries, especially in the LDCs, the majority of which are net food importers. Between 2005 and 2007, commodity prices experienced unprecedented volatility, and the price of nearly every major agricultural commodity sharply increased, creating a global food price bubble (IMF 2009f). At their peak in the second quarter of 2008, the world price of wheat and maize were three times higher than at the beginning of 2003, whereas the price of rice was five times higher. Dairy products, meat, palm oil, and cassava also experienced sharp price hikes (Sharma 2009). Food price inflation is the most regressive of all taxes and disproportionately hurts the poor as a relatively high proportion (some 70 to 80 percent) of their expenses go toward consumption.

Moreover, inflation exacerbates the problem of malnutrition as poor households are forced to buy cheaper foods, such as grains that are rich in calories but contain fewer vitamins and proteins than meat or dairy products. Households living on few dollars a day do not only experience dramatic declines in their purchasing power in the face of even small increases in food prices, the sharp price hikes of basic essentials further cut into what little money these households have left for other necessities like health care, shelter, or school fees for their children. The Food and Agriculture Organization (FAO) has compellingly shown that there were 100 million more people who were hungry (meaning they consume fewer than 1,800 calories a day) in 2009 than in 2008.[11] Overall, this means that more than a billion people, or a sixth of the world's population, were hungry during

---

[11] FAO (Food and Agriculture Organization of the United Nations). 2009. "More People than Ever Are Victims of Hunger," http://www.fao.org/news/story/en/item/20568/icode/

the height of the crisis. The FAO study report notes the problem worsened despite increases in food production in 2008–09. Protectionism and tighter exports of grain and cereals from food-surplus countries such as India resulted in only a modest decline in food prices from the highs of mid-2008. Indeed, average prices at the end of 2008 were still 24 percent higher in real terms than in 2006 (IMF 2009f).

How to Assist the World's Poor

Although the pick-up in export growth since early 2010 suggests that the worst may be over for developing countries, including LDCs that export extractive commodities such as oil and minerals, the slow and hesitant recovery can easily be derailed. As noted earlier, not only are these economies subject to commodity price volatility, the enclave nature of extractive activities means that FDI flows to the sector tend to be limited and generate fewer linkages to the wider the economy. Some extractive industries are capital-intensive with limited job creation. It should be noted that not all poor countries have benefitted from the positive terms of trade. To the contrary, several predominantly agricultural exporters and oil importers have seen a modest deterioration in their terms of trade (World Bank 2012b). Second, and more ominous, are the sovereign debt crisis in Europe and the tepid recovery in the United States as both are the LDCs' most important markets, purchasing 26 percent and 24 percent of their exports respectively. The EU accounted for some 40 percent of all exports from sub-Saharan Africa in 2002 but only about 25 percent in 2010 (World Bank 2012b, 2). The Overseas Development Institute (ODI) estimates that "low and low-to-middle income countries" will suffer cumulative output losses totaling $238 billion in 2012–13 from the crisis in the EU. Besides being the largest export market for countries in the developing world, including many LDCs, the EU is also an important source of aid, FDI, and remittances. The ODI study claims that a 1 percent drop in global export demand could hit growth in poor countries by up to 0.5 percent (Massa, et al., 2012).

Clearly, mitigating the negative effects of the crisis depends on several factors. However, many of these are beyond the control of the world's poorest nations. These include the strength and depth of the global economic recovery, in particular, in the United States and the EU, the resumption of global trade, in particular, expansion of demand in the rich and BRIC countries, especially China, sustained assistance from the G-20 and multilateral financial institutions, and the policy choices that individual LDCs make. Since the LDCs are not responsible for the crisis and given that their economies have been impacted disproportionately, it is not unreasonable to suggest that the G-20 countries, and the United States in particular, have a moral obligation to assist the world's poorest and most vulnerable citizens.

However, despite the fact that the G-7 and G-20 nations (South Africa is the only African nation represented at the G-20) have reiterated their commitments to assist the LDC, to date, their response has been miniscule. ODA disbursement has increased from $25.9 billion in 2005 to $38.6 billion in 2008 and to $40.1 billion in 2009 (UNCTAD 2011, 18), but those amounts are clearly insufficient given the challenges the LDC face – not to mention that "six major recipients accounted for almost half of the total aid received by the LDCs in 2009" (UNCTAD 2011, 18). Similarly, World Bank President Robert Zoellick's repeated calls for the establishment of a Vulnerability Fund for Africa, whereby each developed country devotes 0.7 percent of its stimulus package to provide safety net programs, infrastructure investments, and support for small and medium-sized enterprises and microfinance institutions in the LDCs have gone largely unheeded. The oft-cited claim coming from rich capitals that funds are not readily available sounds hollow in light of the fact that they easily found billions of dollars to bail out their banks and financial institutions in order to "stimulate" their own economies. Given that the stock of foreign-exchange reserves of the LDCs has been considerably depleted, and there are only very limited opportunities to quickly rebuild these reserves (essential to pay for imports such as food, medical supplies, and agricultural inputs), the LDCs need significant additional concessional financing (both grants and very low-interest loans) to simply get through the tough times. The modest 0.7 percent would certainly go a long way to help fill the annual "financing gap" in the funding of much-needed infrastructure and safety-net programs designed to meet the basic needs of the poorest through provision of basic health and nutrition projects.[12]

As noted, since the LDCs' very limited fiscal space (fiscal balances in Africa dropped from a surplus of 2.2 percent of GDP in 2008 to a deficit of 4.4 percent of GDP in 2009), only a handful of countries have been able to implement discretionary countercyclical policies to mitigate the

---

[12] Another way to quickly raise funds was formally suggested in September 2011 by the European Commission president, José Manuel Barroso. He proposed a 0.05 percent tax on financial transactions to raise funds. The tax would be levied on each stock, bond, derivative, or currency transaction – or on financial institutions' so-called casino-style trading. Such a tax could raise billions of dollars to fund safety-net programs, besides increasing development aid for poor countries. The merit of such a tax continues to be hotly debated by the G-20 and others.

socioeconomic impacts of the crisis.[13] Rather, faced with fast deteriorating current accounts and falling exchange rates, some countries, including Ethiopia, Sudan, and the Democratic Republic of Congo, have been forced to pursue tight fiscal policies to contain the fiscal and current account deficits and to protect their foreign reserves (AfDB 2010, 25). Given that the advanced economies have already spent trillions of dollars on domestic fiscal stimulus, would not a similar stimulus help boost the LDCs' ailing economies? The answer is clearly yes. However, without external funding, stimulus support in LDCs can quickly result in an increase in the fiscal deficit that will eventually crowd out private spending and generate inflation – neither of which is conducive to sustained economic growth or poverty alleviation. The fact is that many LDCs (especially those that are export-dependent) are already burdened with unsustainable fiscal deficits, in large part due to deteriorating tax revenues from declining commodity sales. Therefore, it is important that these countries reduce their deficits. Clearly, external financing can help meet this major challenge. Assuming such financing were available, the LDCs should implement a modest fiscal stimulus to boost their economies. Targeted stimulus in urban and rural infrastructure and agriculture would create badly needed jobs and contribute to a platform for future growth. Of course, targeted safety net programs that cushion the poor should be an integral part of the stimulus package. Moreover, concessional funding from donors is essential to prevent a return to the scourge of LDC indebtedness. Although the various forms of debt relief, including the IMF's HIPC and MDRI, have reduced debt burdens for many low-income countries, the global crisis has the potential to greatly exacerbate the situation through increased external borrowing and sharply reduced export and tax revenues.

Currently, some 90 percent of transactions involving trade financing involve the use of trade-related credits (Chauffour and Malouche 2011). In other words, international trade depends heavily on the availability of credit to finance trade. For example, exporters often require advance financing to manufacture products for their buyers. Importers depend on credit to buy goods and equipment such as supplies and machinery. Much of this trade-related credit is issued by banks via letters of credit that assure that businesses are able to pay. However, the crisis has had a negative impact on the price of credit (in particular, dollar-denominated credit), with the cost

---

[13] For example, Tanzania approved a $1.3 billion stimulus package, while "Angola, Lesotho, Mozambique and Sierra Leone, expanded their public works programs on an ad hoc basis, mainly to improve infrastructure and sustain aggregate demand through cash-for-work or food-for-work initiatives largely funded by multilateral donors" (UNCTAD 2010, 25).

of a letter of credit tripling for importers, especially in developing countries (Dorsey 2009). As credit costs have soared, banks and other private creditors are increasingly refusing to honor letters of credit from other banks and financial institutions, and private credit providers are less willing or able to fund trade financing. On the other hand, as credit costs skyrocket, many businesses are finding that the cost is so prohibitive that it exceeds their profit margins. These problems have been further exacerbated by banking-sector deleveraging in the eurozone since it cuts into trade finance flows with adverse impact on developing countries, in particular, the LDCs. Indeed, according to the World Bank, the "eurozone crisis poses a greater threat to developing economies than the 2008 financial crisis."[14] To underscore the importance of trade finance, WTO Director General Pascal Lamy noted in June 2012:

Another message which I will be conveying at the upcoming G-20 Summit is the importance of ensuring availability and affordability of trade finance. The Expert Group on Trade Finance as well as the Aid for Trade and Trade finance workshop which took place on 15 May stressed the importance of keeping multilateral development institutions engaged in trade finance, bearing in mind the development dimension of their programs. The permanent existence of a market gap for poor countries requires long-term public involvement, without which crisis intervention would be meaningless.[15]

As Lamy remarks, the G-20 and multilateral financial institutions can ease this constraint by facilitating export financing where the private sector is reluctant or unable to extend credit.[16] Without such support, world trade will shrink even more than it already has.

Although the G-20 countries have reaffirmed their commitment to free trade and pledged to shield the global economy from the scourge of protectionism, the reality is that protectionist sentiments and pressures have hardly abated – as underscored by the proliferation of regional, plurilateral, and bilateral preferential trade agreements (or the so-called spaghetti bowl

[14]   Mark Tran. 2012. "Eurozone Debt Crisis Poses Serious Threat to Emerging Markets," *The Guardian*, June 19. http://www.guardian.co.uk/globaldevelopment/2012/jun/19/eurozone-debt-crisis-emerging-markets/print

[15]   Pascal Lamy. 2012. "WTO News: Speeches," June 12, http://www.wto.org/english/news_e/sppl_e/sppl234_e.htm

[16]   The World Bank's new Global Trade Liquidity Program (GTLP) has committed up to $50 billion in trade financing for poor countries, and in July 2009, the IMF announced that it would be increasing its lending to low-income countries by allocating $17 billion over five years with zero interest rates on outstanding IMF concessional loans through end-2011, and doubling the borrowing limits of the LDCs under its concessional Poverty Reduction and Growth Facility and Exogenous Shocks Facility programs. However, as of July 2012, much of these critically needed funds had yet to be disbursed.

of trade agreements), the imposition of new and creative barriers to investment or trade in goods and services, the imposition of export restrictions and the implementation of WTO-inconsistent measures to boost exports, and the competitive devaluations of exchange rates to support exports, among others. In the current global climate of shrinking budgets, tepid and uneven recovery, high levels of unemployment, and declining fiscal space, "creeping protectionism" or the incremental buildup of restrictions has the potential to strangle global trade. Indeed, on June 7, 2012, the WTO's Pascal Lamy noted that the rise in trade restrictions now is "alarming," and that since the WTO began monitoring the protectionist reaction to the financial crisis, the scale of trade restrictions is a cause for "serious concern."[17]

No doubt, a return to protectionism would be detrimental to all countries, but the developing countries, and in particular the LDCs, many of whom heavily rely on exports, would be hardest hit. Therefore, it is essential to restart the global trade talks and bring the Doha Round to a successful conclusion. The G-7, indeed the G-20, nations must take the lead in implementing policies to rejuvenate global agricultural growth. In particular, they must eliminate the generous biofuel subsidies that have contributed to the food crisis and the large-scale subsidization of agriculture that has prevented developing countries, especially the LDCs, from expanding their agricultural markets. Within OECD countries, total transfers to farmers (from taxpayers and consumers) averaged about $235 billion per year in 2000–02 (OECD 2007). These enormous subsidies not only deter developing countries from maximizing the gains they can reap from agricultural trade, they also deny consumers in countries that provide these market-distorting supports the benefits from competitively priced food and agricultural products. Additionally, taxpayers are forced to subsidize the high cost of production. By subsidizing producers and frequently dumping excess supply on international markets, the G-20 countries have gravely undermined the efforts of millions of producers in poor countries. The common complaint among LDCs that "the rich countries want capitalism for us and socialism for themselves" has a ring of truth. The rich countries and emerging economies like China and India have a particular responsibility to reduce the trade barriers that harm poor farmers in LDCs. A successful Doha Round will mean less distortion in world food markets and increased international trade. Therefore, meaningful reform in global agricultural trade is the most

[17] Pascal Lamy. 2012. "WTO News: Speeches," June 12, http://www.wto.org/english/news_e/sppl_e/sppl234_e.htm

significant step the G-20 can take to promote global economic growth and development, especially in the least-developed countries.

Finally, for their part, the LDCs must become more proactive in mitigating the negative economic impact of this crisis. Most importantly, they must stay the course on essential public-sector reforms, in particular, reforms designed to improve governance and allocation and use of public resources. This means that fiscal policy must strike a balance between encouraging economic activity and maintaining macroeconomic stability and debt sustainability over the long term. No doubt, in some LDCs there is more room to allow automatic stabilizers to work, but in the majority, stimulus boost will be needed to support growth. Even in countries where debt levels are already unsustainable or where financing constraints are severe, authorities must give priority to strengthening social safety nets to minimize adverse effects on the weak and vulnerable. More broadly, this also means that the LDCs must continue to build capable and responsive states by strengthening transparency and accountability in the management of public resources. They need to strengthen their political and economic institutions, in particular, protection of property rights and rule of law. They need to strengthen regulatory institutions, eliminate highly regressive tax systems, and decisively tackle corruption and nepotism, among other ills that can make LDCs a high-risk and unattractive environment for businesses.

In the case of Africa, the continent will benefit much from deeper regional economic integration. Intraregional trade in the continent remains far below potential due to poor infrastructure, a lack of harmonization of cross-border trade policies, and excessive red tape. Mitigating these bottlenecks should be priority. The Tanzanian president and former African Union chair, Kikwete, has argued for the creation of a "single convergence institution platform" for Southern African Development Community (SADC), Common Market for Eastern and Southern Africa (COMESA), and East African Community (EAC). Such a strategy will not only allow for more coordinated and coherent external trade policy, but also enable Africa to speak with one voice at the WTO, the IMF, and other international bodies. Finally, the LDCs must invest in homegrown solutions. Fundamentally this means investing in the agricultural sector. Because the vast majority of the inhabitants in LDCs are marginal and smallholder farmers with very limited means, increased opportunities in the agricultural sector could boost food production and overall economic growth because they simultaneously promote both food security and income security. Indeed, a viable and sustainable agricultural sector is not only a prerequisite for overall economic growth, but the best bet against the problems of hunger and poverty as it provides a safety net, particularly during a time of global economic uncertainty.

Conclusion

Before the financial crisis engulfed the world, economic prospects in many of the world's poorest nations looked promising. Indeed, LDCs were in a much stronger economic position than they had been for decades. Furthermore, a number of formerly conflict-ridden "failed states" were on the path to post-conflict reconciliation and reconstruction, and the number of countries that had implemented democratic features (that is, competitive elections, improved human rights, a more robust civil society, and freer news media) rose to more than twenty – up from just three in the 1980s. It would be a cruel irony if, just as many of the world's poorest nations began to succeed, their prospects were cut short by a financial crisis in which they had no hand in making. Yet LDCs have the least ability to protect themselves against the adverse effects of the crisis and will need significant concessional financing to weather the crisis. The time is now for members of the international community, especially the G-7 and G-20 nations, to translate their lofty commitments into action.

TEN

G-20 World

Limits to Economic Cooperation in the Post-Crisis Era

It is a familiar story. Following every economic crisis, political leaders, finance ministers, central bank governors, policy makers, academics and other interested parties hurry back to their drawing boards to rethink and redraw the rules or "architecture" governing both the national and international economic order. Their efforts are not always in vain because economic crises, particularly crippling ones, such as the crash of 2008, create their own fortuitous dynamics and offer a rare opportunity to challenge established orthodoxies, think outside the box, put in place much-needed reforms, and, occasionally, profoundly restructure the economy. In the United States the panic of 1907 led to the Federal Reserve Act of 1913 and the creation of the Federal Reserve as the central bank. The Great Depression of the 1930s was the catalyst behind the Glass-Steagall Act, which established the Federal Deposit Insurance Corporation and the separation of commercial and investment banking. More recently, the crisis in the late 1980s led to the enactment of the Federal Deposit Insurance Corporation Improvement Act (FDICIA) of 1991, which established more clear standards for bank supervision, regulation, and capital requirements.

Seen through this prism, there is much truth in former Chief of Staff to President Obama, Rahm Emanuel's quip that "you never want a serious crisis to go to waste." Traumatic events like a financial crisis often mark critical junctures "when old relationships crumble and new ones have to be constructed" (Gourevitch 1986, 9). To Emanuel, the crash of 2008 offered a rare moment. The call for immediate and unambiguous action by an anxious public and a fluid political environment provided an opportunity to rise above the debilitating partisan gridlock of Washington, D.C. and implement far-reaching policy and institutional reforms that the president had been advocating. Indeed, as discussed in Chapter 2, the Obama administration took advantage of this opportunity to put in place a series of legislation designed to jump-start the stalled economy and reform the financial sector.

However, such moments are not readily available to those who are tasked to innovate and reform the global economic order – or in legalese, to build a resilient and balanced international economic and financial architecture. The anarchic and capricious nature of the international system, the cumbersome and frustratingly protracted and often self-serving nature of negotiations between sovereign states, the fact that major stakeholders often have divergent and competing interests and agendas, and that the ambitions of some exceed their capabilities, make common purpose difficult. As Charles Kindleberger (1973, 291), in his masterful study of the economic cataclysm of another era, *The Great Depression of 1929*, compellingly pointed out, "The 1929 depression was so wide, so deep, and so long because the international economic system was rendered unstable by British inability and U.S. unwillingness to assume responsibility for stabilizing it." Kindleberger left a poignant reminder that the absence of global leadership, in particular, failure by the emerging global hegemon (the United States) to assume the mantle of leadership, can make international economic cooperation exceedingly difficult, even in hard and uncertain times.

As it was back then, the world again finds itself in the unenviable situation marked by a conspicuous absence of a global leadership (in the form of an unrivaled hegemon or a consortium of nations) working in tandem to deal with common challenges. The relations between the United States and its main geopolitical rival, China, is one of growing distrust and strategic contention. As Friedberg (2011) has deftly noted, failure to achieve a meaningful entente between these two adversaries is not due to lack of effort, but because of fundamental divergence of interests. Moreover, like fascism in the 1930s, an illiberal authoritarian-capitalist alternative to Western liberalism is already ascendant. Halper has aptly noted that emerging states "are learning to combine market economics with traditional autocratic or semi-autocratic politics in a process that signals an intellectual rejection of the Western economic model."[1] Kagan (2006; 2012); Khanna (2008); Lieber (2007), Mandelbaum (2005; 2010), Meltzer (2008); Rachman (2011), and others have warned that as U.S. primacy wanes so too will the norms, principles, and institutions that the United States fashioned and has so doggedly championed for the past six decades, including a global free-market economy, international institutional cooperation, democracy promotion, and great-power peace. They reiterate

---

[1] Quoted in Ikenberry (2011, 57).

that the U.S.-led international order was fundamentally multilateralist in that the United States did not seek to exploit its preponderant position in a zero-sum fashion. Although the United States did not always abide by multilateral rules, this immensely powerful state created open institutions to which it bound itself and agreed to play by the rules it asked others to accept. In so doing, the U.S. hegemon exercised unprecedented self-restraint and, more often than not, magnanimously complied with the many inconvenient restrictions placed on its prerogatives. It was the hegemon's nonthreatening and accommodating posture that made the U.S.-led international order unique in world history.

However, as the post-war order gradually transforms (and unravels), the work of stabilizing the international economic order is becoming exceedingly difficult. A fatigued and diminished Pax Americana, lacking both political will and economic wherewithal, the European Union preoccupied with its own existential challenges, and a rising and neo-mercantilist China seemingly torn between engagement, quiescence, isolation, and committed to a "China only" strategy is not yet ready or willing to fill the vacuum. This underscores that the post-United States world system lacks a pivotal actor (the United States between 1945 and 1980) or a concert of nations (in the form of the G-7) capable and willing to assume global leadership to facilitate and enforce a stable and relatively consensual rule-based international order essential to global stability and for cooperative and peaceful trade and commerce to thrive.

The assertion that the broad-based and more inclusive G-20 (a pantheon of the world's 20 richest nations) will fill the void is turning out to be overly optimistic. Although the G-20 can speak with one voice, its ability to act with singular purpose is greatly circumscribed because the organization is too institutionally weak and encompasses too many competing interests and agendas to act in unison and with effect. The stark reality is that the current international order, characterized by widening economic multipolarity, an increasingly weary and ambivalent United States, a neo-mercantilist and palpably emboldened China, and a fragmented and divided EU lacks judicious and consequential leadership to deal with the world's many political and economic challenges. If history is a guide, this vacuum warns of not a return to halcyon days of post-war reciprocal multilateralism (which, after all, proved successful because the United States functioned as the first among equals), but of inconclusive short-term realignments at both global and regional levels with a real potential for fissures to morph into egregious zero-sum competitions. This does not augur well for multilateral cooperation, international peace and stability.

"Cooperation" in Hard Times

A large body of scholarship has long contended that the ubiquitous linkages spawned by the inexorable forces of globalization provide strong and irresistible incentives for programmatic collaboration between nation states. Robert Keohane (1984), in his celebrated *After Hegemony*, claimed that cooperation, at least among the advanced capitalist economies, is possible even in the absence of a hegemon. This is because the vacuum is ably filled by multilateral institutions, or "international regimes" through which sovereign states give consent to cooperate with each other. To Keohane, perspicacious global leadership and discrete international regimes are not poor substitutes for raw power; they are ubiquitous mechanisms for facilitating cooperation among "egoistic actors" in an increasingly interconnected and integrated world. In a similar vein, Webb (1995) has noted that expanding economic and financial interdependence has generated a dramatic increase in international monetary coordination in the post-war period.

More recently, Ikenberry (2003, 540) has argued that "as global economic interdependence grows, so does the need for multilateral coordination of policies." He adds that the institutions and norms of "liberal internationalism" (that is, a commitment to open and rule-based global order) are too deeply entrenched and too beneficial to all major players to be made redundant any time soon. With deeper institutionalization, multilateral bodies will be able to produce broadly coordinated and coherent policy responses to both domestic and global economic problems. Ikenberry (2011, 57) unequivocally concludes that "the liberal international order is alive and well. The struggle over international order today is not about fundamental principles. China and other emerging great powers do not want to contest the basic rules and principles of the liberal international order: they wish to gain more authority and leadership within it." Similarly, Zakaria (2008) claims that even as the balance of economic power shifts against the United States, rising powers, and in particular, China will be compelled to operate within the framework of the current liberal international order. However, such viewpoints tend to overlook some inconvenient truths.

First, as Bremmer (2010) and others have pointed out, the peculiar Chinese variant of state capitalism epitomized by the highly centralized and interventionist *guanxi* (network) capitalism top-down Leninist management and, control of the commanding heights of the economy, informal and opaque relationships between the party-state and private networks, and state sponsorship of compliant and "strategic" private business interests is intrinsically incompatible with the competitive and rules-based liberal global economic order.[2] It is plausible that Beijing would want to change the current "rules of the game" once it is in a position to do so (Friedberg 2011). Of course, it is difficult to know whether China's current willingness to play by the rules, or at least tolerate them, is purely strategic and utilitarian, or because it is has become a responsible stakeholder.

Second, no doubt, multilateral cooperation both during and following the global financial crisis has been exemplary, with regular formal summitry comprising heads of states of the G-20, coupled with numerous high-level ministerial meetings involving the IMF, the World Bank, the UN, and related multilateral organizations. Yet, even as these gatherings have produced volumes of official (and occasionally imaginative) statements and declarations, not to mention seductively raising expectations, their actual accomplishments have been disappointing. The G-20 has failed to make real progress on any substantive economic issues that divide the key players. In hindsight, even the solidarity and cooperation demonstrated during those perilous days in the midst of the crisis now seems to be uncomfortably tangential and improvised – unlike the broad and sustained transnational cooperation and collective engagement (under unquestioned yet indulgent U.S. leadership) that marked the creation and subsequent support of the rule-based Bretton Woods system. In fact, it is hard not to be cynical and conclude that the seemingly broad international economic cooperation to mitigate the impact of the financial crisis was dictated primarily by collective fear, and the purposeful large-scale coordinated policy responses such as the currency-swap agreements, interest-rate cuts, and the expansionary fiscal programs introduced by central banks around the world owed less to enthusiastic multilateralism than to narrow and scrupulous short-term national self-interest. And what explains the IMF's new lease on life? After all, the institution not too long ago was deemed redundant. Could the absence of a global hegemon, or even a concert of powers, to assume leadership explain why governments around the world, including the United States, have been only too happy to pass the buck and abdicate responsibility in favor of multilateral bodies such as the G-20, the IMF, and others?

Although liberal internationalists appropriately point out that multilateral institutions and quotidian norms and procedures facilitate global cooperation on many issues at many levels (including during the crash of 2008), their overall assessment regarding the efficacy of multilateral cooperation in effectively addressing contentious economic issues in the post-crisis world seems unduly sanguine. This is not only because their assumption

---

[2] The term "*guanxi*" or network capitalism is also used by McNally (2011).

that liberal norms and institutions have now become universal and are the natural order is exaggerated, but also because complex and contentious multilateral economic coordination and implementation do require effective global leadership – something sorely lacking in what Bremmer and Roubini (2011, 2) have aptly eulogized as the current rudderless "G-Zero world, one in which no single country or bloc of countries has the political and economic leverage – or the will – to drive a truly international agenda."

Perhaps more than anything else, liberal internationalists fail to fully appreciate that the exigencies of domestic (or national) political economy can hinder and undermine effective multilateral cooperation. This problem is particularly acute in today's world. Specifically, correcting the massive global economic imbalances – a major source of domestic economic and structural distortions and an underlying cause of the financial crisis – will not be easy to resolve as the structural roots that gave rise to and have sustained the global imbalances remain intact. Both the borrowing or "deficit" countries (the United States, the United Kingdom, and several eurozone members), and the lending or "surplus" countries (China, Germany, and Japan) will have to first make deep (and painful) domestic structural adjustments in their economies if this problem is to be mitigated. To date, they have tended to blame each other or push the burden on others.

Rebalancing is Hard

The seemingly intractable policy disagreements on rebalancing between the major economic powers underscore the fact that economic rebalancing defies quick fixes. Nobel laureate Michael Spence (2011), in *The Next Convergence*, points out that rebalancing will be exceedingly difficult because the deep structural changes in the domestic and global economy over the last two decades have created a divergence in growth and employment patterns. In the case of the United States, growth and employment has become highly dependent on domestic demand. Spence compellingly shows that between 1990 and 2008 the U.S. economy created 27 million jobs. However, 98 percent were in the non-tradable sectors of the economy, such as the public sector, health care, services, hospitality, and construction. Growth in the tradable sector (manufactured goods for exports and services), was essentially negligible as just 600,000 new jobs were created – much of that in high-end tradable service jobs in finance and information technology. By sharply curbing U.S. domestic demand, the financial crisis has negatively impacted job growth in the non-tradable sector – a problem that will persist in the foreseeable future. In fact, evidence points to a growing problem of job polarization and hollowing out of employment opportunities. Autor (2010) and Jaimovich and Siu (2012) point out that over the past two decades the U.S. economy has increased its demand for high-skilled and high-wage workers and low-skilled and low-wage workers, but demand for the large pool of middle-skilled and middle-wage workers has not only stagnated but declined.

Consumption and spending binges in the United States have been fueled by the availability of cheap credit, facilitated by massive low-interest borrowing from abroad, especially China. This borrowing has resulted in unprecedented levels of public and private debt. In December 2000, the national debt stood at $5.66 trillion. In December 2008, the debt stood at $10.7 trillion, and in March 2010, the gross national debt was more than $13 trillion. As of September 2012, U.S. national debt (the sum of all outstanding debt owed by the federal government) stood at slightly more than $16 trillion. Nearly two-thirds is public debt (owed to the people, businesses, and foreign governments who purchased Treasury bills, notes, and bonds), and the remaining one-third, or $4.74 trillion, are intra-governmental holdings. As of July 2012, some $5.3 trillion or about 48 percent of debt held by the public was owned by foreigners – with China and Japan holding some $1.1 trillion each. According to the nonpartisan Congressional Budget Office (CBO 2012), if the current trajectory is not reversed, by 2020, the annual interest owed on U.S. debt will approach $1 trillion, or roughly 21 percent of projected federal revenue for that year. Undoubtedly, without a meaningful resolution of these structural problems, the United States will continue to remain the world's biggest borrower and largest debtor – with adverse implications for economic growth and job creation.

Reinhart and Rogoff (2009) have warned that when a nation's gross debt reaches 90 percent of its economy, it usually loses about one percentage point of growth a year. In the United States and many other advanced economies, gross debt is either very close or already over this threshold. The U.S. debt has already surpassed 100 percent of GDP – three years before the IMF's (2011h) prediction that U.S. national debt would reach 100 percent of GDP by 2015. This means that the United States needs to reduce its deficit by the equivalent of 12 percent of GDP. On the other hand, Greece, in the midst of a wrenching financial crisis in 2008, needed to reduce its structural deficit by just 9 percent of GDP.

Reducing the distortions in the U.S. economy will not be easy. For starters, Washington must simultaneously tighten fiscal policy to bring its national debt under control, and sharply reduce its large trade deficit to boost growth and generate employment. For the latter, Washington will have to effectively convince its major trading partners (in particular, China) to stop currency manipulation in order to allow the dollar to regain a competitive edge. Spence (2011) argues that, in the short term, the key to reducing these imbalances is through income redistribution, namely tax reform (in particular, taxing consumption more than investment, including giving a "tax holiday" to corporations on their foreign earnings to encourage them to repatriate those earnings back to the U.S.), and targeted and sustained government spending on education and infrastructure – which he argues is essential to boost productivity. In the long term, the key is to reinvigorate the tradable sector, especially the country's manufacturing base, by creating manufacturing jobs that pay competitive wages and benefits. Indeed, President Obama's Presidential Commission on Fiscal Responsibility and Reform, co-chaired by the former senator Republican Alan Simpson as well as President Clinton's former chief of staff, Erskine Bowles, offered a broad proposal to rebalance the U.S. economy (the Commission's report was released in November 2010). The proposal recommended, among other things, (1) $200 billion reduction per year in discretionary spending, (2) $100 billion in increased tax revenues with a 15-cent-per-gallon gasoline tax and the cancelation of tax deductions like the home mortgage interest deduction, (3) maintenance of the Obamacare Medicare cost controls with a possible public option for health-care reform, (4) raising the retirement age for Social Security, (5) raising the payroll tax, but cutting the corporate tax rate from 35 percent to 26 percent, and (6) reducing or replacing the tax expenditures such as preferential tax rates for capital gains and dividends and deductions for state and local taxes with progressive tax credits to generate revenue to eventually reduce rate for all taxpayers. The fact that even the modest Simpson-Bowles proposal was rejected by members of both parties underscores how hard it is to arrive at an agreement on these issues. Domestic rebalancing entails making painful political and economic choices, in particular, which sectors and groups will bear the heaviest burden. If a prudent fiscal policy means a simultaneous increase in tax revenue and deep cuts to entitlements, both the public and the nation's law makers (Democrat and Republican), remain so deeply divided that even a broad consensus on principle remains elusive.

As discussed in Chapter 6, internal and external rebalancing by China, the world's leading surplus economy, will not be easy. Beijing's difficulty is compounded by the possibility that China may be entering into a prolonged period of low growth rates due to the "middle income trap" – a twilight zone where countries are neither able to compete with low-wage countries in basic tradable goods, nor with the advanced high-wage countries in technology-intensive goods and services.[3] Specifically, the sharp rise in China's labor and production costs is making it much harder for Chinese businesses to compete with countries with much lower labor and production costs (Ahuja et al. 2012). China is not only losing global market share in tradable goods, its once overwhelmingly complementary trading relations with other countries are increasingly becoming competitive.[4] Moreover, Eichengreen, Park, and Shin (2011) demonstrate that growth rates of rapidly growing economies decline on average by 2 percent per annum once per-capita income reaches about $17,000 in purchasing power parity (PPP) dollars. China is already close to that threshold. This means that China can no longer expect double-digit growth in GDP – when it did experience such growth rates, after all, that was largely due to its competitive advantage in low-cost manufacturing. Moreover, it remains to be seen if China's manufacturing sector, which is dominated by large (and not very profitable or efficient) state-owned enterprises are agile enough to innovate and become globally competitive. Certainly, China's ability to move up the economic and technological value chain is constrained by the country's institutional weakness, which does not allow for a smooth transition into the ranks of the high-income countries. Preoccupation with such daunting domestic challenges will make resolving the outstanding China-U.S. trade and currency imbalances even more testy and difficult.

China's twelfth five-year plan calls for a decisive internal rebalancing away from export-led growth toward greater reliance on domestic demand via greater household consumption, but translating such goals into reality will be painful and difficult. While some see the recent drop in China's current account surplus (as a share of GDP) as evidence that rebalancing is already at work, such conclusions may be premature. Indeed, closer inspection suggests caution. IMF research has persuasively shown that the fall in China's current account surplus is largely due to high levels of investment, a tepid

---

[3] According to Woo's (2012) "catch-up index" (CUI), China became a middle-income country in 2007–2008. It now faces "five major types of middle-income trap" vulnerabilities:

(a) fiscal stress from the nonperforming loans generated by the interaction between the lending practices of the state banks and the innate desire by state enterprise managers to over-invest and embezzle; (b) the frequent use of macro-stabilization tools that hurt long-term productivity growth; (c) flaws in socio-political governance that exacerbate social tensions; (d) ineffective management of environmental challenges that threaten sustainable development; and (e) inept handling of international economic tensions that could unleash trade conflict (pp. 13–14).

[4] As Krugman (1993) has pointed out, deeper trade integration can also trigger greater specialization of production, resulting in less synchronization of business cycles. This is already happening in China's trade with East Asia.

global demand, and an increase in prices for commodity imports that has outpaced the rise in prices for manufactured goods (Ahuja et al. 2012). The reality is that rebalancing the Chinese economy away from its export dependence (given that its manufactured export sector has been the engine of the country's economy for the past several decades), is easier said than done. Not only will domestic rebalancing entail huge social costs such as short-term job losses and the resultant mass protests that worry political elites, but vested interests, including powerful regional and local elites in the sprawling export zones of China's wealthy coastal provinces, have every incentive to stifle unfavorable central directives. In fact, there is no consensus within the Chinese leadership on either internal or external rebalancing, but the rich coastal provinces, whose economies are based on the export of manufactured goods, are strongly opposed to any such adjustment. Of course, Beijing can expedite external rebalancing by simply allowing the RMB to appreciate – which many see as a prerequisite to resolving the problem (Goldstein and Lardy 2009). The fact that Beijing has refused to do this and continued relying on exchange-rate undervaluation and intervention in foreign-exchange markets to promote exports underscores how difficult rebalancing will be. Not surprisingly, Chinn, Eichengreen, and Ito (2012) predict that the economic imbalances between China and the United States will soon reemerge.

At a minimum, fixing the global imbalances will require cooperative, coordinated, and sustained policy response over years – not only by the United States and China but also the other important players. However, the key deficit and surplus countries continue to pursue and engage in economic policies that are in direct conflict with each other, with China engaging in a particularly insidious race to the bottom (Ferguson and Schularick 2011). This seemingly zero-sum action carries huge risks because it can trigger a disorderly unwinding of the global imbalances. That is, if and when global markets are no longer willing to continue financing U.S. debt, a sell-off of dollar assets and a sharp rise in U.S. interest rates could be triggered – with grave implications for the global economy as the spillover effects would be huge and disastrous. As the following sections illustrate, the G-20 in its current form is simply not up to the task to effectively diffuse this simmering conflict and advance multilateral economic cooperation. In fact, The G-20 has no effective levers to stop competing national interests from pushing against genuine multilateral cooperation. The current decentralized and fragmented international monetary and financial system lacks an effective mechanism or a "neutral" arbiter (like the United States during the Bretton Woods era) to ensure that what each country does to advance its own self-interest does not hurt the collective.

The G-20's Reform Agenda: On Paper

In November 2008 the G-20 held its first summit in Washington, D.C. to address the financial crisis. In a show of solemn solidarity and resolve, the G-20 unanimously agreed that it was time for a "new Bretton Woods" that would be capable of stabilizing financial markets and jump-starting global economic growth. To boost global market confidence, the G-20 cut interest rates, increased liquidity in the financial system, and agreed to increase financial resources for international financial institutions, in particular the IMF.

The G-20 knew that boosting confidence in the financial markets was critical. They were also cognizant of the fact that shielding national and global financial systems from recurrent bouts of speculative excesses and sharp economic contractions was not going to be easy given the deep financial internationalization of markets. After all, the crisis had painfully underscored that not only were the existing international regulatory and supervisory agencies lagging far behind market innovations, but these regulatory bodies had to be significantly strengthened if they were to be effective. In order to reduce market distortions and improve transparency and risk management, the supervisory and regulatory frameworks not only needed more transparent disclosure and reporting rules but also had to be coordinated at the global level to ensure effective macro-prudential supervision. Only such comprehensive harmonization of national and international regulations and the consolidation of surveillance and supervision would make implementation and enforcement much easier as it would reduce incentives for banks and financial institutions to move their operations off-shore to more lax jurisdictions.

To this effect, the G-20 unveiled an ambitious regulatory reform agenda complete with a detailed plan for immediate and medium-term action. This included, among other items: (1) strengthening transparency and accountability, (2) enhancing sound regulation, (3) promoting integrity in financial markets, (4) strengthening international cooperation, and (5) reforming the international financial institutions. At the April 2009 London Summit, the G-20 agreed to "empower" international bodies, including the IMF, the Bank for International Settlements, and various "standard setting" bodies such as the Basel Committee on Banking Supervision (BCBS), the International Organization of Securities Commissions, the International Association of Insurance Supervisors, and the International Accounting Standards Board. Specifically, the G-20 pledged some $5 trillion in fiscal stimulus spending over two years and to increase funding for the IMF and the other multilateral development banks by $1.1 trillion, including tripling the IMF's lending capacity to $850 billion. In a bold move, the G-20 also agreed to transfer about 6 percent of voting power within the IMF to "dynamic emerging-market and developing countries" by the end of 2012. This meant that China would become the IMF's third-largest shareholder – behind the United States and Japan, but ahead of Germany, France, and Great Britain. The BCBS was assigned responsibility for reaching agreement on new capital and liquidity standards, and the Financial Stability Forum (renamed the Financial Stability Board, or FSB, expanded to include all G-20 members) was made into a permanent institution with the powers to report directly to G-20 finance ministers on issues pertaining to regulatory reform and implementation. The FSB was also given primary responsibility for coordinating the actions agreed upon by the G-20. Finally, the G-20 adopted the Declaration on Strengthening the Financial System or G-20 Action Plan, consisting of "47 concrete measures designed to reform all systemically important financial institutions and instruments based on five principles": strengthening transparency and accountability; enhancing sound regulation; promoting integrity in financial markets; reinforcing international cooperation; and reforming international financial institutions. Table 10.1 provides an overview of the core regulatory measures.

At the G-20 Summit in Pittsburgh (September 24–25, 2009), the host – an enthusiastic President Obama – boldly declared that "from now on the Group of 20 will be the primary organization responsible for coordinating global economic policy." British Prime Minister Gordon Brown was even more ebullient, noting that "the old system of international economic cooperation is over. The new system, as of today, has begun... the G-20 is now the premier economic organization for dealing with economic management around the world."[5] With these lofty endorsements, the G-20 formally took over the responsibilities that had been for decades the purview of an elite club made up of the world's wealthiest countries – the G-7 and, more recently, the G-8.[6] Viewed as a far more representative body as

---

[5]   "Leaders' Statement: The Pittsburgh Summit," September 24–25, 2009, http://www.pitts-burghsummit.gov/mediacenter/129639.htm

[6]   The G-7 was formed in 1976, when Canada became a member of the then-Group of Six countries which included France, Germany, Italy, Japan, United Kingdom, and the United States. The G-7 provides a venue for each country to get together, sometimes several times a year, to discuss and formulate macroeconomic policies. The G-8 is different in the sense it was created to allow the heads of governments of the G-7 plus Russia to meet annually and discuss pressing issues of the day. The G-20, created in 1999, includes Argentina, Australia, Brazil, Canada, China, France, Germany, India, Indonesia, Italy, Japan, Mexico, Russia, Saudi Arabia, South Africa, South Korea, Turkey, the United Kingdom, the United States, and one representative of the current EU council. In total, the G-20 represents around 90 percent of global gross national product, 80 percent of world trade (including trade within the European Union), and two-thirds of the world's population.

Table 10.1. *The G-20 "Declaration on strengthening the financial system"*

Financial Stability Board
- Establish, as a successor to the Financial Stability Forum (FSF), a new Financial Stability Board with greater capacity, expanded participation, and a stronger mandate for promoting financial stability

International cooperation
- Complete the creation of supervisory colleges for significant cross-border firms in 2009
- Implement the FSF principles for cross-border crisis management
- Support efforts to develop an international framework for cross-border bank resolution

Prudential regulation
- Maintain current international standards for minimum capital levels until recovery is assured, but then strengthen them
- Once recovery is assured, increase buffers above regulatory minimums, enhance the quality of capital, and develop guidelines for the harmonization of the definition of capital and for minimum capital levels internationally
- Implement recommendations to mitigate procyclicality, including anticyclical buffers
- Supplement risk-based capital requirements with an appropriate leverage ratio
- Improve incentives for risk management of securitization
- Progressively adopt the Basel II capital framework in all G-20 countries
- Develop a global framework for promoting stronger liquidity buffers at financial institutions

Scope of regulation
- Amend regulatory systems for macro-prudential risks and develop suitable tools for controlling such risks
- Ensure that national regulators are able to gather relevant information on all material financial institutions, markets, and instruments to assess systemic risk
- Produce guidelines for assessing whether a financial institution, market, or instrument is systemically important
- Require that hedge funds be registered and subject to oversight, including through disclosure to supervisors
- Require that institutions with hedge funds as counterparties have effective risk management
- Establish central clearing counterparties for credit derivatives that are subject to regulation
- Regularly review boundaries of the regulatory framework and promote good international practices

Compensation
- Endorse and ensure significant progress in implementing the FSF principles on pay and compensation in significant financial institutions by the 2009 remuneration round
- Require supervisors to monitor firms' compensation policies and intervene where necessary

(*continued*)

Table 10.1. *(continued)*

Tax havens and non-cooperative jurisdictions
- Encourage all jurisdictions to adhere to international standards on combating tax evasion, money laundering, and terrorist financing
- Develop a toolbox of effective countermeasures for non-cooperative jurisdictions

Accounting standards
- Reduce the complexity of standards for financial instruments and improve standards for provisioning, off-balance-sheet exposures, and valuation uncertainty
- Strengthen accounting recognition of loan loss provisions by including more credit information
- Achieve clarity and consistency in the application of valuation standards internationally
- Make progress toward a single set of global accounting standards
- Improve the involvement of stakeholders in the process of setting accounting standards

Credit rating agencies
- Subject all credit rating agencies whose ratings are used for regulatory purposes to oversight that includes registration and is consistent with the International Organization of Securities Commissions (IOSCO) Code of Conduct Fundamentals
- Ensure that national authorities enforce compliance by credit rating agencies and require changes to their practices when needed
- Require that credit rating agencies differentiate ratings for structured products and provide full disclosure of their ratings track record and the information and assumptions underpinning the rating process
- Review the role of external ratings in prudential regulation and address any adverse incentives

---

Source: Stephanou (2009, 2) and G-20. 2009. "Declaration on Strengthening the Financial System, London, 2 April 2009," http://www.londonsummit.gov.uk/resources/en/news/15766232/communique-020409

it includes countries from all regions of the world (and which together constitute some 90 percent of global gross national product, 80 percent of world trade, and more than two-thirds of the world's population), the G-20 was seen as better equipped to resolve common challenges in the global age.[7]

In Pittsburgh, the G-20 unveiled yet another plan to promote growth by launching the Framework for Strong, Sustainable and Balanced Growth. The core of this framework is a multilateral process through which G-20 hopes

---

[7] The European Union is represented by the rotating council presidency and the European Central Bank. In addition, the managing director of the IMF and the president of the World Bank, plus the chairs of the International Monetary and Financial Committee and Development Committee of the IMF and World Bank, also participate in G-20 meetings on an ex-officio basis.

to identify objectives for the global economy, the set of policies needed to reach them, and the progress toward meeting these shared objectives – the so-called Mutual Assessment Process (MAP). At the G-20's request, the IMF agreed to provide the technical analysis needed to evaluate how members' policies fit together, and whether, collectively, they can achieve the G-20's goals. Again, at the Seoul Summit (November 2010), the G-20 committed to work with "greater resolve" in addressing global imbalances and reached broad agreement on a set of indicators and guidelines to identify what constitutes "large and persistent imbalances." At the November 2011 Summit in Cannes, the G-20 announced the Cannes Action Plan for Growth and Jobs, and reiterated their support for measures to deal with the eurozone debt problems, strengthening financial regulation, and better managing capital flows.

Certainly, the collective purpose and unity the G-20 demonstrated in responding to the financial crisis and post-crisis developments, including coordinating stimulus programs to jump-start the global economy, synchronizing regulatory reforms to correct distortions in their financial systems, reforming the IMF's governance to include more emerging economies in decision making, and rejecting protectionist policies in favor of balanced and sustainable growth based on free trade, underscore the organization's coming of age and commitment to collective purpose. However, much of these bold measures have yet to be implemented. For example, implementation of the new Basel III standards to strengthen global banking, which the G-20 could have put into effect immediately, has been put off until 2019. The fact is that the G-20 has no formal adjudicating and enforcement mechanism. All agreements passed by the G-20 are done so via consensus, and all agreed-upon "commitments" are nonbinding. In fact, the G-20 does not even have a formal voting system. Therefore, it is very difficult to gauge members' views on particular issues. Given the fact that the G-20's recommendations depend on solicitous peer-pressure and voluntary implementation, governments can cherry pick policies they want enforced. Not surprisingly, Truman (2011, 1) bluntly concludes "that the G-20's journey involved some useful mutual education, but not much in terms of concrete accomplishments." And, with reference to the latest G-20 summit in Los Cabos, Mexico in 2012, Goodliffe and Sberro (2012, 1) note "the diminishing effectiveness and relevance of the G20 as an organ of international governance."

Return of the Divide

Despite the bonhomie, it was only a matter of time before the simmering divisions within the G-20 began to manifest. When the G-20 met in

Seoul in November 2010, the unity and camaraderie so much on display in Pittsburgh had all but vanished. Instead, the old rifts and fault-lines among the world's major economies, among the advanced economies and between the advanced and emerging economies, resurfaced with a vengeance.[8] Despite the by G-20 leaders' rhetorical attempts to put a positive spin on it, the summit ended on a sour note, that is, in acrimony, with heightened divisions over issues of trade and currency.[9] The failure at Seoul was a particularly stinging rebuke to President Obama, who had hoped the Summit would vindicate his "shared jobs agenda" – a goal he saw as "in the interest of all nations." Instead, in Seoul, the U.S. president was on the defensive: first reeling from the failure of the United States and South Korea to conclude a free-trade pact (both sides have been working on this for years), and then seeing the summit reject his jobs agenda and refuse to take a tough line against China's alleged currency manipulation.[10] The *Wall Street Journal* sarcastically asked: "Has there ever been a major economic summit where a U.S. President and his Treasury Secretary were as thoroughly rebuffed as they were at this week's G-20 meeting in Seoul? We can't think of one. President Obama failed to achieve any of his main goals while getting pounded by other world leaders for failing U.S. policies and lagging growth."[11]

To some, the United States' mounting financial woes and eroding influence on the international stage, especially in the economic realm, explains the G-20's rebuff of Obama.[12] Dominique Strauss-Kahn (then the IMF's managing director), noted that the rejection of U.S. proposals was due to

---

[8] Philipp Wittrock. 2010. "Adrift in Seoul: Bickering Likely to Lame G-20 Summit in Seoul, Korea," *Der Spiegel*, 11 November, http://www.spiegel.de/international/world/0,1518,728527,00.html (accessed, January 15, 2011).

[9] Vijay Joshi. 2010. "G-20 Refuses to Back US Push on China's Currency," *Associated Press*, November 12, http://news.yahoo.com/s/ap/as_economic_summits/print (accessed, November 15, 2010). For details on the agreements reached at Seoul, see The G-20 Seoul Summit, *G-20 Seoul Communique: Leaders Declaration*, November 11–12. To be fair, the G-20 did agree on a "Basel III" designed to raise the quality and quantity of bank capital, including giving the Financial Stability Board the authority to tighten supervision of the over-the-counter derivatives market and to reduce reliance on credit rating agencies.

[10] The U.S.-South Korea trade pact collapsed largely because one of President Obama's strongest constituencies, the U.S. auto industry and its labor unions, were opposed to the deal because they felt that the U.S. auto industry was denied fair access into the Korean markets, whereas South Korea was given unfettered access to the U.S. market.

[11] "Embarrassment in Seoul," 2010, *Wall Street Journal*, November 13, http://online.wsj.com/article/SB10001424052748704462704575609770024501384.html.

[12] Ben Feller and Erica Werner. 2010. "Obama's Asian Trip Shows Limits on Global Stage," *Associated Press*, November 14, http://news.yahoo.com/s/ap/20101114/ap_on_bi_ge/us_obama_asia/print (accessed, November 16, 2010).

the fact that "the United States tried to push an idea too fast, at a time when the foundation for cooperation is not as strong as it was during the crisis in 2008–09." He points out that this is not surprising as countries usually come together to protect the global economy in times of great stress, but such cooperation usually diminishes during the recovery phase.[13] The *Wall Street Journal* blamed the Obama administration for the "embarrassment" in Seoul, stating:

Rather than leading the world from a position of strength, Mr. Obama and Treasury Secretary Timothy Geithner came to Seoul blaming the rest of the world for U.S. economic weakness. America's problem, in their view, is the export and exchange rate policies of the Germans, Chinese or Brazilians. And the U.S. solution is to have the Fed print enough money to devalue the dollar so America can grow by stealing demand from the rest of the world. But why should anyone heed this U.S. refrain? The Germans are growing rapidly after having rejected Mr. Geithner's advice in 2009 to join the U.S. stimulus spending blowout. China is also growing smartly having rejected counsel from three U.S. Administrations to abandon its currency discipline. The U.K. and even France are pursuing more fiscal restraint. Only the Obama Administration is determined to keep both the fiscal and monetary spigots wide open, while blaming everyone else for the poor domestic results.[14]

At the heart of President Obama's ambitious jobs agenda was creating a "level playing field" for U.S. exporters. According to Washington, there were two steps to achieving this. First, Beijing must stop its policy of deliberately keeping its currency artificially undervalued, and second, a number of G-20 members, in particular China, must work harder to rebalance their economies or limit their trade surpluses with the United States. In fact, Washington even went to the trouble of proposing specific targets regarding how much a country's current accounts of trade and capital could go into either surplus or deficit, noting that excesses of one or the other could lead to economic instability.[15] The first consideration was particularly critical to Washington, and it was widely known that the Obama administration wanted to make the issue of the undervalued yuan the focal point of G-20 deliberations. The United States, along with other countries, has long

[13] "IMF Chief says US Pushed too Fast at G20," 2010. *The Economic Times*, November 14, http://economictimes.indiatimes.com/articleshow/6919857.cms?prtpage=1 (accessed, November 16, 2010).

[14] "Embarrassment in Seoul," 2010, *Wall Street Journal*, November 13, http://online.wsj.com/article/SB10001424052748704462704575609770024501384.html (accessed, November 15, 2010).

[15] The U. S. suggested that current account surpluses/deficits be capped or limited to 4 percent of GDP.

accused Beijing for deliberately manipulating the yuan at an artificially weak rate to give China an unfair trade advantage.[16]

To Washington, Beijing's neo-mercantilist "cheap yuan" policy cost the United States jobs because by moving production to China, business could take advantage of low labor costs, while the undervalued yuan helped Chinese exporters by making their products less expensive in the United States – thereby eliminating thousands of U.S. jobs. The Obama administration found this unacceptable when U.S. unemployment was stuck at 9.6 percent. Indeed, the president made no secret of his frustration with the slow pace of Beijing's moves to strengthen the value of its currency. If to the White House, the pace of the yuan's appreciation has been too slow and the extent of appreciation too limited, to a growing number of Congressional critics, Beijing is not serious about fixing its overvalued currency – reflected in the fact that the yuan has increased in value by about 1.5 percent since Beijing stopped tying its currency to the U.S. dollar in July 2009. Moreover, Beijing's critics have long pointed out that a stronger or market-determined yuan would encourage Chinese firms to sell more to their own consumers, instead of unduly relying on U.S. and other foreign consumers to buy low-priced Chinese goods. In addition, it would help reduce the U.S. trade deficit with China which in mid-November 2010 stood at an estimated US$268 billion. This did not include the $2.6 trillion China held in foreign-currency reserves.[17]

Contrary to expectations, the leading G-20 economies, including Germany and Japan, refused to back Washington's demand to cajole (and privately arm-twist) Beijing into boosting its currency's value by transitioning to a market-based system.[18] Instead, the G-20 pledged to refrain from "competitive devaluation" of currencies, shunning the Obama administration's wording of "competitive undervaluation" because adopting it would mean explicitly pointing a finger at China's currency policy.

[16] Beijing does this by intervening actively in foreign-exchange markets to prevent its currency from appreciating more quickly by selling the RMB and buying other major currencies (mostly U.S. dollars). This means that Beijing spends enormous amounts of money intervening in the market to keep its currency undervalued.

[17] Of course, a stronger yuan would not only avoid a potential trade war with the United States, it would also help rebalance the disproportionately skewed export-dependent Chinese economy toward domestic consumption – something that Beijing desperately wants. The problem is that a stronger yuan will harm China's exports and thereby job creation.

[18] Just days earlier, U.S. Treasury Secretary Tim Geithner had mentioned that differences between the United States and many G-20 members were "exaggerated" and that he was confident to see a strong consensus in Seoul.

To rub salt into the wound, Beijing charged that the United States was itself engaging in a subtle form of currency manipulation via the U.S. Federal Reserve's easy-money policy. Specifically, Beijing claimed that the Fed's announcement on November 3, 2010 that it was planning to phase in the second round of Quantitative Easing over an eight-month period "if circumstances warranted it" by pumping an additional $600 billion into the U.S. economy was implicitly (and surreptitiously) designed to weaken the dollar to boost the competitiveness of U.S. exports.[19] Similarly, Germany's finance minister Wolfgang Schauble accused the Americans of hypocrisy: "It's inconsistent for the Americans to accuse the Chinese of manipulating exchange rates and then to artificially depress the dollar exchange rate by printing money."[20]

These views resonated with most G-20 members. As *The Economist* aptly noted, "The Fed's policy of 'quantitative easing' contributed to a qualitative hardening of tone among the summiteers."[21] Preoccupied with this issue, the countries made no progress on determining how to reduce the widening gap between nations running large trade surpluses and those running deficits. In other words, on the question of how to rebalance the "persistently large imbalances" in current accounts (which is a broad measure of a nation's trade and investment with the rest of the world), especially correcting the huge trade deficits the United States has with major exporters like China, Japan, and Germany, all the G-20 could agree to was to set "indicative guidelines" to measure the current account imbalances (in consultation with the IMF), but left the details to be determined later. Put more

---

[19] Quantitative easing (QE) refers to a policy when the central bank infuses the banking system with excess reserves such as Treasury and mortgage-backed securities to lower long-term interest rates, and in the process, increase the money supply. The Federal Reserve's monetary policymaking committee or the Federal Open Market Committee (FOMC) announced that it intended to buy an additional $600 billion of longer-term Treasury securities by mid-2011. For details see Bernanke (2010a). In the first phase of quantitative easing, the Federal Reserve purchased medium- to long-term U.S. Treasury and mortgage-backed securities (mostly issued by Fannie Mae and Freddie Mac). As a result its balance sheet increased in size from $800 billion in September 2008 to $2.3 trillion in October 2010. Of course, the Federal Reserve claims that its decision to buy Treasury bonds was designed to lower long-term interest rates and thereby boost economic activity and job creation. Clearly, most of the G-20 countries, notably China, saw this act as an underhanded move by the United States to flood the global economy with dollars and in the process drive down the value of the U.S. dollar and give U.S. exporters an unfair price advantage.

[20] *The Economist*, 2010. "The Ghost at the Feast," November 12, http://www.economist.com/blogs/newsbook/2010/11/g20/print (accessed, November 15, 2010).

[21] Ibid.

bluntly, the G-20 rejected the "binding targets" called for by the United States.[22] Simon Johnson captures the rebuke of the United States, noting

It is hard to imagine how the summit could have gone any worse for the US Treasury and the president.... there was no substantive progress on anything to do with exchange rates. The "indicative guidelines" to be agreed next year are just a way to kick the can down the road. The Chinese are digging in hard on their exchange rate; this is headed towards a mutually destructive trade war.[23]

Kicking the can down the road is an apt description. In mid-February 2011, Beijing once again rejected to use real exchange rates and currency reserves to measure global economic imbalances. Chinese Finance Minister Xie Xuren bluntly stated that the G-20 should use trade figures rather than current account balances, real effective exchange rates, and reserves to assess economic imbalances. Zhou Xiaochuan, the governor of China's central bank, reiterated that Beijing alone would decide the pace of the yuan's appreciation, noting that "external pressure has never been an important factor of consideration and we have never paid special attention to it."[24] At Cannes, Beijing once again rejected the idea of monitoring real effective exchange rates and foreign-exchange reserves. Suffice it to note, without an agreement over how to define economic imbalances, how does the G-20 prescribe effective solutions?

Competing and Contentious Interests

The failure by the G-20 to support President Obama's job agenda, and put pressure on Beijing's trade and currency policies, although triggered by the mounting concern regarding the U.S. Federal Reserve's policy of quantitative easing, is fundamentally rooted in the divergent economic situation, and prospects between the more robust and the lagging or stagnant

[22] These guidelines are to be developed by the G-20 with assistance from the International Monetary Fund, including finance ministers and central bank governors. The G-20 agreed to meet in mid-2011 to discuss progress. For details, see International Monetary Fund (IMF). 2010. *The G-20 Mutual Assessment Process (MAP)*, Washington, DC: IMF External Relations Department http://www.imf.org/external/np/exr/facts/g20map.htm

[23] Simon Johnson, 2010, "G-20: Profound and Complete Disappointment for the US Treasury," (Opinion, Institute for International Economics, November 15, http://www.iie. com/realtime/?p=1858 (accessed, November 16, 2010).

[24] Chinese Finance Minister Xie Xuren said that "the G20 should use trade figures rather than current account balances to assess economic distortions... We think it is not appropriate to use real effective exchange rates and reserves." Daniel Flynn and Abhijit Neogy, 2011, "Chinese stance throws G20 indicator deal into doubt," *Reuters*, February 18, http://www.reuters.com/article/2011/02/18/us-g-idUSTRE71G4FX20110218 (accessed, February 19, 2011).

economies within the G-20 – what Federal Reserve Chair Bernanke has aptly termed a "two-speed global recovery." The failure to reach a broad compromise between competing national interests is due to lack of effective leadership. Specifically, we not only have a two-speed recovery, but also a two-track dialogue with the parties talking past each other. The United States, Europe, and Japan are still struggling to recover from the effects of the global financial crisis while the emerging economies, especially Asian economies (as well as Brazil), have been enjoying robust economic growth. Most troubling, the world's largest economy, the United States, seemed to have lost momentum, with GDP growth slowing to an annual rate of about 2 percent over the June and November 2010. This only served to compound the problems of the anemic economy, negatively impacting the already weak U.S. housing and labor markets. In the United States, an estimated 30 percent of homeowners face negative or near-zero equity in their homes, and unemployment looks increasingly structural rather than cyclical.

Despite the Federal Reserve's multipronged strategy, including a dramatic easing of monetary policy, maintaining official interest rates close to zero since late 2008, and purchasing more than a trillion dollars in Treasury securities and U.S.-backed mortgage-related securities, the U.S. economy has remained stubbornly stagnant. As Bernanke (2010) noted, "On its current economic trajectory, the United States runs the risk of seeing millions of workers unemployed or underemployed for many years ... as a society, we should find that outcome unacceptable." Arguably, running out of options, the Federal Reserve saw little option but to use other instruments to stimulate economic activity, including quantitative easing. However, most (if not all) of the G-20 members saw the U.S. Federal Reserve's ambitious expansionary monetary policy reflected in its $600 billion asset-purchase plan as an even greater threat to global economic growth and recovery than China's alleged mercantilist trade and currency policy. After all, why did emerging economies like Brazil, South Korea, and India and advanced economies such as Germany and Japan – who a few short weeks ago had a common cause with Washington regarding Beijing's mercantilist trade and currency policies, make a sharp volte-face at Seoul?[25]

Advanced economies, including Germany and Japan, and emerging economies like China, Brazil, and India, with healthy trade surpluses and

---

[25] In fact, German Chancellor Merkel said she had "praise for the Chinese. They've shown exemplary engagement with Europe" and they've proven to be a "good companion for our budgetary policy." Philipp Wittrock, 2010, "Adrift in Seoul: Bickering Likely to Lame G-20 Summit in Seoul, Korea," *Der Spiegel*, November 11, http://www.spiegel.de/international/world/0,1518,728527,00.html (accessed, November 12, 2010).

strong currencies (at least relative to the U.S. dollar), concluded (correctly) that the Federal Reserve's ambitious bond-buying program would give U.S. exporters an unfair advantage by driving down the value of the dollar and that a stronger U.S. dollar would, in turn, undermine their exports. The G-20 economies have every reason to be concerned about the rising levels of public debt in the United States. They also know that the United States' aggressive monetary easing, vividly illustrated by the Obama administration's willingness to print new money to cover its deficits and hide the real value of its debt, is laying the foundations for inflationary pressures, both nationally and globally. Not surprisingly, Chancellor Merkel

dispatched her finance minister, Schäuble, and economics minister, Rainer Brüderle, to argue against the Americans' demands. Then she personally made clear that Germany would not be yoked to any sort of export quotas at the G-20 summit. Speaking at the Business Summit, a meeting of top executives held on the sidelines of the G-20, Merkel made it clear that fixed upper limits for trade surpluses or deficits would be "neither economically justified nor politically appropriate" and "would be irreconcilable with the goal of free global trade."[26]

Emerging economies are particularly concerned that U.S. Federal Reserve's purchase of Treasury bonds would push Treasury interest yields so low that investors would be forced to pump massive volumes of speculative capital (or "hot money") in the form of capital, portfolio equity, fixed-income investments and stocks into emerging markets. Indeed, if this were to happen on a large enough scale, it would negatively impact these economies, exacerbating exchange rate volatility and sharply shooting up the value of their currencies (thereby undermining their exports), besides creating dangerous asset bubbles in their economies. Overall, the emerging economies, having rebounded from the global credit crisis, prefer tighter policies to the loose ones adopted by the United States. Quite justifiably, these economies remain deeply concerned about their ability to respond to inflows that will inevitably drive up their exchange rates and threaten their export base. Over time, it could also potentially trigger inflationary pressures and create bubbles in their economy (especially real estate), besides making the economy's stability contingent on the sentiments of foreign investors. Indeed, G-20 members like South Korea, Indonesia, and Brazil which experienced firsthand the debilitating impact of "hot money" during the Asian financial crisis of 1997–98 certainly do not want to see a recreation of such conditions.

[26] Philipp Wittrock, 2010, "Adrift in Seoul: Bickering Likely to Lame G-20 Summit in Seoul, Korea," *Der Spiegel*, November 11, http://www.spiegel.de/international/world/0,1518,728527,00.html (accessed, November 12, 2010).

Beijing deftly seized upon this rather unanticipated opportunity to accuse the Obama administration of pursuing policies harmful to free trade. Zhang Tao, director of the international department of People's Bank of China, noted that Washington "should not force others to take medicine for its own disease," warning that disorderly capital inflows resulting from the Fed's action could hurt emerging markets. Zhang added that "as emerging countries are important for the global economic recovery that will greatly increase the downward risks in the world economy."[27] To show that its concerns are not simply rhetorical, Beijing reiterated that it has taken a number of proactive steps, including increasing capital for bank reserves, raising benchmark interest rates to soak up excess liquidity in the economy, and tightening rules on real-estate purchases for foreigners to cool down its overheated real-estate market.[28] The coming together of unlikely allies made up of advanced and emerging economies (of course, minus the United States) ultimately resulted in the final G-20 communiqué – which formally approved that emerging economies, especially those with overvalued exchange rates could impose "carefully designed macroprudential measures" (i.e. capital controls) to protect their economies from the inflows of "hot money." This was a significant departure from the norm as capital controls are deeply frowned upon (especially by the United States and the IMF) because they are viewed as antithetical to the principles of free trade.

The Divide Will Not Go Away

On the final day of the Seoul Summit, a visibly disappointed U.S. president sternly noted that the yuan "is undervalued. And China spends enormous amounts of money intervening in the market to keep it undervalued ... the issue of the [yuan] is one that is an irritant not just to the United States, but is an irritant to a lot of China's trading partners and those who are competing with China to sell goods around the world." President Obama also subtly issued a warning to the G-20, in particular China, against relying too much on exports to the United States for global growth. He noted that "one of the important lessons the economic crisis taught us is the limits of

---

[27] Phillip Inman and Patrick Wintour, 2010, "G20 Trade Deal Unlikely," *Guardian*, November 11, http://www.guardian.co.uk/world/2010/nov/11/g20-trade-deal-doubtful/print (accessed, November 12, 2010).

[28] Specifically, Beijing ordered commercial banks to transfer an additional 0.5 percent of their assets by November 29 to the People's Bank of China, the country's central bank. The central bank uses these reserves to buy about $1 billion a day worth of dollars, euros, and other hard currencies – purchases designed to prevent the renminbi from appreciating.

depending primarily on American consumers and Asian exports to drive economic growth .... Going forward, no nation should assume that their path to prosperity is simply paved with exports to America" (Takenaka and Bryanski 2010). Politely responding to Obama, Chinese President Hu Jintao reiterated Beijing's commitment to expand domestic demand growth and to a gradual reform of its exchange-rate regime. Clearly, this was not enough for the Obama administration. Obama's national security adviser, Tom Donilon, later told a news briefing that China needed to show tangible progress on reforming the exchange rate before Hu visits Washington in January 2011 as it would be an important time to look at exactly what the quantum of progress has been on this."[29]

On November 19, 2010, Bernanke (2010), at a European Central Banking Conference in Frankfurt, not only vigorously defended his policy of quantitative easing, but also in no uncertain terms blamed China and other emerging markets for undervaluing their currencies and causing the imbalances responsible for the global crisis. Bernanke noted that "currency undervaluation by surplus countries is inhibiting needed international adjustment and creating spillover effects that would not exist if exchange rates better reflected market fundamentals." Moreover, Bernanke blamed the large capital inflows to emerging economies and to these countries' poorly adjusted foreign-exchange policy as foreign investors are looking for not only "return differentials that favor emerging markets," but also "additional returns expected from exchange rate appreciation." To Bernanke, resolving this problem must entail emerging economies allowing their exchange rates to "reflect market fundamentals." This explains why a number of countries, including Brazil, China, India, Indonesia, South Africa, Japan, Malaysia, Taiwan, and Thailand, among others, have recently put in place capital controls on foreign investments in their bond markets to curb currency appreciation (Cline and Williamson 2010). For example, Brazil, deeply concerned that foreign investors were pushing up the prices of securities, began limiting capital inflows by taxing investors' purchase of the country's stocks and bonds. Brazilian authorities are also concerned that a massive influx of foreign capital would inflate the value of its currency, the real (in fact, Brazil's flexible exchange rate was fast rising against both the dollar and the euro), making Brazilian exports uncompetitive and thereby

---

[29] Daniel Ten Kate and Kathleen Chu, 2010, "U.S. Pushes China for Yuan Appreciation before Hu's January Visit to Obama," *Bloomberg*, November 13, http://www.bloomberg.com/news/print/2010-11-13/u-s-pushes-china-for-yuan-appreciation-before-hu-s-january-visit-to-obama.html (accessed, November 15, 2010).

dampening the country's economic growth.[30] In the meantime, the yuan remains artificially undervalued to promote Chinese exports.

During the meeting of finance ministers and central bank governors from the G-20 in Paris (February 18–19, 2011), Treasury Secretary Geithner once again criticized China, stating that the yuan was still "substantially undervalued" and that the measures taken by Beijing to adjust the value of its currency by allowing it to appreciate against the dollar was not enough. Beijing remained defiant, noting that currency reform was an internal matter. Geithner correctly noted that the real effective exchange rate is the best measure to evaluate a currency against its trading partners, but China vociferously disagreed.[31] Beijing reiterated its usual complaint that "hot money" inflows (an indirect reference to U.S. Federal Reserve's $600 billion bond purchase program) risk destabilizing the economies of emerging countries. At Beijing's insistence, the final G-20 communiqué made no mention of the real effective exchange rate or foreign-currency reserves.[32]

Instead, the G-20 agreed on only board references to exchange rates and the current account as a measure to assess economic imbalances, but with emphasis on indicators such as public debt, fiscal deficits, private saving and borrowing, trade balance, and balance of payments such as net investment flows. Again on Beijing's insistence, the indicators were not binding targets, but guidelines for coordinated economic policies to reduce distortions, in particular, disruptive fluctuations in capital flows. At its Ministerial Meeting (April 2011), the G-20 finance ministers reached an agreement on a set of indicators to monitor global economic imbalances. Specifically, the IMF was given responsibility to identify imbalances by drawing on a wide range of indicators, including internal factors, such as public debt and fiscal deficits, private savings rate and private debt, and external factors, such as trade balance and net investment income flows and transfers. Needless to say the indicators are broad and convoluted enough to give China wiggle room. It is, therefore, not surprising that despite the stated commitment by all key players to enhanced exchange-rate flexibility and reforms to the international monetary system to avoid disruptive swings in capital flows and exchange rates, competitive devaluations continue unabated.

[30] Brazil's currency has appreciated nearly 50 percent on a trade-weighted basis since December 2008.

[31] Liz Alderman, 2011, "As G20 Leaders Set Deal, Geithner Criticizes China," *New York Times*, February 19, http://www.nytimes.com/2011/02/20/business/global/20euro.html?_r=1&pagewanted=print (accessed, February 20, 2011).

[32] Daniel Flynn and Abhijit Neogy, 2011, "Chinese Stance Throws G20 Indicator Deal into Doubt," *Reuters*, February 18, http://www.reuters.com/article/2011/02/18/us-g-idUSTRE71G4FX20110218 (accessed, February 20, 2011).

In the early 1970s, the problem of mounting current account mismatches was resolved with the collapse of the Bretton Woods system, and in the 1980s, international coordination of exchange-rate movements, such as the G-5 Plaza agreement of 1985 and the G-7 Louvre agreements in 1987, played a decisive role. Of course, the United States used its considerable influence over Japan (especially as the provider of the "security umbrella") for Tokyo to agree to the Plaza Accord, which resulted in Japanese institutional investors taking big losses on their assets. China, on the other hand, faces no such deterrence. Indeed, the global imbalances currently are due to policy-driven lack of exchange-rate flexibility. However, the inability of the G-20 to address the problem it was established to address, coupled with the continuing acrimonious exchanges between the world's major economies, is threatening to resurrect destructive protectionist policies like those that worsened the Great Depression in the 1930s. Specifically, given that the surplus and deficit countries are pursuing directly conflicting economic policies (that is, deliberately resisting the relative price changes that are essential for a successful rebalancing), the obvious danger is that the worst-hit countries, including the United States, may resort to protectionism to facilitate rebalancing.

Although the G-20 has made the requisite pledges not to pursue protectionist policies and made a commitment to diligently work toward concluding the long-stalled Doha Round on trade liberalization, this has hardly stopped the G-20 and other countries from erecting trade barriers, if not engaging in outright protectionism. Bussiere et al. (2011, 826) note that despite the commitment made by the G-20 to "refrain from raising new barriers to investment or to trade in goods and services, imposing new export restrictions, or implementing WTO inconsistent measures to stimulate exports," seventeen of these twenty nations have announced protectionist measures, and by August 2009, thirteen member countries of the G-20 implemented these measures. In fact, from "November 2008 to December 2009, 390 trade-damaging state measures were announced or implemented by G-20 members, plus several more by non-G-20 members" (Bussiere et al. 2011, 839). Similarly, Hoekman (2012, 17–18) notes that of the "1,243 trade measures that were imposed between the onset of the crisis in late 2008 and the end of the fourth quarter of 2011 ... about three-quarters of these restricted trade... the Group of 20 advanced and emerging economies account for most of these trade measures." These divisions have been magnified, because, as Lawrence (2012, 1) notes, "America has traditionally provided leadership in the WTO and multilateral trade negotiations, but the current talks, the Doha Round, are moribund and US leadership conspicuously absent." Compounding this are the nonbinding nature of G-20 commitments, including the lack of a dispute settlement and sanctioning mechanism. Not surprisingly, what Baldwin and Evenett (2009) have termed "murky protectionism" remains a pervasive problem and the Doha Round talks stalled.

More ominously, in such an environment, missteps could spark a tit-for-tat retaliation between two of the world's largest economies, which is in nobody's interest as it will send the global economy back into recession. Yet, as Robert Reich (the former U.S. secretary of labor), pessimistically notes:

China and the U.S. are the only big players in the currency game. And with neither of them stepping up to bat, the game is in dangerous territory. Other nations will now do whatever they can to reduce the value of their currencies in order to stimulate more exports and therefore create more jobs... the truth is that much more needs to be done to ease tensions that are moving the global economy closer to the brink of outright protectionism. The key responsibility falls to China and America – both in terms of what they do internationally and also what they do domestically. So far, both have failed.[33]

More bluntly, if "currency wars" are to be avoided, Beijing must allow for more than just minimal RMB appreciation. As the United States has already made its position on the issue clear, there is high probability that the next step may be punitive Congressional intervention. Influential U.S. senators Chuck Schumer (Democrat) and Charles Grassley (Republican) already have legislation on the books that would impose anti-dumping duties on some Chinese goods and countervailing tariffs on all of them if China does not allow its currency to appreciate. Indeed, a large bipartisan majority in the U.S. House of Representatives has already approved legislation to enact retaliatory tariffs on Chinese exports unless Beijing revalues the yuan.

During their semiannual talks in mid-April 2011, G-20 finance ministers again "chastised the United States for not doing enough to shrink its massive overspending and warned that budget strains in rich nations threaten the global recovery." Brazil's finance minister, Guido Mantega, in particular, criticized the United States:

[Mantega] offered sharp words in a thinly veiled attack on the United States [stating] "Ironically, some of the countries that are responsible for the deepest crisis since the Great Depression, and have yet to solve their own problems, are eager to prescribe codes of conduct to the rest of the world."

[33] Robert Reich, 2010, "G-20 Failure Moves Global Economy To Brink Of Protectionism," *The Christian Science Monitor*, November 15, http://www.csmonitor.com/layout/set/print/content/view/print/343499 (accessed, November 15, 2010).

Suffice it to note, Geithner replied back with his own veiled criticism of China and other countries on global imbalances by noting they must adopt "greater exchange rate flexibility."[34]

In the meantime, despite the problems with the yen in the aftermath of the earthquake and the problems in the eurozone (namely, the realization that Greece and others may have to restructure their debt obligations), the dollar has continued its steady decline against most major currencies. While this is due in part to near-zero interest rates in the United States (compared to higher rates elsewhere), other factors are also at play. On April 18, when Standard & Poor's warned that the U.S. government's coveted AAA rating status was in jeopardy because of concerns regarding the Obama administration's and Congressional Republicans' failure to reach an agreement on deficit reduction, including concerns about United States' exploding budget deficit, the dollar experienced a sharp sell-off. Adding to the dollar woes, Beijing has continued to put pressure on Washington implicitly warning of a diversification away from dollars, besides allowing the yuan to gradually appreciate. Of course, this creates more challenges for the dollar. On one hand, a rising yuan means that Beijing needs fewer dollars to offset yuan strength; on the other, China's competitors, in particular other Asian exporters, are also letting their currencies gain strength against the dollar. Thus, despite Washington's long-held demand that Beijing must allow the yuan to rise against the dollar (and other currencies) to boost U.S. exports and thereby help reduce the United States' massive trade deficit, the dollar's continued decline poses an unanticipated challenge, further widening the divide between the United States, China, and other G-20 member countries.

China's Defiant Stand: Because It Can

Beijing has shown no indication of backing down on its currency policy – without which external or global rebalancing will be impossible. Instead, deeply worried that the exploding U.S. government deficits have the real potential to lead to inflation and sharply reduce the purchasing power of its dollar-denominated financial assets, Beijing clearly has a back-up plan. On March 14, 2009, Chinese Premier Wen Jiabao bluntly noted that he was "worried" about the safety of China's more than $1 trillion investments in

---

[34] Lesley Wroughton, 2011, "World Finance Chiefs Chastise U.S. On Budget Gap," *Reuters*, April 16, http://www.reuters.com/article/2011/04/16/us-imf-usaidUSTRE73F1TN20110416 (accessed, April 20, 2011).

U.S. government debt and that Beijing was watching economic developments in the United States closely. Wen expressed concern that the massive stimulus expenditures in the United States could lead to soaring deficits – which, in turn, could sink the dollar's value and thereby the value of China's investments. With so much at stake, Wen broke with protocol by lecturing Washington on financial management, urging the Obama administration to keep focus on important matters such as providing guarantees that China's investments in the United States would keep their value. Wen unambiguously noted: "We have lent a huge amount of money to the U.S. Of course we are concerned about the safety of our assets. To be honest, I am definitely a little worried… the United States must maintain its good credit, honor its promises and guarantee the safety of China's assets."[35]

On March 24, 2009, further underscoring Beijing's fear that the rapidly growing U.S. budget deficits could drive down the dollar and with it the value of China's investments (especially in U.S. Treasuries), Zhou Xiaochuan, the governor of the People's Bank of China, called for the creation of a new international reserve currency (which he termed a "super-sovereign reserve currency") to replace the dollar because "an international reserve currency that is disconnected from individual nations is able to remain stable in the long run, thus removing the inherent deficiencies caused by using credit-based national currencies."[36] On June 26, 2009, the People's Bank again renewed its call for a new global currency, noting that the IMF should manage more of members' foreign-exchange reserves. Countries acquire portfolios of foreign exchange when they limit the appreciation of the currencies in the face of balance-of-payments surpluses. China, which holds a massive portfolio of foreign exchange in mostly dollar-denominated assets, claimed that the credit-based national reserve currencies (like the dollar) not only contributed to global imbalances, but also to financial crises. To Zhou, a new currency reserve system controlled by the IMF would not only be more stable, but also more economically viable because it would be used for international trade, financial transactions, and commodity pricing. In essence, Zhou's proposal suggested a gradual replacement of the dollar with Special Drawing Rights (SDRs), a concept introduced by the IMF in 1969 as an international reserve to support the Bretton Woods fixed-exchange rate

[35] Michael Wines, 2009. "China's Leader Says He Is 'Worried' Over U.S. Treasuries," *New York Times*, March 14, http://www.nytimes.com/2009/03/14/business/worldbusiness/14china.html?_r=1&pagewanted=print (accessed, April 15, 2011).

[36] Zhou's statement is published in English and Chinese on the People's Bank of China's Web site. Zhou Xiaochuan. 2009. "Reform the International Monetary System," March 23, http://www.pbc.gov.cn/english/detail.asp?col=6500&id=178 (accessed, April 15, 2011).

regime. Zhou's proposal would expand the basket of currencies that currently constitutes the basis of SDR valuation to all large economies (such as Russia) and set up a settlement system between SDRs and other currencies so they could be used in international trade and financial transactions. This would mean, first, for countries to entrust a portion of their SDR reserves to the IMF to manage collectively on their behalf, and second, that SDRs would gradually replace existing reserve currencies.

Cognizant that this may take some time, Beijing has been contemplating and experimenting with a number of other strategies, including short-term arrangements to diversify its investment portfolios away from U.S. dollars Put more bluntly, as Chen and Peng (2007) note, Beijing has been seriously examining its options regarding the cost of maintaining the dollar-based system.[37] Beginning in 2004, Beijing began experimenting with convertibility by establishing an offshore RMB market in Hong Kong, and over the following years the offshore market has expanded. In 2007, the China Development Bank issued the first offshore RMB-denominated bonds (called the "dim-sum" bond). In 2009, Beijing signed currency-swap agreements totaling about 650 billion yuan (about $95 billion) with Hong Kong, Argentina, Indonesia, South Korea, Malaysia, and Belarus (Fung and Yau 2012). The agreements will allow these countries to settle accounts with China using the yuan rather than the dollar. Further, in July 2009, the People's Bank took another step toward internationalizing its currency and reducing reliance on the U.S. dollar with the announcement of new rules to allow select companies to invoice and settle trade transactions in RMB through financial institutions in Shanghai, Hong Kong, and Macao (Chen and Cheung 2011).

This means that importers and exporters will now be able to place their orders with approved Chinese companies and settle payment in RMB. In addition, Hong Kong banks will now be allowed to issue yuan-denominated bonds – clearly a step toward building an offshore yuan market, while foreign banks will be allowed to buy or borrow yuan from mainland lenders to finance such trade (Cheung, Ma, and McCauley 2011; Dobson and Masson 2009). While the Central Bank has assured that this does not mean

---

[37] It should be noted that China is hardly alone. Both Russia and India have also called for an end to the dollar's dominance in the international monetary system. Russian President Dmitry Medvedev, on several occasions, has noted that the dollar system is "flawed" and that a new supranational currency should be created. Similarly, a senior economic adviser to Indian Prime Minister Manmohan Singh has urged the government to diversify its $264.6 billion foreign-exchange reserves (2008 figures) and hold fewer dollars. Like China, both have claimed that world currencies need to adjust to help unwind trade imbalances that have contributed to the global financial crisis.

full convertibility of the RMB, but is intended to provide stability for local exporters hit hard by the dollar's widely fluctuating value, it does underscore Beijing's growing concern about the future of the greenback and is in line with China's ambition to make the yuan an internationally traded currency. All of this means that the United States cannot perpetually rely on the exorbitant privilege the dollar provides to help service its external debt.

With China's foreign-exchange reserves heavily invested in U.S. dollar-denominated bonds, Beijing faces potentially massive capital losses if the dollar were to depreciate. Thus, confidently quoting Keynes's famous aphorism, "When you owe the bank a thousand pounds you are at its mercy, when you owe the bank a million pounds, it is at your mercy," some find comfort in the fact that the United States has such a tight choke hold on China that Beijing will have no choice but continue to buy U.S. dollars and government bonds in order to avoid a precipitous drop in the value of its already massive investments in U.S. securities. For its part, Beijing is not sitting idly by, but taking concerted action to reduce its dependence on U.S. assets, in particular, the low-yield dollar-denominated U.S. Treasury Bills. It is important to note that Beijing purchased such a large amount of Treasuries because it is not allowed to invest in other U.S. assets – the Chinese state-run oil company CNOOC, for instance, was denied the right to buy Unocal in 2005. Suffice it to note, Beijing has already noted its displeasure with this policy and warned it will no longer tolerate it. Furthermore, Beijing has been gradually diversifying its portfolio to make it less dependent on the U.S. dollar. Part of this long-term strategy has been to increase its gold holdings. Given China's massive investment in U.S. government bonds, Beijing has a vested interest in maintaining – or at least not endangering – the value of the Treasuries it holds, but common sense does not always dictate government action.

Indeed, China has its own pressing problems that may eventually lead Beijing to reconsider putting so much of its funds in low-yielding (and underperforming) U.S. securities. First, China's banking sector is dangerously leveraged as a result of the 4 trillion yuan ($630 billion) stimulus launched in 2008 to counter the ill-effects of the global financial crisis. The banking sector is not only heavily exposed to the country's highly speculative property sector, but also to the off-balance sheet "shadow banking" transactions conducted by municipal and local governments and well-connected insiders. It has been estimated that by using various local government financing vehicles (LGFVs), authorities get around prohibitions on excessive borrowing, resulting in accumulation of some 10.7 trillion yuan (about $1.65 trillion) in bad loans by the end of 2010 – a figure equivalent to 25 percent of China's annual economic output. If China's real-estate bubble bursts, local governments default on their debts, the balance sheets of Chinese banks deteriorate, and nonperforming loans pile up, Beijing will have much less to lend and may be forced to repatriate its funds.

The United States should know from its own history that creditor status gives a sovereign much power and influence. Kirshner (1997; 2003) persuasively shows that creditor countries have constantly sought to influence other states by strategically targeting the stability and value of their currencies through interventions in the foreign-exchange market – as the United States did so effectively against Great Britain during the 1956 Suez crisis. Friedberg (2012, 55–56) notes that China "uses commercial relations for its strategic advantage... The fact that such an action would probably do at least much damage to the Chinese economy does not guarantee that in the heat of a crisis, Beijing would not attempt it." In fact, Beijing did try to impose sanctions on Japan via its large position in Japanese government bonds during the Diaoyu/Senkaku islands dispute in September 2012. Clearly, Beijing has the capacity to use currency to advance its strategic goals. Contrary to conventional wisdom, Beijing does not have to take extreme action to have a consequential impact on the U.S. economy. If China reduces its purchases or sells even a modest portion of its position, Treasury prices would fall, and yields would sharply rise, resulting in higher borrowing costs for the U.S. government and a slowdown in economic activity. This underscores that Beijing's current mercantilist policy of using exchange-rate undervaluation and intervention in foreign-exchange markets to promote exports could trigger a "disorderly unwinding" of the global imbalances. That is, if and when global markets are no longer willing to continue financing U.S. debt, it could trigger a sell-off of dollar assets and a sharp rise in U.S. interest rates – with grave implications for the global economy as the spillover effects would be disastrous.

A Perilous Future

Even in the midst of a rapidly deteriorating situation in the eurozone and dire warnings of another global crisis, the G-20 leaders at their June 17–19, 2012 summit in Mexico failed to do anything substantive (besides issuing a joint statement that they "will act together to strengthen recovery and address financial market tensions") to ease market worries. Instead, petty squabbling and finger-pointing were on full display as some leaders chastised Europe to take "all necessary measures" to quell the crisis in the eurozone. Canada's refusal to commit extra funds to the IMF because they would be used to prop up Europe's shaky economies prompted the head of the EC, José Manuel Barroso, to fire back with: "Frankly, we are not coming here to receive lessons in terms of democracy and in terms of how to run an economy because the European Union has a model that we are very proud of." Knowing that stakes for him were high with the upcoming election, President Obama tried to mediate a solution to the European crisis – without much effect. Similarly, there was no progress on the President's two other foreign policy challenges, ending the violence in Syria and nuclear talks with Iran. As the *New York Times* (Cooper 2012) aptly noted, "For all his influence as the leader of the biggest economy in the world, Mr. Obama sometimes seemed a bystander, there to exhort and cajole the other European leaders (especially the German chancellor) but little else."

The U.S. Federal Reserve's continuation of its quantitative easing (QE) series of programs has led to a tit-for-tat response by other G-20 members. From November 2008 through March 2010, QE1 bought $1.75 trillion in long-term Treasuries, as well as debt issued by Fannie Mae and Freddie Mac and fixed-rate mortgage-backed securities (MBS) guaranteed by those agencies. From November 2010 through June 2011, QE2 bought $600 billion of U.S. government debt in the form of long-term Treasuries. In September 2012, the Federal Reserve announced a new program, QE3, or "open-ended bond purchases" (totaling $40 billion in mortgage-backed securities per month) to run on a continuing basis until there is "substantial improvement" in labor market conditions. While QE1 and QE2 involved the purchase of specific types of securities within a defined time period, QE3 has no limits – meaning the Fed can buy unlimited amounts of mortgages, Treasuries or other securities for as long as they see fit.

Arguably, the U.S. Federal Reserve's activism has pushed other advanced-economy central banks to rely increasingly on QE measures, besides requiring their banks to buy up their own government's debt by implicitly allowing banks to not count the sovereign debt against their Basel capital requirements. For example, the European Central Bank (ECB) has implemented three asset-purchase programs since 2011, providing more than €1 trillion in low-cost financing to eurozone banks. Between March 2009 and January 2010, the Bank of England purchased some £200 billion of assets, mostly U.K. government bonds or *gilts*. Japan's new prime minister, Shinzo Abe, has long blamed the yen's appreciation on the easy monetary policies of the United States and the eurozone. To counter this "unfair practice," he instructed that the Bank of Japan (BOJ) ease up on monetary policy by doubling its inflation objective and expanding its asset-purchase program. With its benchmark interest rate already close to zero, Japan's central bank has little choice but to engage in the purchase of government bonds to inject liquidity into the economy and it its hopes to push Japan out of persistent deflation. In April 2012, the BOJ announced the purchase of $61 billion of assets to inject more liquidity in the economy, besides maintaining interest rates of between zero and 0.1 percent. In September 2012, the BOJ added $128 billion more to its program of asset purchases, and in December 2012, it increased its QE program by another ¥10 trillion ($118 billion). By the end of 2012, the BOJ's easing program had pumped an estimated $1.2 trillion (¥101 trillion) into the economy. Nonetheless, this still was deemed insufficient. In early January 2013, Tokyo approved an "emergency" stimulus of ¥10.3 trillion ($116 billion) to create demand and boost the moribund economy, and on January 22, the BOJ set a 2-percent inflation target and agreed to open-ended asset purchases. However, already burdened with a public debt twice the size of the country's economy (and the largest in the OECD), such loose monetary policy has the real potential to trigger a buildup of asset bubbles and inflation – similar to what happened in the late 1980s.

Although the Fed has long claimed that its rationale for injecting liquidity in the economy and maintaining low interest rates is aimed at encouraging investment and job growth, and the BOJ claims that its central goal is to stem persistent deflation (and there is no reason not to believe either justification), one of the consequences of the Fed's actions is that it also pushes down the value of the dollar, just as the BOJ's aggressive actions will further devalue the yen. In the end, the worsening of the competitive position of other major currencies could very well force a new round of competitive devaluations as countries weaken their currencies to boost exports. Hardly surprisingly, Bernanke's (2012) pitch that "this policy not only helps strengthen the U.S. economic recovery, but by boosting U.S. spending and growth, it has the effect of helping support the global economy as well" has fallen on deaf ears. Others see his actions as a continuation of Washington's destructive "beggar-thy-neighbor" policy. Predictably, Brazil's finance minister, Guido Mantega, dubbed the policy "selfish" as it negatively impacts emerging markets by undermining their exports and overall growth by destabilizing capital and currency flows. He warned that "Brazil, for one, will take whatever measures it deems necessary to avoid the detrimental effects of these spillovers." Similarly, the Russian finance minister, Anton Siluanov, noted that "everything is getting done, from my perspective, blindly, without regard to the consequences it could have." Bernanke rejected these criticisms. Without naming China directly he argued that countries can prevent asset bubbles and inflation by allowing the value of their currencies to rise in response to capital flows in. The problem, Bernanke noted, is that some emerging market economies have deliberately kept the value of their currencies low to gain unfair trade advantages.[38] It is not unreasonable to suggest that such a hard and uncompromising position can further exacerbate tensions among the G-20 countries, potentially unleashing a destructive currency and trade war.

Indeed, during their mid-February 2013 meeting, the G-20 finance ministers and central bankers once again reaffirmed their pledge to "refrain from competitive devaluation," besides going to great lengths to downplay concerns that the actions of some were weakening the value of their currencies. However, there is no denying that one of the side effects of aggressive monetary easing is that it weakens a country's currency. To markets, facts talk louder than deeds. The reality is that the BOJ's aggressive monetary policy has led to a sharp fall of the yen against the dollar and other major currencies. As the yen has depreciated, the dollar and the euro have appreciated – and talk of "currency war" is palpable. Whether the G-20 has the ability to bring its members' exchange rates into alignment or if these actions signal further spiraling toward beggar-thy-neighbor policies is an open question

The discord and acrimony on display at G-20 Summits and beyond is symptomatic of a much deeper trend in the international system – the unraveling of the liberal multilateral partnership that guided the global economy for much of the second half of the twentieth century. The U.S. hegemon no longer towers over potential contenders, and is no longer in the position to unilaterally dictate global economic policy. As hegemonic stability theory has long contended, the absence of a hegemon or even a concert of powers with the ability to exercise restraint and leadership in the global political and economic arena indicates that meaningful cooperation between large, divergent, and competing economic national interests will be ever more contentious and difficult to resolve. Rather, with a growing leadership vacuum at the center of global economic policymaking, the world is entering a period that will be marked with unprecedented uncertainty and ambiguity. Whether the G-20 or a smaller bloc of powers can find a new equilibrium and fashion some sort of workable internationalist and multilateral compact in the form of pragmatic reciprocal partnerships or task-specific concerts, or whether the widening polarization spins out of control in the form of protracted trade and currency conflicts is the essential question of our time.

---

[38] Timothy Ahmann, 2012. "Bernanke Defends Fed Stimulus as China, Brazil Raise Concerns," *Reuters*, October 14, http://news.yahoo.com/federal-reserves-bernanke-says-u-stimulus-boon-global-042324105-business.html (accessed, October 15, 2012).

Bibliography

Abdelal, Rawi. 2007. *Capital Rules: The Construction of Global Finance*. Cambridge, MA: Harvard University Press.

Abramowitz, Alan. 2011. *The Disappearing Center: Engaged Citizens, Polarization and American Democracy*. New Haven, CT: Yale University Press.

Acemoglu, Daron. 2009. *Modern Economic Growth*. Princeton, NJ: Princeton University Press.

Acharya, Viral, Thomas Cooley, Matthew Richardson, and Ingo Walter. 2010. *Regulating Wall Street: The Dodd-Frank Act and the New Architecture of Global Finance*. Hoboken, NJ: John Wiley and Sons.

Acharya, Viral and Nirupama Kulkarni. 2012. "What Saved the Indian Banking System: State Ownership or State Guarantees?" *The World Economy*, vol. **35**, no. 1, pp. 19–31.

Acharya, Viral, Matthew Richardson, Stijn Van Nieuwerburgh, and Lawrence White. 2011. *Guaranteed to Fail: Fannie Mae, Freddie Mac and the Debacle of Mortgage Finance*. Princeton, NJ: Princeton University Press.

Acharya, Viral and Matthew Richardson. 2009a. "Causes of the Financial Crisis," *Critical Review*, vol. **21**, nos. 2–3, pp. 195–210.

eds. 2009b. *Restoring Financial Stability: How to Repair a Failed System*. Hoboken, NJ: John Wiley and Sons.

Adenauer, Isabell, Norbert Funke, and Charles Amo Yartey. 2009. "In a Spin." *Finance and Development*, March, vol. **46**, no. 1, pp. 16–17.

African Development Bank (AfDB). 2010. *African Economic Outlook 2010*. Tunis: Tunisia.

Ahluwalia, Montek. 2011. "Prospects and Policy Challenges in the Twelfth Plan," *Economic and Political Weekly*, vol. **46**, no. 21, pp. 88–105.

Ahmed, Liaquat. 2009. *Lords of Finance: The Bankers Who Broke the World*. New York: Penguin Books.

Ahuja, Ashvin, Nigel Chalk, Malhar Nabar, Papa N'Diaye, and Nathan Porter. 2012. "An End to China's Imbalances?" IMF Working Paper, WP/12/100. Asia and Pacific Department, Washington, DC: International Monetary Fund.

Akerlof, George and Robert Shiller. 2010. *Animal Spirits: How Human Psychology Drives the Economy, and Why It Matters for Global Capitalism*. Princeton, NJ: Princeton University Press.

Akin, Cigdem and M. Ayhan Kose. 2007. "Changing Nature of North-South Linkages: Stylized Facts and Explanations," IMF Working Paper, WP/07/280, Washington, DC: International Monetary Fund.

Alderman, Liz. "In Ireland, Low Corporate Taxes Go Untouched," *New York Times*, November 25, 2010. http://www.nytimes.com/2010/11/26/business/global/26tax. html?_r=1&pagewanted=all

Alesina, Alberto and Howard Rosenthal. 1995. *Partisan Politics, Divided Government, and the Economy*. New York: Cambridge University Press.

Alessandria, George, Joseph P. Kaboski, and Virgiliu Midrigan. 2010. "The Great Trade Collapse of 2008-09: An Inventory Adjustment?" *IMF Economic Review*, vol. **58**, no. 2, pp. 254-94.

Aliber, Robert. 2009. *The New International Money Game*. 7th ed. New York: Palgrave Macmillan.

Allen, Franklin and Douglas Gale. 2009. *Understanding Financial Crises*. New York: Oxford University Press.

Allen, Roy. 2010. *Financial Crises and Recession in the Global Economy*. 3rd ed. Northampton, MA: Edward Elgar Publishing.

Allen, William and Richhild Moessner. 2011. "The International Liquidity Crisis of 2008-2009," *World Economics*, vol. **12**, no. 2, pp. 183-98.

Alp, Harun, Selim Elekdag, and Subir Lall. 2011. "Did Korean Monetary Policy Help Soften the Impact of the Global Financial Crisis of 2008-09?" IMF Working Paper, Asia and Pacific Department, WP/12/5, Washington, DC: International Monetary Fund.

Altman, Roger. 2009. "The Great Crash, 2008," *Foreign Affairs*, vol. **88**, no. 1, pp. 2-14.

Alturki, Fahad, Jaime Espinosa-Bowen, and Nadeem Ilahi. 2009. "How Russia Affects the Neighborhood: Trade, Financial, and Remittance Channels," IMF Working Paper, WP/09/277, Washington, DC: International Monetary Fund.

Amable, Bruno. 2003. *The Diversity of Modern Capitalism*. New York: Oxford University Press.

Andrews, David. 2008. *Orderly Change: International Monetary Relations since Bretton Woods*. Ithaca, NY: Cornell University Press.

Andrews, Edmund. 2009. *Busted Life: Inside the Great Mortgage Meltdown*. New York: W. W. Norton.

Arora, Vivek and Roberto Cardarelli, eds. 2011. *Rebalancing Growth in Asia: Economic Dimensions for China*. Washington, DC: International Monetary Fund.

Asian Development Bank (ADB). 2009. *Asian Development Outlook 2009: Rebalancing Asia's Growth*. Manila: ADB.

Åslund, Anders. 2012. "Why a Breakup of the Euro Area Must Be Avoided: Lessons from Previous Breakups," *Policy Brief*, no. PB12-20, Washington, DC: Peterson Institute for International Economics.

   2007. *Russia's Capitalist Revolution*. Washington, DC: Peterson Institute for International Economics.

Åslund, Anders and Valdis Dombrovskis. 2010. *How Latvia Came through the Financial Crisis*. Washington, DC: Peterson Institute for International Economics.

Åslund, Anders, Sergei Guriev, and Andrew Kuchins, eds. 2010. *Russia after the Global Economic Crisis*. Washington, DC: Peterson Institute for International Economics.

Asmundson, Irena, Thomas Dorsey, Armine Khachatryan, Ioana Niculcea, and Mika Saito. 2011. "Trade and Trade Finance in the 2008–09 Financial Crisis," IMF Working Paper, WP/11/16, Washington, DC: Strategy Policy and Review Department, International Monetary Fund.

Autor, David. 2010. "The Polarization of Job Opportunities in the U.S. Labor Market," *The Hamilton Project* and *The Center for American Progress*, April, pp. 1–40.

Axilrod, Stephen. 2009. *Inside the Fed: Monetary Policy and its Management, Martin through Greenspan to Bernanke*. Cambridge, MA: MIT Press.

Baldwin, Richard, ed. 2009. *The Great Trade Collapse: Causes, Consequences and Prospects*. VoxEU.org Ebook.

Baldwin, Richard and Simon Evenett. 2009, "Introduction and Recommendations for the G20," in Richard Baldwin and Simon Evenett, eds., *The Collapse of Global Trade, Murky Protectionism, and the Crisis: Recommendations for the G20*, London: CEPR, pp. 1–9.

Bank of England. 2008. *Quarterly Bulletin (2008 Q4)*, vol. 48, no. 4. www.bankofengland. co.uk/publications/quarterlybulletin/index.htm

Bank of Korea (BOK). 2009. *Financial Stability Report*. Seoul.

Bank of Spain. 2011. "Quarterly Report on the Spanish Economy," *Economic Bulletin*, April. Madrid: Banco De Espana.

2009. *Annual Reports 2008*. Madrid: Banco De Espana.

Barro, Robert. 2009. "Demand Side Voodoo Economics," *The Economist Voice*, vol. 6, no. 2, pp. 1–5.

Bartels, Larry. 2008. *Unequal Democracy: The Political Economy of the New Gilded Age*. Princeton: Princeton University Press.

Barth, James, Gerard Caprio Jr., and Ross Levine. 2012. *Guardians of Finance: Making Regulators Work for Us* Cambridge, MA: MIT Press.

Barth, James, Tong Li, Wenling Lu, Triphon Phumiwasana, and Glenn Yago. 2009. *The Rise and Fall of the U.S. Mortgage and Credit Markets: A Comprehensive Analysis of the Meltdown*. Santa Monica, CA: Milken Institute.

2008. *A Short History of the Subprime Mortgage Market Meltdown*. Santa Monica, CA: Milken Institute.

Bartlett, Donald and James Steele. 2012. *The Betrayal of the American Dream*. New York: PublicAffairs.

Bateman, Bradley, Toshiaki Hirai, and Maria Cristina Marcuzzo, eds. 2010. *The Return To Keynes*. Cambridge, MA: Harvard University Press.

BCBS (Basel Committee on Banking Supervision). 2011. *Basel III: A Global Regulatory Framework for More Resilient Banks and Banking Systems*. Basel, Switzerland: Bank for International Settlements. http://www.bis.org/publ/bcbs189.pdf

2005. *Basel II: International Convergence of Capital Measurement and Capital Standards: A Revised Framework – Comprehensive Version*. Basel, Switzerland: Bank for International Settlements. http://www.bis.org/publ/bcbs128.pdf

Bastasin, Carlo. 2011. *Saving Europe: How National Politics Nearly Destroyed the Euro*. Washington, DC: Brookings Institution Press.

Belousov, D. R. 2010. "On the Development of the Crisis of the Russian Economy in 2008–2009," *Studies on Russian Economic Development*, vol. 21, no. 1, pp. 14–27.

Bergsten, Fred and Joseph Gagnon. 2012. "Currency Manipulation, the US Economy, and the Global Economic Order," *Policy Brief*, no. PB12-25, Washington, DC: Peterson Institute for International Economics.

Berglöf, Erik and Anatoli Annenkov. 2011. "Baltic Lessons for Europe's Future Economic Governance," *Europe's World*, Issue 17, Spring, pp. 70–77.

Berglöf, Erik, Yevgeniya Korniyenko, Alexander Plekhanov, and Jeromin Zettelmeyer. 2009. "Understanding the Crisis in Emerging Europe," Working Paper, 109, London, European Bank for Reconstruction and Development.

Berglöf, Erik, Alexander Plekhanov, and Alan Rousso. 2009. "Russia: A Tale of Two Crises," *Finance and Development*, vol. **46**, no. 2, pp. 16–19.

Berkmen, Pelin, Gaston Gelos, Robert Rennhack, and James Walsh, 2009. "The Global Financial Crisis: Explaining Cross-Country Differences in Output Impact," IMF Working Paper, WP/09/280, Washington, DC: International Monetary Fund.

Berman, Sheri. 2006. *The Primacy of Politics: Social Democracy and the Making of Europe's Twentieth Century*. New York: Cambridge University Press.

Bernanke, Benjamin. 2012. "U.S. Monetary Policy and International Implications," speech at the "Challenges of the Global Financial System: Risks and Governance under Evolving Globalization," A high-level seminar sponsored by Bank of Japan-International Monetary Fund, Tokyo, Japan, October 14, http://www.federalreserve.gov/newsevents/speech/bernanke20121014a.htm

    2010a. "Rebalancing the Global Recovery," speech at the Sixth European Central Bank Central Banking Conference, Frankfurt, Germany, November 19, http://www.federalreserve.gov/newsevents/speech/bernanke20101119a.htm

    2010b. "Aiding the Economy: What the Fed Did and Why," November 5, http://www.federalreserve.gov/newsevents/other/o_bernanke20101105a.htm

    2009a. "Asia and the Global Financial Crisis," speech at the Federal Reserve Bank of San Francisco's Conference on Asia and the Global Financial Crisis, Santa Barbara, California, October 19, http://www.federalreserve.gov/newsevents/speech/bernanke20091019a.htm

    2009b. "Financial Reform to Address Systemic Risk," speech at the Council on Foreign Relations, Washington, DC, March 10, http://www.federalreserve.gov/newsevents/speech/bernanke20090310a.htm

    2005. "The Global Savings Glut and the U.S. Current Account Deficit," speech given at the Sandridge Lecture, Virginia Association of Economists, Richmond, VA, March 10, http://www.federalreserve.gov/boarddocs/speeches/2005/20050414/default.htm

Bindi, Federiga. 2010. *Italy and the European Union*. Washington, DC: Brookings Institution Press.

Bitner, Richard. 2008. *Confessions of a Subprime Lender: An Insider's Tale of Greed, Fraud and Ignorance*. New Jersey: John Wiley and Sons.

Bivens, Josh. 2011. *Failure by Design: The Story behind America's Broken Economy*. Ithaca: NY: Cornell University Press.

Blanchard, Olivier. 2009. "The Perfect Storm," *Finance and Development*, vol. **46**, no. 2, pp. 37–39.

Blinder, Alan. 2009. "Six Blunders en Route to a Crisis," *The New York Times*, January 25, p. 7.

Blinder, Alan and Mark Zandi. 2010a. "How the Great Recession Was Brought to an End," Moody's Analytics Special Report, July 27.

    2010b. "Stimulus Worked," *Finance and Development*, vol. **47**, no. 4, pp. 14–17.

Bliss, Robert and George Kaufman. 2009. *Financial Institutions and Market, 2007–2008: The Year of Crisis*. New York: Palgrave Macmillan.

Bofinger, Peter, Lars P. Feld, Wolfgang Franz, Christoph Schmidt, and Beatrice Weder di Mauro. 2011. "A European Redemption Pact," November 9. http://voxeu.org/index.php?q=node/7253

Bonner, William and Addison Wiggin. 2006. *Empire of Debt: The Rise of an Epic Financial Crisis*. Hoboken, NJ: John Wiley and Sons.

Bookstaber, Richard. 2008. *A Demon of Our Own Design: Markets, Hedge Funds and the Perils of Financial Crisis*. Hoboken, NJ: John Wiley and Sons.

Booth, Laurence. 2009. "The Secret of Canadian Banking: Common Sense?" *World Economics*, vol. **10**, no. 3, pp. 1–17.

Bord, Vitaly M. and Joao A. C. Santos. 2012. "The Rise of the Originate-to-Distribute Model and the Role of Banks in Financial Intermediation," *Economic Policy Review*, Federal Reserve Bank of New York, July, pp. 1–14.

Bordo, Michael, Angela Redish, and Hugh Rockoff. 2011. "Why Didn't Canada Have a Banking Crisis in 2008 (or in 1930, or 1907, or …)?" NBER Working Paper, no. 17312, Cambridge, MA: National Bureau of Economic Research.

Bordo, Michael and Barry Eichengreen. 2002. "Crises Now and Then? What Lessons from the Last Era of Financial Globalization?" NBER Working Paper, no. 8716, Cambridge, MA: National Bureau of Economic Research.

    1999. "Is Our Current International Economic Environment Unusually Crisis Prone?" in David Gruen and Luke Gower, eds. *Capital Flows and the International Financial System*, Canberra: Reserve Bank of Australia, pp. 18–74.

Breisinger, Clemens, Marie-Helen Collion, Xinshen Diao, and Pierre Rondot. 2010. "Impacts of the Triple Global Crisis on Growth and Poverty in Yemen," IFPRI Discussion Paper 00955, Washington, DC: International Food Policy Research Institute.

Bremmer, Ian. 2010. *The End of the Free Market: Who Wins the War Between States and Corporations?* New York: Portfolio.

    2009. "State Capitalism Comes of Age: The End of the Free Market," *Foreign Affairs*, vol. **88**, no. 3, pp. 40–55.

Bremmer, Ian and Nouriel Roubini. 2011. "A G-Zero World," *Foreign Affairs*, vol. **90**, no. 2, pp. 2–7.

Brixiova, Zuzana Laura Vartia and Andreas Worgotter. 2010. "Capital Flows and the Boom–Bust Cycle: The Case of Estonia," *Economic Systems*, vol. **34**, no. 1, pp. 55–72.

Brooks, Petya Koeva. 2009. "Households Hit Hard by Wealth Losses," *World Economic Outlook*, June 24. Washington, DC: International Monetary Fund Research Department.

Brunnermeier, Markus. 2009. "Deciphering the Liquidity and Credit Crunch 2007–2008." *Journal of Economic Perspectives*, vol. **23**, no. 1, pp. 77–100.

Bussiere, Matthieu, Emilia Perez-Barreiro, Roland Straub, and Daria Taglioni. 2011. "Protectionist Responses to the Crisis: Global Trends and Implications," *The World Economy*, Vol. **34**, Issue 5, May, pp. 826–52.

Caballero, Ricardo. 2009. "The "Other" Imbalance and the Financial Crisis," unpublished paper, December 29, Dept. of Economics, MIT.

Caballero, Ricardo and Arvind Krishnamurthy. 2009. "Global Imbalances and Financial Fragility," *American Economic Review*, vol. **99**, no. 2, pp. 584–88.

Caballero, Ricardo, Emmanuel Farhi, and Pierre-Olivier Gourinchas. 2008. "Financial Crash, Commodity Prices, and Global Imbalances," *Brookings Papers on Economic Activity*, Fall, pp. 1–55.

Caijing. 2009. "Financial Crisis: Impact on China," April 11, p. 1.

Calomiris, Charles. 2008. "Not (Yet) a 'Minsky Moment,'" in Andrew Felton and Carmen Reinhart, eds. *The First Global Financial Crisis of the 21st Century*. www.voxeu.org/index.php?q=node/739

   ed. 2007. *China's Financial Transition at a Crossroads*. New York: Columbia University Press.

Campbell, Doug. 2007. "Armed against ARMs," *Region Focus*, Federal Reserve Bank of Richmond, Fall, vol. 2, no. 4, pp. 18–20.

Campbell, John. 2004. *Institutional Change and Globalization*. Princeton, NJ: Princeton University Press.

Cannato, Vincent. 2010. "A Home of One's Own," *National Affairs*, Spring, no.3, pp. 69–86.

Cargill, Thomas and Takayuki Sakamoto. 2008. *Japan since 1980*. New York: Cambridge University Press.

Cargill, Thomas, Michael Hutchison, and Takatoshi Ito. 2000. *Financial Policy and Central Banking in Japan*. Cambridge, MA: MIT Press.

Cassidy, John. 2009. *How Markets Fail: The Logic of Economic Calamities*. New York: Farrar, Straus and Giroux.

Cassis, Youssef. 2007. *Capitals of Capital: A History of International Financial Centres*. Cambridge: Cambridge University Press.

Chinese Banking Regulatory Commission (CBRC), Annual Report, 2008.

Congressional Budget Office (CBO). 2012. *An Update to the Budget and Economic Outlook: Fiscal Years 2012 to 2022*, August, Washington, DC: Congressional Budget Office.

   2010. *The Budgetary Impact and Subsidy Costs of the Federal Reserve's Actions during the Financial Crisis*. May, Washington, DC: Congressional Budget Office.

   2009a. *The Budget and Economic Outlook: Fiscal Years 2009 to 2019*. January. http://www.cbo.gov/ftpdocs/99xx/doc9957/01–07-Outlook.pdf

   2009b. *The Budget and Economic Outlook: An Update*. August 25. http://www.cbo.gov/ftpdocs/105xx/doc10521/2009BudgetUpdate_Summary.pdf

   2009c. *A Preliminary Analysis of the President's Budget and an Update of CBO's Budget and Economic Outlook*. March. http://www.cbo.gov/ftpdocs/100xx/doc10014/03–20-PresidentBudget.pdf

   2009d. *An Analysis of the President's Budgetary Proposals for Fiscal Year 2010*. June. http://www.cbo.gov/ftpdocs/102xx/doc10296/06–16-AnalysisPresBudget_for-Web.pdf

   2009e. *Measuring the Effects of the Business Cycle on the Federal Budget*. June. http://www.cbo.gov/ftpdocs/102xx/doc10299/06–23-BusinessCycle.pdf

   2008. *The Budget and Economic Outlook: An Update*. September. http://cbo.gov/doc.cfm?index=9706&type=0

   2001. *The Budget and Economic Outlook: Fiscal Years 2002–2011*. January. http://www.cbo.gov/ftpdocs/27xx/doc2727/entire-report.pdf

Cecchetti, Stephen G. 2009. "Crisis and Responses: The Federal Reserve in the Early Stages of the Financial Crisis." *Journal of Economic Perspectives*, vol. **23**, no. 1, pp. 51–75.

Central Bank of the Russian Federation. 2010. *Annual 2009 Report.* Moscow: Government of Russia.

Central Bank and Financial Services Authority of Ireland (CBFSAI). 2006. *Financial Stability Review.* Dublin. http://www.centralbank.ie/ fns_srep1.asp

Chaffin, Joshua. 2010. "Dublin Pays €17.5bn for Own Rescue," *Financial Times*, November 29. http://www.ft.com/cms/s/fbcb7732-fb3e-11df-b576-00144feab49a,dwp_uuid=bd2f85d2-8e90-11db-a7b2-0000779e2340,print=yes.html

Chan, Kam Wing. 2010. "The Global Financial Crisis and Migrant Workers in China: 'There Is No Future as a Labourer; Returning to the Village Has No Meaning." *International Journal of Urban and Regional Research*, vol. **34,** no. 3, pp. 659–77.

Chancellor, Edward. 2000. *Devil Take The Hindmost: A History of Financial Speculation.* New York: Penguin.

Chand, Sheetal. 2009. "The IMF, the Credit Crunch and Iceland," *World Economics*, vol. **10**, no. 3, pp. 19–41.

Charlton, Angela. 2012. "Troubled Europe Summit: Merkel vs Everyone Else." *Associated Press*, June 28. http://news.yahoo.com/troubled-europe-summit-merkel-vs-everyone-else-233837687 – finance.html

Chauffour, Jean-Pierre and Mariem Malouche, eds. 2011. *Trade Finance during the Great Trade Collapse.* Washington, DC: The World Bank.

Chen, Hongyi and Wensheng Peng. 2007. "The Potential of the Renminbi as an International Currency." *China Economic Issues*, no. 7/07. Hong Kong: Hong Kong Monetary Authority.

Chen, Shaohua and Martin Ravallion. 2009. "The Impact of the Global Financial Crisis on the World's Poorest." World Bank Development Research Group. Washington D. C. http://www.voxeu.org/index.php?q=node/3520

2008. "The Developing World Is Poorer than We Thought, but No Less Successful in the Fight against Poverty," Policy Research Working Paper 4703, Washington, DC: The World Bank.

Chen, Xiaoli and Yin-Wong Cheung. 2011. "Renminbi Going Global." *China & World Economy*, vol. **19**, no. 2, pp. 1–18.

Cheung, Yin-Wong, Guonan Ma, and Robert McCauley, 2011. "Renminbising China's Foreign Assets." *Pacific Economic Review*, vol. **16**, no. 1, pp. 1–17.

Chinn, Menzie, Barry Eichengreen, and Hiro Ito. 2012. "Rebalancing Global Growth," in Otaviano Canuto and Danny Leipziger, eds. *Ascent after Decline: Regrowing Global Economies after the Great Recession.* Washington, DC: The World Bank, pp. 35–86.

Chinn, Menzie and Jeffery A. Frieden. 2011. *Lost Decades: The Making of America's Debt Crisis and the Long Recovery.* New York: W.W. Norton.

Chinn, Menzie and Hiro Ito. 2007. "Current Account Balances, Financial Development, and Institutions: Assaying the World 'Saving Glut.'" *Journal of International Money and Finance*, vol. **26**, no. 4, pp. 546–69.

Cho, Dongchul. 2009. "The Republic of Korea's Economy in the Swirl of Global Crisis," ADBI Working Paper, no. 147. Tokyo: Asian Development Bank Institute. http://www.adbi.org/working-paper/2009/08/19/3272.korea.recovery.gfc/

Chorafas, Dimitris. 2009. *Financial Boom and Gloom, the Credit and Banking Crisis of 2007–2009 and Beyond.* New York: Palgrave Macmillan.

Chwieroth, Jeffrey. 2009. *Capital Ideas: The IMF and the Rise of Financial Liberalization.* Princeton, NJ: Princeton University Press.

Clarida, Richard. ed. 2007. *G7 Current Account Imbalances: Sustainability and Adjustment.* Chicago: University of Chicago Press.

Clark, Nicola. 2011. "Sarkozy and Merkel Call for Closer Euro Coordination," *The New York Times,* August 16. http://www.nytimes.com/2011/08/17/business/global/merkel-arrives-in-paris-to-begin-economic-talks-with-sarkozy.html

Clarke, Peter. 2009. *Keynes: The Twentieth Century's Most Influential Economist.* New York: Bloomsbury.

Cline, William. 2010. *Financial Globalization, Economic Growth and the Crisis of 2007–09.* Washington, DC: Peterson Institute for International Economics.

2005. *The United States as a Debtor Nation.* Washington, DC: Institute for International Economics.

Cline, William and John Williamson. 2010. "Currency Wars," *Policy Brief,* no. PB10–26. Washington, DC: Peterson Institute for International Economics.

Cohan, William. 2011. *Money and Power: How Goldman Sachs Came to Rule the World.* New York: Random House.

2008. *House of Cards: A Tale of Hubris and Wretched Excess on Wall Street.* New York: Random House.

Cohen, Ariel and Lajos F. Szaszdi. 2009. "Russia's Drive for Global Economic Power: A Challenge for the Obama Administration," *Backgrounder #2235.* January 30. Washington, DC: The Heritage Foundation.

Contessi, Silvio and Hoda El-Ghazaly. 2010. "The Trade Collapse: Lining Up the Suspects," *The Regional Economist,* April, St. Louis: Federal Reserve Bank of St. Louis, pp. 10–11.

Cooper, Helene. 2012. "Leaders Make Little Headway in Solving Debt Crisis," *New York Times,* June 19. http://www.nytimes.com/2012/06/20/world/leaders-make-little-headway-in-solving-europe-debt-crisis.html

Cooper, Richard. 2008. "Global Imbalances: Globalization, Demography and Sustainability," *Journal of Economic Perspectives,* vol. **22**, no. 3, pp. 93–112.

2007. "Living with Global Imbalances," *Brookings Papers on Economic Activity* **2**, pp. 91–110.

Cooper, William. 2009. "Russia's Economic Performance and Policies and Their Implications for the United States," CRS Report to Congress, RL34512, June 29. Washington, DC: Congressional Research Service.

Coval, Joshua, Jakub W. Jurek, and Erik Stafford. 2009. "Economic Catastrophe Bonds," *American Economic Review,* vol. **99**, June, no. 3, pp. 628–66.

Crawford, Alan and Simon Kennedy. 2011. "Europe Boosts Bailout Fund With 'Firewall' Bond Purchases, Eases Greek Aid," *Bloomberg,* March 12. http://www.bloomberg.com/news/print/2011-03-12/europe-boosts-bailout-fund-with-firewall-bond-purchases-eases-greek-aid.html

Crook, Clive. 2012. "How Germans Botched the Spanish Bank Bailout," *Bloomberg,* June 12. http://www.bloomberg.com/news/print/2012-06-12/how-germans-botched-the-spanish-bank-bailout.html

Crotty, James. 2009. "Structural Causes of the Global Financial Crisis: A Critical Assessment of the New Financial Architecture," *Cambridge Journal of Economics,* vol. **33**, Issue 4, July, pp. 563–80.

Crouch, Colin. 2005. *Capitalist Diversity and Change*. New York: Oxford University Press.

Congressional Research Service (CRS). 2012. *Sovereign Debt in Advanced Economies: Overview and Issues for Congress*. CRS Report R41838 by Rebecca M. Nelson.

2011. *State and Local Government Debt: An Analysis*. CRS Report R41735 by Steven Maguire.

2009a. *The Global Financial Crisis: Analysis and Policy Implications*. CRS Report RL34742 by Dick K. Nanto.

2009b. *Economic Stimulus: Issues and Policies*. CRS Report R40104 by Jane G. Gravelle, Thomas L. Hungerford, and Marc Labonte.

2009c. *The Global Financial Crisis: Analysis and Policy Implications*. CRS Report RL34742 by Dick K. Nanto.

2009d. *Financial Turmoil: Federal Reserve Policy Responses*. CRS Report RL34427 by Marc Labonte.

2009e. *American Recovery and Reinvestment Act of 2009 (P.L. 111-5): Summary and Legislative History*. CRS Report R40537 by Clinton T. Brass, Carol Hardy Vincent, Pamela J. Jackson, Jennifer E. Lake, Karen Spar, and Robert Keith.

2009f. *Troubled Asset Relief Program: Legislation and Treasury Implementation*. CRS Report RL34730 by Baird Webel and Edward V. Murphy.

2009g. *Financial Market Intervention*. CRS Report RS22963 by Baird Webel and Edward V. Murphy.

2009h 17 July. *Financial Regulatory Reform: Analysis of the Consumer Financial Protection Agency (CFPA) as Proposed by the Obama Administration and H.R. 3126*, CRS Report R40696, by David H. Carpenter and Mark Jickling.

2008. *The Emergency Economic Stabilization Act and Current Financial Turmoil: Issues and Analysis*. CRS Report RL34730 by Baird Webel and Edward V. Murphy.

Dadush, Uri and William Shaw. 2011. *Juggernaut: How Emerging Markets Are Reshaping Globalization*. Washington, DC: Carnegie Endowment for International Peace.

Darvas, Zsolt. 2011. "A Tale of Three Countries: Recovery after Banking Crises." *Bruegel Policy Contribution*, Issue 2011/19, pp. 1–18

Das, Satyajit. 2010. *Traders, Guns and Money: Knowns and Unknowns in the Dazzling World of Derivatives*. Harlow, UK: Prentice Hall.

Davidson, Paul. 2009. *The Keynes Solution, the Path to Global Economic Prosperity*. New York: Palgrave Macmillan.

2009a. *John Maynard Keynes*. New York: Palgrave Macmillan.

Davies, Howard and David Green. 2010. *Banking on the Future: The Fall and Rise of Central Banking*. Princeton: Princeton University Press.

Davis, Steven. 2009. *Banking in Times of Turmoil, Strategies for Sustainable Growth*. New York: Palgrave Macmillan.

De Haan, Arjan. 2010. "A Defining Moment? China's Social Policy Response to the Financial Crisis." *Journal of International Development*, vol. **22**, issue 6, pp. 758–71.

Deawtripont, Mathias, Jean-Charles Rochet, and Jean Tirole. 2010. *Balancing the Banks: Global Lessons from the Financial Crisis*. Princeton, NJ: Princeton University Press.

Delong, Bradford and Stephen Cohen. 2010. *The End of Influence: What Happens When Other Countries Have the Money*. New York: Basic Books.

Delpla, Jacques and Jakob von Weizsäcker. 2010. "The Blue Bond Proposal." *Bruegel Policy Brief*, May, no. 3.

Demyanyk, Yuliya. 2009. "Quick Exits of Subprime Mortgages." *Federal Reserve Bank of St. Louis Review*, vol. **91**, no. 2, pp. 79–93.

Demyanyk, Yuliya and Otto Van Hermet. 2008. "Understanding the Subprime Mortgage Crisis." Working Paper no. 2007–05. St. Louis: Federal Reserve Bank of St. Louis.

Desai, Padma. 2011. *From Financial Crisis to Global Recovery*. New York: Columbia University Press.

    2003. *Financial Crisis, Contagion, and Containment: From Asia to Argentina*. Princeton, NJ: Princeton University Press.

Devarajan, Shanta. 2009. "Africa and the Global Economic and Financial Crisis." Washington, DC: The World Bank. http://africacan.worldbank.org

Diao, Xinshen, Yumei Zhang and Kevin Chen. 2012. "The Global Recession and China's Stimulus Package: A General Equilibrium Assessment of Country Level Impacts." *China Economic Review*, vol. **23**, issue 1, pp. 1–17.

Dimsdale, Nicholas. 2009. "The Financial Crisis of 2007–9 and the British Experience." *Oxonomics*, vol. **4**, issue 1, June pp. 1–9.

Dobson, Wendy. 2009. *Gravity Shift: How Asia's New Economic Powerhouses Will Shape the Twenty-First Century*. Toronto: University of Toronto Press.

Dobson, Wendy and Paul Masson. 2009. "Will the Renminbi Become a World Currency?" *China Economic Review*, vol. **20**, no. 1, pp. 124–35.

Dobson, Wendy and Anil Kashyap. 2006. "The Contradictions of China's Gradualist Banking System." *Brookings Papers on Economic Activity*, vol. **2**, pp. 103–62.

Dooley, Michael, David Folkerts-Landau, and Peter Garber. 2005. *International Financial Stability: Asia, Interest Rates, and the Dollar*. New York: Deutsche Bank Global Research.

Dorsey, Thomas. 2009. "Trade Finance Stumbles." *Finance and Development*, vol. **46**, no. 1, pp. 18–20.

Dowd, Kevin and Martin Hutchinson. 2010. *Alchemists of Loss: How Modern Finance and Government Regulation Crashed the Financial System*. Chichester, UK: Wiley.

Eatwell, John and Murray Milgate. 2011. *The Rise and Fall of Keynesian Economics*. New York: Oxford University Press.

Economic and Social Commission for Western Asia (ESCWA). 2009. "The Impacts of the Financial Crisis on ESCWA Member Countries: Challenges and Opportunities." March 14. Beirut, Lebanon.

The Economist. 2012. "The euro crisis: A winner in France, alarm in Greece," May 6 http://www.economist.com/blogs/charlemagne?page=6

    2010a. "A Very European Crisis." February 4. http://www.economist.com/node/15452594/print

    2010b. "The Euro: Emergency Repairs." 13 May. http://www.economist.com/node/16106575/print

    2010c. "The Euro and the Future of Europe." 13 May. http://www.economist.com/node/16116773/print

    2009a. Congo's Faltering Economy: Too Big to Fail." April 16. http://www.economist.com/world/mideast-africa/displaystory.cfm?story_id=13496903

    2009b. "The Foreclosure Plan: Can't Pay or Won't Pay?" February 19, http://www.economist.com/node/13145396

Eichengreen, Barry. 2012. "Europe's Trust Deficit." *Project Syndicate*, 12 March http://www.project-syndicate.org/print/europe-s-trust-deficit

2011a. "The Euro's Never-Ending Crisis." *Current History*, vol. **110**, no. 732, pp. 91–96.

2011b. *Exorbitant Privilege: The Rise and Fall of the Dollar and the Future of the International Monetary System*. New York: Oxford University Press.

2010. "Europe's Inevitable Haircut." *Project Syndicate*, December 2. http://www.project-syndicate.org/commentary/eichengreen25/English

2006. *The European Economy Since 1945: Coordinated Capitalism and Beyond*. Princeton: Princeton University Press.

1996. *Globalizing Capital*. Princeton: Princeton University Press.

Eichengreen, Barry, Donghyun Park, and Kwanho Shin. 2011. "When Fast Growing Economies Slow Down: International Evidence and Implications for China." NBER Working Paper no. w16919. http://ssrn.com/abstract=1801089

Eichengreen, Barry and Kevin O'Rourke. 2009. "A Tale of Two Depressions." *VoxEU*, March, www.voxeu.org/index.php?q=node/3421.

El-Erian, Mohamed. 2011. "Europe Must Consider Radical Options." *The Financial Post*, July 15. http://www.pimco.com/EN/Insights/Pages/Europe-Must-Consider-Radical-Options.aspx

2010. "Many More Chapters Left in the Greece Drama," May 3. http://www.pimco.com

Ellis, Charles. 2008. *The Partnership: The Making of Goldman Sachs*. New York: Penguin.

Emmons, William and Bryan J. Noeth. 2012. "Household Financial Stability: Who Suffered the Most from the Crisis?" *The Regional Economist*, St. Louis Federal Reserve, July, pp. 11–17.

Eskesen, Leif Lybecker. 2009. "Countering the Cycle – The Effectiveness of Fiscal Policy in Korea," IMF Working Paper no. 09/249, Washington, DC: International Monetary Fund.

Esping-Andersen, Gosta. 1990. *The Three Worlds of Welfare Capitalism*. Princeton, NJ: Princeton University Press.

Europe's World. 2011. "Europe's World Background Briefing," no. 18, Summer, p. 56.

European Central Bank (ECB). 2012. *Monthly Bulletin: December, 2012*. Frankfurt am Main: European Central Bank.

2011. *The Monetary Policy of the ECB*. Frankfurt am Main: European Central Bank.

2010. *Monthly Bulletin: December, 2010*. Frankfurt am Main: European Central Bank.

European Commission (EC). 2010. *The Economic Adjustment Programme for Greece*. Brussels: European Commission.

2009. *Economic Crisis in Europe: Causes, Consequences and Responses*. Luxembourg: European Commission Directorate-General for Economic and Financial Affairs.

2008. *EMU@10: Successes and Challenges after Ten Years of Economic and Monetary Union*. Luxembourg: European Commission Directorate-General for Economic and Financial Affairs.

European Commission. 2012. *Statistics of the European Commission*. Brussels: European Commission. http://epp.eurostat.ec.europa.eu

Eurostat-Euro Indicators. 2012. The European Commission: Luxembourg.

Evans-Pritchard, Ambrose. 2008. "Europe Helpless as Financial Crisis Spreads across Atlantic" *International Herald Tribune*, October 3, p. 26.

Ewing, Jack. 2011. "Greece Nears a Tipping Point in Its Debt Crisis." *The New York Times*, 18 September, p. A10.

2010. "French and Germans Most Exposed in Euro Debt Crisis," *New York Times*, June 14, p. B8.

Ezekwesili, Obiageli. 2009. "Africa: Dealing with the Global Economic and Financial Storm" The World Bank. http://go.worldbank.org/UBWOLYVQ30

2009a. "The Urgency of Harnessing Africa's Natural Resources to Fight Poverty." The World Bank. http://go.worldbank.org/X9R69JWR80

Faiola, Anthony. 2010. "Spain, Portugal Face Pressure for Bailouts," *Washington Post*, November 27, http://www.washingtonpost.com/wpdyn/content/article/2010/11/26/AR2010112605032_pf.html

Farrell, Greg. 2010. *Crash of the Titans: Greed, Hubris, and the Fall of Merrill Lynch, and the Near-Collapse of Bank of America*. New York: Random House – Crown Business.

Federal Deposit Insurance Corporation (FDIC). 2011. "The Orderly Liquidation of Lehman Brothers Holdings Inc. under the Dodd–Frank Act." *FDIC Quarterly*, vol. 5, no. 2, pp. 31–49.

Feldstein, Martin. 2012. "The Failure of the Euro." *Foreign Affairs*, vol. 91, no. 1, p. 105–16.

2010. "For a Solution to the Euro Crisis, Look to the States." *The Washington Post*, Tuesday, May 18, p. A19.

2008. "Resolving the Global Imbalance: Dollar and U.S. Savings Rate." *The Journal of Economic Perspectives*, vol. 22, no. 3, pp. 113–26.

1997. "The EMU and International Conflict," *Foreign Affairs*, vol. 76, no. 6, pp. 60–73.

Feng, Cai, ed. 2010. *Transforming the Chinese Economy*. Leiden, Netherlands: Brill.

Ferguson, Charles. 2012. *Predator Nation: Corporate Criminals, Political Corruption, and the Hijacking of America*. New York: Crown.

Ferguson, Niall. 2008. *The Ascent of Money: A Financial History of the World*. New York: Penguin Press.

Ferguson, Niall and Moritz Schularick. 2011. "The End of Chimerica." *International Finance*, vol. 14, no. 1, pp. 1–26.

Financial Crisis Inquiry Commission (FCIC). 2011. *The Financial Crisis Inquiry Report, Final Report of the National Commission on the Causes of the Financial and Economic Crisis in the United States*. Washington, DC: U.S. Government Printing Office.

Financial Times. 2008. "The Fatal Banker's Fall," October 1, Gapper, John, http://www.ft.com/intl/cms/s/0/ccc6d456-8fd7-11dd-9890-0000779fd18c.html#axzz2TEIMhQd6.

Findlay, Ronald and Kevin O'Rourke. 2010. *Power and Plenty: Trade, War, and the World Economy in the Second Millennium*. Princeton: Princeton University Press.

Fleming, Michael and Nicholas J. Klagge. 2010. "The Federal Reserve's Foreign Exchange Swap Lines." *Current Issues: Federal Reserve Bank of New York*, vol. 16, no. 4, pp. 1–7.

Flood, Robert P. and Peter M. Garber. 1994. *Speculative Bubbles, Speculative Attacks, and Policy Switching*. Cambridge, MA: MIT Press.

Foster, John and Fred Magdoff. 2009. *The Great Financial Crisis: Causes and Consequences*. New York: Monthly Review Press.

Freeman, Richard. 2010. "It's Financialization." *International Labour Review*, vol. **149**, no. 2, pp. 165–183.

Friedberg, Aaron. 2012. "Bucking Beijing." *Foreign Affairs*, vol. **91**, no. 5, pp. 48–58

2011. *A Contest for Supremacy: China, America, and the Struggle for Mastery in Asia.* New York: W.W. Norton & Company.

Friedman, Benjamin. 1988. *Day of Reckoning: The Consequences of American Economic Policy under Reagan and After.* New York: Random House.

Friedman, Jeffrey, ed. 2009. *What Caused the Financial Crisis?* Philadelphia: University of Pennsylvania Press.

Friedman, Milton. 1962. *Capitalism and Freedom.* Chicago: University of Chicago Press.

1957. *A Theory of the Consumption Function.* Princeton, NJ: Princeton University Press.

Friedman, Milton and Anna J. Schwartz. 1963. *A Monetary History of the United States: 1867–1960.* Princeton, NJ: Princeton University Press.

Fukumoto, Tomoyuki and Ichiro Muto. 2011. "Rebalancing China's Economic Growth: Some Insights from Japan's Experience." Bank of Japan Working Paper Series, no.11-E-5. Tokyo: Bank of Japan.

Fung, Hung-Gay and Jot Yau. 2012. "Chinese Offshore RMB Currency and Bond Markets: The Role of Hong Kong." *China & World Economy*, vol. **20**, no. 3, pp. 107–22.

G-20. 2009. "Declaration on Strengthening the Financial System, London, 2 April 2009" http://www.londonsummit.gov.uk/resources/en/news/15766232/communique-020409

Gaddy, Clifford G. and Barry W. Ickes. 2010. "Russia after the Global Financial Crisis." *Eurasian Geography and Economics*, vol. **51**, no. 3, pp. 281–311.

Galbraith, James. 2012. *Inequality and Instability: A study of the World Economy Just Before the Great Crisis.* New York: Oxford University Press.

Galbraith, John Kenneth. 1961. *The Great Crash.* Boston: Houghton Mifflin Co.

Gans, Herbert. 2008. *Imagining America in 2033: How the Country Put Itself Together after Bush.* Ann Arbor, MI: University of Michigan Press.

Garnaut, Ross and David Llewellyn-Smith. 2009. *The Great Crash of 2008.* Melbourne: Melbourne University Press.

Garnham, Peter. 2010, "Greece Crisis Takes Toll on Euro." *Financial Times*, April 24, http://www.ft.com/intl/cms/s/0/49b0f326-4f39-11df-b8f4-00144feab49a.html#axzz2TEIMhQd6.

Garon, Sheldon. 2011. *Beyond Our Means: Why America Spends While the World Saves.* Princeton, NJ: Princeton University Press.

Geiger, Michael. 2008. "Instruments of Monetary Policy in China and Their Effectiveness: 1994–2006," Discussion Paper No. 187, Geneva: United Nations Conference on Trade and Development.

Gidadhubli, R.G. 2010. "Russia: Social Impact of Economic Crisis." *Economic and Political Weekly*, vol. **xlv**, no. 11, pp. 27–29.

Gill, Martha. 2011. "French Banks Weigh On Bourses." *Financial Times*, August 13. http://www.ft.com/cms/s/0/79c94dba-c4fe-11e0-ba5100144feabdc0.html#ixzz1Uww AA7Sx

Gilman, Martin. 2010. *No Precedent, No Plan: Inside Russia's 1998 Default.* Csmbridge, MA: MIT Press.

Gilpin, Robert. 1987. *The Political Economy of International Relations*, Princeton, NJ: Princeton University Press.

Gnos, Claude. 2009. *Monetary Policy and Financial Stability*. Northampton: MA: Edward Elgar Publishing.

Goldstein, Morris and Nicholas Lardy. 2009. *The Future of China's Exchange Rate Policy*. Washington, DC: Peterson Institute for International Economics.

   2005. "China's Role in the Revived Bretton Woods System: A Case of Mistaken Identity," Working Paper 05-2, Washington, DC: Peterson Institute for International Economics.

Goldsworthy, Brenton and Daria Zakharova. 2010. "Evaluation of the Oil Fiscal Regime in Russia and Proposals for Reform," IMF Working Paper, WP/10/33, Washington, DC: International Monetary Fund.

Goodhart, Charles. 2009. *The Regulatory Response to the Financial Crisis*. Northampton, MA: Edward Elgar.

Goodliffe, Gabriel and Stéphan Sberro. 2012. "The G20 after Los Cabos: Illusions of Global Economic Governance." *The International Spectator: Italian Journal of International Affairs*, vol. **47**, no. 4, pp. 1–16.

Goodman, John. 1992. *Monetary Sovereignty: The Politics of Central Banking in Western Europe*. Ithaca, NY: Cornell University Press.

Gorton, Gary. 2010. *Slapped by the Invisible Hand: The Panic of 2007*. New York: Oxford University Press.

   2009. "The Subprime Panic." *European Financial Management*, vo. **15**, no. 1, pp. 10–46.

Gorton, Gary and Andrew Metrick. 2010. "Regulating the Shadow Banking System." *Brookings Papers on Economic Activity*, Washington, D.C. Brookings Institution, pp. 261–97.

Gould, Erica. 2006. *Money Talks: The International Monetary Fund, Conditionality, and Supplementary Financers*. Stanford: Stanford University Press.

Gourevitch, Peter. 1986. *Politics in Hard Times: Comparative Responses to International Economic Crises*. Ithaca, NY: Cornell University Press.

Gourinchas, Pierre-Olivier and Hélène Rey. 2007. "International Financial Adjustment." *Journal of Political Economy*, vol. **115**, no 4, pp. 665–703.

Grace, John. 2005. *Russian Oil Supply: Performance and Prospects*. New York: Oxford University Press.

Gramlich, Edward. 2007. *Subprime Mortgages: America's Latest Boom and Bust*, Washington, DC: Urban Institute Press.

Greenspan, Alan. 2011. "Activism." *International Finance*, vol. **14**, no. 1, pp. 165–82.

   2010a. "The Crisis." *Brookings Papers on Economic Activity*, Washington, DC: Brookings Institution, Spring, pp. 1–49.

   2010b. "The Crisis: Comments and Discussion." *Brookings Papers on Economic Activity*, Spring, pp. 201–46.

   2008. "Testimony on Sources of Financial Crisis." House Committee on Government Oversight and Reform, October 23, Washington, DC

   2007. *The Age of Turbulence: Adventures in a New World*. London: Allen Lane.

   2004. "Globalization and Innovation." Remarks at the Conference on Bank Structure and Competition, Federal Reserve Bank of Chicago, Chicago, May 6. http://www.federalreserve.gov/boarddocs/speeches/2004/200405062/default.htm

Grigore, Eleches. 2008. *From Economic Crisis to Reform: IMF Programs in Latin America and Eastern Europe*. Princeton, NJ: Princeton University Press.

Grimes, William. 2008. *Currency and Contest in East Asia: the Great Power Politics of Financial Regionalism*. Ithaca, NY: Cornell University Press.

Gros, Daniel and Stefano Micossi. 2009. "The Beginning of the End Game," in Andrew Felton and Carmen M. Reinhart, eds. *The First Global Financial Crisis of the 21st Century*. VoxEU.org, http://www.voxeu.org/reports/reinhart_felton_vol2/First_Global_Crisis_Vol2.pdf

Gros, Daniel and Thomas Mayer. 2010. "Towards a Euro(pean) Monetary Fund," *Policy Brief* no. 202. Brussels: Centre for European Policy Studies (CEPS).

Grossman, Richard. 2010. *Unsettled Account: The Evolution of Banking in the Industrialized World Since 1800*. Princeton, NJ: Princeton University Press.

Gruber, Joseph and Steven Kamin. 2007. "Explaining the Global Pattern of Current Account Imbalances," *Journal of International Money and Finance*, vol. **26**, no. 4, pp. 500–22.

Hacker, Jacob and Paul Pierson. 2010. *Winner-Take-All Politics: How Washington Made the Rich Richer – and Turned Its Back on the Middle Class*. New York: Simon and Schuster.

Hall, Peter. 1989. *The Political Power of Economic Ideas: Keynesianism across Nations*. Princeton, NJ: Princeton University Press.

Hall, Peter and David Soskice, eds. 2001. *Varieties of Capitalism: The Institutional Foundations of Comparative Advantage*. New York: Oxford University Press.

Hallerberg, Mark, Carlos Scartascini, and Ernesto Stein. 2009. *Who Decides the Budget?*. Cambridge, MA: Harvard University Press.

Hanson, Philip. 2011. "Russia: Crisis, Exit and … Reform?" *Journal of Communist Studies and Transition Politics*, vol. **27**, nos. 3–4, pp. 456–75.

Harold, James. 2009. *The Creation and Destruction of Value: the Globalization Cycle*. Cambridge, MA: Harvard University Press.

Hausmann, Ricardo, Jason Hwang, and Dani Rodrik. 2007. "What You Export Matters." *Journal of Economic Growth*, vol. **12**, no. 1, pp. 1–25.

Helleiner, Eric. 1994. *States and the Reemergence of Global Finance*. Ithaca, NY: Cornell University Press.

Hix, Simon. 2008. *What's Wrong with the European Union and How to Fix It*. Cambridge, UK: Polity Press.

Hoekman, Bernard. 2012. "Trade Policy: So Far So Good," *Finance and Development*, vol. **49**, no. 2, pp. 17–19.

Hoffman, Philip T, Postel-Vinay Gilles, and Jean-Laurent Rosenthal. 2009. *Surviving Large Losses: Financial Crises, the Middle Class, and the Development of Capital Market*. Cambridge, MA: Harvard University Press.

Holinski, Nils, Clemens Kool, and Joan Muysken, 2012. "Persistent Macroeconomic Imbalances in the Euro Area: Causes and Consequences." *Federal Reserve Bank of St. Louis Review*, vol. **94**, no. 1, pp. 1–20.

Honohan, Patrick. 2009. "Resolving Ireland's Banking Crisis." *The Economic and Social Review*, vol. **40**, no. 2, pp. 207–31.

Honohan, Patrick and Brendan Walsh. 2002. "Catching Up With the Leaders: The Irish Hare," *Brookings Papers on Economic Activity*, Washington, DC, Brookings Institution, Part 1, pp. 1–57.

Hoshi, Takeo and Anil K. Kashyap. 2004. "Japan's Financial Crisis and Economic Stagnation." *Journal of Economic Perspectives*, vol. **18**, no. 1, pp. 3–26.

1999. "The Japanese Banking Crisis: Where Did It Come From and How Will It End?" NBER Working Paper, no. 7250. Cambridge, MA: National Bureau of Economic Research.

Huang, Yasheng. 2011. "Rethinking the Beijing Consensus," *Asia Policy*, no. 11, January, pp. 1–26.

Hubbard, Glenn and Duggan William. 2009. *The Aid Trap: Hard Truths about Ending Poverty*. New York: Columbia Business School Press.

eds. 2001. *Corporate Financing and Governance in Japan*. Cambridge, MA: MIT Press.

Hufbauer, Gary Clyde and Kati Suominen. 2010. *Globalization at Risk: Challenges to Finance and Trade*. New Haven, CT.: Yale University Press.

Hufbauer, Gary Clyde and Jeffry Schott. 2009. "Buy American: Bad for Jobs, Worse for Reputation." *International Economics Policy Briefs,* no. PB09–2, Washington, DC: Institute for International Economics.

Hufbauer, Gary Clyde and Yee Wong. 2004. "China Bashing." *International Economics Policy Briefs*, no. PB04–5. Washington, DC: Institute for International Economics.

Hyman, Louis. 2011. *Debtor Nation: The History of America in Red Ink*. Princeton, NJ: Princeton University Press.

Ikenberry, John. 2011a. "The Future of the Liberal World Order." *Foreign Affairs*, vol. **90**, no. 3, pp. 56–68.

2011b. *Liberal Leviathan: The Origins, Crisis and Transformation of the American World*. Princeton, NJ: Princeton University Press.

2003. "Is American Multilateralism in Decline?" *Perspectives on Politics*, vol. **1**, no. 3, pp. 533–50.

Immergluck, Dan. 2009. *Foreclosed: High-Risk Lending, Deregulation, and the Undermining of America's Mortgage Market*. Ithaca, NY: Cornell University Press.

Inman, Phillip and Jill Treanor. 2010. "Allied Irish Banks Suffers Massive Withdrawals." *The Guardian*, November 19. http://www.guardian.co.uk/business/2010/nov/19/ireland-banks-bailout-imf/print.

International Monetary Fund (IMF). 2012. *Global Financial Stability Report: Restoring Confidence and Progressing on Reforms*. Washington, DC: International Monetary Fund.

2011a. "Spain: Selected Issues." IMF Country Report No. 11/216, Washington, DC: International Monetary Fund.

2011b. "Italy: Staff Report for the 2011 Article IV Consultation; Informational Annex; Public Information Notice; Statement by the Staff Representative; and Statement by the Executive Director for Italy." IMF Country Report No. 11/173, Washington, DC: International Monetary Fund.

2011c. "Greece: Fourth Review Under the Stand-By Arrangement and Request for Modification and Waiver of Applicability of Performance Criteria," IMF Country Report No. 11/175, Washington, DC: International Monetary Fund.

2011d. "People's Republic of China: Financial System Stability Assessment," IMF Country Report No. 11/321, Washington, DC: International Monetary Fund.

2011e. "Russian Federation: Financial System Stability Assessment," IMF Country Report No. 11/291, Washington, DC: International Monetary Fund.

2011f. "Greece: Fifth Review Under the Stand-By Arrangement, Rephasing and Request for Waivers of Nonobservance of Performance Criteria; Press Release on the Executive Board Discussion; and Statement by the Executive Director for Greece," IMF Country Report No. 11/351, Washington, DC: International Monetary Fund.

2011g. "Republic of Korea: 2011 Article IV Consultation – Staff Report and Public Information Notice on the Executive Board Discussion," IMF Country Report No. 11/246, Washington, DC: International Monetary Fund.

2011h. "The United States: 2011 Article V Consultation," IMF Country Report No. 11/201, Washington, DC: International Monetary Fund.

2010a. "Greece: Staff Report on Request for Stand-By Arrangement," IMF Country Report No. 10/110, Washington, DC: International Monetary Fund.

2010b. "Greece: Second Review Under the Stand-By Arrangement – Staff Report; Press Release on the Executive Board Discussion; and Statement by the Executive Director for Greece," IMF Country Report No. 10/372, Washington, DC: International Monetary Fund.

2010c. "Ireland: Request for an Extended Arrangement – Staff Report; Staff Supplement; Staff Statement; and Press Release on the Executive Board Discussion," IMF Country Report No. 10/366, Washington, DC: International Monetary Fund.

2010d. "Russian Federation: Financial Sector Stability Assessment Update," IMF Country Report No. 10/96, Washington, DC: International Monetary Fund.

2010e. "Russian Federation: 2010 Article IV Consultation – Staff Report; and Public Information Notice on the Executive Board Discussion," IMF Country Report No. 10/246, Washington, DC: International Monetary Fund.

2010f. *Regional Economic Outlook: Europe – Fostering Sustainability*. Washington, DC: International Monetary Fund.

2010g. *World Economic Outlook: Recovery, Risk and Rebalancing*. Washington, DC: International Monetary Fund.

2010h. *Impact of the Global Financial Crisis on the Gulf Cooperation Council Countries and Challenges Ahead, Middle East and Central Asia Department*. Washington, DC: International Monetary Fund.

2010i. "Arab Republic of Egypt: 2010 Article IV Consultation – Staff Report; Public Information Notice on the Executive Board Discussion; and Statement by the Executive Director for the Arab Republic of Egypt," IMF Country Report No. 10/94, Washington, DC: International Monetary Fund.

2009a. *Global Financial Stability Report: Navigating the Financial Challenges Ahead*. Washington, DC: International Monetary Fund.

2009b. *International Financial Statistics (CD-ROM)*. Washington, DC: International Monetary Fund.

2009c. "Russian Federation: 2009 Article IV Consultation," IMF Country Report No. 09/246, Washington, DC: International Monetary Fund.

2009d. *World Economic Outlook: Crisis and Recovery*. Washington, DC: International Monetary Fund.

2009e. *World Economic Outlook Update, July*. Washington, DC: International Monetary Fund.

2009f. *The Implications of the Global Financial Crisis for Low-Income Countries*. Washington, DC: International Monetary Fund.

2009g. *Regional Economic Outlook: Sub-Saharan Africa.* Washington, DC: International Monetary Fund.

2009h. *World Economic and Financial Surveys: Regional Economic Outlook for Asia and the Pacific – Global Crisis.* Washington, DC: International Monetary Fund.

2009i. "India: Staff Report for the 2008 Article IV Consultation" Country Report No. 09/18, Washington, DC: International Monetary Fund.

2009j. "IMF Executive Board Concludes 2008 Article IV Consultation with India" Public Information Notice (PIN) No. 09/35, Washington, DC: International Monetary Fund, http://www.imf.org/external/np/sec/pn/2009/pn0935.htm

2009k. "Japan: 2009 Article IV Consultation: Staff Report; Staff Statement; and Public Information Notice on the Executive Board Discussion," IMF Country Report No. 09/210, Washington, DC: International Monetary Fund.

2009l. *World Economic Outlook.* Washington, DC: International Monetary Fund.

2009m. "IMF Team Completes the 2009 Article IV Consultation Discussions with Japan," Press Release No. 09/179, Washington, DC: International Monetary Fund, http://www.imf.org/external/np/sec/pr/2009/pr09179.htm

2009n. "Republic of Korea: 2009 Article IV Consultation – Staff Report; Staff Statement; Public Information Notice on the Executive Board Discussion; and Statement by the Executive Director for the Republic of Korea," IMF Country Report No. 09/262, Washington, DC: International Monetary Fund.

2009o. "IMF Presses Korea to Continue Rebalancing Economy," *IMF Survey Magazine: Countries and Regions,* August 9. Washington, DC: International Monetary Fund. http://www.imf.org/external/pubs/ft/survey/so/2009/car080909a.htm

2009p. "Arab Republic of Egypt: 2008 Article IV Consultation," IMF Country Report No. 09/25, Washington, DC: International Monetary Fund.

2009q. *Global Financial Stability Report: Responding to the Financial Crisis and Measuring Systemic Risks.* Washington, DC: International Monetary Fund.

2009r. "Republic of Yemen: 2008 Article IV Consultation – Staff Report: Public Information Notice on the Executive Board Discussion and Statement by the Executive Director for the Republic of Yemen," IMF Country Report No. 09/100, Washington, DC: International Monetary Fund.

2009s. "Executive Board Concludes 2008 Article IV Consultation with the United Arab Emirates" Public Information Notice (PIN) No. 09/47, Washington, DC: International Monetary Fund.

2009t. "United Arab Emirates: 2008 Article IV Consultation: Staff Report; Staff Statement; and Public Information Notice on the Executive Board Discussion," IMF Country Report No. 09/124, Washington, DC: International Monetary Fund.

2009u. "IMF Sees Spending by Middle Eastern Oil Exporters Softening Global Financial Crisis Impact" Press Release, No. 09/28, February 9, Washington, DC: International Monetary Fund. http://www.imf.org/external/np/sec/pr/2009/pr0928.htm

2008a. *Global Financial Stability Report.* World Economic and Financial Surveys, Washington, DC: International Monetary Fund.

2008b. "Austria: Financial System Stability Assessment – Update," IMF Country Report No. 08/190, Washington, DC: International Monetary Fund.

2008c. *International Financial Statistics (CD-ROM).* Washington, DC: International Monetary Fund.

2008d. *IMF Financial Stability Report 2008*. Washington, DC: International Monetary Fund, http://www.imf.org/external/pubs/ft/gfsr/2008/02/index.

2008e. "Republic of Korea: 2008 Article IV Consultation – Staff Report; Staff Supplement; Public Information Notice on the Executive Board Discussion; and Statement by the Executive Director for the Republic of Korea," IMF Country Report No. 08/297, Washington, DC: International Monetary Fund.

2008f. "Republic of Korea: Selected Issues," Country Report No. 08/296, Washington, DC: International Monetary Fund.

2008g. *World Economic Outlook Database*. October. Washington, DC: International Monetary Fund.

2008h. *World Economic Outlook Update*. November. Washington, DC: International Monetary Fund.

2007a. *Global Financial Stability Report*. October. World Economic and Financial Surveys, Washington, DC: International Monetary Fund.

2007b. *World Economic Outlook 2007*. April. Washington, DC: International Monetary Fund.

2006. "Ireland: 2006 Article IV Consultation – Staff Report; Staff Supplement; and Public Information Notice on the Executive Board Discussion," IMF Country Report No. 06/293, Washington, DC: International Monetary Fund.

Issing, Otmar. 2008. *The Birth of the Euro*. New York: Cambridge University Press.

Iverson, Torben. 1999. *Contested Economic Institutions: The Politics of Macroeconomics and Wage Bargaining in Advanced Democracies*. New York: Cambridge University Press.

Jabko, Nicolas. 2006. *Playing the Field: A Political Strategy for Uniting Europe, 1985–2005*. Ithaca, NY: Cornell University Press.

Jacobs, Lawrence and Theda Skocpol. 2011. *Reaching for a New Deal: Ambitious Governance, Economic Meltdown, and Polarized Politics*. New York: Oxford University Press.

Jaffee, Dwight and Mark Perlow. 2008. "Investment Bank Regulation after the Bear Stearns Rescue." *Central Banking*, vol. 18, pp. 38–44.

Jaimovich, Nir and Henry Siu. 2012. "The Trend Is the Cycle: Job Polarization and Jobless Recoveries." NBER Working Paper no. 18334, National Bureau of Economic Research, pp. 1–36.

James, Harold. 2012. *Making the European Monetary Union*. Cambridge, MA.: Harvard University Press.

Janeway, William. 2012. *Doing Capitalism in the Innovation Economy*. New York: Cambridge University Press.

Jarrow, Robert. 2011. "The Economics of Credit Default Swaps." *Annual Review of Financial Economics*, vol. 3, pp. 235–57.

Jayaram, Shruthi, Ila Patnaik, and Ajay Shah. 2009. "Examining the Decoupling Hypothesis for India." *Economic and Political Weekly*, vol. 44, no. 44, pp. 109–16.

Johnson, Simon and James Kwak. 2010. *13 Bankers: The Wall Street Takeover and the Next Financial Meltdown*. New York: Vintage.

Jones, Daniel Stedman. 2012. *Masters of the Universe: Hayek, Friedman and the Birth of Neoliberal Politics*. Princeton, NJ: Princeton University Press.

Jones, Erik. 2012. "Italy's Sovereign Debt Crisis." *Survival: Global Politics and Strategy*, vol. 54, issue 1, pp. 83–110.

2010. "Merkel's Folly." *Survival: Global Politics and Strategy*, vol. **52**, no. 3, pp. 21–38.

Judt, Tony. 2005. *Postwar: A History of Europe Since 1945*. New York: Penguin Press.

Jun-kyu, Lee. 2010. "Korea's Economic Stability and Resilience in Time of Crisis," *Korea's Economy 2010*, vol. **26**, Washington, DC: Korea Institute for International Economic Policy, pp. 8–13.

Kagan, Robert. 2012. *The World America Made*. New York: Alfred A. Knopf.

2006. *Dangerous Nation: America's Place in the World from Its Earliest Days to the Dawn of the Twentieth Century*. New York: Alfred A. Knopf.

Kang, Myung-koo. 2009. "Global Financial Crisis and Systemic Risks in the Korean Banking Sector." *KEI Academic Paper Series*, vol. **4**, no. 5, Washington, DC:Korea Economic Institute of America.

Kasjanovs, Igors and Anna Kasjanova. 2011. "The Crisis in Latvia: Reasons and Consequences." *World Economics*, vol. **12**, no. 3, pp. 105–212.

Kato, Takatoshi. 2009. "Impact of the Global Financial Crisis and Its Implications for the East Asian Economy." Keynote Speech by Deputy Managing Director, International Monetary Fund, at the Korea International Financial Association, First International Conference, Seoul, Korea, October 16. http://www.imf.org/external/np/speeches/2009/101609.htm

Kawai, Masahiro and Shinji Takagi. 2009. "Why Was Japan Hit So Hard by the Global Financial Crisis?" ADBI Working Paper Series, no. 153, Tokyo: Asian Development Bank Institute.

Keidel, Albert. 2011. "China's Exchange Rate Controversy: A Balanced Analysis." *Eurasian Geography and Economics*, vol. **52**, no. 3, p. 347.

Kelly, Morgan. 2010. "Whatever Happened to Ireland?" May 17 http://www.voxeu.org/index.php?q=node/5040;

2007. "Banking on Very Shaky Foundations." *Irish Times*, September 7, p. 17.

Kenny, Charles. 2011. *Getting Better: Why Global Development is Succeeding – and How We Can Improve the World Even More*. New York: Basic Books.

Keohane, Robert. 1984. *After Hegemony: Cooperation and Discord in the World Political Economy*. Princeton, NJ: Princeton University Press.

Kasekende Louis, Ndikumana Léonce, and Rajhi Taoufik. 2009. "Impact of the Global Financial and Economic Crisis on Africa," Working Papers Series no. 96. Tunis, Tunisia: African Development Bank.

Kenworthy, Lane. 2006. "Institutional Coherence and Macro-economic Performance." *Socio-Economic Review*, vol. **4**, no. 1, pp. 69–91.

Keynes, John Maynard. 1936. *The General Theory of Employment, Interest and Money*. New York: Harcourt Brace.

Khalil, Akram Hanna. 2009. "The Global Financial Crisis: Effects on the Egyptian Economy." *Egyptian Commentary*, Issue 119, 25 January. http://acpss.ahram.org.eg/eng/ahram/2004/7/5/EGYP140.HTM

Khamis, May and Abdelhak Senhadji. 2010. "Learning From the Past." *Finance and Development*, vol. **47**, no. 1, pp. 50–52.

Khanna, Parag. 2008. *The Second World: How Emerging Powers are Redefining Global Competition in the 21st Century*. New York: Random House.

Kiff, John and Vladimir Klyuev. 2009. "Foreclosure Mitigation Efforts in the United States: Approaches and Challenges," IMF Staff Position Note, SPN/09/02. Washington, DC: International Monetary Fund.

Kindleberger, Charles. 1973. *The World in Depression: 1929–1939*. Berkeley: University of California Press.

Kindleberger, Charles and Robert Aliber. 2005. *Manias, Panics, and Crashes*, 5th ed. Hoboken, NJ: John Wiley and Sons.

Kirby, Peadar. 2002. *The Celtic Tiger in Distress: the Growth of Inequality in Ireland*. Basingstoke: Palgrave.

Kirkegaard, Jacob Funk. 2010. "How Europe Can Muddle Through Its Crisis," *Policy Brief*, no. PB10–27, Washington, DC: Peterson Institute for International Economics.

Kirshner, Jonathan, ed. 2003. *Monetary Orders: Ambiguous Economics, Ubiquitous Politics*. Ithaca, NY: Cornell University Press.

1997. *Currency and Coercion: The Political Economy of International Monetary Power*. Princeton, NJ: Princeton University Press.

Kling, Arnold and Nick Schulz. 2009. "Markets Fail. That's Why We Need Markets." *Christian Science Monitor*, 28 December. http://www.csmonitor.com/Commentary/Opinion/2009/1228/Markets-fail.-That-s-why-we-need-markets

Knott, Jack. 2012. "The President, Congress, and the Financial Crisis: Ideology and Moral Hazard in Economic Governance." *Presidential Studies Quarterly*, vol. **42**, no. 1, pp. 81–100.

Kojima, Akira. 2009. "Japan's Economy and the Global Financial Crisis." *Asia Pacific Review*, vol. **16**, no. 2, pp. 15–24.

Kolb, Robert, ed. 2011. *Financial Contagion: The Viral Threat to the Wealth of Nations*. Hoboken, NJ: John Wiley and Sons.

Konzelmann, Sue, Marc Fovargue-Davies, and Gerhard Schnyder. 2012. "The Faces of Liberal Capitalism: Anglo-Saxon Banking Systems in Crisis." *Cambridge Journal of Economics*, vol. **36**, no. 1, pp. 495–524.

Koo, Richard. 2009. *The Holy Grail of Macroeconomics: Lessons from Japan's Great Recession*. Hoboken, NJ: John Wiley and Sons.

Kose, M. Ayhan and Eswar Prasad. 2010. *Emerging Markets: Resilience and Growth amid Global Turmoil*. Washington, DC: Brookings Institution Press.

Kose, M. Ayhan, Christopher Otrok, and Eswar Prasad. 2008. "Global Business Cycles: Convergence or Decoupling?" IMF Working Paper, WP/08/143, Washington, DC: International Monetary Fund.

Kotlikoff, Laurence and Scott Burns. 2012. *The Clash of Generations: Saving Ourselves, Our Kids, and Our Economy*. Cambridge, MA: MIT Press.

Kotz, David. 2009. "Economic Crises and Institutional Structures: A Comparison of Regulated and Neoliberal Capitalism in the U.S.," in J. Goldstein and M. Hillard, eds. *Heterodox Macroeconomics: Keynes, Marx and Globalization*. London: Routledge, pp. 176–188.

Kowsmann, Patricia, Costas Paris, and Stephen Fidler. 2011. "Euro Zone Reaches Deal on Greek Debt," *The Wall Street Journal*, July 21, p. 4.

Krippner, Greta. 2011. *Capitalizing on Crisis: The Political Origins of the Rise of Finance*. Cambridge, MA: Harvard University Press.

Krugman, Paul. 2012a. "What Ails Europe?" *The New York Times*, February 26. http://www.nytimes.com/2012/02/27/opinion/krugman-what-ails-europe.html?_r=1&pagewanted=print

2012b. *End This Depression Now*. New York: W.W. Norton.

2011. "Legends of the Fail." *The New York Times*, November 10, p. A35.

2010. "Eating the Irish." *New York Times*, November 26. http://www.nytimes.com/2010/11/26/opinion/26krugman.html?pagewanted=print

2010a. "Chinese New Year." *The New York Times*, January 1. http://www.nytimes.com/2010/01/01/opinion/01krugman.html

2010b. "The Euro Trap," *The New York Times*, April 30. http://www.nytimes.com/2010/04/30/opinion/30krugman.html

2009a. *The Return of Depression Economics and the Crisis of 2008*. New York: W.W. Norton.

2009b. "How Did Economists Get It So Wrong," *New York Times Magazine*, September 6, pp. 36–43.

2009c. "Stressing the Positive," *The New York Times*, May 8, p. A31.

2008a. "The International Financial Multiplier," available at www.princeton.edu/~pkrugman

2008b. *The Return of Depression Economics and the Crisis of 2008*. New York: W.W. Norton.

1993. "Lessons of Massachusetts for EMU," in Francesco Giavazzi and Francisco Torres, eds. *Adjustment and Growth in the European Monetary Union*, New York: Cambridge University Press, pp. 241–61.

1984. "The International Role of the Dollar: Theory and Prospect," in John Bilson and Richard Marison, eds. *Exchange Rate Theory and Practice*. Chicago: University of Chicago Press, pp. 261–78.

Kuttner, Kenneth and Adam Posen. 2001. "The Great Recession: Lessons for Macroeconomic Policy from Japan," *Brookings Papers on Economic Activity*, No. 2, pp. 93–185.

Kwong, Charles. 2011. "China's Banking Reform: The Remaining Agenda." *Global Economic Review*, vol. **40**, no. 2, pp. 161–78.

Landon, Thomas. 2012. "New Bailout Is a Reprieve for Greece, but Doubts Persist." *The New York Times*, February 21. http://www.nytimes.com/2012/02/22/business/global/greece-dodges-bullet-with-new-bailout-but-doubts-remain.html?_r=1&pagewanted=print

Lane, David. 2011. "The Impact of Economic Crisis: Russia, Belarus and Ukraine in Comparative Perspective." *Journal of Communist Studies and Transition Politics*, vol. **27**, nos. 3–4, pp. 587–604.

Laqueur, Walter. 2012. *After the Fall: The End of the European Dream and the Decline of a Continent*. New York: St. Martin's Press.

Lardy, Nicholas. 2010. "The Sustainability of China's Recovery from the Global Recession," *Policy Brief*, no. PB10-7, Washington, DC: Peterson Institute for International Economics.

2006. "China: Toward a Consumption-Driven Growth Path," *Policy Briefs in International Economics*, no. PB06-6, Washington, DC: Institute for International Economics Policy.

2005. "China: The Great New Economic Challenge" in C. Fred Bergsten, ed. *The United States and the World Economy: Foreign Economic Policy for the Next Decade.* Washington, DC: Institute for International Economics, pp. 121–142.

László, Andor. 2009. "Hungary in the Financial Crisis: A (Basket) Case Study." *Debatte: Journal of Contemporary Central and Eastern Europe,* vol. **17**, no. 3, pp. 285–96.

Lavelle, Kathryn. 2004. *The Politics of Equity Finance in Emerging Markets.* New York: Oxford University Press.

Lavoie, Marc. 2009. *Introduction to Post-Keynesian Economics.* New York: Palgrave Macmillan.

Lawrence, Robert. 2012. "How Can Trade Policy Help America Compete?" *Policy Brief,* no. PB12–21, Washington, DC: Peterson Institute for International Economics.

Lee, Jong-Wha and Cyn-Young Park. 2009. "Global Financial Turmoil: Impact and Challenges for Asia's Financial Systems," *Asian Economic Papers,* vol. **8**, no. 1, pp. 9–40.

Lee, Jong-Wha and Changyong Rhee. 2007. "Crisis and Recovery: What We Have Learned from the South Korean Experience?" *Asian Economic Policy Review,* vol. **2**, no. 1, pp. 146–64.

Levchenko, Andrei, Logan Lewis, and Linda Tesar. 2010. "The Collapse of International Trade during the 2008–09 Crisis: In Search of the Smoking Gun." *IMF Economic Review,* vol. **58**, no. 2, pp. 214–53.

Lewis, Michael. 2010. *The Big Short: Inside the Doomsday Machine.* New York: W.W. Norton.

Lieber, Robert. 2007. *The American Era: Power and Strategy for the 21st Century.* New York: Cambridge University Press.

Liebowitz, Stan. 2008. "Anatomy of a Train Wreck: Causes of the Mortgage Meltdown," Policy Report, Washington, DC: Independent Institute, pp. 1–29.

Lin, Justin Yifu. 2012. *Demystifying the Chinese Economy.* New York: Cambridge University Press.

Lin, Justin Yifu, Hinh T. Dinh, and Fernando Im. 2010. "US-China External Imbalances and the Global Financial Crisis." *China Economic Journal,* vol. **3**, no. 1, pp. 1–24.

Lin, Justin Yifu, Fang Cai, and Zhou Li. 2003. *The China Miracle: Development Strategy and Economic Reform.* Hong Kong: Chinese University Press.

Lo, Chi. 2009. *Asia and the Subprime Crisis: Lifting the Veil on the Financial Tsunami.* New York: Palgrave Macmillan.

Lowenstein, Roger. 2010. *The End of Wall Street.* New York: Penguin.

Lund, Susan and Charles Roxburgh. 2010. "Debt and Deleveraging: The Global Credit Bubble and its Economic Consequences." *World Economics,* vol. **11**, no. 2, pp. 1–30.

Lynch, David. 2010. *When the Luck of the Irish Ran Out: The World's Most Resilient Country and Its Struggle to Rise Again.* New York: Palgrave Macmillan.

Lynn, Matthew. 2010. *Bust: Greece, the Euro, and the Sovereign Debt Crisis.* New York: Bloomberg Press.

MacSharry, Ray and Padraic White. 2000. *The Making of the Celtic Tiger: The Inside Story of Ireland's Boom Economy.* Dublin: Mercier Press.

McDonald, Lawrence and Patrick Robinson. 2009. *A Colossal Failure of Common Sense: The Inside Story of the Collapse of Lehman Brothers.* New York: Crown Business.

McKee, Bob. 2010. "The Unfolding Sovereign Debt Crisis." *World Economics*, vol. **11**, no. 4, pp. 37–50.

McKinnon, Robert. 2005. *Exchange Rates under the East Asian Dollar Standard: Living with Conflicted Virtue*. Cambridge, MA: MIT Press.

McKinnon, Ronald. 1979. *Money in International Exchange*. New York: Oxford University Press.

McKinsey Global Institute. 2010. *Debt and Deleveraging: The Global Credit Bubble and its Economic Consequences*. Mckinsey and Company. January, pp. 1–94.

McKissack, Adam and Jessica Xu. 2011. "Chinese Macroeconomic Management through the Crisis and Beyond." *Asian-Pacific Economic Literature*, vol. 25, Issue 1, May, pp. 43–55.

McLean, Bethany and Joe Nocera. 2010. *All the Devils are Here: The Hidden History of the Financial Crisis*. London: Penguin.

McNally, Christopher. 2011. "China's Changing *Guanxi* Capitalism: Private Entrepreneurs between Leninist Control and Relentless Accumulation." *Business and Politics*, vol. **13**, no. 3, pp. 1–28.

Ma, Guonan. 2007. "Who Pays China's Bank Restructuring Bill?" *Asian Economic Papers*, vol. **6**, no. 1, pp. 46–71.

Ma, Guonan and Wang Yi. 2011. "Why is the Chinese Saving Rate so High?" *World Economics*, vol. **12**, no. 1, pp. 1–26.

Madrick, Jeff. 2010. *The Age of Greed: The Triumph of Finance and the Decline of America, 1970 to the Present*. New York: Knopf.

   2008. *The Case for Big Government*. Princeton, NJ: Princeton University Press.

Majone, Giandomenico. 2009. *Europe as the Would-Be World Power: The EU at Fifty*. New York: Cambridge University Press.

Makin, Anthony. 2009. *Global Imbalances, Exchange Rates and stabilization Policy*. New York: Palgrave Macmillan.

   2007. "Does China's Huge External Surplus Imply an Undervalued Renminbi?" *China and the World Economy*, vol. **15**, no. 3, pp. 89–102.

Mallaby, Sebastian. 2010. *More Money than God: Hedge Funds and the Making of a New Elite*. New York: Penguin.

Mandelbaum, Michael. 2010. *The Frugal Superpower: America's Global Leadership in a Cash-Strapped Era*. New York: Public Affairs.

   2005. *The Case for Goliath: How America Acts as the World's Government in the Twenty-first Century*. New York: PublicAffairs.

Marer, P. 2010. "The Global Economic Crises: Impacts on Eastern Europe." *Acta Oeconomica*, vol. **60**, no. 1, pp. 3–33.

Marquand, David. 2011. *The End of the West: The Once and Future Europe*, Princeton, NJ: Princeton University Press.

Marron, Donald. 2010. "America in the Red." *National Affairs*, no. 3, Spring, pp. 3–19.

Martin, Andrew and George Ross, eds. 2004. *Euros and Europeans: Monetary Integration and the European Model of Society*. New York: Cambridge University Press.

Martin, Reiner. 2010. "Boom and Bust in the Baltic Countries – Lessons to be Learnt." *Intereconomics*, vol. **45**, no. 4, pp. 220–26.

Marsh, David. 2009. *The Euro: The Politics of the New Global Currency*. New Haven, CT: Yale University Press.

Mattli, Walter and Ngaire Woods, eds. 2009. *The Politics of Global Regulation*. Princeton, NJ: Princeton University Press.

Martinez-Diaz, Leonardo. 2009. *Globalizing in Hard Times the Politics of Banking-Sector Opening in the Emerging World*. New York: Cornell University Press.

Massa, Isabella, Jodie Keane, and Jane Kennan. 2012. "The Euro Zone Crisis and Developing Countries," Working Paper 345, London: Overseas Development Institute.

Mauldin, William. 2008. "Russia Providing $200 Billion for Banks, Builders." *Bloomberg*, 7 October. http://www.bloomberg.com/apps/news?pid=newsarchive&sid=a16Bn NfBwIkw

Mayer, Martin. 1997. *The Bankers: The Next Generation*. New York: Truman Talley Books/Dutton.

Mayhew, David. 2008. *Parties and Policies: How American Government Works*. New Haven, CT: Yale University Press.

Mehrling, Perry. 2011. *The New Lombard Street: How the Fed Became the Dealer of the Last Resort*. Princeton, NJ: Princeton University Press.

Meltzer, Allan. 2009. "What Happened to the Depression?" *Wall Street Journal*, August 31. http://online.wsj.com/article/SB10001424052970204251404574342931435353 734.html

2008. "End of the American Century," *World Economics*, vol. **9**, no. 4, pp. 1–11.

2003. *A History of the Federal Reserve, Volume 1: 1913–1951*. Chicago: University of Chicago Press.

Mian, Atif and Amir Sufi. 2012. "What Explains High Unemployment? The Aggregate Demand Channel," NBER Working Paper, no. 17830, Cambridge, MA: National Bureau of Economic Research.

2009. "House Prices, Home Equity-based Borrowing, and the U.S. Household Leverage Crisis," NBER Working Paper, no. 15283, Cambridge, MA: National Bureau of Economic Research.

Mian, Atif, Amir Sufi, and Francesco Trebbi. 2010. "The Political Economy of the Subprime Mortgage Credit Expansion," Working Paper, no. 10–21. Chicago: The University of Chicago Booth School of Business.

Michael, Oliver. 2007. *Economic Disasters of the Twentieth Century*. Northampton, MA: Edward Elgar Publishing.

Milanovic, Branko. 2011. *The Haves and the Have-Nots: A Brief and Idiosyncratic History of Global Inequality*. New York: Basic Books.

Minsky, Hyman P. 1986. *Stabilizing an Unstable Economy*. New Haven, CT: Yale University Press.

1982. *Can It Happen Again? Essays on Instability and Finance*. Armonk, NY: M. E. Sharpe.

1975. *John Maynard Keynes*. New York: Columbia University Press.

Mishkin, Frederic. 2011a. "Over the Cliff: From the Subprime to the Global Financial Crisis." *Journal of Economic Perspectives*, vol. **23**, no. 1, pp. 49–70.

2011b. *Macroeconomics: Policy and Practice*. Boston: Addison-Wesley.

2006. *The Next Great Globalization: How Disadvantaged Nations Can Harness Their Financial Systems to Get Rich*. Princeton, NJ: Princeton University Press.

Mitchell, Daniel J. 2009. "Spending Is Not Stimulus: Bigger Government Did Not Work for Bush, and It Will Not Work for Obama," *Cato Institute Tax and Budget Bulletin*, No. 53. Washington, DC: Cato Institute.

Mitra, Pradeep. 2010. "The Impact of Global Financial Crisis and Policy Responses: The Caucasus, Central Asia and Mongolia." *Global Journal of Emerging Market Economies*, vol. **2**, no. 2, pp. 189–230.

Mitra, Pradeep, Marcelo Selowski, and Juan Zalduendo. 2009. *Turmoil at Twenty: Recession, Recovery and Reform in Central and Eastern Europe and the former Soviet Union*. Washington, DC: The World Bank.

Mohan, Rakesh. 2008. "Global Financial Crisis and Key Risks: Impact on India and Asia," Remarks by Deputy Governor Reserve Bank of India presented at IMF-FSF High-Level Meeting on the Recent Financial Turmoil and Policy Responses, Washington DC, October 9.

Mohieldin, Mahmoud. 2008. "Point of View: Neighborly Investments." *Finance and Development*, vol. **45**, no. 4, pp. 40–42.

Monsarrat, Alexei and Skinner Kiron. 2010. *Renewing Globalization and Economic Growth in a Post-Crisis World*. Pennsylvania: Carnegie-Mellon University Press.

Montgomery, Lori and Anthony Faiola. 2009. "Geithner Says China Manipulates Its Currency," *The Washington Post*, January 23, p. A08. http://www.washingtonpost.com/wpdyn/content/article/2009/01/22/AR2009012203796.html

Moravcsik, Andrew. 2012. "Europe after the Crisis: How to Sustain a Common Currency." *Foreign Affairs*, vol. **91**, no. 3, pp. 54–68.

Morgan, Glyn. 2005. *The Idea of a European Superstate: Public Justification and European Integration*. Princeton, NJ: Princeton University Press.

Morrison, Wayne. 2008. *CRS Report for Congress: China-U.S. Trade Issues*. Order Code 33536. Washington, DC: Congressional Research Service.

Morrison, Wayne and Marc Labonte. 2011. *China's Currency Policy: An Analysis of the Economic Issues*. December 19, No. RS21625. Washington, DC: Congressional Research Service. p. 2.

  2009. *China's Currency: A Summary of the Economic Issues*. No. RS21625. Washington, DC: Congressional Research Service.

  2008. *China's Holdings of U.S. Securities: Implications for the U.S. Economy*. Order Code RL34314. Washington, DC: Congressional Research Service. www.fas.org/sgp/crs/row/RL34314.pdf.

Morse, Edward. 2009. "Low and Behold: Making the Most of Cheap Oil." *Foreign Affairs*, vol. **88**, no. 5, pp. 36–52.

Mortenson, Gretchen and Joshua Rosner. 2011. *Reckless Endangerment: How Outsized Ambition, Greed and Corruption Led to Economic Armageddon*. New York: Times Books, Henry Holt and Company.

Moses, Abigail. 2012. "Greece Deal Triggers $3B in Default Swaps: ISDA." *Bloomberg*, March 9, http://www.bloomberg.com/news/print/2012-03-09/greek-debt-deal-might-trigger-3-billion-of-default-swaps-under-isda-rules.html.

Motonishi, Taizo and Hiroshi Yoshikawa. 1999. "Causes of the Long Stagnation of Japan during the 1990s: Financial or Real?" *Journal of the Japanese and International Economies*, vol. **13**, no. 3, pp.181–200.

Mourlon-Druol, Emmanuel. 2012. *A Europe Made of Money: The Emergence of the European Monetary System*. Ithaca, NY: Cornell University Press.

Muolo, Paul and Mathew Padilla. 2008. *Chain of Blame: How Wall Street Caused the Mortgage and Credit Crisis*. Hoboken, NJ: John Wiley.

Munchau, Wolfgang. 2010. *The Meltdown Years*. New York: McGraw-Hill.

Mundell, Robert. 1961. "A Theory of Optimum Currency Areas." *American Economic Review*, vol. **54**, no. 4, pp. 657–65.

Naughton, Barry. 2009. "In China's Economy, the State's Hand Grows Heavier." *Current History*, vol. **108**, issue 719, pp. 277–83.

Newman, Katherine. 2008. *Laid Off, Laid Low: Political and Economic Consequences of Employment Insecurity*. New York: Columbia University Press.

Nicoll, Alexander. 2008. "The Importance of the Financial Crisis." *Survival*, vol. **50**, no. 6, pp. 5–14.

Nolan, Brian, Philip J. O'Connell, and Christopher Whelan, eds. 2000. *Bust to Boom: The Irish Experience of Growth and Inequality*. Dublin: Institute of Public Administration.

Norberg, Johan. 2009. *Financial Fiasco: How America's Infatuation with Homeownership and Easy Money Created the Economic Crisis*. Washington, DC: Cato Institute.

Northcott, Carol Ann, Graydon Paulin, and Mark White. 2009. "Lessons for Banking Reform: A Canadian Perspective." *Central Banking*, vol. **19**, no. 4, pp. 1–12.

Nutting, Rex. 2012. "European Bank's Shaky Finances." *The Wall Street Journal*, March 3. http://online.wsj.com/article/SB10001424052970203986604577255233089782226.html?mod

Nye, Joseph. 2011. *The Future of Power*. New York: Public Affairs.

O'Hagan, John W., ed. 2000. *The Economy of Ireland: Policy and Performance of a European Region*. Dublin: Gill and Macmillan.

O'Hearn, Denis. 1998. *Inside the Celtic Tiger: The Irish Economy and the Asian Model*. London: Pluto Press.

O'Riain, Sean. 2004. *The Politics of High Tech Growth: Developmental Network States in the Global Economy*. Cambridge, MA: Cambridge University Press.

O'Sullivan, K.P.V. and Tom Kennedy. 2010. "What Caused the Irish Banking Crisis." *Journal of Financial Regulation and Compliance*, vol. **18**, no. 3, pp. 224–42.

O'Toole, Fintan. 2009. *Ship of Fools: How Stupidity and Corruption Sank the Celtic Tiger*. London: Faber and Faber.

Obstfeld, Maurice, Jay C. Shambaugh, and Alan M. Taylor. 2010. "Financial Stability, the Trilemma, and International Reserves." *American Economic Journal: Macroeconomics*, vol. **2**, no. 2, pp. 57–94.

Orenstein, Mitchell. 2009. *Pensions, Social Security, and the Privatization of Risk*. New York: Columbia University Press.

Organization for Economic Co-Operation and Development (OECD). 2012. *OECD Sovereign Borrowing Outlook 2012*. Paris: Organization for Economic Co-Operation and Development.

2010. *Economic Survey of China*. Paris: Organization for Economic Co-Operation and Development.

2009a. *Economic Survey of Japan 2009*. Paris: Organization for Economic Co-Operation and Development.

2009b. *Economic Survey: Greece*. Paris: Organization for Economic Co-Operation and Development.

2009c. *Economic Survey of Russia 2009: Stabilization and Renewed Growth: Key Challenges*. Paris: Organization for Economic Co-Operation and Development.

2008a. *Economic Survey of Korea, 2008*. Paris: Organization for Economic Co-Operation and Development.

2008b. *Competition Issues in the Financial Sector: Key Findings*. Paris: Organization for Economic Co-Operation and Development.

2007. *Agricultural Policies in OECD Countries: Monitoring and Evaluation 2007*. Paris: Organization for Economic Co-Operation and Development.

2005. *OECD Economic Survey: China*. Paris: Organization for Economic Co-Operation and Development.

2005a. *Recent Tax Policy Trends and Reforms in OECD Countries*. Paris: Organization for Economic Co-Operation and Development.

Orhangazi, Ozgur. 2008. *Financialization and the US Economy*. Northampton, MA: Edward Elgar Publishing.

Overholt, William. 2010. "China in the Global Financial Crisis: Rising Influence, Rising Challenges." *The Washington Quarterly*, vol. **33**, no. 1, pp. 21–34.

Owens, Jeffrey. 2005. "Fundamental Tax Reform: The Experience of OECD Countries." *Tax Foundation Background Paper*, No. 47. Washington, DC: Tax Foundation.

Padoa-Schioppa, Tommaso. 2004. *The Euro and its Central Bank: Getting United after the Union*. Cambridge, MA: MIT Press.

Palan, Ronen, Murphy Richard, and Chavagneux Christian. 2009. *Tax Havens: How Globalization Really Works*. New York: Cornell University Press.

Panagariya, Arvind. 2008. *India: The Emerging Giant*. New York: Oxford University Press.

Park, Yung-Chul. 2009. "Global Economic Recession and East Asia: How Has Korea Managed the Crisis and What Has it Learned?" Working Paper, no. 409, Seoul: Bank of Korea, Institute for Monetary and Economic Research.

Park, Yung-Chul and Chi-Young Song. 2011. "Prospects for Monetary Cooperation in East Asia." ADBI Working Paper Series, no. 314. Manila: Asian Development Bank Institute.

Pat, K.A. 2009. "Why Indian Banks Are Healthy in This Global Crisis." *Economic and Political Weekly*, vol. **44**, no. 17, pp. 21–22.

Patil, R. H. 2010. "Financial Sector Reforms: Realities and Myths." *Economic and Political Weekly*, vol. **45**, no. 18, pp. 48–61.

Patrick, Stewart. 2008. *The Best Laid Plans: The Origins of American Multilateralism and the Dawn of the Cold War*. Lanham, MD: Rowman and Littlefield.

Patterson, Scott. 2010. *The Quants: How a New Breed of Math Whizzes Conquered Wall Street and Nearly Destroyed It*. New York: Crown Publishers.

Paulson, Henry. 2010. *On the Brink: Inside the Race to Stop the Collapse of the Global Financial System*. New York: Business Plus.

2008. Testimony by Secretary Henry Paulson before the Senate Banking Committee on Turmoil in the U.S. Credit Markets: Recent Actions Regarding Government Sponsored Entities, Investment Banks, and Other Financial Institutions. 23 September. U.S. Department of the Treasury http://www.treasury.gov/press-center/press-releases/Pages/hp1153.aspx

Peláez, Carlos. 2009. *Regulation of Banks and Finance, Theory and Policy after the Credit Crisis*. New York: Palgrave Macmillan.

Petrakov, N.Ya. 2010. "The Possibilities of Dealing with the Impact of the Economic Crisis in Russia." *Studies on Russian Economic Development*, vol. **21**, no. 1, pp. 1–4.

Phillips, Kevin. 2008. *Bad Money: Reckless Finance, Failed Politics and the Global Crisis of American Capitalism*. New York: Viking Adult.

Piketty, Thomas and Emmanuel Saez. 2003. "Income Inequality in the United States," *Quarterly Journal of Economics*, vol. **118**, no. 1, pp. 1–39.

Pisani-Ferry, Jean and Adam Posen, eds. 2009. *The Euro at Ten: The Next Global Currency?* Washington, DC: Institute for International Economics.

Polanyi, Karl. 1944. *The Great Transformation*. Boston: Beacon Press.

Portes, Richard. 2009. "Global Imbalances," in Mathias Dewatripont, Xabier Freixas, and Richard Portes, eds. *Macroeconomic Stability and Financial Regulation: Key Issues for the G-20*. London: Centre for Economic Policy Research, pp. 19–26.

Posner, Richard. 2010. *The Crisis of Capitalist Democracy*. Cambridge, MA: Harvard University Press.

2009. *A Failure of Capitalism: The Crisis of '08 and the Descent into Depression*. Cambridge, MA: Harvard University Press.

Prasad, Monica. 2012. *The Land of Too Much: American Abundance and the Paradox of Poverty*. Cambridge, MA: Harvard University Press.

Rachman, Gideon. 2011. *Zero-Sum Future: American Power in an Age of Anxiety*. New York: Simon and Schuster.

Rajan, Raghuram. 2010. *Fault Lines: How Hidden Fractures Still Threaten the World Economy*, Princeton, NJ: Princeton University Press.

2005. "Has Financial Development Made the World Riskier?" *The Greenspan Era: Lessons for the Future*. Kansas City: Federal Reserve Bank of Kansas, pp. 313–69.

Rajan, Ramkishen. 2009. *Exchange Rates, Currency Crisis and Monetary Cooperation in Asia*. New York: Palgrave Macmillan.

Rajan, Ramkishen and Sasidaran Gopalan. 2010. "India's International Reserves: How Large and How Diversified?" *Global Economy Journal*, vol. **10**, issue 3, pp. 1–16.

2009. "India and the Global Financial Crisis: Impact and Responses." *South Asia*, vol. 10, no. 14, pp. 6–8.

Ram, Mohan T.T. 2009. "The Impact of the Crisis on the Indian Economy." *Economic and Political Weekly*, vol. **44**, no. 13, pp. 107–14.

Ratanpal, Amit. 2008. "Indian Economy and Indian Private Equity," *Thunderbird International Business Review*, vol. **60**, no. 6, pp. 353–58.

Ratha, Dilip, Sanket Mohapatra, and Anil Silwal. 2009. "Migration and Remittance Trends 2009." *Migration and Development Brief*, No. 11. Washington, DC: World Bank: Migration and Remittances Team. http://www.worldbank.org/prospects/migrationandremittances.

Raudla, Ringa and Rainer Kattel. 2011. "Why Did Estonia Choose Fiscal Retrenchment after the 2008 Crisis?" *Journal of Public Policy*, vol. **31**, no. 2, pp. 163–86.

Ravallion, Martin. 2009. "Bailing out the World's Poorest." *Challenge*, vol. **52**, no. 2, pp. 55–80.

Read, Collin. 2009. *Global Financial Meltdown: How We Can Avoid The Next Economic Crisis*. New York: Palgrave McMillan.

Reddy, Y.V. 2009. "India's Financial Sector in Current Times." *Economic and Political Weekly*, vol. **44**, no. 45, pp. 13–15.

Reich, Robert. 2010. *Aftershock: The Next Economy and America's Future*. New York: Vintage.

Reichley, James. 1981. *Conservatives in an Age of Change: The Nixon and Ford Administrations*. Washington, DC: The Brookings Institution.

Reinhart, Carmen and Vincent Reinhart. 2010. "5 Myths about the European Debt Crisis." *The Washington Post*, May 9, p. B03.

Reinhart, Carmen and Kenneth Rogoff. 2009. *This Time is Different: Eight Centuries of Financial Folly*. Princeton, NJ: Princeton University Press.

Reserve Bank of India (RBI). 2009a. *Annual Report of the RBI for the Year 2008–09*. New Delhi.

2009b. *Macroeconomic and Monetary Developments: Second Quarter Review*. New Delhi.

2009c. *Report of the Committee on Financial Sector Assessment*. New Delhi.

2008. *Report on Trend and Progress of Banking in India: 2007–2008*. New Delhi.

Reyes, Paul. 2010. *Exiles in Eden: Life Among the Ruins of Florida's Great Recession*. New York: Henry Holt and Company.

Rhodes, William. 2011. *Banker to the World: Leadership Lessons From the Front Lines of Global Finance*. New York: McGraw-Hill.

Riedel, James. Jing Jin and Jian Gao. 2007. *How China Grows: Investment, Finance and Reforms*. Princeton, NJ: Princeton University Press.

Roberts, Russell. 2008. "How Government Stoked the Mania." *Wall Street Journal*, October 3. http://online.wsj.com/article/SB122298982558700341.html

Rochet, Jean-Charles. 2008. *Why Are There So Many Banking Crises? The Politics and Policy of Bank Regulation*. Princeton, NJ: Princeton University Press.

Rodrik, Dani. 2011. *The Globalization Paradox: Democracy and the Future of the World Economy*. New York: W.W. Norton.

2007. *One Economics, Many Recipes: Globalization, Institutions and Economic Growth*. Princeton, NJ: Princeton University Press.

Rogoff, Kenneth. 2010. "The Euro at Mid-Crisis." *Project Syndicate*, December 2, http://www.project-syndicate.org/commentary/rogoff75/English

Romer, Christina. 2009. "Fiscal Policy and Economic Recovery." *Business Economics*, vol. **44**, no. 3, pp. 132–35.

Rosato, Sebastian. 2010. *Europe United: Power Politics and the Making of the European Community*. Ithaca, NY: Cornell University Press.

Rother, Björn. 2009. *The Determinants of Currency Crises: A Political Economy Approach*. New York: Palgrave Macmillan.

Roubini, Nouriel and Stephen Mihm. 2010. *Crisis Economics: A Crash Course in the Future of Finance*. New York: Penguin Press.

Roubini, Nouriel and Brad Setser. 2004. *Bailouts or Bail-ins? Responding to Financial Crises in Emerging Economies*. Washington, DC: Institute for International Economics.

Saccomann, Fabrizio. 2008. *Managing International Financial Instability*. Northampton, MA: Edward Elgar Publishing.

Sachs, Jeffrey. 2009. "Achieving Global Cooperation on Economic Recovery and Long-Term Sustainable Development." *Asian Development Review*, vol. **26**, no. 1, pp. 3–15.

2005. *The End of Poverty: Economic Possibilities of Our Time*. New York: Penguin.

Sapir, Andre. 2011. "Europe after the Crisis: Less or More Role for Nation States in Money and Finance." *Oxford Review of Economic Policy*, vol. **27**, no. 4, pp. 608–19.

Sapir, Jacques. 2008. "Russia and the World Financial Crisis: Impact, Opportunities and Risks.", Paris: École des Hautes Études en Sciences Sociales. http://www.iris-france. org/docs/pdf/forum/2008_02_14_russia.pdf

Sarotte, Mary Elise. 2011. *1989: The Struggle to Create Post-Cold War Europe*. Princeton, NJ: Princeton University Press.

Schenk, Catherine. 2010. *The Decline of Sterling: Managing the Retreat of an International Currency, 1945–1992*. New York: Cambridge University Press.

Schwartz, Anna. 2009. "Origins of the Financial Market Crisis of 2008." *Cato Journal*, vol. **29**, no. 1, pp. 19–23.

2007. "The Role of Monetary Policy in the Face of Crises." *Cato Journal*, vol. **27**, no. 2, pp. 157–63.

Schwartz, Herman. 2009. *Subprime Nation: American Power, Global Capital, and the Housing Bubble*. Ithaca, NY: Cornell University Press.

Schwartz, Nelson and Liz Alderman. 2011. "France Keeps a Watchful Eye on Turmoil in Italy." *The New York Times*, November 13, p. B1.

Scott, James C. 1998. *Seeing Like a State: How Certain Schemes to Improve the Human Condition Have Failed*. New Haven, CT: Yale University Press.

Secchi, Carlo and Villafranca Antonio. 2009. *Liberalism in Crisis*. MA: Edward Elgar Publishing.

Sestanovich, Stephen. 2008. "Russia and the Global Economic Crisis." *Expert Brief*, Naw York: Council on Foreign Relations.

Setser, Brad. 2008. "Impact of China Investment Corporation on the Management of China's Foreign Assets," in Morris Goldstein and Nicholas Lardy, eds. *Debating China's Exchange Rate Policy*. Washington, DC: The Peterson Institute, pp. 201–18.

Setser, Brad and Rachel Ziemba. 2009. "GCC Sovereign Funds: Reversal of Fortune." *CGS Working Paper*, New York: Council on Foreign Relations Press.

Sharma, Shalendra. 2010. "China as the World's Creditor and the United States as the World's Debtor: Implications for Sino-American Relations." *China Perspectives*, no. 4, pp. 100–16.

2009a. *China and India in the Age of Globalization*. New York: Cambridge University Press.

2009b. "The Other Global Crisis: Combating the Food and Humanitarian Crisis," *International Journal*, vol. **64**, no. 2, pp. 501–20.

2007. *Achieving Economic Development in the Era of Globalization*. London: Routledge.

2004. "Resolving Sovereign Debt: Collective Action Clauses or the (SDRM) Sovereign Debt Restructuring Mechanism." *Journal of World Trade*, vol. **38**, no. 4, pp. 627–46.

2003. *The Asian Financial Crisis: Crisis, Reform and Recovery*. Manchester: Manchester University Press.

Sharma, Shalendra and Nicholas Imparato. 2009. "The World's Poorest Nations and the Global Financial Crisis." *World Economics*, vol.**10**, no. 4, pp. 25–44.

Sharma, Shalendra and Sally Tam. "The Eurozone's Next Domino: Why Portugal is Not Greece." *World Economics*, vol. **13**, no. 2, pp. 125–53.

Sheard, Paul. 2009. "Japan and the Global Financial Crisis." *Global Asia*, vol. **4**, no. 1, pp. 1–7.

Sheng, Andrew. 2009. *From Asian to Global Financial Crisis: An Asian Regulator's View of Unfettered Finance in the 1990s and 2000s.* New York: Cambridge University Press.

Shih, Victor. 2010. "China's 8,000 Credit Risks." *The Wall Street Journal,* February 9. http://online.wsj.com/article/SB10001424052748703427704575052062978995460. html

Shiller, Robert. 2012. *Finance and the Good Society.* Princeton, NJ: Princeton University Press.

    2008. *The Subprime Solution: How Today's Global Financial Crisis Happened, and What to Do about It.* Princeton, NJ: Princeton University Press.

Silber, William. 2012. *Volcker: The Triumph of Persistence.* New York: Bloomsbury Press.

Sinclair, Timothy. 2008. *The New Masters of Capital: American Bond Rating Agencies and the Politics of Creditworthiness.* Ithaca, NY: Cornell University Press.

Singer, David Andrew. 2007. *Regulating Capital: Setting Standards for the International Financial System.* Ithaca, NY: Cornell University Press.

Skidelsky, Robert. 2009. *Keynes: The Return of the Master.* New York: Allen Lane.

Sommer, Martin. 2009. "Why Has Japan Been Hit So Hard by the Global Recession?" IMF Staff Position Note, No. SPN/09/05, Washington, DC: International Monetary Fund.

Sorkin, Andrew. 2011. "In a Bill, Wall Street Shows its Clout." *New York Times,* July 4. http://dealbook.nytimes.com/2011/07/04/in-a-bill-wall-street-shows-clout/

    2009. *Too Big to Fail: The Inside Story of How Wall Street and Washington Fought to Save the Financial System – and Themselves.* New York: Viking.

Soros, George. 2011. "Three Steps to Resolving the Eurozone Crisis," *Financial Times,* August 14, http://www.ft.com/cms/s/0/ba30bc32-c4f7–11e0-ba51–00144feabdc0. html#ixzz1V7JSQ7vE

    2009. "The Game Changer." *Financial Times,* 28 January, http://www.ft.com/intl/cms/ s/0/49b1654a-ed60–11dd-bd60–0000779fd2ac.html#axzz2TEIMhQd6.

    2008. *The New Paradigm for Financial Markets: The Credit Crisis of 2008 and What It Means.* New York: Public Affairs.

Spence, Michael. 2011. *The Next Convergence: The Future of Economic Growth in a Multispeed World.* New York: Farrar Straus Giroux.

Spiegel, Peter. 2011. "The Quest for a Second Greek Bail-out Is Beset by Conflict and Confusion." *Financial Times,* July 19. http://www.ft.com/cms/s/0/f297fb6a-b248– 11e0-9d80–00144feabdc0.html#ixzz1So2w7km6

Spiegel, Peter, Quentin Peel, Patrick Jenkins, and Richard Milne. 2011. "EU Leaders Agree to New Greek Bail-out," *Financial Times,* July 21. http://www.ft.com/cms/ s/0/952e0326-b3af-11e0–855b00144feabdc0.html#ixzz1SmCYNHDp

Steil, Benn. 2010. "Debt and Systemic Risk: The Contribution of Fiscal and Monetary Policy." *Cato Journal,* vol. **30**, no. 2, pp. 391–96.

Steil, Benn and Manuel Hinds. 2009. *Money, Markets and Sovereignty.* New Haven, CT: Yale University Press.

Stein, Jerome. 2011. "The Diversity of Debt Crises in Europe." *Cato Journal,* vol. **31**, no. 2, pp. 199–215.

Stenfield, Edward. 2010. *Playing Our Game: Why China's Economic Rise Doesn't Threaten the West.* New York: Oxford University Press.

Stephanou, Constantinos. 2009. "The Reform Agenda: Charting the Future of Financial Regulation." Crisis Response: Public Policy for the Private Sector, Note Number 2, Washington, DC: The World Bank.

Stiglitz, Joseph. 2010. *Freefall: America, Free Markets, and the Sinking of the World Economy*. New York: W.W. Norton.

———. 2009. "Obama's Ersatz Capitalism." *New York Times*, April 1, p. A31.

Stoner-Weiss, Kathryn. 2009. "Russia and the Global Financial Crisis: The End of Putinism"? *The Brown Journal of World Affairs*, vol. **15**, no. 2, pp. 103–15.

Stott, Michael. 2008. "Russia acknowledges financial crisis has hit hard," Reuters, November 21, http://www.reuters.com/article/idUSTRE4AK4L620081121

Stulz, Rene. 2010. "Credit Default Swaps and the Credit Crisis." *Journal of Economic Perspectives*, vol. **24**, no. 1, pp. 73–92.

———. 2009. "Financial Derivatives: Lessons from the Subprime Crisis." *The Milken Institute Review*, First Quarter, pp. 58–70.

Sturzenegger, Federico and Jeromin Zettelmeyer. 2006. *Debt Defaults and Lessons from a Decade of Crises*. Cambridge, MA: MIT Press.

Subbarao, Duvvuri. 2009. "Emerging Market Concerns: An Indian Perspective," Remarks by Dr. D. Subbarao, Governor, Reserve Bank of India at G-30 International Banking Seminar in Istanbul on October 5. http://rbi.org.in/scripts/BS_SpeechesView.aspx?Id=441

Subramanian, Arvind. 2011. *Eclipse: Living in the Shadow of China's Economic Dominance*. Washington, DC: Peterson Institute for International Economics.

———. 2010a. "Greek Deal Lets Banks Profit from "Immoral Hazard." *Financial Times*, May 6. Posted on Peterson Institute for International Economics Web site, http://www.iie.com/publications/opeds/oped.cfm?ResearchID=1566

———. 2010b. "New PPP-Based Estimates of Renminbi Undervaluation and Policy Implications." *Policy Brief*, no. PB10–8, Washington, DC: Peterson Institute for International Economics.

———. 2009. "India's Goldilocks Globalization," Washington, DC: Peterson Institute for International Economics. http://www.iie.com/publications/opeds/oped.cfm?ResearchID=1238

Summers, Lawrence. 2011. "How to Save the Eurozone." *The Financial Times*, 18 July. http://www.ft.com/cms/s/2/324f9054-b0a7–11e0-a5a700144feab49a.html#ixzz1SPfMRnFq

Syed, Murtaza, Kenneth Kang, and Kiichi Tokuoka. 2009. "Lost Decade" in Translation: What Japan's Crisis Could Portend about Recovery from the Great Recession," IMF Working Paper, WP/09/282, Washington, DC: International Monetary Fund.

Takenaka, Kiyoshi and Gleb Bryanski. 2010. "U.S. and China stick to guns on global balancing at APEC," November 13, Reuters. http://www.reuters.com/article/2010/11/13/us-apec-idUSTRE6AC0BB20101113

Talbott, John R. 2009. *Contagion: The Financial Epidemic That is Sweeping the Global Economy … and How to Protect Yourself From It*. Hoboken, NJ: John Wiley.

Taleb, Nassim Nicholas. 2010. *The Black Swan: The Impact of the Highly Improbable*, 2nd ed. New York: Random House.

Tanzi, Vito and Ludger Schuknecht. 2000. *Public Spending in the 20th Century: A Global Perspective*. Cambridge: Cambridge University Press.

Taylor, Alan. 2011. "The Financial Rebalancing Act." *Foreign Affairs* vol. **90**, no. 4, pp. 91–99.

Taylor, John. 2012. "A Better Grecian Bailout." *Wall Street Journal*, February 22. http://online.wsj.com/article/SB10001424052970204909104577236852645109964.html

——— 2011. "An Empirical Analysis of the Revival of Fiscal Activism in the 2000s," *Journal of Economic Literature*, vol. **49**, no. 3, pp. 686–702.

——— 2009. *Getting Off Track: How Government Actions and Interventions Caused, Prolonged, and Worsened the Financial Crisis*. Stanford, CA: Hoover Institution Press.

Tett, Gillian. 2009. *Fool's Gold: How the Bold Dream of a Small Tribe at J.P. Morgan Was Corrupted by Wall Street Greed and Unleashed a Catastrophe*. New York: Free Press.

Thibodeau, Patrick. 2008. "Greenspan: Bad Data Hurt Wall Street Computer Models." *New York Times*, 23 October http://www.nytimes.com/external/idg/2008/10/23/23idg-Greenspan-Bad.html.

Thomas, Jason. 2010. "Managing the Federal Debt." *National Affairs*, Fall, no. 5, pp. 20–34.

Thomas, Landon and Raphael Minder, 2012. "Cost of Spain's Housing Bust Could Force a Bailout," *New York Times*, April 24. http://www.nytimes.com/2012/04/25/business/global/cost-of-spains-housing-bust-could-force-a-bailout.

Tomz, Michael. 2007. *Reputation and International Cooperation: Sovereign Debt Across Three Centuries*. Princeton, NJ: Princeton University Press.

Trenin, Dimtri. 2009. "Russia Reborn: Reimagining Moscow's Foreign Policy." *Foreign Affairs*, vol. **88**, no. 6, pp. 64–78.

Truman, Edwin. 2011. "G-20 Reforms of the International Monetary System: An Evaluation," *Policy Brief*, no. PB11–19. Washington, DC: Peterson Institute for International Economics.

——— 2010. *Sovereign Wealth Funds: Threat or Salvation?* Washington, DC: Peterson Institute for International Economics.

Ueda, Kazuo. 2009. "Solving Japan's Economic Puzzle." *Far Eastern Economic Review*, Posted May 1, http://www.feer.com/essays/2009/may/solving-japans-economic-puzzle.

United Nations Conference on Trade and Development (UNCTAD). 2011. *The Least Developed Countries Report 2011: The Potential Role of South-South Cooperation for Inclusive and Sustainable Development*. Geneva, Switzerland.

——— 2010. *The Least Developed Countries Report 2010: Towards a New International Development Architecture for LDCs*. Geneva, Switzerland.

United Nations – Economic and Social Commission for Asia and the Pacific (UN-ESCAP). 2009. *Economic and Social Survey of Asia and the Pacific, 2009: Addressing Triple Threats to Development*. New York.

United States. 2009a. Remarks of President Barack Obama,Address to Joint Session of Congress, February 24. http://www.whitehouse.gov/the_press_office/remarks-of-president-barack-obamaaddress-to-joint-session-of-congress

——— 2009b. *A New Era of Responsibility: Renewing America's Promise*. Washington, DC: U.S. Government Office of Management and Budget.

——— 2008a. "*Housing Government-Sponsored Enterprises: A Single Regulator Will Better Ensure Safety and Soundness and Mission Achievement*," Statement of William B. Shear, Director, Financial Markets and Community Investment. March 6.

Washington, DC: U.S. Government Accountability Office. http://www.gao.gov/ new.items/d08563t.pdf

2008b. *The Economic Stimulus Act of 2008* (Pub.L. 110–185, 122 Stat. 613, enacted February 13. Washington, DC: U.S. Government Printing Office.

2008c. *The Housing and Economic Recovery Act of 2008* (Pub.L. 110–289, enacted July 30, Washington, DC: U.S. National Archives and Records Administration Government Printing Office.

2008d. Mid-Session Review, Budget of the U.S. Government, Fiscal Year 2009, July 2008. U.S. Government, Office of Management and Budget. www.whitehouse.gov/ omb/budget/fy2009/pdf/09msr.pdf.

United States Department of the Treasury. 2012. "Report to Congress on International Economic and Exchange Rate Policies," May 25. Washington, DC: U.S. Department of the Treasury, Office of International Affairs. http://www.gpo.gov/fdsys/pkg/ CRPT-112hrpt494/html/CRPT-112hrpt494.htm

2010. "Statement of Treasury Secretary Geithner On the Report to Congress on International Economic and Exchange Rate Policies," April 3. http://www.treasury. gov/press-center/press-releases/pages/tg627.aspx

2009a. "Financial Stability Plan." Fact Sheet, February 10. Washington, DC: U.S. Department of the Treasury, http://financialstability.gov/docs/fact-sheet.pdf

2009b. "Secretary Geithner Introduces Financial Stability Plan." Press Release, February 10. Washington, DC: U.S. Department of the Treasury, http://www.treas. gov/press/releases/tg18.htm

2009c. "*Homeowner Affordability and Stability Plan.*" Fact Sheet, February 18. Washington, DC: U.S. Department of the Treasury, http://www.treasury.gov/initia- tives/eesa/homeowner-affordability-plan/FactSheet.pdf

2008a. "Statement by Secretary Henry M. Paulson, Jr. on Treasury and Federal Housing Finance Agency Action to Protect Financial Markets and Taxpayers." September 7. Washington, DC: U.S. Department of the Treasury, http://www.ustreas.gov/press/ releases/hp1129.htm

2008b. "*Government Sponsored Enterprise Credit Facility.*" Fact sheet, September 7. Washington, DC: U.S. Department of the Treasury Office of Public Affairs, http:// www.ustreas.gov/press/releases/reports/gsecf_factsheet_090708.pdf

2008c. "*Treasury Senior Preferred Stock Purchase Agreement.*" Fact sheet, September 7. Washington, DC: U.S. Department of the Treasury, Office of Public Affairs, http://www.treas.gov/press/releases/reports/pspa_factsheet_090708%20hp1128. pdf

United States Federal Reserve. 2009. "Changes in U.S. Family Finances from 2004 to 2007: Evidence from the Survey of Consumer Finances." *Federal Reserve Bulletin*, February, pp. 1–56.

United States Financial Crisis Inquiry Commission. 2011. "Final Report of the National Commission on the Causes of the Financial and Economic Crisis in the United States," January. http://www.gpoaccess.gov/fcic/fcic.pdf

Verdier, Daniel. 2002. *Moving Money: Banking and Finance in the Industrialized World.* New York: Cambridge University Press.

Veron, Nicolas. 2012. "Europe's Single Supervisory Mechanism and the Long Journey Towards Banking Union." *Policy Brief*, no. PB12–24, Washington, DC: Peterson Institute for International Economics, pp. 1–9.

Vincelette, Gallina Andronova, Alvaro Manoel, Ardo Hansson, and Louis Kuijs. 2010. "China: Global Crisis Avoided, Robust Economic Growth Sustained." Policy Research Working Paper, no. WPS5435, Washington, DC: The World Bank.

Wade, Robert and Silla Sigurgeirsdottir. 2012. "Iceland's Rise, Fall, Stabilization and Beyond." *Cambridge Journal of Economics*, vol. **36**, issue no. 1, January, pp. 127–44.

Wade, Robert. 2008. "Financial Regime Change." *New Left Review*, vol. **53**, Sept–Oct, pp. 5–21.

Walker, Marcus, Charles Forelle, and David Gauthier-Villars. 2010. "Europe Bailout Lifts Gloom," *The Wall Street Journal*, 9 May. http://online.wsj.com/article/SB100 01424052748704879704575236602686084356.html

Wallison, Peter. 2009. "Cause and Effect: Government Policies and the Financial Crisis." *Critical Review*, vol. **21**, nos. 2–3, pp. 365–76.

Walter, Andrew. 2008. *Governing Finance East Asia's Adoption of International Standards.* Ithaca, NY: Cornell University Press.

Wang, X. 2007. "China as a Net Creditor: An Indication of Strength or Weaknesses?" *China and the World Economy*, vol. **15**, no. 6, pp. 22–36.

Warnock, Francis and Veronica Warnock. 2009. "International Capital Flows and US Interest Rates." *Journal of International Money and Finance*, vol. **28**, no. 6, pp. 903–19.

Webb, Michael. 1995. *The Political Economy of Policy Coordination: International Adjustment since 1945.* Ithaca, NY: Cornell University Press.

Wessel, David. 2009. *In Fed We Trust: Ben Bernanke's War on the Great Panic.* New York: Crown/Random House.

Whelan, Karl. 2010. "Policy Lessons from Ireland's Latest Depression." *The Economic and Social Review*, vol. **41**, no. 2, pp. 225–54.

White, Lawrence. 2011. "Preventing Bubbles: What Role for Financial Regulation." *Cato Journal*, vol. **31**, no. 3, pp. 603–19.

    2008. "How Did We Get into This Financial Mess?" Cato Institute Briefing Papers, no. 110, November 18, Washington, DC: Cato Institute.

Wilcox, James. 2009. "Underwriting, Mortgage Lending, and House Prices: 1996–2008." *Business Economics*, vol. **44**, no. 4, pp. 189–200.

Wilmarth, Arthur. 2011. "The Dodd-Frank Act: A Flawed and Inadequate Response to the 'Too-Big-to-Fail' Problem." *Oregon Law Review*, vol. **89**, no. 3, pp. 951–1057.

Wines, Michael. 2009. "China's Leader Says He Is 'Worried' Over U.S. Treasuries," *New York Times*, March 14. http://www.nytimes.com/2009/03/14/business/worldbusiness/14china.html?_r=1&pagewanted=print

Woertz, Eckart. 2008. "Impact of the US Financial Crisis on GCC Countries." *GRC Report*, Dubai: Gulf Research Center, pp. 1–21.

Wolf, Martin. 2008. *Fixing Global Finance.* Baltimore: John Hopkins University Press.

Woo, Wing Thye. 2012. "China Meets the Middle-Income Trap: The Large Potholes in the Road to Catching-up." *Journal of Chinese Economic and Business Studies*, vol. **10**, no. 4, pp. 313–36.

Woo, Wing Thye and Wei Zhang. 2011. "Combating the Global Financial Crisis with Aggressive Expansionary Monetary Policy: Same Medicine, Different Outcomes in China, the UK and USA." *The World Economy*, vol. **34**, no. 5, pp. 667–86.

2010. "Time for China to Move from Macro-Stability to Macro-Sustainability: Making Macro-Stimulus Work and Maintaining Its Effects." *Journal of the Asia Pacific Economy*, vol. **13**, no. 4, pp. 349–68.

Woodford, Michael. 2010. *Interest and Prices: Foundations of a Theory of Monetary Policy*. Princeton, NJ: Princeton University Press.

Woods, Thomas. 2009. *Meltdown: A Free-Market Look at Why the Stock Market Collapsed, the Economy Tanked, and Government Bailouts Will Make Things Worse*. Washington, DC: Regnery Publishing.

World Bank. 2012a. "World Bank Sees Progress Against Extreme Poverty, But Flags Vulnerabilities." Press Release No: 2012/297/DEC, Washington, DC: The World Bank.

2012b. *Global Economic Prospects: Uncertainties and vulnerabilities*. Washington, DC: The World Bank, Sub-Saharan Africa Annex.

2011. *World Development Indicators*. Washington, DC: The World Bank. http://data-bank.worldbank.org/ddp/home.do?Step=2&id=4&hActiveDimensionId=WD I_Series

2010. *Global Economic Prospects: Fiscal Headwinds and Recovery*. (Regional appendix: Middle East and North Africa). Washington, DC: The World Bank.

2009a. *Global Development Finance: Charting a Global Recovery*. Washington, DC: The World Bank.

2009b. *China Quarterly Update*. Washington, DC: The World Bank.

2009c. "The Reform Agenda," in *Crisis Response*, No. 2. Washington, DC: The World Bank.

2009d. *Economic Developments and Prospects: Middle East and North Africa Region – Regional Integration for Global Competitiveness, 2008*. Washington, DC: The World Bank.

2008a. *World Development Indicators 2008 CD-ROM*. Washington, DC: The World Bank.

2008b. *The Little Data Book on Africa: 2008*. Washington, DC: The World Bank.

2008c. *China Quarterly Update*. Beijing: The World Bank Office. www.worldbank.org/china

2007. *Global Development Finance 2007*. Washington, DC: The World Bank.

World Bank in Russia. 2009a. *Russian Economic Report*, No. 20, November. http://www.worldbank.org.ru

2009b. *Russian Economic Report*, No. 19, June. http://www.worldbank.org.ru

2008. *Russian Economic Report*, No. 17, November. http://www.worldbank.org.ru

World Economic Forum (WEF). 2009. *The Africa Competitiveness Report, 2009*. Geneva: World Economic Forum.

World Trade Organization (WTO). 2010. *World Trade Report 2010*. Geneva: World Trade Organization.

2009. "The Impact of the Financial Crisis on Least-Developed Countries," December 2, Geneva: World Trade Organization.

http://www.wto.org/english/thewto_e/minist_e/min09_e/impact_fin_crisis_e.pdf.

Wright, Robert. 2010. *Bailouts: Public Money, Private Profit*. New York: Columbia University Press.

Wynne, Mark. 2009. "The Financial Crisis, Trade Finance and the Collapse of World Trade." *Globalization and Monetary Policy Institute 2009 Annual Report*. Dallas: Federal Reserve Bank of Dallas.

Xing, Yuqing. 2010. "Facts about the Impacts of FDI on China and the World Economy," *China: An International Journal*, vol. **8**, no. 2, pp. 309–27.

Yang, Mu and Tin Seng Lim. 2010. "Recession Averted? China's Domestic Response to the Global Financial Crisis," in Zheng Yongnian and Sarah Tong, eds. *China and the Global Economic Crisis*. Singapore: World Scientific Publishers, pp. 25–46.

Yao, Xianguo and Xin Wu. 2011. "Transition of China's Financial System after the Global Financial Crisis." *The World Economy*, vol. **34**, issue 5, pp. 792–804.

Yavlinsky, Grigory. 2011. *Realeconomik: The Hidden Cause of the Great Recession (and How to Avert the Next One)*. New Haven, CT: Yale University Press.

Yi, Kei-Mu. 2009. "The Collapse of Global Trade: The Role of Vertical Specialization," in Richard Baldwin and Simon Evenett, eds. *The Collapse of Global Trade, Murky Protectionism, and the Crisis: Recommendations for the G20*. VoxEU.org e-book, pp. 45–48. http://www.voxeu.org/epubs/cepr-reports/collapse-global-trade-murky-protectionism-and-crisis-recommendations-g20

Yingzi, Tan and Dingding Xin. 2009. *China Daily*, February 3 (online). http://www.chinadaily.com.cn/china/2009–02/03/content_7440106.htm

Yu, Yongding. 2009. *China's Policy Responses to the Global Financial Crisis*, Richard Snape Lecture, November 25. Melbourne: Productivity Commission,.

Zakaria, Fareed. 2008. *The Post-American World*. New York: W.W. Norton.

Zandi, Mark. 2008. *Financial Shock: A 360° Look at the Subprime Mortgage Implosion, and How to Avoid the Next Financial Crisis*. New Jersey: FT Press.

Zettelmeyer, Jeromin, Piroska Nagy and Stephen Jeffrey. 2010. "Addressing Private Sector Currency Mismatches in Emerging Europe." European Bank for Reconstruction and Development, Working Paper, no. 115, London: EBRD.

Zingales, Luigi. 2009. "Capitalism After the Crisis." *National Affairs*, Fall, no. 1, pp. 22–35.

Zuckerman, Gregory. 2009. *The Greatest Trade Ever: The Behind-the-Scenes Story of How John Paulson Defied Wall Street and Made Financial History*. New York: Random House – Crown Business.

Index